D1234039

So Much to Do, So Little Time

Edited and annotated by
Michael Hayden

So Much To Do,
So Little Time

The Writings of Hilda Neatby

UNIVERSITY OF BRITISH COLUMBIA PRESS
Vancouver

SO MUCH TO DO, SO LITTLE TIME
THE WRITINGS OF HILDA NEATBY

This book has been published with the help of grants from the Canada Council and the University of Saskatchewan.

Canadian Cataloguing in Publication Data

Neatby, Hilda, 1904–1975.
    So much to do, so little time

            Bibliography: p.
            ISBN 0-7748-0171-9

    1. Canada — Intellectual life — Addresses, essays, lectures.   2. Neatby, Hilda, 1904–1975.
    3. Historians — Canada — Biography.   1. Hayden, Michael, 1934 —   II. Title.

FC95.4.N42   971.06   C82-091383-9
F1021.2.N42

ISBN-0-7748-0171-9

Printed in Canada

CONTENTS

LIST OF ILLUSTRATIONS

1. Hilda with brother Allan and sister Kate.
2. Neatby family en route from England, 1906.
3. Neatby homestead, 1916.
4. Hilda Neatby, 1925.
5. Letter to Kate, 22 January 1933.
6. B.A. Honours degree certificate.
7. Regina College in the mid-1930's.
8. University of Saskatchewan campus, 1928.
9. Massey Commission members.
10. Hilda Neatby with nephew Blair Neatby.
11. Hilda Neatby receiving Order of Canada.

PHOTOGRAPHIC CREDITS

Plates 1, 2, and 3 are reproduced with the kind permission of Mr. Leslie Neatby. Plates 4, 5, 6, 7, 9, 10, and 11 are reproduced courtesy of the Saskatchewan Archives Board, and Plate 8 courtesy of the University of Saskatchewan archives.

PREFACE

As an American-born male historian of seventeenth-century France with no particular love for things English, it is quadruply presumptuous of me to attempt to present Hilda Neatby to the world. Fortunately, the purpose of this book is to allow Hilda to present herself.

This book is not only about Hilda; essentially, this book is by Hilda. My words, where they appear, are merely a vehicle for allowing Hilda to speak one more time. This time she will be speaking not solely on one subject — on education, or religion, or the role of women, or the history of Quebec — which is how most people have heard and judged her in the past. She will be speaking about all of these things and more. This book is Hilda on the world as she saw it and as she lived in it. She represents an important part of Canada's recent past and provides a commentary on its present. What she has said warrants being heard as a whole rather than in pieces. If wrong she deserves to be refuted, not ignored, nor vilified.

I consistently refer to Hilda Marion Ada Neatby, C.C., M.A., Ph.D., LL.D., F.R.S.C., as Hilda. I choose this rather than the too cold Neatby, the socially correct Miss Neatby (it often seemed to me that those who called her this did so condescendingly), or the academically correct Doctor or Professor Neatby. During the debate over *So Little for the Mind*, she protested that critics whom she had never met thought nothing of calling her Hilda. However, at least in her later years, she wanted her colleagues to use her first name. It took me a long time to get up the courage to do so to her face; it is now a habit. I hope that she will not mind.

The first chapter is biographical, beginning with Hilda on herself and continuing with an account of those events, people and ideas that seem to have made the most difference in her life. The rest of the book consists essentially of the writings of Hilda Neatby. The second section contains seven chapters: Hilda *as* a woman, Presbyterian, westerner, Canadian, student and letter writer, teacher, and historian. The third section has four chapters: Hilda *on* education in the schools, universities, Canadian history, and the world around her. Each chapter consists of one or more selections from her published and unpublished works, preceded by an introduction. Because civilization, Christianity, duty, history, and Canada were constant themes for Hilda, the divisions are not airtight. A final chapter discusses, in a tentative fashion, her formation, her ideas, and her relationship with her times. More needs to be known about her times before Hilda can be fitted into them.

Most of the material for this book was found in the collection deposited by

Hilda Neatby in the Saskatchewan Archives in Saskatoon. Some of her correspondence is to be found in the Archives of the University of Saskatchewan. A
number of letters from Hilda to Frank Underhill in the Public Archives of
Canada were brought to my attention by Dale Miquelon; other letters in that
repository to A.L. Burt and Eugene Forsey I found myself. The material in the
Sound Archives was tracked down by Josephine Langham. A number of letters
to Eugene Forsey were sent to me by Blair Neatby. Roger Graham and Ivo
Lambi gave me access to correspondence in their possession. Some of Hilda's
published writings are in the Saskatchewan Archives; the rest I found in the
journals where they appeared. The part of the bibliography of published works
that is most likely to be incomplete is the section on book reviews. The bibliography of unpublished works, made up mostly of speeches, depends solely on the
archival collections and is incomplete.

Those who have helped me have been many. Hilda's brothers and sisters,
Leslie, Allan, Margery, and especially Kate, provided important information.
Kate's husband Ted and daughter Ruth also aided me. Among her longtime
friends and colleagues, Kay and Roger Graham, Bernadine Bujilla, W.A.
Riddell, Francis Leddy, Greta Rempel, and Margaret Belcher were of particular
help. Among the friends of the 1960's special mention must be made of Ivo and
Jackie Lambi, Hugh and Suzanne Johnson, Mary Hallett, Joe and Cathy Fry,
and Del Gradish, and especially Peg MacVean who provided not only information but typing and preparation of the index. Dick Rempel provided memories of the 1940's. My wife Joan helped especially in the final stages. The
archivists of the Saskatchewan Archives Board, especially Darcy Hande, were
patient and helpful. To these and all the others who have provided aid and
encouragement, especially Maria Lipp, and Dale Miquelon who was of special
help in revising the chapters on history and Canadian history — thank you.

PART ONE

Some Words about Hilda

Introduction

And Not To Yield is the subtitle of Hilda Neatby's last book, a history of Queen's University. However well those words may fit that university, there is no question that the editors who prepared the manuscript for publication and who chose the title also caught, unintentionally, Hilda's spirit.

The preface of that book and an obituary written by her friend of many years, Roger Graham, contain the first open references to the suffering that Hilda went through without either yielding or deviating from her duty. Only her friends knew of her sleepless nights, of her long and severe colds and infections, and, in the end, of her cancer.[1]

In the early 1950's when she was buried in requests to speak throughout the country, she occasionally begged off by replying truthfully that her doctor had ordered her to cut back on her activity. Most often she simply said that she could not be away from her classes, from her students. She meant it. From mid-September to mid-May Hilda and her students were inseparable. No matter how dense they were, no matter how many times she had to lead them through the wording of the Quebec Act, they were her students, and she was going to make something of them. No matter what it cost her, shy as she was, to appear in the classroom, she was pulled there by duty and by something else. A good teacher, she said, is a born performer, half afraid perhaps, but an actor. An actor with a purpose — an actor who had a civilizing mission. Even the fools had to be suffered and suffered gladly — most of the time — because occasionally a really good student would come along. And when that happened a teacher had to be ready to help — or perhaps ready not to hurt; to prepare, but not to get too much in the way. A teacher too involved in committee work or using term time for research not directly related to the classes being taught would miss the opportunity; the opportunity to keep one of the most important institutions in the world going — the university.

She carefully defined the university one day to an administrator who appeared at a salary negotiating session when Hilda was one of the faculty representatives. The administrator began "The university is prepared to offer you..." whereupon Hilda cut in "My students and I are the university, not you and the other administrators" — she and her students and the other professors and their students, together, searching for truth in difficult times, without yielding.

Even in the darkest times there was hope, and there were alternatives. At the end of the 1940's, she was involved in a search for alternatives or additions to the university to help in the search for civilization. Between 1949 and 1951 she was one of five members of the Royal Commission on National Development in the

Arts, Letters and Sciences — the Massey Commission. This commission more than any other single body, commission or task force, through the creation of the Canada Council and support for the National Film Board and less commercial television, has both moulded and advanced Canadian culture. The end result left much to be desired, but Hilda knew the world was like that.

Hilda truly cared for learning and scholarship, and she could become very upset at those who interfered with it. She tried hard to help anyone who was willing to make an effort. However, those who pretended were in danger, particularly those who had gone to university and who were now placed in charge of students, especially the very young. Some of the professors of education in Canada have neither forgotten nor forgiven Hilda for what was the most monumental outburst of intellectual indignation in Canada in the 1950's.

The Massey Commission did not deal directly with education since that was within provincial jurisdiction, but the members heard enough on their trips across Canada to become convinced that something had to be said. The chairman, Vincent Massey, soon to be Governor General, encouraged Hilda to study the problem of the schools. She did. The result was *So Little for the Mind*. Though she titled its sequel *A Temperate Dispute* and wondered why professional educators would not join with her in discussion, there is little to wonder at. Hilda published for all to read exactly what she thought: "The present preoccupations with body building and character moulding are useless and may even be dangerous so long as we neglect and starve the mind."[2]

Hilda not only cared about her students and all students from grade one upward, she also strove to improve education. She not only cared about the search for truth; she was also involved in it. Hilda was a historian. She taught and wrote history. Those two activities took up the greatest part of her life. She was interested in the history of the whole world, especially the western world; but above all she was a historian of her own country. She would grumble that no really good history of Canada had been written and that Canada had no great historians because not enough had worked long enough. She also thought that Canadian history had been misused: "Canadian history which, properly understood, could help to develop in Canadians a sense of unity and of international understanding, has been used too long to stir up petty resentments against each other, against Great Britain and against the United States."[3] There was a remedy — broader and more critical histories of Canada.

Born in England and profoundly influenced by things English, Hilda was a Canadian and very proud of it. She was also a westerner from the prairies, and a Saskatchewanian. Hilda was a woman and aware of that too both because she was very feminine and because others reproached her with it. She spoke of women in society long before it became fashionable, for example in 1952:

> Women in the modern age of their emancipation are intellectually and emotionally competent, as they have always been. They now operate in a much larger social frame, and some women have not realized, perhaps, that

the frame is larger. They are tempted to excuse themselves from actions on the grounds that women cannot do certain things, that men do things better, that women are emotional, trivial, etc. . . . This is no time for feminine indolence or for masculine vanity. There is so much to do, and for doing it there is so little time.[4]

Hilda was conscious of time and its passing, partly because it is a preoccupation of a historian but even more because she had a clear picture in her mind of what the world should be, and she was impatient for change.

There were limitations; there were experiences that she had not had. She remarked in amazement concerning sexual practices about which she had no knowledge before she read Mary McCarthy's *The Group*. She had not thrown the book down in disgust or horror, however, when she found that it described actions that were to her literally and figuratively unthinkable. Her upbringing and the way of life she had chosen limited somewhat her knowledge of both the earthier and more mundane things in life; yet she never ran from reality, and she was always ready to learn.

Above all Hilda was deeply religious. She was Presbyterian to the core, but she came slowly to appreciate other religions. Living, friends, and her growing awareness of history gradually broadened Hilda's religious tolerance to the point that she felt at home in the 1960's introducing a Sikh intellectual or addressing an Anglican synod. Still she never swerved from allegiance to her own faith.

There were and still are many who would resist the use of words like "warm human being" to describe Hilda Neatby. They would rather use vindictive, overbearing, nasty, unfair, mannish, bigoted, over-intellectual. Hilda had (and has) enemies — some deserved, some not. When she rode forth to do battle for the intellect, civilization, or Christianity both the enemy and the bystander (innocent or merely slow-witted) were liable to be attacked. Once attacked by Hilda, they tended to remember.

Hilda was not always right, but, for a human being, she was consistent and determined. These two tendencies, when combined with her convictions, led to the creation of more partisans and enemies than disinterested acquaintances. At the risk of being attacked by both camps, I have taken a position somewhere in the middle, though I lean toward Hilda. My choice of ground is based on personal knowledge, talking with those who knew her best, analysis of all remaining information on her life, a careful reading of every known scrap of her writing, and a consideration of the conditions and influences that surrounded her.

Hilda's closest friends knew her as a person far better than I did, but they have not read all that she wrote. Her colleagues, students, and those who have read parts of her work know some of her facets. Through this book it should be possible to gain a fuller idea of the impatient woman with so much to do who, if she had not been so modest, could have adopted the motto "And not to yield" — and yet who did yield: to circumstances when she had to; to change when it was necessary; to friends if at all possible; and always to truth.

| *A Short Biography of Hilda Neatby*

Hilda Neatby was not well known until the Massey Commission began its work in 1949. But by then she was in her mid-forties with a well defined personal identity. Finding how she became the person she was presents difficulties. Her letters are of some help, but with the exception of 1924-25 and 1932-35 there are few extant from the first two-thirds of her life. She did not begin to save her correspondence until the early 1950's.

Some traces of Hilda show up in university records. The memories of her friends have been a source of information for her early life. The Neatby family has supplied the world with four books about itself, and Hilda appears briefly in three of them.[1] Through talking with her surviving brothers and sisters, I have learned much more. Hilda often spoke of her personal experiences, but she wrote very little about them. One exception was in the second half of the 1960's when, under duress from a persistent woman in Quebec, she produced five pages titled "H. Neatby Biographical Notes." These "notes" present a placid happy life:

"Born: 1904 Sutton, Surrey, England.

My parents, with eight children of whom I was the youngest but one, came out to Canada in 1906 settling in the small town of Earl Grey in Saskatchewan. Later my parents moved to a totally unsettled area just opened for farming. It was some miles west of the present Watrous, Saskatchewan. The country was rolling, at that time full of the small ponds which local people call sloughs. Much of the land was stony and the first task of the farmer was to remove the stones on the surface and those which were just below the surface after which cultivation proceeded. In the early days most people used oxen. Later the luxury of horses was introduced. Living was extremely primitive although some people had frame houses. Many, however, used the cheap and traditional sod shack. . . .

My primary school education was received in the little school which served our rural district. There was no high school available in the neighbourhood at that time. My high school training was somewhat scrappy, carried out with the assistance of elementary school teachers and of course my parents, with the addition of one year at a collegiate institute in Saskatoon. My family moved to Saskatoon in 1919. In the summer of 1920 I had my one experience as a rural teacher, a very young and very ignorant one. I had not even the usual normal school training.

In the autumn I entered the University of Saskatchewan. I graduated with a B.A. Honours degree in History in 1924. I was fortunate enough to be given a provincial government scholarship to Paris for 1924–25. The first time I saw Paris I saw it as an extremely unsophisticated young woman of twenty whose previous urban experience had been confined to Saskatoon. The shock was sufficiently great to be painful but I recovered and have the fondest memories of my year there."[2]

The outrageous and impossible conditions in which Hilda was actually raised have been realistically detailed by her older brother Leslie and her younger sister Kate. Only one who was there could describe them adequately.

Briefly, her father failed as a physician in England because he was not interested in the profession into which he had been pushed by a domineering, austere, determined physician father.[3] As children continued to come, his wife, who had both a medical heritage and medical talent and was aware of it, pushed the family to Earl Grey, Saskatchewan, in 1906. By 1908 it was evident that her husband was still a failure as a doctor. As Andrew Neatby turned more and more to his books while neighbours patronized a new doctor, Ada Neatby again pushed the family, this time onto a remote homestead. The farm was run by the two oldest boys Walter and Allan (all of 14 and 12 years of age), without experience, much food, or adequate clothing. The family lived in an uninsulated shack in temperatures down to -40° while their father read, "his only refuge in increasingly deep depression induced by unfamiliar and unwelcome surroundings."[4] In winter their mother stayed in bed to keep the youngest child warm. The oldest sister, Edith, sixteen when they moved to the farm, was in charge of the house. The other children, Margery, Kenneth, Leslie, Hilda, and eventually Kate, did chores in and outside the house.

One infant died before the family came to Canada, another died in Manitoba en route to Earl Grey; two others would die in Saskatchewan, one a few hours after birth, the other after a few months. The other eight not only survived their upbringing but showed remarkable talents and most lived (and some continue to live) long lives. They have all admitted in one way or another that they were formed partly by the necessity of surviving, but especially by their mother's determination to raise them again to the middle-class status from which they had fallen, by the religious training provided by their father, and by his constant reading aloud to them from the three-thousand-volume library he had brought with him from England.

They were also affected by the unfamiliar society in which they found themselves. In 1937 Edith described life in Earl Grey in 1907:

> The people you met dressed as you did, therefore by our ideas they were our equals, but their information was less than our former charwoman's, therefore they weren't, their housekeeping was good, therefore they were our kind, their houses were desolate, therefore they weren't: Of course the only way is to plunge in headlong and sort yourself out afterwards, but neither father nor mother could do that. Father tied everything to his religion, mother to her gentility, and they couldn't break loose.[5]

As for Hilda, her brothers and sisters say that she missed the hardest of the physical work and that along with her sister Kate she escaped early enough to miss the roughness of western life. That statement needs modification. After a long period of harassment by a bully in the schoolyard, Hilda made the mistake of running from him only to find herself with her back to a wall, facing a semi-circle of children mimicking her every action and word. Much later she described the effect of the confrontation:

> I can't explain it, but it is the most dreadful experience I have ever had and associated with the rather queer life we lived, I think it gave me a fear of my fellow man that is permanent. Such things are brutalizing at the time, but I suppose in the long run they may be good. I don't think I could ever persecute a minority.[6]

Hilda did not persecute minorities; she preferred to take on the majority. She never again ran from a bully, no matter how much it hurt.

Hilda devoted herself to studying at an early age and with determination. Much later she said that one of her earliest desires had been to attend the University of Saskatchewan.[7] Long before she was aware of the universities, Hilda exhibited what Leslie described as accomplishment achieved not through genius but "by sheer brutal hard work carried on with a tenacity of which the rest of us were incapable."[8] In the process she at times dominated those around her. Leslie speaks of her as the "acknowledged autocrat" of the family; Kate of "firmness of character so great as to be unkindly called obstinacy."[9] Yet Kenneth would add, "She is unique in our family in that she occasionally indulges in fits of modesty."[10] And throughout her life she joined in when the family was having fun. Above all she loved to hear her father read.

Hilda was a determined, ambitious person motivated, her family agrees, by a sense of duty and her religious convictions. She supported her parents and helped others in the family for five years in the 1920's. She provided loans and gifts of money when her brothers were struggling to establish themselves. She lovingly took care of her mother for many years with only intermittent help. And to her nephews and nieces Aunt Hilda was a favourite.

On his deathbed, Hilda's father told her that if he had allowed himself to have a favourite among his children, he would have chosen her because she reminded him of his father. Something compelled this admiration for his father and his daughter. Hilda shared with her grandfather the ability to push herself far beyond the usual limits. She gained, in time, more understanding, more humanity than he had had. Perhaps this was because she was a woman, perhaps it came from her father's reading, perhaps from her study of history. Most probably it came from her Christianity. To say that being a Presbyterian, the religion of her maternal grandparents, softened Hilda gives an idea of the hardness of her paternal grandfather's religion. As for her father, he was a Baptist who moved towards Presbyterianism in all but name: "Father's insistence on meticulous observance of what he regarded his religious duty was probably vital to us psychologically as a balance to his frequent periods of depression in which is insisted that life had ended for him when he left England, that he was a failure, and that nothing much mattered."[11]

Hilda summed up her training during a convocation address in 1969: "I was taught not self-expression but self-control, not confrontation but respect for my seniors, not to go after flower power or student power or sit-ins or live-ins but to do my duty." As she immediately went on to say, she had changed; she had learned to tolerate in others dress, decorum and ideas that would have shocked her parents. But she remained "old-fashioned enough to believe in self-control, in courtesy, in respect, and in attention to duty."[12]

The Neatby family moved to Saskatoon in 1919 after eleven years on the farm so that the four youngest could attend high school and university. The older children were on their own, married or soon to be, and until Hilda began to provide some money in late 1926, the family survived on a share of the income from the family farm, then run by Walter, on what could be gained from a little tutoring by Mr. Neatby (most of his time was spent in the university library), on money from the boys' summer jobs, and, especially, on the income from Mrs. Neatby's dressmaking and taking in boarders.

Mrs. Neatby had been behind the move to Saskatoon. Kate said it was because she wanted greater opportunities for the second half of her family.[13] In conversation Leslie put it bluntly — their mother had pushed education so that the family could get back to its class. In his book he put it differently:

> It is difficult to conjecture what would have become of us but for our mother's determination. The excellent training in mind and spirit which our father had casually imparted had left us no conception of earning a living except on the soil. Our mother's resolution and unquenchable ambition for her children gave us the required vision and impulse.[14]

Hilda's years at the University of Saskatchewan, 1920–24, can be easily enough described. She came with a wide background in English literature, a deep and narrow religious commitment, and many prejudices. She worked very hard and had a few good friends with whom she ate lunch and occasionally went skating. Her only extracurricular activity seems to have been the Historical Society, of which she was secretary-treasurer in 1923–24. Her history professors remembered her as a slow starter, shy, but in the end brilliant.[15] She won a scholarship every year and upon graduation won the Copeland Scholarship as the "most distinguished student taking the degree B.A. or B.Sc. with Honours or Distinction." There are few traces of her beyond this in the records or in living memories except as a member of the Neatby clan. Few who were at the university in the 1920's have forgotten them, though the memories vary. President Murray put it positively, if blandly, that they were "a family that has attained high distinction in academic courses."[16] Others took a more emotional stand, either for or against the family. In a student body of less than a thousand they most certainly stood out. The yearbook in 1924 used mock Chaucerian words describing Hilda in a spirit totally unlike any other graduate: "Her fame brought alle wondering to her feet."[17] More than fifty years later a friend said, "She was serious yet not lugubrious. Yet I cannot remember ever hearing her really laugh." Another remembers Hilda's gaiety, but it was connected with her classes. She continued, "A brilliant and critical mind and yet full of generosity to others. Education to her was significant and she hoped to improve the standard of education in the public schools in Saskatchewan." A third said, "A thoughtful, intelligent woman, dedicated to her work as a student of history. She was well read and I found her an interesting person to talk to."[18]

Looked at from the perspective of their effect on Hilda, her university years were very important. She learned from A.S. Morton the necessity of attention to the detail of a document.[19] It was, however, the influence of Frank Underhill that had the greatest impact. Years later she described him as "a strange combination of a clear cold intellectual and the ardent idealist." She did not accept his solution to Canada's problems after World War I: "isolationism and Fabian socialism." But she was not put off by what some saw as cynicism. She saw the point of his logic and sharp wit: "Underhill never lost his evangelistic fervour, his conviction that mankind could be enlightened." She also admired the care he took with all students despite his scornful remarks about the average undergraduate:

> No one who prepared essays for Underhill could remain unconscious of the need for clear and disciplined thought, for the most precise organization of materials, for the most rigid economy (in the best sense) in the use of words. He was severe in his criticism, but I believe he was never discouraging to honest effort.
>
> A shy man and really reluctant to give offence, he had taught himself that reluctance was intellectual cowardice, a temptation to be resisted. Such resistance to temptation resulted occasionally in remarks of almost brutal frankness.

This almost seems to be Hilda describing herself. His influence on her is unmistakable. "With no moralizing at all he ground into us the idea that anything short of perfection was inadequate." She added, unnecessarily, that she had never been able to escape these standards. She differed with many of his opinions but not with "truth was to be valued for its own sake."[20] In later years Hilda wrote to Professor Morton and her doctoral adviser A.L. Burt on the proper occasions. She wrote to Underhill whenever she was in an intellectual crisis — and he answered.[21]

When she applied for a Paris Scholarship from the Province of Saskatchewan in April 1924 she asked A.S. Morton and her French professor J.A. MacDonald to write letters of reference for her. Morton outlined the work that she had done. She had concentrated on seventeenth and eighteenth-century French history, doing most of her reading and all of her writing in French (a paper every week in the winter, every two weeks in the summer). In 1922–23 she read Saint Simon in detail and went on to Madame de Motteville and the Abbé de Choisy. In 1923–24 she wrote almost weekly papers on such standard seventeeth-century French topics as Colbert's administration, justice, and commerce. In the last months of her undergraduate work she concentrated on a bibliographical study which culminated in a thirty–eight page paper in French on historical sources for the reign of Louis XIV.[22]

Morton concluded his letter of recommendation of 1924 by saying "She has grown until she constantly impresses me as putting a real intellectual quality into her work. She is a young woman with a mind." She was "self-contained and somewhat reserved. In manner she is shy, but I have rarely had one who was quicker to speak her mind as the subject of her paper was being discussed and readier to debate a disputable point.[23]

Her French teacher, after noting that she had an excellent command of French and that she spoke the language well and with ease, added "with Miss Neatby before me in class I have always felt the challenge of a strong and original mind, performing with ease the work of the class, and capable of ranging far beyond." He concluded, "Miss Neatby is young in years, but she seems to have a remarkably old head."[24]

Inspired by her father's reading, Hilda had read widely; she had inherited determination from her grandfather and her mother. She received rigorous training from Morton; the ideals came from Underhill. She must also have been difficult company for anyone except her family and the few friends who shared her ideas and her prejudices and who felt her hidden warmth.

Hilda had come to the university to qualify for high school teaching. Her first class from Morton had convinced her that she wanted to be a university history professor. In later years she would describe the years between 1920 and 1946 with the statement that she had been fortunate — after a few difficulties, she got what she wanted.

The difficulties were many, though it did not seem so to her in the summer of 1924. The first blow came when the Paris scholarship was not renewed for a second year, making it impossible for her to get the degrees she wanted. From 1925 to the end of the 1940's she laboured against heavy odds created by the economic situation, her sex, and personality clashes.

The Paris Scholarship had been instituted by the Province of Saskatchewan as a war memorial and to improve high school teaching in the province. In 1924 three of the ten applicants were successful, each receiving $600.00 and a promise of $600.00 more later in the year.[25] After some inquiries in Paris, Hilda set for herself the goal of the *Certificat d'études françaises* and a *licence* in history. Failure to get a renewal of the scholarship (in fact, there were no renewals until 1930, shortly before the programme closed) meant that Hilda could not try for a *licence*.

When she was choosing the subject for her *licence*, under Morton's influence, she considered nineteenth-century European history but decided that "it is too horribly uninteresting."[26] She decided to continue her study of Colbert, but now she worked on his dealings with Canada. She had taken her first Canadian history in her last year in university only because Underhill was teaching the course. Otherwise she might never have studied the subject. Many years later she told Roger Graham that if her choice had been free she would have chosen mid-nineteenth-century Canadian history. How her choices became less free will shortly be seen.

Hilda left Montreal for Europe on 2 August, 1924. She spent the second half of August and most of September with her relatives in England, returning to visit them in April and much of the summer of 1925. The rest of her year was spent almost exclusively in Paris studying at the Collège de la Guilde and the Sorbonne. She lived in a student pension on Boulevard St. Michel.

A number of letters from Paris to her family have been preserved.[27] The year sounds familiar to anyone who has had a similar experience: great plans that had to be restricted because one year is short, the French educational system is mysterious, and the bureaucracy is difficult.[28] Despite her professors' glowing remarks about her French she had the usual difficulties:

> When I ought to talk both ideas and language desert me. I am reminded of what Miss Carr said to me when she was critizing my first English essay, "The chief trouble with you is that you have essentially no ideas, and you do not know how to express the few that you have got."[29]

Her letters to her family are full of concerns about laundry and grey Parisian weather, mixed with descriptions of marvellous sights and thrilling excursions.

All in all her time in England surrounded by relatives sounds happier. Her grandmother described two automobile trips taken to see medieval churches:

> I think Clement must be very amusing. He and Hilda on both our big occasions sat together behind, and we could not help noticing that conversation *never* flagged. There was hardly a breather during the hour and a

half going or returning. And much laughter, so Edwin would have said that was good for both of them.[30]

One value of the year in Paris for Hilda was that for the first time she came into close contact with people who thought differently, people whom she could not dismiss as being beneath concern. It was difficult. "As far as Christian friends go I suppose there are Christian people in Paris, but I haven't come across any."[31] Concerning a Protestant girl who went to early Mass so that she could go both to the Louvre and to church on Sunday, "I am narrow-minded I know, but it does amaze me to see people who were brought up to know better doing such idiotic things. For people who were brought up R.C.'s it is different of course."[32] She wrote to her sister Margery about the visit of an English aunt to Paris, "Unfortunately she is practically a Roman Catholic . . . . Of course Marcelle Durif with whom I room is an R.C. but then she admits it so you know where you are."[33]

Bit by bit Marcelle's and France's influences made some difference. As she broadened her experience, though, she also remained herself as in a letter to her sister Kate: "As to your dilemma about whether to get married or get a scholarship. I advise the latter very decidedly. Don't let marriage interfere with the really serious things of life."[34]

The year was quickly over. Hilda received a *Certificat d'études phonétique élémentaire* with a mediocre mark of 47 out of 70 and a *Certificat d'études françaises*, based on an essay, in which she earned the highest rating for a non-French student.[35] She returned to Saskatoon ready to enter normal school and then to teach high school. Despite the disappointment, there was still some hope in her letters. She was going to find a way to get back to Paris to continue her historical studies. In the meantime she planned to work on her M.A. in history while going to normal school. "As I must be in Saskatoon for Normal I may as well do something useful with my year."[36]

In the biographical notes that she composed in the 1960's Hilda gracefully slid over the difficult quarter century between 1925 and 1949:

On my return to Saskatoon I took a course in the local normal school with the intention of becoming a high school teacher of history. However it chanced that the year I was ready to take a position one of the professors in the French department, Dr. Margaret Cameron, was given a year's leave of absence to complete her doctoral studies in Paris. I was asked to accept an instructorship at the university in French. I spent an interesting, painful, and delightful year learning to teach at the expense of some hundred and twenty kindly and I think rather chivalrous freshmen, of whom a considerable number were older than myself.

The next year favour also fortuned me in the unexpected resignation of the professor of Canadian history. I served as a temporary replacement for four years because the onset of the depression made it difficult for the university to secure a man of the experience and quality that they desired. At the end of four years I received a teaching assistantship at the University of Minnesota where I spent three altogether delightful years with pleasant companions and kind and amiable if exacting professors. The pleasures of those years were sharpened by the extreme insecurity of the time. We had to make our happiness from hour to hour. We all wanted to teach history in a university. None of us had positions or any prospect of positions or any hope that there would be any positions. During the years that I was at Minnesota the budget was progressively cut. The university feared that its standing as a graduate school would be permanently impaired.

My research for the doctoral thesis was carried on under the direction of A.L. Burt whose specialty was the Old Province of Quebec, 1760–1791. Under his direction I did a study on the administration of justice during the later part of that period. This required a summer visit to Ottawa. The Burts in the goodness of their hearts invited me to accompany them and their four lively children in their large car and I have the happiest recollections of those transcontinental journeys which took me from St. Paul in Minnesota to the Y.W.C.A. in Ottawa where impecunious females were given adequate and even very comfortable lodging and food for a very modest sum.

I worked long hours in the Archives during those summers aided by the regulation which allowed students free access at any time. Ottawa was not the beautiful and bustling city that it is today. It was severely struck by the depression and I have vivid recollections of the park benches covered with unemployed and hopeless looking men. Once again I and my fellow students at the Archives experienced the keen pleasures of youth and energy and ambition sharpened by the constant sense of uncertainty and insecurity.

On receiving my degree in 1934 I still had no prospect of employment. After a somewhat anxious summer in Saskatchewan I was given a half-time position at Regina College which had just been taken over by the University of Saskatchewan with the assistance of a grant from the Carnegie Foundation. My half-time position involved, as I recall, very hard work, fifty to sixty hours a week but again great pleasure and great happiness in young and able colleagues and in our students.

Altogether I taught at Regina College history and French for twelve years with one interval of a year during the Second World War when I was invited to act as a temporary replacement for one of the professors in the History department at the University of Toronto. This year was of great interest to me and great value.

Shortly after my return I was transferred to the University of Saskatchewan at Saskatoon where I have ever since been Professor in the History department."

In her first year back in Saskatoon Hilda took a history class and a political science class, both from Underhill, along with her work at the Normal School. Then the eternal need of the University for temporary people intervened. In 1926–27 Hilda taught French while Professor Cameron was on leave. Then for four years from 1927–28 to 1930–31 she taught history, always as a temporary replacement for Frank Underhill, who had gone to the University of Toronto. In the first two years she taught a lecture class in Canadian history and a reading class in Canadian Constitutional history. Hilda has described her experience teaching French. Morton, as department head, described her first year teaching history: "Miss Neatby seems to have followed closely the constitutional side of Canadian history which is the most difficult and the least interesting." The forty students in the lecture class "found it somewhat dull." However, the one student in the reading class found it interesting. As for Hilda, "She feels Canadian history does not offer the wider and more interesting issues and asked to be allowed to take English History."[37]

Hilda got $150.00 per month for twelve months during 1926–27 and 1927–28. In 1929–30, now with an M.A., her salary was $2,000, and in her last year $2,100. These salaries were average for the time for someone with her qualifications.[38]

Having finished her thesis, "Imperial Sentiment in Canada, 1867–1896," Hilda planned to go on to doctoral work. She knew that this would be necessary if she were going to continue to teach at a university. According to University of Saskatchewan regulations, she had already taught for one more year than allowed as a temporary member of faculty. The question was where to go for her degree. She wanted to go to Toronto and study Imperial history with Underhill, but Morton advised her that Canadian universities hired their own under-graduates after they finished their graduate work and that therefore Toronto would never hire her. So she should study in the United States where there would be more opportunity for her if she had a U.S. degree.[39] The implication was that Saskatchewan would not be hiring her back. Since she really wanted to work with Underhill, she wrote to President Murray:

> It would be of very great assistance to me to know whether, in event of my future record being satisfactory, there would be any prospect of another appointment for me at this University, or whether your plans for the history department make that out of the question.[40]   .

What Hilda was delicately referring to was that President Murray's daughter, Jean, who had replaced Underhill during the spring of 1926, was returning from her doctoral studies at the University of Chicago. Murray's answer to Hilda was not put in writing. He told her to see him as soon as convenient. His answer must have been that there would be no chance of a place for Hilda because she chose the University of Minnesota for doctoral studies. Resentment was to simmer in the Neatby family for years. Hilda herself was to feel for years that Morton's and Murray's attitude toward her had been "Goodbye and good riddance." Whatever her attitude toward President Murray, Hilda liked his daughters Jean and Lucy.[41]

Hilda had written to Underhill in January 1930 thanking him for encouraging her to apply for a Toronto fellowship and saying that she was going to discuss things with Morton.[42] In October 1930 she reported to Underhill that she had been advised (by Morton though she did not mention his name) that a U.S. degree would be of more use to her than a Toronto one for a position in the States.[43] Underhill agreed and Hilda replied:

> It is a great disappointment in every way, and especially on that account, to give up the idea of coming to Toronto. I feel, however, that if a Toronto student has not a good chance of a position in the United States it would be better to try for an American university as in Saskatchewan at least even the better high school positions seem to be more or less closed to women.[44]

Two days later she wrote the letter to Murray quoted above, and, shortly after, applied and was accepted for doctoral work at the University of Minnesota. She also received an assistantship which provided tuition and support. Her plan was to work with A.L. Burt, formerly of the University of Alberta. She wished to do something concerning the relationship between Great Britain and Canada. Morton had interested her in a study of the policy of the Colonial Office between 1849 and 1867, and she asked Underhill what he thought. Evidently he replied that she should consult with Burt, who in turn gently pushed her into his period, 1767–1800, where he could be of more help.[45] Hilda had a longing for the study of nineteenth-century Canadian and English history but put it in the background for many years with the words, "I think that the later period is more difficult and more important but I am very much interested in the earlier one."[46]

The period 1931–34 at the University of Minnesota, like the year in Paris, was another time of growth through experience with the unfamiliar for Hilda. It is also the longest single period in her life covered by a series of letters.[47] During these years Hilda studied intensely, again with attention to detail. She attended the theatre, visited the art museum, heard concerts, but above all she found herself in the middle of a new kind of life — that of the United States. These years mark the beginning of her love-hate relationship with that country which would persist until the time of her last article.

Sometimes her letters were about a minute point of Quebec history, sometimes about happy hours spent in the Archives in Ottawa during the summers, sometimes about sitting with friends, smoking and discussing life's problems and mysteries, and sometimes about her panic as her orals approached, or her despair at her adviser's attitude as she tried to write her thesis. Early on she learned the American female usage of the term "the curse," was fascinated by it, and continually referred to it. Other words made temporary incursions into her vocabulary as when she said she could not "jazz off to Maine" to visit a friend next summer.[48] She also wrote to her sister on one occasion in words that might surprise those who knew her formally in later years: "I do agree with you that shabby underwear and shoes have a really demoralizing effect."[49] In one letter she admitted being pulled by the desire to relive her Sundays in Saskatoon "with two churches and a Sunday school and reading improving books to you and singing hymns in between time."[50] In the next letter she told her sister of the wonderful unspiritual activities she was indulging in on Sunday (after church). The people who were responsible for the new kind of Sunday were the Burts, who, though religious,[51] did not meet her standards. She clung to these, though by the end of her Minnesota days she did admit that "my Presbyterianism has grown cold."[52]

Life began well at Minnesota even if the ways were strange and not up to Hilda's standards. As she wrote to Frank Underhill in November of 1931:

I am having a very good time here almost too good to be true. Everyone in the department is very kind, and all the people that I take classes with seem to be really good. At present I am doing only general reading in Canadian history with Mr. Burt, but after Christmas I hope to start reading for my thesis which will be, I think, something on the judicial system under the Quebec Act.

You asked me to give you my impressions of an American university . . . . This place is so big it is very hard to get into touch with the general life of the University. . . . I have found my sections decidedly disappointing. I don't know whether their high school training is bad, or whether a different type comes to the university here. . . .

The graduate classes and all the graduate work generally are so pleasant that I ought not to criticize them, but I cannot help wishing that they would try a little harder to make people do their own thinking and learn to write down their own thoughts. . . .

We read and answer questions on what we have read. The reading is very well planned and you get trained to be accurate and thorough which I feel is very good for me, but I think one might have that without giving up the other.[53]

By the second year Hilda thought better of the students, and she was beginning to realize how much she had to learn for her written and oral preliminary examinations in the spring of 1933. Fear drove her to alternating bouts of heavy studying and mild diversions ranging from cigarettes to movies and plays.

Men do not seem to have played an important role in Hilda's personal life. About marriage she wrote:

Either we are naturally sexless or we were brought up in a sexless way. For it is quite amazing to me what a large part that sort of thing seems to play in the average unmarried woman's life. I can understand a craving to be married to a particular person, but I think the general urge to marriage is rather a tragedy, and yet when you think about it it seems to be almost universal.[54]

Her comment on her present prospects were "I should like to get married too if I could find someone sufficiently interesting and sufficiently devoted, but no one here fills either qualification although they are all very good company."[55] The devotion would have had to extend to a deep understanding of her shyness and insecurities as well as her convictions, and the interest would have to be generated by a willingness to debate everything and do it well. But there were definite limits: "I think people whose chief charm is their brain are delightful to know, but not to marry."[56] In another context she had written to Kate: "With our upbringing we can be perfectly at home with people who are evangelical and non-cultured or cultured and non-evangelical, but if they are neither the one nor the other you just don't meet."[57]

The man who would have interested Hilda would have had to be interesting, devoted, cultured, and evangelical. She met some who had three out of the four qualifications, but evidently none with all four who were free. According to her sister Kate, there were at least two proposals in Hilda's life, "but neither apparently was tempting."[58]

She was very interested in her sister Kate's courtship in England and in sexual concerns of her female friends in Minnesota. She liked to associate with men, she liked to be flattered by them, but above all she liked to argue with them. Hilda could not live without intellectual argument. She believed that it was impossible to argue with women and that if she argued too much with men they would be put off,[59] but argue she must. Shortly before she died, Hilda interrupted dictation of farewell letters to her friends to discuss the marital problems of the woman who was transcribing the letters. After listening to her, Hilda's one comment was "Yes men do not like women who are intelligent."

Whenever it was that Hilda decided that marriage would not be for her, if in fact she did, she was concerned that she not become "high schoolish," the words she once used to describe a single, aging, intellectual high school teacher who never could shake off her teaching habits.[60] And when she spoke of single life as she approached thirty, she did not use words like enjoying or living, she used "facing."[61]

The Burts, or more accurately Mrs. Burt, who influenced her husband, tried both to relax and to broaden Hilda through dinners, teas, symphonies, and visits. They were particularly supportive when her father died in early 1932. They continued to support her during her second year although Hilda began to be worried that Mr. Burt, as she would always refer to him, did not really have her interests at heart.

The second year ended with success in her preliminary examinations. Her comment to her sister was "All my exams were too easy to be exciting, but long enough to be frightfully tiring."[62] She had applied for a fellowship from the Royal Society of Canada to finance a year of research for her thesis which at the time she was describing as "An investigation of the Treasury Accounts in London with a view to determining how much Quebec was costing Great Britain prior to the Constitutional Act of 1791 and how the money was spent."[63] Despite strong letters from Burt, Morton, and Underhill, and an all out attempt by President Murray who was on the selection committee, she failed to get the fellowship. The two fellowships in her section went to Harry Wolfson in Economics and Roy Daniells in English. In the end a third fellowship was found for G.F.G. Stanley in History despite a strong protest from Murray, who argued that Hilda, ranked second in History behind Stanley, was the better candidate on the strength of the letters since Burt, who had taught both, ranked Hilda higher. Another factor was that Stanley had already had more opportunities (through the Rhodes Scholarship) to prepare himself for research. But the committee was firmly under the control of the eastern members who, in effect, simply kept Murray informed of what they were doing.[64] It is interesting to note that among others who did not obtain a fellowship were such future notables as John Kenneth Galbraith, Burton Kierstead, Samuel Hayakawa, Earle Birney, Beatrice Corrigan, and Margaret Ormsby.

The failure to get a Royal Society fellowship marked the beginning of a period of troubles. Hilda received $400.00 from the University of Minnesota as an "Emergency Fellow in History." Upon arriving on campus after a summer of research in Ottawa she found a very gloomy group of students. Everyone had come to realize that there simply were no jobs. She tried sharing an apartment with two girls whom she liked very much, but she found that she had to live alone to work well. She felt that she was always the odd one out because of her study habits. Burt was unsympathetic to her personal problems and was determined to make her revise her thesis. Eventually, she would attribute the first to Burt's personality and chalk up the second to experience. She even came to admit grudgingly that her thesis had needed revision.[65] At the time, though, these experiences were traumatic. The presentation of the conclusion of her thesis to Burt in April 1934 brought a difficult year to an abrasive end. Years later Burt's youngest child, Jean, recalled the occasion. She remembered Hilda telling Burt off and storming out of the house. The girl had been thrilled because Hilda had been "the first student, let alone the first woman, who had ever talked back to my father." Hilda corrected the daughter's memory saying that though she had argued forcefully on the occasion, it was Burt who had had enough and who sent her home to think things over and to stop being so obstinate. A letter to Kate at the time confirms Hilda's version.[66]

The thesis, "The Administration of Justice Under the Quebec Act," was finished, with a revised conclusion, and Hilda was awarded her degree. Then there was nothing. A second application to the Royal Society failed. Knox College in Illinois asked the University of Minnesota History Department for "a man" in British and Medieval history, both fields in which Hilda had done much of her work. The department replied that they had no man but an excellent woman. After much pressure (Knox sent its graduates to Minnesota for graduate study and worked at keeping good relations, and a woman professor at Minnesota was both a graduate of Knox and a friend of the chairman) Knox agreed to consider Hilda's application. After many months with no reply, and despite continued inquiries from Minnesota, Hilda heard at the end of June that a male Minnesota Ph.D. in American History had been hired to teach the courses.[67] She was not surprised. She had written to Kate a year earlier: "The regrettable fact is that as the U's here are not going into any new lines and those at home are pretty well on the rocks a Ph.D. in Canadian history is practically an unsalable article and when it is saddled with the wrong sex things are even worse."[68]

By the time she heard from Knox, she was back in Saskatchewan looking for almost any kind of teaching job. In May of 1933 Hilda had been able to say "I think I could be quite happy in a Saskatchewan high school even though I hadn't planned on it."[69] But the Knox experience depressed her, and, furthermore, she found that there were no teaching jobs available except the one type she refused to apply for — rural elementary schools paying $400.00 a year. The only reason she did not apply for those was that most of them were not giving the teachers the $400.00. She thought she would be better off working at the Bible Institute where her mother was employed.[70]

Hilda heard a rumour that the University of Saskatchewan, which had just taken over the bankrupt Regina College from the Methodist Church, was looking for someone to teach history. Correspondence with President Murray revealed that they were keeping the man already there.[71] In desperation, Hilda accepted, at $25.00 a month and board, a job as supervisor and meal planner for a house for girls coming to Saskatoon to prepare for high school. She had begun work when a letter arrived from Murray offering her $900.00 and room and board for nine months of teaching at Regina. She grabbed it.[72]

When the University of Saskatchewan had taken over Regina College, President Murray had reluctantly decided to keep the former English and history teacher to teach history at both Regina and Luther College and to serve as warden of the boys' residence. In September it was decided that his load was too heavy. The teacher, David Smith, would teach grade twelve history and English and correspondence courses. Hilda was hired to teach Modern European history at Regina College, Luther College, and in Moose Jaw for a total of nine hours a week, to teach five hours of grade twelve French, and to handle the correspondence work in History 2 and grade twelve French.

The Hilda who arrived in Regina in the fall of 1934 was described almost fifty years afterwards by Greta Rempel, later one of Hilda's close friends:

It was during the depression, and Hilda, like the rest of us, was low in funds. This was reflected in her shabby dress and shoes, and in her short, straight hair. She seemed at the time quite weary; but this could not hide Hilda's inner strength and goodness. When she spoke her face lit up and she charmed everyone.[73]

When Hilda took up her position at Regina College, she was expected to fit back into the Saskatchewan mold or, more accurately, the Regina version of the Canadian way of life. In the 1920's and 1930's, for a woman it meant propriety, church, teas, meetings with speeches, and more propriety. Escape was to be found only through walks around Wascana Lake or discussions. The discussions were of three varieties: intellectual arguments with Ferguson of Classics at table in the Residence, intellectual-moral-religious discussions with Mr. and Mrs. Smith in their rooms or on the sunporch of the College infirmary, and gossip with a friend, Clara Hill, about the improprieties of certain others: "You would think that a man of his age would have some faint inkling of the proper way of paying addresses to a lady."[74]

Hilda did not rebel. She could live within the restrictions. While in Minnesota she had developed; she had relaxed a bit. She sighed with relief when comparing Mrs. Burt's hospitality with the formality of the Mortons and Simpsons in Saskatoon.[75] She had even relaxed her Presbyterianism a little. That came back in full force in Regina, partly under the influence of the minister of the church she attended.

During her first year, at least, she felt at home only with the college misfit — the person she had been hired to help eliminate because he was supposedly a poor teacher and unlearned: "The Smiths are really a great comfort. They read and talk and think as we do, and no one else here does."[76] She could not really fit into the mold of Regina society. She did not like the round of teas that one was supposed to attend: "I and others helped to serve in our best clothes. I get to hate these things more and more, but I suppose they can't be helped." Bit by bit she found people like Jake Rempel, a Mennonite biologist who did not fit either, to keep her mind active. Hilda found another escape too. She quickly gained a reputation as a speaker and constantly gave speeches, often the same one and not infrequently on topics — like the Spanish Civil War — that she knew little about until a few weeks before the speech was scheduled. She did not really approve of this, nor of being only partially prepared to teach modern European history. But in both cases she did what she could — and she did work hard. Her former confidence that she would be an academic of high standing and high standards was being tempered by reality and by a tendency to speak and to argue for the sake of doing so.[77] Perhaps this was the result of a professional malady of professors. It could have been her defence against the overly confining world of Regina polite society. If she had to participate, she could at least partly set the tone of the occasion by her speeches.

For the most part, life was teaching and the preparation it demanded. Hilda taught all morning three days a week, and one afternoon; two more mornings were taken up with the journey to and from Moose Jaw for 8:30 classes; and she spent hours and hours marking. Here and there there was some shopping, some badminton in the gymnasium, and a bit of gymnastics in hopes of controlling her weight which had gone from 140 pounds to 154. But mostly, when not teaching or marking, she was trying to prepare for classes in modern European history and preparing for or giving speeches in Regina and Moose Jaw.

At first the students did not seem too bad, but by the end of the first year she was appalled at the change she perceived in the educational system of Saskatchewan. She did not just complain; she pushed for the development of the library. By the end of her first year she had a reform of the history curriculum in mind for Regina — alternating courses in Canadian and English or Imperial history backed up by tutorial groups devoted to methods of study — which was accepted by Morton who was her nominal superior.[78]

Jake Rempel, who came both to Regina and later to Saskatoon at the same time as Hilda, wrote after her death: "At both places we often stood side by side fighting for reform that was so badly needed."[79] She found friends and she attracted students. By her last year in Regina, it could be said "The veterans loved her classes because she encouraged them to think things through for themselves. She never objected to their questioning her statements or position as long as they were prepared to defend their position."[80]

Hilda became part of a small, close-knit group. She had opportunities to argue; she had opportunities to teach. She had her religion and she had her mother to care for. She had friends like Jake and Gerta Rempel who invited her to parties that featured games such as charades which Hilda enjoyed. She was not unhappy. Minneapolis had been a bit too open for Hilda. Regina was a bit too closed, not morally but intellectually. However, she found outlets as the chairman of the current events group of the University Women's Club, as a speaker, and as an associate editor and columnist of the *Bulletin* of the Saskatchewan Teachers' Federation. In 1935 she published an article in the *Canadian Historical Review*. In 1936 she somehow got to Cracow for a meeting of university women. In 1937 her thesis, slightly revised and polished, the footnotes occasionally sharpened, appeared as a book. During the early 1940's she kept the teachers of Saskatchewan abreast of the development of the war. During the same time she reached for a national audience through the *Dalhousie Review*. Her first attempt, "The European Problem," was turned down in 1941, but her article "The Democratic Cycle" was published in 1943; another article, "Education for Democracy," appeared in 1944.

There had been talk of having Hilda teach history and political science classes in Saskatoon in 1942–43 while George Simpson, the head since Morton's retirement, was in Ottawa, but his return to Saskatoon because of poor health precluded that. The seconding of a number of University of Toronto historians to

External Affairs led to Hilda's being offered and accepting a one-year appointment there for 1944–45.

Toronto's department head, Chester Martin, approached Hilda about a second year. She told him that he would have to get the approval of the authorities in Saskatoon. She herself told President Thomson of the University of Saskatchewan that she wanted to stay in Toronto but that she wished her "personal preferences to be disregarded" and the choice made "solely in the interests of the university." Saskatchewan's official answer to Toronto was that while they knew that Miss Neatby had benefited from her stay there and that Toronto's need was great, Saskatchewan's was greater because Regina College was bursting with newly returned veterans. Real motives were more mixed. Dean Basterfield of Regina worried in a letter to Thomson that Hilda was being used by Toronto. The president's reply clearly indicated Saskatchewan's motives, such as they were:

> I think that Miss Neatby has to make up her mind whether she wants to serve the University of Saskatchewan or the University of Toronto. At the same time, I believe that if we act too strongly the University of Toronto may settle the matter by taking Miss Neatby away from us. That is not desirable.

In the end another year of leave was denied Hilda even though the people who had replaced her in 1944–45 were still available and though two other faculty members were granted leaves during 1945–46. President Thomson told Hilda that the greatly increased enrolment made her return necessary and clinched the matter with a statement sure to have an effect on Hilda: "Your generous mind will realize the spirit in which [our decision] has been made."

Hilda still hoped that the University of Toronto would call her back permanently. No woman should have hoped that then, or for a long time after. Dean Basterfield had been right. It fell to Frank Underhill to break the news to her. By then Hilda had returned to Regina where she taught twenty-one hours a week and served as acting Dean of Women. The University of Saskatchewan did grant Hilda's request that a way be found for her mother to live with her in residence.[81]

Then enrolment began to soar in universities. Unlike the situation in 1940, when it had been a question of replacing the retiring Morton, Saskatoon now wanted Hilda back — after having given up trying to find a suitable man. In the fall of 1946 Hilda returned to Saskatoon, not without misgivings and only after an uncharacteristic decision on her part. After she had accepted Saskatoon's offer in June 1946, she was approached by the University of Alberta. If a firm offer had been forthcoming, she would have accepted it despite having agreed to come to Saskatoon.

This decision to ignore a commitment was the result of Hilda's conviction that she was not welcome at the University of Saskatchewan. When approached by President Thomson in May, she had told him that she would rather teach political science than history. But at that point she remained quiescent as seen in a telegram Thomson sent to Dean Thompson about the negotiations, "she has no special desire to join department where not welcome nevertheless will accept our decision." Hilda believed that Simpson did not want her. Thomson tried to assure her that it was not so. However, he wrote to Dean Thompson, "Simpson still wants Lightbody — to avoid excessive feminity in his staff." Charles Lightbody was being considered for a one-year appointment as a stop-gap measure, but there had been much opposition to his appointment on the grounds that he might not fit into the university community and his lack of publications.

The Head of Economics and Political Science did not want Hilda in his department because she would not fit into his long-term plans for expansion. Hilda told Thomson that she felt personally and professionally frustrated in Regina and wanted out. President Thomson was torn by his fear of losing Hilda on one side and his knowledge that not only Simpson but Jean Murray also did not want Hilda back in Saskatoon. In the end, despite her protestations that political science was her real interest, Hilda came back to teach history, because she needed to escape Regina and because she wanted more advanced students; the university invited her only because it could find no other suitable candidate.[82]

During the few years before her appointment to the Massey Commission, Hilda became involved, albeit gingerly, in the life of the University of Saskatchewan. President Murray and Professor Morton were dead, but as she wrote to Ruth Underhill, "I feel that the personal problems which made me decide to go to Edmonton if I could, are still there." Nevertheless, she managed again to come to terms with the world, adding "however, no doubt they [the problems] are everywhere."[83] She described the situation to Mrs. Underhill in the fall of 1948:

> I am busy and enjoying life. I'm supposed to be concentrating on Saskatchewan history but I find it extremely hard to concentrate on anything at all. Charles [Lightbody] and Georgie [Simpson] seem very happy. I don't see as much of them as I should. The students are delighted with Charles, and say he knows everything, which I think must be nearly true. Certainly, like the Bourbons, he forgets nothing.[84]

Then came the offer from Vincent Massey to be a member of the Royal Commission on National Development in the Arts, Letters and Sciences. At first Hilda was dubious about taking a year off from teaching for something that seemed so vague, particularly when after the first meeting she was warned that the chairman had his report already sketched out. She was also worried about her reception as a woman and a westerner. She later told Kate that for a time everyone she met appeared to wonder if she had something crawling on her.[85] It was, however, a release from an uncomfortable position. As she told Mrs. Underhill, she could not really get going with her research on western Canadian history. She was the first editor of *Saskatchewan History*. She did write an article on doctors in the Northwest Territories and was planning to go on to the lawyers, but her heart was not in it. Her heart would be in the work of the Massey Commission, which became virtually a full-time position from the summer of 1949 to the end of January 1951.

Where did the impetus for the commission come from? Partly it came from the people. "We were conscious of a pervading hunger existing throughout the country for a fuller measure of what the writer, the artist and the musician could give."[86] There was opposition. Hilda was later to summarize it as coming from barbarians, devotés of nineteenth-century, *laissez-faire* liberalism, and French-speaking Canada. The first were "those who from ignorance, stupidity, prejudice or greed or sheer carelessness shut their eyes to the wholeness of life and society." The second were those who wanted contributions to the arts to come from those who were interested and who kept pointing to the United States, ignoring the fact that in the United States, unlike Canada, businessmen who made large fortunes contributed significantly to the arts. The third group were not barbarians, nor in favour of *laissez-faire*, but they could not "accept or accept completely the concept of Canadian nationalism inherent in the terms of reference of the Massey Commission."[87]

The commission came into being partly because there was a desire for it, but the desire was translated into reality in a truly Canadian manner. At the National Liberal Convention in August 1948, the Canadian University Liberal Federation proposed a body like the commission. They were voted down. Brooke Claxton, then Minister of National Defence, liked the idea. He discussed it with Jack Pickersgill and Lester Pearson, both of whom, for a mixture of intellectual and political reasons, liked it too. They knew that Mackenzie King would not accept it, so they waited until Louis St. Laurent became prime minister in November 1948. St. Laurent was looking for a vehicle to provide federal money to provincial universities hit hard by a rise in student numbers. He also realized that broadcasting needed to be investigated. While he was not very happy about the possibility of money being given to ballet, he nevertheless went along with the project. On Claxton's advice, Vincent Massey was chosen as the head of the commission and was given a fairly free hand in choosing the other members, Père Georges-Henri Lévesque, O.P., Norman MacKenzie, Arthur Surveyer, and Hilda.[88]

Why Hilda was chosen for the commission is not known. At first it seems logical, until one remembers that in 1949 she was not well known outside of Regina and Saskatoon, except to a few historians and those who were very interested in what was happening to education and who read the *Dalhousie Review*. Hilda always said that she was chosen because she filled so many quotas — western, woman, academic. There may be some truth in that. But Vincent Massey wanted more than just a quota filler. He must have been impressed by the articles of 1943 and 1944.[89]

Once the commission was in existence it could and did respond to the great public interest shown in 114 public meetings in sixteen cities held mostly during the fall and winter of 1949–50. The resulting report was the outcome of 110 private meetings of the commission during May, June, and July 1950, and the fall and winter of 1950–51. The commission members wrote the report,basing the first part on the briefs presented, and the second — the recommendations — on their reaction to what they had heard. From what her sister, Kate, and her fellow commission member Father Lévesque, have said, and from the drafts in Hilda's papers, it is evident that Hilda had a significant influence on both the content and the wording of the report. The final choice of crucial words was often hers, though only after many battles with the English-language secretary, Archibald Day. As for content Fr. Lévesque has said, 'Au moment de la rédaction de notre rapport nous lui avons d'ailleurs confié la première écriture de plusiers chapitres importants." He added that Massey particularly appreciated her "esprit de synthèse comme aussi la qualité de son analyse des documents et des témoinages." Finally he added, "Je me souviens que, souvent, durant les travaux de la Commission Massey, elle réussissait victorieusement à tenir tête à ses collègues masculins." Further proof of her influence is found in the fact that over 20 per cent of the report deals with the acquisition and preservation of historical documents for the use of professional historians. Archives played a small part in the mandate of the commission and restriction to a professional group was contrary to the spirit of the rest of the report. The other contradiction that points to Hilda's influence is the recommendation that the existing crowded reading room in the Public Archives be maintained while the rest of the report talks about new and better facilities. Hilda loved that room and did not want to see it go.[90]

Travelling about the country, listening continually, questioning carefully, Hilda learned that there were more ways of life than her own that were worthy of respect. She even found herself almost supporting the soap opera as a necessary means of escape for isolated women.[91] She came to appreciate the role of sports in life.[92] She advocated that French-language stations present programmes where the pace of conversation would be very slow for the sake of those whose French was weak but who wished to improve. But throughout the sessions her greatest concern was for the preservation of documents for historians. And she got that into the final report in full measure.

The *Report of the Royal Commission on National Development in the Arts, Letters and Sciences* is one of the best written reports of royal commissions in existence. Donald Creighton said of the report that it "surveyed the dismal scene with panoramic amplitude and pitiless detail. In measured terms and with copious evidence [it] expressed concern for the first time at the heavy pressure of American influence on Canadian life."[93] It is easy now to forget that the commission was the first to warn of the dangers of American cultural influence in the postwar period. But this is confirmed by Frank Underhill.[94] The first fifteen pages of what Arthur Lower called a "classic report"[95] set the tone: Canada is becoming a mature, wealthy country whose inhabitants have more and more leisure and therefore time for cultural development. Canada's size, small population, language, location, and history make it vulnerable to American cultural invasion. The good that comes from the U.S. (including a significant sum of money from foundations such as Rockefeller and Carnegie for Canadian cultural development) must be acknowledged. "It cannot be denied, however, that a vast and disproportionate amount of material coming from a single alien source may stifle rather than stimulate our own creative effort; and passively accepted without any standard of comparison, this may weaken critical faculties."[96]

The next 250 pages are an organized and pointed summary of the 462 briefs presented by twelve hundred witnesses to the commission, of the work by four advisory committees, and of forty special studies. There follow 112 pages of the committee's reflections on the material presented to them and, finally, 146 recommendations. Between the recommendations and a series of appendices there are printed the reservations of commission member Arthur Surveyer, concerning radio, television, and the National Film Board. His reservations point up the thrust of the recommendations made by the rest of the committee. Surveyer wanted what is more and more coming to pass — freedom for private broadcasters and film makers to do what they wish how they wish. The present day "made in Canada" films, weekly hook-ups with American radio networks that present the most popular records in the States, the competition between CTV and CBC to see who can import the worst of Americana along with the growing popularity of cable TV (which has bought off those who might have complained with one channel for PBS) should soon prove that the rest of the commission was prophetic when it said "We are now spending millions to maintain a national independence which would be nothing but an empty shell without a vigorous and distinctive cultural life."[97]

The rest of the report, supported by all the members of the commission, has had a more lasting effect. Its thrust was that a distinctive and high-level Canadian culture, influenced by the English, French, and Americans but also by Canadian experience, must be developed in Canada and made available to as many as possible. The presupposition was that although much development was needed — to be paid for by government grants for study and work — a Canadian culture already existed. Its spread beyond Toronto, Ottawa, and Montreal should begin immediately. The key was money: money from the government because no one else would provide it; money to build museums and libraries; money to develop symphonies, ballet companies, and theatre groups; money to provide scholarships and fellowships; money to send art collections, artistic troupes, and books across the country. All of this would be backed up and furthered by a national radio and television network which would provide not only ordinary entertainment, news, and even soap operas, but also Canadian plays, concerts, and ballets.

The commission was accused of being elitist, too much influenced by Vincent Massey's anglophilism, and determined to impose culture on unwilling Canadians. Vincent Massey and Hilda Neatby were anglophiles, perhaps Arthur Surveyer, despite his Quebec roots and education, was too. His official biographical account, unlike his brother's, is at pains to ignore his connections with the political and religious establishment of French-speaking Quebec. But Father Lévesque was not an anglophile, and he had real influence on the commission partly because Massey and Hilda were very attentive to what he said, partly because he dug in his heels and insisted that Quebec be heard.

It was not only Quebec that was heard. The commissioners learned that many Canadians were concerned about the quality of their lives and that they did not intend to be dictated to; a substantial number of them were not going to have symphonies and ballets forced upon them. Hilda and Vincent remained intellectuals and aristocratic, but they came to realize that there were limits. "Our hope is that there will be a widening opportunity for the Canadian public to enjoy works of genuine merit in all fields, but this must be a matter of their own free choice." The commissioners hoped exposure would create demand: "appetite grows by eating. The best must be made available to those who wish it."[98]

Critics who did not complain that the report advocated continued government control of broadcasting or was too elitist said that it did not go far enough. The commission, however, was "keenly aware of the practical problems of the moment, and have had them constantly in mind in the preparation of this document. We have reduced our recommendations to the minimum. . . . Our military defences must be made secure; but our cultural defences equally demand national attention; the two cannot be separated. Our recommendations are the least we can suggest in conformity with our duty; more, indeed, should be done."[99]

The recommendation for the establishment of "The Canada Council for the Encouragement of the Arts, Letters, Humanities and Social Sciences" was probably the most important contribution of the commission. Thirty-five per cent of the commission's recommendations concerned radio and TV. Because of their effect on the total population, they might seem worthy of being ranked as most important. They were not, however, followed long enough. Aid to universities and for study and development of the arts, letters, humanities, and social sciences made up only 15 per cent of the recommendations, but they continue to have effect. As a result of the grants Canada has been changed. There is more and better education for far more Canadians. There are more scholars and artists who have been able to be more productive. Canada is a better place to live because of university grants and the impetus given to the development of cultural activities by the Canada Council and its new offshoot — the Social Sciences and Humanities Research Council of Canada.

The history of the Massey Commission cries out to be written. When it is, the names of Massey, Lévesque, and Neatby will stand out. MacKenzie's and

Surveyer's roles need clarifying. Hilda, standing firm alongside Père Lévesque and Vincent Massey, made the report possible. Witness Massey's letter to Hilda calling her back for one final session to help in the fight to the finish against Surveyer; restrained as always but, for him, pleading, "I would be only too happy to spare you this visit, but it seems to be quite clear that the meeting will be quite important . . . ." Fr. Lévesque was more open:

> Je me suis aperçu que M. Massey (soit dit confidentiellement) était completement effaré à la seule penseé de ne pouvois compter sur votre presence. J'ai très nettement l'impression que, psychologiquement et intellectuellement, il a absolument besoin de vous pour mener à bon fin cette réunion que l'effraie un peu. Il veut à tout prix nous voir tous deux à coté de lui.[100]

Any doubts that Hilda played an important part in writing the report will be dispelled by the fact that shortly after Vincent Massey became Governor General he asked Hilda to write speeches for him. Hilda wrote a large number of the 575 speeches that Vincent Massey gave as Governor General between 1952 and 1959. The collaboration began at Massey's summer home, Batterwood, in August 1952 when Hilda prepared speeches for his first trip across Canada as Governor General. She then suggested that she continue to write speeches for him. He quit looking for a young man to do the work and happily, though secretly, used Hilda. The method was for Hilda to send ideas and drafts to Massey and then, every so often, when she was in the East or as the result of a special trip, to spend several days with him either in Ottawa or at Batterwood near Port Hope, Ontario. At other times the speeches would be discussed only through the mail or on occasion over the phone. She never told anyone but her sister Kate about this, but the letters and diaries she left in the Saskatchewan Archives make her role clear.[101]

Hilda found the work difficult but enjoyable: "I have, however, realized increasingly how interesting and important the whole problem is, I mean the problem of saying things appropriate to a Canadian in your position, and yet things that will be useful, and that are really characteristic of yourself."[102] That she was more than an amanuensis can be seen in another letter "Frankly, your reluctance, which I quite understand, and with which I have complete sympathy, to be theological, philosophical or professorial, make it extremely difficult to say anything significant to such an audience, especially when you must preserve the academic character that has been so obvious in your recent speeches."[103] Supposedly Hilda prepared drafts. In actuality, she wrote speeches, tailored to fit Massey, that expressed what they both thought. Massey added and subtracted a bit, but he did not change them in any substantial way.

Hilda's attendance upon the Governor General did not escape attention. His wife had died in 1951. There were rumours. That Hilda knew of them is shown in her reply to an inquiry from Eugene Forsey:

Your letters are full of pleasant surprises, but I must admit that the one on the Governor General is not news to me. I can only hope that it has not been revealed to him. I can see the horror on his face — although I must add that we are very good friends, and I have a standing invitation to see him when I am in the East. Perhaps that is how the story started. But he can't marry *all* the people who go to see him! To return to the story, last winter I was dashing into my office and out again for an early morning lecture when a determined looking man barred my way, saying he wished to put a personal question. I urged him to do so without delay, if he must, spent three minutes explaining in detail that the tale as Mark Twain put it had been greatly exaggerated, and then rushed off to deal with the adventures of John A. Macdonald. Later I heard from the editor that my story was convincing and that the "reliable source" (in Winnipeg he said) had been duly discounted. However I welcome the repetition as it brings to me the story about Charlotte Whitton — Many thanks.[104]

As Hilda said, they were good friends. In their letters there was always restraint except on the one occasion when Hilda felt that she had been mistreated, but she did not send that letter. She began the drafts of her letters "Your X," but the final copies always began "Your Excellency." As for Massey, his letters at first began with a typed "Dear Miss Neatby," progressing to an occasional handwritten "Dear Miss Neatby." Standing by itself is the last letter, dated 24 February 1967, after a year and a half of silence. It begins with a handwritten "Dear Hilda" and ends "Affectionately." For Vincent Massey that was a lot.

In private Hilda treasured a signed picture of Massey. She sent a scathing letter (marked personal and confidential) to the editor of *Saturday Night* in February 1955 refusing to write an article for the magazine because of the editor's off-hand and contemptuous dismissal of the Massey Commission Report and what she regarded as an unsubstantiated malicious attack on Massey as Governor General.[105] In later years she disapproved privately of Massey's inability to transcend the limitations of his background. Publicly, reviewing Massey's autobiography in *Queen's Quarterly*, Hilda admitted Massey's errors of judgment in the 1930's (she was alluding to his anti-semitism) but admired the way in which he did not try to excuse himself. She clearly understood that in addition to Canada he loved "another society and another age." Hilda shared that love. As she wrote to him when she proposed that she continue as his speech writer, "I have confidence because I know that you generally like what I do."[106] She knew that people found Massey's insistence on symbolic actions stuffy. She had suffered from them herself. She insisted though, in the *Queen's* review, that it was his "simplicity and a sense of humour" that counted.[107]

It would be pleasant to imagine a romance between the two. Whatever Massey's inclination, Hilda had set her standards years before: a serious candidate would have to be evangelical, cultured, sufficiently interesting, and sufficiently devoted. Massey came closer than most to meeting them. Perhaps Hilda wanted nothing to get in the way of the life she had chosen for herself: scholarship and teaching in a university. Perhaps they were both too shy. Perhaps the fact that Massey was later romantically involved with another woman who became a friend of Hilda's meant that he had never seen Hilda in that light, perhaps not. Or maybe the experience in 1953 of Massey writing letters to her for the sake of the record to cover his oversight in not following through on arrangements for a meeting and then his failure to discuss the reasons for his actions convinced her that he would never be sufficiently devoted: "Each of us has his own type of vanity. Mine is not so much wounded by direct criticism as it is by indirect dealing which I find it very difficult to bear with patience."[108] The person whom she had met in the 1950's who was sufficiently devoted was Fr. Lévesque. As the only two unmarried people connected with the commission, they attended all the receptions together, he referring to her as "my presbyterian boss," she to him as "my catholic padre." But he, alas, was most distinctly, neither evangelical nor available.

The strong bond between Hilda and Vincent Massey which was based on similar attachments and thoughts resulted in one other collaboration. If Hilda provided Vincent's words while he was Governor General, he provided the encouragement and the money that made it possible for Hilda to write *So Little for the Mind*.

Hilda had been interested in education below the university level for many years. Her own experiences and those of her family were a part of the reason. Her brother Leslie's career as a teacher and a principal, and his violent reaction to the educational bureaucracy and its pronouncements were particularly important. Hilda's experience as associate editor of the Saskatchewan Teachers' Federation *Bulletin* in the 1940's had an influence. Above all she was influenced by what she had observed in her university classes.[109] And then came the Massey Commission. Her articles in *Dalhousie Review* had probably attracted Massey's attention to her. In the second of them she sounded the theme of the book that he would encourage her to write: "We thus, undemocratically, allow a large number of our citizens to be automatically excluded from any formal education beyond that of the elementary school. On the other hand, for the pupils in high school in the name of democracy we maintain a disastrous equalitarianism."[110]

Although the commission tried to stay away from the problems of education because it was a provincial matter, there was no escaping the condition of education and the reaction of many to it.[111] In discussing what they heard, Massey and Hilda must have realized just how similar their ideas were. Massey also discovered how well Hilda could write. He pushed her to write a book on the state of primary and secondary education in Canada and, on the condition of secrecy, provided the money needed for the research through the Massey Foundation.[112]

Hilda began her work on the book in the summer of 1951 soon after the Massey Commission's work was finished and immediately after her classes for the year were over. She was helped by Donald Greene, a Ph.D. student at Columbia, who had taught English for a time at the University of Saskatchewan, and by Marian Younger. The former helped with the research and wrote parts of the book including the original draft of Chapter 7.[113] The latter gathered statistics, checked sources, and typed. The whole effort cost Massey $2,349.14. That was $149.14 more than budgeted, much to Hilda's chagrin.[114]

Along with the drafts for his speeches, Hilda sent Massey drafts of the chapters of the book. By the spring of 1952 a draft of the whole book was ready. Hilda sent copies both to Massey and to a friend who was a teacher in Moose Jaw. Hesitantly, but firmly, the teacher cautioned Hilda about the tone of the book, "You may, by your bitterness, alienate more people than you convince." She warned that some statements were too general in their condemnations, "There is more than one suggestion here of 'generalizing from too few cases.'" Massey persuaded her not to include a forty-three page critique of the ideas of the influential American educator and philospher John Dewey (1859-1952), who both Hilda and Massey held responsible for what they perceived as the faults of Canadian education. He urged her on, however, praising her "hard hitting style" and "arresting phrases."[115]

Longmans Green and Macmillan turned the book down as too controversial, but Clarke Irwin accepted it. The editor became a little worried just before publication that its criticism was too strong, but Hilda held firm.[116] The book appeared on 17 October 1953. The result was both amazing and devastating to Hilda. It was amazing because so many copies were sold (7,794 in its first year, a very substantial number in Canada at that time) devastating because she had not expected such a violent reaction from the people she attacked, including not only signed articles and letters but anonymous notes such as the one she received consisting only of a quotation that the sender claimed, incorrectly, was from the *Taming of the Shrew*:

> Frustrated virgin,
> thrice-ambitious — vain.
> Whose mindless thought
> spawned by neurotic spleen
> loosened the clots
> of her encrusted brain.[117]

Reaction to the book was best described by Frank Underhill:

> The book has been received with rapture by most of the working teachers and by most of the parents of middle-brow intellectual status or better. But the swivel-chair educators who were the chief victim of Miss Neatby's onslaught regard her as pious Catholic churchmen regard Voltaire.[118]

As the fury increased Eugene Forsey became Hilda's champion, introduced himself to her, and urged her onward.[119] Frank Underhill, to whom she always went in time of trouble, was a little more cautious, but he too liked what he read, though he felt that Hilda was too conservative both politically and religiously and also too hard on Dewey. Hilda admitted that by removing the critique of Dewey her treatment of him had become superficial, but "I still think he *was* all the things I said he was."[120]

Supported by friends, Hilda stood up to the criticism. She accepted requests to speak across the country.[121] She wrote an article for *Maclean's* attacking her attackers.[122] Their rage and either inept or malicious misuse of evidence could only give support to Hilda's contention that schools in Canada no longer provided intellectual training.

Later Hilda admitted that "I made fun of Canadian educators for calling themselves experts"[123] and that she had emphasized only one aspect of the problem: "This work was done under considerable pressure as a result of conversations with friends who thought that our predicament was a serious one but that the best way to bring public opinion to bear on the matter was to emphasize the ludicrous side."[124] Yet she was unrepentant and she continued the above account with the words "On the whole I think the treatment justified." She even admitted to Forsey that she liked the fight.[125] While emphasizing the ludicrous, Hilda looked at her work from another angle. She meant it as a serious attack based on her deepest convictions. As she wrote to Underhill:

> I think that I could have made a perfectly satisfactory rationalist case — I know I could — but it seemed to me insincere to write seriously about the most serious of subjects without making clear my own convictions. At the same time I was most anxious to make a purely rational case. I therefore asked myself at every stage whether you (as the most fanatical rationalist I know) would accept my case on a rationalist basis. I could almost say that I have never been able to shake my past — I still write essays for you.[126]

By the summer of 1955 Hilda was tired. She still had to care for her mother and teach her classes. She turned down an extensive eastern speaking tour in the winter of 1955–56 because of her teaching responsibilities.[127] The burst of outrage from educators was dying down. Letters still came, though more slowly, and Hilda continued to answer them.[128] By that summer some 12,000 copies of *So Little for the Mind* had been sold as well as about 1,000 of *Debt of Reason* and 1,700 of *Temperate Dispute*, two collections of her speeches published at the urging of Clarke Irwin. *So Little* would continue a slow but steady sale reaching 14,753 by 1975. A paperback was published in 1968, and by 1975 2,117 copies of it had been sold.

Hilda had less and less to do with education in the schools though every so often she would be asked to speak or to comment. Sputnik, the world's first space satellite, launched by Russia in 1957, led to grave questions about the quality of western science education. Hilda received a telegram from the Toronto *Daily Star*:

> Request wire me collect your view how Canadian education can best meet threat Russian advances in field. What are shortcomings and strengths our system. Should we swing to science and neglect humanities. How about homework — heavier curriculum, teaching methods, length of courses. Would appreciate full comment soonest.[129]

In the late 1950's she was asked to write newspaper articles on the reports of royal commissions on education in both Manitoba and Alberta. She was not happy with what she read.[130] Perhaps her best summary of what she had been saying came in a letter of 1963 to Arthur Lower commenting on an article he had drawn to her attention:

> The education process has gone into a down-spin because ill educated and incompetent professors of education attract, as he says, only the weaker students and have to recruit their ranks from these students. I think the fundamental difficulty, however, lies even deeper. It has been very difficult to get people of first class minds to give themselves to the entirely necessary work of providing a generous education for people of mediocre ability who necessarily make up the bulk of the school population. This impatience of really able people with the task of teaching those who are less able is a problem that one finds everywhere and is, I think, the index of selfishness. It is difficult to get people to dedicate themselves to an important work which they do not find interesting.[131]

One last reminder of her time of fame and infamy came to Hilda in 1966 when McClelland and Stewart were preparing to publish her book on Quebec in the late eighteenth century as part of their series on Canadian history. Clarke Irwin, out of the blue, insisted that Hilda's contract for *Temperate Dispute* gave them a thirty-day option on her next book. After much consternation and with advice from McClelland and Stewart, Hilda sent a letter on 4 October 1966 demanding an acceptance by 14 October of an immediate non-returnable advance against royalties of $50,000, $25,000 more on publication, complete control of the text, and the inclusion of a preface explaining the way in which Clarke Irwin got control of the book. By 11 October Clarke Irwin had given up their option.[132]

After the excitement of the first half of the 1950's came the payment — illness. Hilda had first suffered from significant illness while a graduate student. Many of the same symptoms — headaches, inability to sleep, colds — came for the same reason, overwork. The combination of teaching, lecturing, writing, working on Massey's speeches, participating in the first executive of the Faculty Association of the University of Saskatchewan, and taking care of her mother, who was in failing health, told on her. Her mother died 19 March 1956. Kate described the effect on Hilda as that of losing a child. Hilda's diary shows that she was collapsing, but she kept moving between Saskatoon, Port Hope, Ottawa, and Princeton, N.J., where Kate lived. Fortunately she had already secured a sabbatical. She spent the fall and early winter of 1956 resting at Kate's house doing some work in Princeton's library. By Christmas she was back home "feeling blind with fatigue" taking 222's and sleeping pills. In February her doctor told her that she should not do any studying or undertake any speaking engagements until the fall. Hilda decided to travel. She left for England and Europe on 18 March, stopping off for three days in Ottawa to work on speeches. She spent two weeks in England, followed by six weeks in Italy and two months in England. Italy was a great joy to her. "I find in Italians all the charm I hoped to find in Frenchmen (and didn't). . . ."[133]

She was back in Saskatoon by mid-August, still feeling tired.[134] In September she plunged into university life again. What free time she had was often spent with her family, playing Scrabble, cards, or just visiting. Church was a constant. Marking papers and writing speeches for university audiences took a significant amount of time. Her health remained poor. In 1959 she was depressed and took benzedrine for the condition. By 1966 she had moved on to 282's, this time for arthritic pain. Exercise and aspirin saved her from often feeling doped. Headaches and insomnia continued, the latter treated by doing 500-piece jigsaw puzzles and by reading Agatha Christie.[135] Yet Hilda did not pause. Vincent Massey had fewer speeches to give in his last two years as Governor General, but 1957–58 was a busy time with conferences and the writing of both popular and scholarly articles. Her presentation of "Christian' Views of History: Toynbee and Butterfield" to the Royal Society in June 1958 was a highpoint. The sudden collapse and death of her brother Kenneth that fall was a painful shock.[136]

When Professor Simpson became sick in 1957 it was apparent that Hilda would have to be his successor as head of the History Department of the University of Saskatchewan. She took over officially in July 1958 after having slowly assumed more and more authority from late 1957 onward. She tried to reorganize the department and ran head on into a major conflict with Charles Lightbody. Until July of 1962 when Lightbody retreated to Regina, there was constant trouble over who would teach what, how, and to whom.[137]

Hilda wrote ironically to Underhill in 1958 about a job candidate, "She is of the wrong sex."[138] Her reaction to both the "woman problem" and to the troubles she faced in the history department between 1959 and 1962 were best expressed in a response to an invitation to be a member of a C.A.U.T. Committee on the Status of Women (which she accepted):

> The difficulty of determining the precise status of women at any given time is
> that if a woman has failed to get a position she will naturally tend to attribute

it to her sex rather than to any want of qualifications. However, I well remember being warned as a graduate student at the University of Minnesota that women as women were undesirable colleagues. They were likely to make trouble in any department. Experience has taught me that there is always likely to be trouble when human beings of either sex are gathered together.[139]

In the 1960's the major problem with the faculty was getting and keeping enough good people to teach the rapidly expanding student body. With a substantial number of jobs to choose from, many were not particularly interested in Saskatchewan. But Hilda attracted some, relatively good pay attracted others, and a sense of adventure, the rest. Her standards were "I am interested in his intellectual quality first of all but also in his willingness to devote himself seriously and conscientiously to his teaching duties." She added that a candidate also had to be able to get along with the other members of the department.[140] Hilda was careful and personally involved in each choice. Consequently, she was never quite sure about the few hired during her two years of leave in the mid-1960's.

Hilda found that she had to hire Americans because there were few Canadians trained in non-Canadian history, and those who were often did not want to come to Saskatoon. Her answer to critics was "We must look for the best people regardless of where they have taken their training. I also agree that we should be providing more and better training for Canadian students."[141]

Being a department head in the 1960's meant that the faculty had to be a major concern. But Hilda's real interest was in the students. Her favourites were the freshmen and the honours students. She would later say that it was for the latter that the department was built up, contrary to the practice of "our neighbours" who concentrated on graduate students.[142] It was only reluctantly that she went along with the department in the expansion of graduate work to include a Ph.D. programme.

Hilda is remembered by more people as a teacher than as a department head. In her public lectures in the early 1950's Hilda had had some problems. She had attempted not to read her text, but in extemporizing she had to concentrate on what she was saying and so allowed her voice to become too soft and her speech too fast. On the radio she excelled.[143] In the classroom she was effective because she was dealing with familiar material and did not have a large hall to contend with. Students remember the excitement of her lectures. Her approach to history tended to remain constitutional when possible, and when not, it was closely tied to what the historical personalities involved had written. This was leavened by an appreciation of the people she was talking about. In other words her lectures were much like her historical writing.

A student of the late 1950's remembers that Hilda never used the same notes for a course twice and that she wrote three and a half pages of constructive criticism of an essay that she marked A–. Remembering the late 1920's, a former student wrote "I enjoyed in particular a three hour evening once a week with Professor Hilda and two other students; an essay or written criticism every session, professor and three students, no holds barred." Hilda's method of teaching first-year students, whether in the 1920's or 1960's, was "to train the student to read with perception, to amplify the material of the text with basic documents, and to write clearly and logically." Hilda was concerned about students and their problems, but she insisted upon academic standards. Appeals such as "This is the last class I need to graduate, can't the 47 be made a 50?" meant little to her because standards were at stake — you either knew or you did not, and if you did not then you got a mark below fifty. And not just any mark. Hilda was far more convinced than most professors in the humanities that she could assign an exact mark. A 47 was given because that mark indicated exactly how much the student knew.[144]

Dedication to her responsibilities as teacher and head of the department meant that Hilda had to turn down most requests for speeches. She was not forgotten, though. In 1967 she was made a member of the Order of Canada, was chosen as Saskatchewan Woman of the Century, and awarded centennial medals by the Council of Jewish Women of Canada and the Canadian Women's Press Club. In 1974-75 she was awarded honourary doctorates by three universities.[145]

Perhaps the headship had come just in time. Canada was changing. If Hilda had continued to give speeches, fewer people would have listened to her ideas on intellectual excellence. However, at the University of Saskatchewan those who favoured less content and more discussion would have to find a counter to her dictum on teaching, "communication from those who do know to those who do not." Those who wanted a university bookstore full of chocolates and sweatshirts had to face her wrath.[146]

When Hilda could find the time she was busy again as a practising historian. Time was hard to find, though, because in addition to her work in Canadian history, Hilda insisted on teaching the first-year European survey and an honours seminar in Victorian Britain. During the late 1950's and 1960's Hilda was on many national committees of the Royal Society, the Canadian Historical Association (of which she became the first woman president in 1962), the Presbyterian Church, the Canadian Association of University Teachers, and the Humanities Association of Canada. She was involved in the establishment of the Faculty Association at the University of Saskatchewan in 1951–52 but to her regret she was never chosen to be a member of an important committee at the University of Saskatchewan. Those closest to her may well have been afraid of either her insistence on standards or her ability and inclination to argue her point. According to Francis Leddy, the reason that she was not chosen to be a member of the first Canada Council was that "it was argued that she would prove to be an uncomfortable and contentious colleague on a council of twenty-one, certain to take more than her share of time in argument." Dr. Leddy believes that the matter was left open until the last moment and that only on the day

St. Laurent presented the list to cabinet was he chosen to fill the place Hilda might have had.[147]

Between 1949 and 1956 Hilda talked about and did a little work on the life of Walter Scott, the first premier of Saskatchewan. The attraction was that the documents were available without travel. This was of course before photo-copying, when microfilming was rare, and when research grants were almost non-existent for historians. Technology and Hilda's Canada Council have so changed things that it takes an effort of the imagination to recall those days. The biography of Scott was to be followed by a history of the province of Saskatchewan in which the University of Toronto Press was interested. Then in 1956 Hilda was approached by W.L. Morton to write a volume on Quebec between 1760 and 1791 for the planned Canadian Centenary Series to be published by McClelland and Stewart. This she could not resist.[148]

She began work immediately but slowly. Her presidential address to the Canadian Historical Association in June 1963 on Bishop Briand was one of the first fruits. It was only when she combined a sabbatical year with a year of leave without pay between 1963 and 1965 that she was able to plunge into her work.[149] Bishop Briand became her favourite historical character, and she hoped to write his biography. This did not happen, but after the Quebec book was published she did significant work on the Quebec merchant Pierre Guy and on the influence of the American Revolution on Canada.[150]

Finally, in 1969, Hilda was sure that she had found someone whom she could trust and who would accept the job to replace her as head of the History Department — Ivo Lambi. She happily went back to full-time teaching and research. She had written to Roger Graham in 1967, "How right you are about release from bondage! I think I never felt it so much as now when it is I hope nearly over."[151]

Then came an offer that she could not refuse — a three-year appointment in the history department of Queen's University with duties consisting of the writing of the history of Queen's University combined with a very restricted amount of teaching — one seminar. The offer came in January 1969. It had been proposed by Gerald Tulchinsky, a former faculty member at Saskatchewan who was then at Queen's. It was quickly supported by Roger Graham, also at Queen's after many years at Saskatchewan, and by others. She had been asked previously to teach at Queen's for a term in 1956, but had refused because she had decided to take a leave for research on western history. Then had come the invitation to write on Quebec, and the headship.[152] This time she accepted, taught one more year in Saskatchewan, arranged for a leave of absence for her last year before retirement, and in the summer of 1970 set off for Kingston.

Unfortunately Hilda's departure from the University of Saskatchewan seemed to her to be almost as difficult as her entry had been. This time it was the bureaucracy that worried her, specifically the personnel department which was slow in arranging the details of her pension. She exaggerated the problem, but it took her two years to feel easy about the situation.[153] Hilda remained concerned about the University of Saskatchewan, worried about its political problems, and provided funds for a history scholarship to be named for Frank Underhill in memory of his twelve years in Saskatchewan where, she felt, he learned much about people and where he had left a distinctive mark because of his "intellectual power" and "sheer energy."[154]

Kingston proved to be a lonely place for Hilda. Kay Graham worked hard to get her involved in the social life of the city and the university, but people did not respond. Hilda may well not have minded. When not in the archives Hilda did needlepoint and bargello or read. She spent most of her Sundays with the Grahams.

Four months were different, from September through December 1970, because she shared them with a visiting professor from Oxford, A.F. Madden. They had met years before when Hilda's nephew Blair Neatby had been Madden's student. Hilda and Freddie were kindred spirits living lonely lives because of the isolation produced by the reserved (if not withdrawn) society of Queen's and Kingston. Together they enjoyed themselves, sharing apples, yogurt, and Jane Austen, having dinner, having breakfast, discussing everything from the Quebec Act to life after death, and, on one memorable occasion, bringing a dress dummy to a dinner party. It meant a great deal to Hilda. She carefully filled her diary in those days and later went back to add a few notes. She stopped her entries abruptly when Freddie left for England.[155]

After Professor Madden left Hilda was not feeling well, but she worked hard on the history of Queen's. One person who had close contact with her in those days used two words to describe what kept Hilda going, "ambition and ruthlessness." Whatever the truth of this, she was not so driven that she refrained from travel. She went to Europe in the spring of 1971 and to Greece and Turkey in the spring of 1972. In late August 1973, she learned that she had cancer of the uterus. Hilda had already made plans to return to Saskatoon to finish her writing. In early fall 1973 she went home, sick but determined to finish the book on Queen's. She cancelled her plans to spend the winter in the cottage in the Maddens' property in England.

The Lambis were her solace now. She had moved from charades with the Rempels and boiled chicken and coffee in the 1930's and 1940's, to a glass of sherry and a bit of wine with the Grahams in the late 1950's, to gourmet meals in the 60's as she tried to take care of her growing faculty. She had found this difficult, functioning both as a professional person and, in effect, a professional person's spouse, but she had suffered from coolness as a young faculty member and did not want her colleagues to feel the same way. Now she relaxed a bit, went to movies like "The Graduate" and "Who's Afraid of Virginia Woolf?", and had two (and even three) drinks of scotch with the Lambis, joining Jackie Lambi in a cigarette or two.

In April, May, and June 1974 she, along with Kate and Ted, visited the

Maddens' cottage in England. In the fall of 1974 she was feeling well. The cancer was in remission. She delivered a convocation address and received an honorary doctorate at the University of Windsor and accepted an honorary degree from Carleton University shortly afterward. Then on 5 December 1974 she learned that she would die soon. At first she did not stop, continued to work on the Queen's history, accepted tentatively a request that she be an honoured guest at the Canadian Historical Association meeting in June, and agreed to give the convocation address and receive another honorary doctorate from the University of New Brunswick on 15 May 1974.[156]

By mid-April she was quite sick. She arranged for a woman to transcribe a series of letter to her friends saying goodbye and thanking them for their friendship. When she had done her duty she rested, hoping until the end that her strength would come back so that she could finish the second volume of the Queen's history. On 14 May 1975 she died.

Before going on to her writings and to a tentative conclusion about her place in Canadian history perhaps the comments of her friends and family several years after her death should be recorded:

Hilda was North Country to the core, she could not cheat, she always turned out the lights. Hilda did what had to be done. She did the best that she could with what she had. She achieved what she did by sheer hard brutal work and perseverance, not brilliance. "Apart from her keen intellect, her most salient feature was that she never gave up." She was tough but not malicious. She was critical and demanding of herself first and then of others. She had exceptional "vigueur intellectuelle . . . acuité de . . . perception des hommes et des évènements . . . franchise et . . . loyauté indéfectibles . . . force de caractère . . ." Behind her façade she was warm, human, feminine. She spoke of a desire to spend her retirement taking care of old people.[157]

In a way she was like the writer she admired the most, Jane Austen, always observing, always describing. More, though, she was like the women in Shakespeare whom she admired so much. Women with feminine charm, moral worth, and great competence. She had described them in those terms to her sister Kate in the 1930's. She came closest to describing her spirit in a speech in 1952 when she told an audience of women of "the need for getting things done, and done promptly without too much theorizing": "There is so much to do and for doing it there is so little time."

PART TWO

Hilda as . . .

2 | *As Woman*

Hilda came early to realize the disadvantages that women faced in a man's world. Her father had made no such distinctions, but there was no escaping them in the university environment where she spent so much of her life. Although there were some women on the faculty, their numbers were few, and they were at times barely tolerated even though those as talented as Hilda were superior to many of their male colleagues. The faculty club and various societies were closed to them. Further, as Hilda admitted in a letter to Frank Underhill in 1958, there was in effect a quota system that made it impossible for her to add a third woman to the history department, whatever the person's qualifications, even though as department head she had the power to hire.

But she did not let such limitations prevent her from trying to do what she wanted with her life, nor did they lead her to reduce the demands she made either on herself or her sisters. The fullest expression of her ideas are to be found in a speech to the Canadian Federation of University Women delivered in Ottawa in August, 1952, which is reproduced in this chapter. The speech sums up most of what Hilda thought on this subject. From the time she first carefully thought about women's roles until her death, she basically accepted the ideas she expressed in this speech:

> Women in the modern age of their emancipation are intellectually and emotionally competent, as they have always been. . . . There is no time for feminine indolence or for masculine vanity. There is so much to do, and for doing it there is so little time.[1]

Hilda was elitist in her conception of women as in all other areas of life. She was thinking of the women university graduates, and of these women she expected important things, as she made clear in a speech to the Edmonton University Women's Club on 11 January 1954:

Women should, I think, ask themselves whether, apart from particular causes they are content to see a decline in a great civilization parallel in time the period when for the first time they can play in it an active and even a dominant role. Of course they are not content. But they should ask, too, whether this age is marked by a strenuous effort on the part of women, particularly educated women, to understand the nature of their own civilization, to realize its possibilities for the good life, and to combat the evils which may threaten it. Are our roots dying because responsible women have decided that we should discard our past heritage or because they are merely ignorant of it and careless about it? Women have leisure, power, prestige. Their moral influence, always great, is unimpaired. Is it not their especial responsibility to see our society as a whole, past and present, to make themselves responsible to preserve what is good and reject what is bad or useless? It is a cause of rejoicing that their legal, constitutional powers are ample and increasing. It is, however, of supreme importance that they be brought to bear on the topics about which women know most — those institutions concerned with the care, the training and the teaching of children and young people.[2]

Hilda developed her ideas on women and their place in society in relation to her own experiences as an intellectual and a single working woman, who had few close relationships with men, who cared for her mother for more than twenty years, who loved children, though she was not often nor continuously in close contact with them, who grew up in pioneer conditions, but who, as her brother Leslie put it, escaped soon enough to have missed the realities of most people's lives.

When her service on the Massey Commission and her writing of *So Little for the Mind* both brought her to think carefully about the role of woman in society and created a demand for the expression of those ideas, Hilda found a ready audience at the meetings of women's groups made up of ordinary people. Speaking to mothers and teachers about education she said: "The blame lies with women who teach and allow the misuse of a good thing"; "Mothers do or should know more than anyone else does about what goes on in schools"; and "One hundred years ago the responsibility for current educational policies would have rested primarily with men. Today it rests primarily with women."[3]

Each state in life has its duties and limitations, but all women should use the talents that they have. She wrote in 1961 about those married women who were qualified and who wanted to teach in a university. "Personally I would be inclined to choose the most competent person and accept the babies as they came."[4] For that to be possible society had to change: "Much of the discrimination . . . does seem to be irrational, and I think that the exposure of it in your report is most important and valuable."[5]

There was one other aspect of women's work that Hilda did not speak about as much but which she carried out in her own life — that of taking an active role in religion as she did most fully in her last years. In 1953 she had already pointed women in that direction in a speech she gave to an Anglican group, the Women's Auxiliary:

I think women's responsibility for Christian witness is fundamentally in the care and creation of their homes because that is a work that no one else can do — I do not think it ends there. By tradition the channels through which women's witness may flow have been carefully defined and somewhat narrow. They may speak to one or ten of sin and salvation, but not to too many — unless perhaps the many are heathen — and not to men — unless perhaps they are telling men about the heathen — and not in a church, or if in a church not in a very holy place. These things are changing. Of the older communions I believe that my own church has the distinction of not having yielded on inch — and even they, I hear, have set up a committee.

Should these things be changed and what should be the attitude of women in the matter?

If women are members of the Church theirs, I believe, is the duty and privilege of all church members to seek guidance in prayer, and to do nothing rashly. At the same time if they seek guidance they must expect direction and they cannot renounce responsibility for listening and obeying. It is said that Elizabeth Fry went through agonies when she felt called upon to speak to the Friends in meeting. It was allowed, of course, because the Quakers fear to restrain the spirit, but it was most unusual and evidently somewhat repulsive. Elizabeth Fry and many other saints have gone through the agony and the ecstasy of listening to and obeying the spirit — and all women, like all men, are called to be saints. Nothing, I think, could be more disastrous than to bring the issue of women's rights — even without the vanity and pugnacity that so often accompany them — into the Christian Church. But in an age when Christian women are active in all secular callings it seems to me that they should constantly and humbly seek for guidance in the matter of their supreme responsibility in serving the Church in this day of crisis and opportunity.[6]

Few people, female or male, could follow Hilda all the way into her intellectually and physically demanding world, but many were attracted by her ideas and their forceful expression. She may have been both ahead of her time and old-fashioned at the same time: an "old" feminist, telling women what they could do for society rather than telling society what it should do for women; "new" in her uncompromising standards. She was beyond old and new in her dedication to duty. She was both in and out of touch with the realities of the lives of most women. She had an impact, however, on those women whose life touched hers — be they housewives, scholars, students, business women, or the departmental secretary who was amazed that Hilda understood that she could believe that there was more to life than making coffee for unappreciative male faculty members.

ARE WOMEN FULFILLING THEIR OBLIGATIONS TO SOCIETY?

The longer this question is considered the more presumptuous does it seem, in one short lecture, to attempt any reply to it. What an array of other questions it calls up! What is society? What are women's obligations to it? And, not wholly irrelevant, as I hope to show, what are women? This, the most baffling question of all, which women blithely ignore, and which men torture themselves trying to answer, is really the crux of the whole matter.

It is impossible to approach even the simpler aspects of the problem without recalling the position of women during the whole course of human civilization. I say civilization, advisedly, in order to set aside the interesting phenomena to be observed in certain primitive societies where women have played unusual roles. In civilized societies, as we know them, women have been ordinarily, to use John Stuart Mill's expression, in a condition of subjection.

In such a condition their precise situation has varied greatly. They may have been treated with regard and esteem, and with certain rights recognized and given efficient protection in law; or they may have been nearly or completely in the condition of chattel slaves. The *Encyclopaedia Britannica* in a somewhat terse and unpoetic treatment of the subject "women" comments on "a long history of dependence and subordination"; "a struggle for the recognition of equality of opportunity with men and for equal rights irrespective of sex" and of difficulties in obtaining this recognition "due to historical causes combined with the habits and customs which history has produced." These statements after examination show only that even in the western world, where they have had by far the happiest lot in terms of freedom, women have been kept practically in a position of legal and social tutelage until the last hundred years. Exactly why this has been so is a tantalizing question. It is not possible to assign precise causes either for the long subjection, or for the relatively rapid emancipation. Proponents of women's rights have, indeed, answered these questions simply and shortly. Subjection was due to the tyranny of men, and emancipation has been won by the energy of women. Neither proposition is wholly without truth, but historians and sociologists will agree that they over-simplify the facts.

The actual facts of the emancipation, however, can be stated very simply indeed. Although the movement has taken different courses in different societies owing to varying social and economic conditions and to what may conveniently be called historical accident, women in the western world, and in many other places where western influence has operated, now expect, equally with men, control of their persons, of their children and their property, freedom to enter into contracts, to enjoy the use of all public utilities, and to join public associations including educational institutions and professional organizations. They have also won with the vote the right in theory to appointment to most public offices. They have been insisting on these things patiently and impatiently for well over a century. It is reasonable to say now that in many countries the battle is won, and there remains only the mopping-up process which must deal piecemeal with social prejudices and institutional anachronisms.

But there is another side to the medal. The period of the emancipation of women happens to have coincided with a crisis in our civilization which seems to have resulted in a very serious decline of morals and of culture. It was hopefully suggested at least by the more exuberant feminists, that with women exercising increasing control the world would grow astonishingly better. They were prepared to promise justice in society, purity in politics, and peace on earth, among other things. The sad truth is that in many ways the world has grown astonishingly and alarmingly worse. Many women are disappointed and perhaps even disillusioned, and some men are turning rather peevishly on the women who, they say, have demanded new rights while clinging to old privileges. These men now ask, in effect, what women think they are doing except talk?

The answers of many women come readily enough, and are not entirely unreasonable: "Give us time," they say; or, "Give us our rights in practice as in theory": or, simply, "Be patient, we are doing our best." There is, however, a distinct tendency to answer in a new and rather delightfully feminine vein. A year or two ago an important American quarterly instituted a discussion on the matter. One of two women writers, describing herself as an ex-feminist, stated bluntly that women's chief if not her only job was the bearing and rearing of children. What else she might do with her freedom in her spare time was her business. She could not, however, be expected to do two serious jobs. As for the unmarried career woman forced to "postpone or curtail, or deny the full expression of a primary instinct which other human beings express as a matter of course" too much must not be expected of her, either. "Women's rights indeed!" says the new feminist in effect. "What right have these brutal monsters of men to drag us from our homes and children and insist that we set their silly world to rights. We are setting it to rights, but in the home." This may be an overstatement of the position, but it is a fair indication of the general direction of some of the statements that one reads.

These new feminists are joined by at least one man. An American scientist has recently published an article entitled "The Natural Superiority of Women." As a scientist, he explains, with a half apology to his fellow males, that women are physically superior to men, the superiority apparently being traceable to a more symmetrical sex chromosome. From this premise the writer proceeds with a certainty which must be intuitive, for it assuredly is not logical, to assert woman's moral superiority; the conclusion finally drawn is that she must not mind much about matters of the intellect, but must set about saving the world using her gifts of mother love to teach men how to love humanity. Our great-grandparents could and did put the matter much more clearly, but they could hardly have been more definite on woman's place.

What is impressive about the discussion of women's rights and duties today, along with general goodwill to women's equality and an unwillingness to set the clock back, is a regretful feeling that not much has been accomplished to make the world better; and a kind of groping back to a clearer definition of the things by which the anti-feminists used to set so much store — woman's home duties, and her moral influence. Most of all, however, one senses a feeling of bewilderment. We were subjected; we are now emancipated; beyond a much pleasanter and fuller life for many individuals, and particularly for unmarried women, what does this mean to women as a group and to society as a whole? Are women better and more useful people? And is society materially improved by their new condition and new contributions?

The answer to these questions must be sought in a broad view of history and of society. After all, human nature so far as we can tell, has changed very little in the whole long period of recorded history. And that entire period, as has been said, has seen women kept more or less in subjection. The historian and the sociologist may both ask why, but probably neither will be entirely satisfied with the cryptic comment of the *Encyclopaedia Britannica* on "historical causes." I am not going into this problem in any detail. One must, however, consider the probable biological and psychological factors. After all, the balance of sexes in society, which an international committee has recently referred to as their di-unity, is a very delicate one. It does seem probable that women have an advantage and a significance so obvious and so overwhelming that men have made a necessary if crude retort by maintaining them in physical and legal subjection. It might be argued, further, that women have unconsciously accepted, and even built on this tradition of subjection because they have understood the necessity of maintaining a psychological balance.

I am not qualified to discuss this very difficult subject. The theory is illustrated in the experience of most women. Men seem to get on best when women afford them covert provocation for their activities, rather than open assistance or direction. And women, recognizing men's remarkable gifts, especially in their creative faculties, and moreover, being practical people and anxious to get things done, have been prepared to supply the covert provocation. They do not particularly resent working behind the scenes; on the contrary, they may derive a certain satisfaction from doing so.

Granting, however, that the traditional subjection of women to men has very profound biological and psychological roots, its social manifestations have, of course, varied enormously from one civilization to another, and from century to century. And, it would indeed be hard to imagine any biological or psychological cause that could begin to explain some of the excesses and absurdities that the historian has to record. Here we must blame the accidents of history, or, more directly, the evils of human nature.

I think it is fair to say that in western civilization at least the accidents of history and the evils of human nature must bear a very heavy responsibility. The essential character of our civilization is completely hostile to any formal subjection of women. It is generally said that our moral and social ideals can be summed up in the single word freedom. In the growth of this freedom two factors have been chiefly operative: the rational humanism of the Greek Stoics with its doctrine of essential equality; and the spiritual unity of Christianity with its doctrine of love. These two factors have been operating, however slowly and imperceptibly, for two thousand years and more. They are in essence necessarily inimical to any subjection of one sex by the other. The rationalist must judge all men on the basis of their capacity for rational conduct. Even if we grant that woman's reason is on the average weaker than man's, the principle must still render absurd any general disqualification on the basis of sex. The Christian, although the system of the Church long retained, and still retains to some extent the Judaic suspicion of woman as the temptress, specifically as well as by implication denies any real inequality. "In Christ Jesus" (says St. Paul, who was responsible for rather minute regulations on the submission of women) "there is neither male nor female, Jew nor Greek, bond nor free."

These profoundly important influences, rational and Christian, have operated together throughout the whole liberal and democratic movement, of which the feminist movement is only a special and recent development. They provided the philosophic and moral basis for the proclamation of freedom and equality for all men, which, slowly, was recognized as including all women. One thing more, however, was needed to translate equality in material terms. Economic necessity allowed the framers of the Declaration of Independence to agree ultimately to a union which left the negroes in bondage. In the same way, equality for classes and for sexes would have been very difficult to translate into social and political terms without the technological advances which have enabled the machine to absorb so much of the work formerly left to the obedience of the slave and to the patience of the woman. Indeed the early factory with all its abuses gave to many women of the working classes, married as well as single, their first conviction of economic equality, and their first enjoyment of economic independence — limited, of course, in the case of the married woman by the husband's control over her wages.

Three things then have contributed to the development of feminism as well as democracy; the rationalist admission of the essential equality of all reasonable beings; the Christian recognition of the equality and unity in Christ of all members of the human race; and the possibility of freedom from physical and material bondage provided in the scientific and machine age. And yet today feminism, like democracy, is faced with a kind of intellectual and moral crisis: How did we get here and why? What do we want now? Feminism like democracy has disappointed some of its most ardent exponents. And critics of feminism as of democracy are not sure whether we should go on with the mixture as before, or whether we should now try something new. It is worth while to look for a moment at the weaknesses which have become apparent in each movement.

The most commonly recognized weakness of democracy is equalitarianism. In contemplating our superiors, almost all of us are divided between admiration and resentment. In the face of superior wisdom we waver between obedience and defiance. An aristocratic system with all its vices does encourage the virtues of admiration of the good and obedience to the wise. Democracy, with all its virtues, may encourage the corresponding vices of contempt for, or indifference to, both. It is a platitude to say that equality may well lead to equalitarianism, because levelling down is so much easier than levelling up.

Is there a corresponding weakness in the feminist movement to this levelling down? The one of which feminists are accused, and of which they seem to be increasingly conscious is that although they promised, if given equal rights with men, to run society quite differently and much better, they have rather tended instead to assert their identity with men, and to try to prove that they can do the same things as men, more efficiently. One of their critics accuses them of adopting man's materialist standards; of interesting themselves in more money, bigger and better jobs, more prestige, and of measuring their success in terms of these things, instead of in terms of better human society. The result, says their critic, is a levelling off of sex differences, an extinction of sex, without regarding the fact that an extinction of sex is an extinction of humanity in whose survival and improvement we are presumably all interested.

Is there any truth in this accusation? Before reading this critic I had been reflecting on the whole puzzling question of the subjection of women to which I have already referred. It occurred to me, as it undoubtedly has occurred to thousands of others, that the women whom Shakespeare knew or created were unsurpassed if not unsurpassable, not only in feminine charm and moral worth but also in their amazing competence. One may pass over Lady Macbeth, who might with advantage to herself and others have been a little less competent; and Cleopatra, whose adequate subjection would have been a distinct boon to society, although an undoubted loss to literature. But there are the two Portias: Brutus's wife refusing to be overpowered by her husband's towering mind and character and demanding as a right his respect and confidence; and the brilliant Portia of the *Merchant of Venice* undertaking instantly and without fuss to deal with a crisis which the men concerned had nobly but incompetently allowed to get out of hand. And there are countless other women of mind and character which command instant respect. As one critic says of Shakespeare's women, they are almost all as a group completely feminine, and yet "almost all practical, impatient of mere words, clear-sighted as to ends and means." It was perhaps no accident that they should have been created at the moment when two great forces in our western civilization met most powerfully in England: The rationalism of the Renaissance and the religious enthusiasm of the Reformation. However that may be, Shakespeare is, I suppose, a great emancipator of women in that no one who has read his plays seriously could honestly maintain their inferiority or deem them as a group incompetent for any task they might decide to undertake. It is, however, interesting that Shakespeare's women are at once lovable and competent as women. No one can forget their sex for a moment. Rosalind's assumption of men's clothes and mannerisms in *As You Like It* makes her only more obviously and strikingly feminine.

· Returning to the male critic, then, is it possible that women whose obvious equality has been increasingly recognized in western society may have become a little bewildered by the suddenness of the formal emancipation so that they really have been inclined to confuse equality with identity? They can, as Shakespeare has shown us, hardly be greater than they were with all the formal bonds still on them. Emancipation has only given them a much wider frame within which to operate. That, we all agree, is as it should be, and it is notable that Shakespeare's women, like other great women, were pretty impatient of their restrictions at times. But it is, however, important to remember that it is still what women are, and what they are as women, that counts. If in our wider frame, we forget that fact, we will still produce nothing but a shallow and distorted picture.

This fact is, as I have suggested, being increasingly emphasized by feminists, but still, I think, with a measure of confusion. Ashley Montague, the scientist whose views on the superiority of women have been mentioned, reiterates that they are better than men, and must teach men how to create a new society through love of humanity. Dorothy Thompson, in other words, says much the same thing. But must we be so self-conscious? Why can we not operate in the new wide frame as in the old narrow one simply and quietly as individuals bent on doing the job that needs doing; bringing to that job our rational faculties, which are identical with those of men, and also our feminine qualities. A woman does not need to do what has been called man's work in a man's way. She does necessary work, much of which has been wrongly assigned to men, in her own way, claiming no special virtue or privilege beyond that of using all her human and womanly powers.

Such a course would indeed return us to the tradition of the original feminists. I am thinking of some of the women before the days of the "women's movement," who had no thought of acting as exponents of women's rights, but only of getting things done and of giving women all the power necessary for that purpose. Elizabeth Fry went to places where no lady should go because things needed to be done there which only a woman could do. Florence Nightingale demanded and secured authority even over men because only by exercising such authority could she bring relief to starving and tortured soldiers. Harriet Beecher Stowe became a feminist leader as a by-product of her determination to remove what she deemed a moral disgrace from her nation. Josephine Butler demonstrated a woman's right to speak publicly about things at that time regarded as unmentionable in public even by men, because only by so doing could she protect other women from degradation and destruction.

This is no criticism at all of movements for women's rights as such. I think, however, that feminists, like exponents of democracy, have constantly to remind themselves that freedom is dangerous without a purpose, and that a right is meaningless without a duty. And, considering women's duties in society in the light of their characters and traditions it is difficult to come into complete agreement for example with those who urge her to teach men how to love humanity. In the art of theorizing about love or anything else, women have never been in the same street with men. As for loving humanity, women have, indeed, an instinctive love of their families which is very strong; and good women extend their sympathies very widely. But surely women's best claim to render public service does not lie in any special moral virtue or any particular knowledge. It lies rather in the fact that tradition and temperament and experience keep constantly before women the need for getting things done, and done promptly without too much theorizing. In that respect women do seem, on the whole, to have a decided advantage over men. It was women's conception of things to be done that only they could or would do that really gave moral force and energy to the whole feminist movement. It is over-intellectualization of the movement, and exclusive preoccupation with legal rights, a too minute analysis of the relative virtues and capacities of the sexes that may weaken it. Over a century ago Carlyle begged his fellow-countrymen to stop wrangling about political theories and economic doctrines and consider the "condition of England" question. Today, I think, women should stop concerning themselves, except incidentally, about whether they are better or worse, more clever or more stupid than men and take up the "condition of humanity" question as individuals who have a responsibility for it.

This brings me belatedly, and after rather a tortuous journey, to the questions to be discussed in our panels. Are women, and in particular university women, fulfilling their obligations to society? If not, what can they do collectively and as individuals?

As I have suggested, fundamental to the problem is "What are women?" I have not answered the question, but I have tried to suggest that in the present crisis they can do no good by trying to identify themselves with men or by assuming some special moral virtue or special revelation. It is better for them as individuals, working now in a larger frame than ever before, to bring their undeniable practical gifts to bear on human problems. And within this larger frame along with their practical gifts, women do retain certain special advantages and opportunities that their husbands, for example, have not.

It would be rash for me to suggest that married women have ample leisure.

It is, however, true that most married women at some stage in their careers have a leisure and a flexibility of working days and hours not enjoyed by the unmarried "career woman" or by men. It is also true that if the married woman has a family she has had intimate experiences of the problems of children and young people at all stages in their growth. she has moreover had contacts with other women of varying groups as well as to some extent with men. As a university woman she should have the education as well as the intelligence to learn from these contacts.

Leisure time, flexibility of hours, varying personal and social contacts: these do constitute special opportunities which in our present social and economic system come if not to all women at all times, at least to many women at some time, and certainly to women more than to men. They need not by themselves make a woman a particularly useful person. They must obviously be exploited and supplemented by serious reading and thinking, by group discussions and attendance at lectures and by recourse to all the other sources of enlightenment on which educated women in general draw very freely. These two are excellent in themselves; they give pleasure, they make the individual more interesting to herself and to others; they make her a better person in her small circle. And yet in the larger circle of society they still only constitute a preparation for service rather than service itself.

What are women's special opportunities for service, as a rule? The primary ones, I suppose we would all agree, are still in the family. Some twenty to thirty years ago the one-child family, if the expression is not a contradiction in terms, had a certain vogue among educated people. It is now remarkable to note the enthusiasm with which so many young people of education and of limited means are preparing to have and are having real families. It is certainly not surprising that the mothers see little time for much beyond their families. I should like to suggest that establishing a moral tone and moral practices in her family is a woman's first obligation to society, and one which she should not allow anyone else to assume as theirs. In reading what is called educational literature I am shocked at the way in which it is assumed that the school is entirely or almost entirely responsible for matters that should be learned at home — a sense of duty, respect, courtesy, regard for the rights of others, honesty, generosity and so forth. Women who are mothers are the individuals to whom society should look with confidence for this duty. The tendency of the schools to assume it, and of women as free individuals in a free society to encourage them in doing so, can only hurt education without much helping morals.

Another obvious concern of women in charge of families is the formal education of children and young people. Education is now one of our major national industries. On its proper conduct depends our freedom and happiness in the future. There is, however, increasing doubt among university teachers, and teachers in other institutions, whether we are really doing what we want to do. There is some doubt about whether we even want the right things. When you are in the educational machine you feel like a very small wheel indeed. The right hand hardly knows what the left hand does. No one person has time or opportunity to survey the whole scene. But women who bring up families from kindergarten to Ph.D. have a complete view of the process from one particular angle. With all the helpful activities of Home and School Clubs, I still wonder whether educated women are taking seriously the education of their children. Before their emancipation they had no legal control at all, and therefore less responsibility. Now they are as fully responsible as their husbands. If they are prepared to let the state take full charge, should they not inform themselves fully and exercise some critical judgment about what the state is doing? No one can possibly have a better chance of knowing what goes on in the schools than women; but about all the general and non-specialized comment on education in this country seems to be written by men.

Still within the family and closely related to education is the question of culture, of the disinterested cultivation of the arts, letters and sciences. In the Massey Report there was much emphasis, rightly I think, on the part played by the voluntary societies; emphasis might well have been put on the role of women in such societies. It perhaps should have been noted also that the cultural climate of our community is largely determined by the climate of the home. After all, the home is the natural place for the formation of lifelong tastes and interests. It is the only place where one can sit and reflect and enjoy in a fashion completely natural and spontaneous. It is at once the root and the fruit of civilized society in our country. And women, gifted or otherwise, are the individuals who in our present state of society have a large, perhaps the largest share in determining the cultural atmosphere of the home. I am in entire agreement with the ex-feminist whom I have quoted who said that woman's chief industry was bearing and rearing children; but her article left me with the impression that she took a somewhat narrow and biological view of her job.

What about the obligations of women outside the family? There, of course, one encounters the second group of women, the unmarried group, who, although they may have family obligations have not families in the proper sense of the word.

The special obligations of the unmarried career woman are, I think, difficult to define. It is, I suppose, a question of whether she has some special function or special opportunity. She should, no doubt, like her male colleagues, do her duty as a free individual in a free society. She works, very often, in a framework made by and for men, and if she is sensible she will use her discretion and tact in adjusting herself to it as far as is right and reasonable. In this situation, however, she has certain special functions. First, it is she who must probably bear the brunt of the mopping-up operation I have already mentioned. She does meet social and professional prejudice, and she may have to combat or to endure what seems to her like discrimination against her on account of her sex. She needs to remember that there are issues involved beside which her own career is not very important. One which appeals to her practical sense, is the importance of getting jobs done regardless of who gets the credit or of who gets the most pay. The second — which may seem at times to run counter to the first — is the necessity of conducting herself so that women who come after her will find it easier, not harder to make their contributions: that is, she must not demand too much, and she must not yield too much. She must not appear as the cheap and patient drudge on the one hand, nor, on the other, as the creature who thinks of nothing but pay and prestige. Finally, she has the delicate task of maintaining without obtruding the character and quality of her sex. I don't know how one does all these things. I know only that I have seen women who make a remarkably good attempt at them, and others who are less successful. I think we would all agree that they are very important.

But apart from the obligations of the mopping-up process in the emancipation of women the career woman as an individual has certain special information, and certain advantages. She does very often live in a man's world professionally, but many of her social contacts must be with women of all groups. She has, therefore, like the married woman a broad, if relatively superficial view of society. In public service of any sort her sympathy and imagination, developed by wider social contacts are an invaluable supplement to the special or technical information that may be possessed by her colleagues.

What about the married career woman? Her first responsibility is presumably an intelligent adjustment to circumstances: to her family situation, to her own and her husband's temperament, and to their economic problems. This matter will, no doubt, be dealt with in the panel discussions. Two observations occur to me. One is that recently, to my amazement, I have met or learned of married women who are completely ignorant of the family business, or of the financial position in which they might expect to find themselves on the death of their husbands; these women took the position that it was not for them to inquire. It is difficult for an unmarried person to make sweeping statements in such a matter, but it does seem reasonable to assert that every member of a free society should have precise information on his or her economic position in order to fulfil all necessary obligations related to it. My other observation is a development of the same point. A young woman whose husband had died very suddenly leaving her with a young child was offered a job by his firm if she would learn to type. She refused, and went home to live on her family, and ultimately on her son. Consciously or unconsciously, she was like the other women trading on her sex, and denying her emancipation. It seems proper that women by precept and example should protest against such demonstrations of femininity.

Women, married and unmarried, have to solve the difficult problem of how best they can render public service in the local community, the province, and the nation. This is the topic of one of the panels and will be dealt with in detail there. Obviously women being no longer barred by their sex have a definite obligation to place their time and talents and training at the public service. The problem of the home responsibilities of the married woman is always difficult. It should, however, be remembered that too much of the public service in a local community may be done, and not too well done, by men tired after a long day's work, when it could well be handled at least in part by their wives who do, after all, often conduct most of the business of the family. Like the married woman's career, it is a matter for individual adjustment according to particular circumstances. The only general statement that can be made, I think, is that we should all use our common sense, and avoid selfishness and laziness — an extremely difficult, but very important proceeding.

Women's responsibilities in international affairs are much discussed today, and are of the first importance. Here, in particular, we must face the difficult problem raised by the fact that women are not adequately represented, according to their number, in public service. They are, however, increasingly highly and efficiently organized. What should women's organizations do in this matter? It would be highly objectionable to suggest a fixed quota. Should they rather organize themselves to bring about the employment of women whom they judge capable of making an important contribution? We all, of course, desire peace but I find the arguments that women will promote peace by womanly interests and by womanly virtue unconvincing. Women's loyalties and affections can be channelled just as easily into a narrow regard for their own families, a narrow partyism, and a narrow nationalism, as into any broad love of humanity. In fact, our practical instincts rather invite us to the narrow, the concrete, the apparently attainable objective. It might be argued that women should take particular pains to keep informed on international affairs just because our personal and intimate interests sometimes make abstract problems distasteful to us, and because, being uninformed we can all too easily be stampeded into a narrow emotional viewpoint. Ample information and a broad understanding should help women to reject narrow and personal interpretations, and to bring imagination and sympathy to bear intelligently on human problems. They can then use their practical administrative talents, which are much needed, on projects where time and money are so easily spent, and so often wasted. This is an area where women's organizations could and should make an important contribution.

I should like to bring together the threads of a too diffuse discussion by reminding you of three or four propositions which I have placed before you.

1. The subjection of women does seem to represent in human society a kind of unconscious compensation for their biological and psychological advantages. What might be termed historical inertia as well as human selfishness allowed it to develop in a wholly irrational fashion, and resulted in absurd discriminations which have been very difficult to remove.

2. The emancipation of women was a distinctive aspect of the democratic movement in western civilization. Theoretically it is implicit in the rational humanism and in Christianity which have been formative influences in western

civilization. The essential fact of equality has been revealed in western art, and especially in literature. Shakespeare is an obvious example, but there are plenty of others. The social and legal recognition of equality, however, waited for the material advances of the machine age, and for the general democratic reorganization of society.

3. Just as democratic practice suffers levelling down and from dispersed responsibility, so may feminism suffer from a ruthless identification of sexes and from a confusion of freedom and equality which are only means to an end, with the essential social ends for which they are rightly demanded.

4. Women in the modern age of their emancipation are intellectually and emotionally competent, as they always have been. They now operate in a much larger social frame, and some women have not realized, perhaps, that the frame is larger. They are tempted to excuse themselves from action on the ground that women cannot do certain things, that men do things better, that women are emotional, trivial, etc. It seems to me that it is the job of the C.F.U.W. to help women to see themselves as individuals, free to work, and to suffer, and to make mistakes. Free and responsible, they must sum up all their assets and liabilities of character, of intellectual ability, of knowledge and experience, of economic and social position; and they must then devote themselves disinterestedly and intelligently, without self-consciousness, to the difficult and arduous tasks that confront free people everywhere. This is no time for feminine indolence or for masculine vanity. There is so much to do, and for doing it there is so little time.[7]

3 | *As Presbyterian Christian*

What is to be said about Hilda as a Presbyterian? She was one — fully and completely — and it showed. She was sure of herself and where she stood. She knew that she was right in religion as well as in education, in grammar, style, in salary negotiations — in life. At the same time she was sadly convinced of her own failure to attain the unattainable, to be perfect. All of this could be, and often was, infuriating to ordinary mortals because she was so sure that her approach was the only moral and the only civilized one. At the same time, she tried so hard, expected so much of herself, was so conscious of what to her were serious flaws in herself, and was so kind that one had to admire her. One had to, unless too infuriated by her expression of the duties of others; unless there had been too many clashes. Then people were liable to stand in corridors and shout to the world "Hilda Neatby is a third rate hack" as a colleague in the History Department is reported to have done. After a heated debate with Hilda in a College of Arts and Science meeting, one of three women members of the faculty, when upbraided for arguing in front of the male members, said to the second, "I don't consider Hilda to be a woman — she is a Neatby."

In part she was the way she was because she was a Neatby. She had been raised by her mother and father to have a sense of her worth which tempered her humility. Being English and educated and poor on the prairies brought a form of pride, combined with a feeling of persecution, and a concern for others. Her character was also formed by her intelligence, her single state, and her femininity. Under everything there was a rock-solid foundation of Presbyterianism.

She did not turn a blind eye to the faults of Presbyterians, however. In reply to a request to express herself on the possibility of having a Presbyterian residence on campus Hilda wrote:

> I am not now thinking of whether we ought to go in to sustain weak Presbyterians or to create new ones. I am wondering whether we are willing to let other churches carry all the burden of what sometimes looks like a losing battle. I am wondering whether as Protestants (*and* Presbyterians!) we are content to do nothing on a campus where a notice was circulated recently by a university official asking for hospitality for visiting university teams over the weekend. He added "The Roman Catholics will need to go to church."[1]

Hilda's sister Kate thinks that she was tempted by Low-Church Anglicanism — the language of the Prayer Book and a bit of ritual. Hilda wrote in 1955: "I am an oecumenical Presbyterian with a profound respect for the Church of England liturgy."[2] Her brother Leslie said that she was not strong denominationally, but that she could not have been either a Roman Catholic or a Pentecostal — the first because she could not submit, the second because she needed reason.

Despite the Anglican temptation, Hilda remained a convinced Presbyterian. Presbyterianism came to Hilda partly as a family inheritance, partly as a choice. She remained Presbyterian because it helped to define her. The religion expressed as essential element of her being. Presbyterianism was difficult, even impossible, but it was definite, and for her it stood for individual responsibility, for striving, and for freedom. Most Canadian Presbyterians joined the new United Church in the mid-1920's. Hilda's reason for not doing so is not recorded. Most likely she regarded the new church as a compromise.

There is no need to reprint a series of selections. One, a sermon "Inheritance and Stewardship," says it all. As a matter of fact Hilda wrote little about Presbyterianism.[3] Perhaps she did not wish to impose it on anyone. Perhaps she felt that it was not meant for most people. They had more than enough trouble with the bland Christianity of twentieth century Canada.

Christianity was an essential part of Hilda's life and thought — it was the integrating factor. Its importance to her is apparent in every chapter of this book. For that reason a separate chapter is not devoted to it in Part Three. The other selections in this chapter show Hilda's idea of Christianity conceived of as something broader than the Presbyterian faith.

Hilda remained constant in her faith but became more tolerant as time went on. Even in the 1930's she could admit that she was narrow-minded about religion and that Protestantism left much to be desired, especially in its external manifestations. She wrote to Kate about a Student Christian Movement leader, "I doubt if he has much religion but he seemed sincere, and I like him better than the general run of S.C.M. secretaries."[4] Her long friendships with Roman Catholics such as Bernadine Bujilla and Fr. Lévesque and Mennonites like the Rempels must have helped to make her more religiously tolerant. Greater contact with non-Christians from the 1950's onward led her to a greater respect than she had had for all who believed, who had a code, whether it was the scientific method or an Eastern religion. Yet she remained a convinced and practising Presbyterian; an elder in her last years when, somewhat to her amusement, Presbyterians finally permitted women to hold such an office.

The second selection, illustrating Hilda's ideas about Christianity in general, is a letter to Kate in 1933, full of concern because of her sister's lack of interest in attending church services and describing Hilda's views on the importance and difficulties of Christianity.

The third selection "The Protestant Church: A Historical Essay," is a simplified history of the development of Protestantism; simplified partly because it was intended for a popular audience, partly because Hilda's conception of continental European history tended to be somewhat vague, even if she stated it forcefully. A more accurate statement would be that for Hilda, as for many of her colleagues, in those areas of history which she taught only on a survey level, she had a tendency to continue to accept the history learned as a student. In Hilda's case the history of the European continent, except for the eighteenth and nineteenth centuries, tended to remain the version of the 1920's. What is important about this selection is that it reveals Hilda's conception of the essence of the Reformation — standing by a position firmly and clearly stated.

The fourth selection, "Address: St. Andrew's College Dinner, February 17, 1956," delivered to a group of graduating United Church divinity students, begins with some very bad professional jokes. Hilda went through a phase in the 1950's when she evidently felt it necessary to begin speeches in such a way. These set pieces were very inferior to her real humour. Once over the jokes, the speech became a warning that the world was far more complicated than the ministers-to-be imagined and that they would need not only faith but intelligence and knowledge to succeed in their calling.

The next two selections are typical of a relatively large number of talks Hilda directed to those still in university during her last years at the University of Saskatchewan. She urged the students to take heart, to be humble, and to know what they really valued. She called on them to choose Christianity and stand firmly for it in the face of a collapsing civilization. The admonitions and prescriptions remain general because the audiences were United Church and inter-denominational. For herself there was no easy way, ever. For others a somewhat easier road was permissible, if necessary.

In the last selection, "Sermon: Third Avenue United Church, May 24, 1970," Hilda simply stated her belief: God loves human beings and saves humans from themselves. He has made them free and given them the possibility of eternal life. Then she explains why she believed as she did: because her parents taught her that way, because they lived that way, because the Holy Spirit had inspired her, and because her faith was rational, historical, and buttressed by miracles.

Hilda's faith was a simple one that she could explain simply. It was also profound; this she could explain also but usually within the context of her historical studies. Above all it was a faith lived exactingly and lovingly.

INHERITANCE AND STEWARDSHIP

It is the custom in an anniversary year like this to look back and to look forward: to look back and see what we have received and have done, and to look forward with plans for the future. In the passage of the Old Testament read today, we have the story of the Children of Israel in a great national meeting with their king, Solomon, affirming through him the fundamental and central tradition which made them what they were: faith in the power and goodness of God and His willingness forgivingly to renew His covenant with His people when, having sinned, they repented. The New Testament passage, perhaps strangely, takes up the same theme, but it is an ominous warning of the danger of forgetting or neglecting the fact of God's power and goodness, but adding one of the most famous of all renewals of the invitation to return. It is in the light of these passages, so reminiscent of the story of the people with whom Presbyterians are often associated, that we could look at our own position in this century, looking backward and looking forward.

When we consider the particular inheritance of the Presbyterian Church, we have to go back to the time of the great and somewhat sensational reforms of the 16th century which splintered the ancient church of western Europe, and produced a number of Christian communions which stood for a re-definition of faith and order in the Church. Our own Presbyterian Church is one of the Calvinist group, marked by certain particular emphases or developments of Christian truths which had a profound effect on the life of the Church and on the practice of individual members. It was these central beliefs that gave the Church its character. Without them it would have had no particular reason for existing:

The Calvinists and Presbyterians re-emphasized their deep sense of the majesty and goodness and power of God;

They re-emphasized their profound sense of the helplessness and sinfulness of man, and his inability to do anything for himself in his predicament;

They re-emphasized their belief in the overruling providence of God in the destiny of man in His will so to operate in the lives of His elect that finally in His divine plan all things would come under His rule and His law.

Much might be said on these great themes if we had time and I were capable of saying it. I want, however, to speak of the specific practical outcome. One might say that the people who emphasized these great truths produced what could be called in all reverence a "do-it-yourself" kind of religion, whose practices differed markedly from the ones that had been in vogue in the later mediaeval church.

In the practical working out of their beliefs, the Presbyterians found no place for a priestly group to intercede and stand between man and God. They found no place for elaborate church buildings or images, or vestments, or candles, or incense, or, for a time, music, or much liturgy. They found no place for auricular confession or penances or absolution, and they observed no special feast days or holy days.

Instead they saw the company of the elect as a very simple grouping of ministers, elders and ordinary church members. Of this group every man, woman and child was expected daily to stand before God in prayer alone, confessing and thanking and petitioning, and every family was expected to have its daily family worship. In this company there was a Bible in every home, if not in every hand. This was the Word on which people fed, daily as individuals and in families.

And on Sunday, or as it was more commonly called, the Sabbath, the elect went seriously to church, where they found no decoration, no lights, no music, no incense, but a somewhat, perhaps, austere minister in the decent black gown and white bands which were in those days the ordinary dress of the scholar. The Sabbath was the weekly retreat. It was not a day for any light pleasure, but was sober waiting on God and ministration of the Word, so that a man might renew himself in the power of God and the knowledge of His will.

And on the six other days of the week, he would continue to worship in the usual exercises of religion, and also in sober, honest, diligent work.

Much of this has changed through the centuries, and, I think we would all say, quite rightly and appropriately. The early Protestants did throw out in their terror of corruption and idolatry much that was very good. Their predecessors had come to see that music and colour and beauty and laughter are God's gifts, and are not to be despised but are to be thankfully accepted. It is probable, indeed it is certain, that in this matter we probably overrate the austerity of the early reformed churches, or at least the austerity of some church members. There were certainly some whose austerity could not be overrated.

The urgent problem today, however, is whether in making these changes we may have wasted our heritage. We may have obscured our means of vision. We may have forgotten what we really live for and by. An estate may be inherited and passed from hand to hand over the centuries. During the centuries it may be greatly changed, in buildings, in areas and modes of cultivation, in the plants grown, in the trees, in the processing of the crops, and yet it may be still a good and fruitful place to live in. It may still perform its original purpose better than ever in providing for bodily health and comfort and joy; in noting changes of the past, and in contemplating changes in the future, all that matters is the essential purpose and the means by which that is achieved.

Today whatever *we* think about what we have done with our heritage, there is no doubt about our public image, or at least our public image in some quarters. We know, for Pierre Berton has told us, that we are old-fashioned, hypocritical, not with it, dead but don't know it.

I think that I agree with Pierre Berton, mostly. At least I agree with him in his serious charges. All of us are partly, and part of us are entirely hypocritical. Many of us are dead and half-dead. I don't think I would agree with Pierre Berton about the reason for this. I suggest the reason is that we have neglected our estate. We have confused the plants with the weeds. We have concentrated on negative things and forgotten that one lives on positives and then negatives take care of themselves.

THE ESSENTIAL HERITAGE

Prayer — In the past in our tradition we threw out priestly masses and penance and indulgences and litanies, because we said a man must come before God daily in solitude, in order to prepare himself for the public worship, thanksgiving, confession and petition on Sunday. We played down emphasis on outward forms in order to give the inward convictions free play. We said, "No one tells me what and when to pray. I decide for myself." And then we don't pray, and so what have we left? Nothing. At least our Roman Catholic friends have a crucifix on the wall and kneel to say a prayer when they enter their own, always open, churches. We have just gone negative. And then we say, "No priest intercedes for us." But do we intercede for ourselves, for our ministers, for each other, and how much, and how often?

The Bible — We say that no priest or pope tells us what the Bible says and what it means, or what is our duty to God and our neighbour. We say, "I read the Bible and decide under God for myself." So I don't read the Bible, or do I, but how often and how much? And if I don't what have I got left? It might even be better for a pope or a priest to tell me what I should be doing, if I do nothing to find out for myself.

The church — And we say no one tells us how often and when to go to church. We decide that for ourselves. And so we decide not to go, or not to go very often, and when we do go, we don't, we say, get much out of it. But how much this says of our neglect, our destruction of our tradition. What is there in our belief that says we go to church to get something out of it? That is, in any obvious sense. If we believe that the fundamental truth of the universe is a mighty and righteous but merciful God standing over against sinful and helpless men and women, then we would meet together primarily to acknowledge this fact. No doubt that acknowledgement would bring us benefits, but prayer is more than pushing out a begging bowl. And how can we get or give benefits in public worship if that worship does not gather up all the private prayers and meditations and Bible studies of the week? How much we have neglected our heritage in this way! How much I, especially, have neglected it! I have come to think that everyone in the congregation should be obliged to preach a sermon occasionally. It is astonishing how much one learns. I see no reason why the minister should have this advantage all to himself.

I think our forefathers both overseas and in our own land have passed on to us through prayer and patient striving a very rich inheritance, what our Roman Catholic friends would call "a treasury of Grace." I think we have lived, in the past century, too much on it, without doing a great deal with it. We have in fact wasted our estate, or as a lawyer would say, we have "committed waste" and now we wander about, thinking it doesn't look as prosperous as it used to, and wondering if we should do something, but what.

In fact, Presbyterians have been working on this, and last June they held a congress at Queen's University in Kingston, where a number of serious people made a number of serious speeches making a number of important suggestions.

Personally I am strongly in favour of change, but change to be useful for our purposes has got always to be made in harmony with some fundamental belief and some primary purpose consistent with that belief. Otherwise you go round in a circle. I was somewhat dismayed in reading one of these addresses by a professor of divinity who seems, although I hesitate to say it, to have forgotten the essential character of our heritage. This is part of what he says:

> You see, this is what gets me, and here you and your groups, too, let's face it, you think the big problem of the church is that people aren't going to church

enough. Why should they go to church, again? I didn't catch it. That is the good layman, you know, the one who regularly turns up and supports all your little organizational schemes. . . . What is this all about? What about the man so committed to civic life that he just hasn't time for church except perhaps now and again on a Sunday morning. Is he a bad layman? God help us if that's our judgment on that man.

God help us, too, if we don't recognize good done by anyone whether or not he is a Presbyterian, whether or not he ever goes to church, whether or not he is a Christian. There is such a thing as uncovenanted grace. But Presbyterians as Presbyterians operate within the covenant.

When I read this, I ask is this man a Presbyterian? Is he really a Christian, in the ordinary accepted sense, or should I say is he in these words expressing truly his Christian belief? Of course there are many things that we should change. There are no practices in themselves that are sacred, but the oldest thing in the Presbyterian tradition, the oldest thing in the Christian tradition, is the practice of Christians who are moved by the spirit meeting regularly in an agreed place for joint prayer to God in expectation that they will be enlightened and invigorated by the Holy Spirit, which is their sole reliance for doing and being good.

There is a danger in all revolutionary change, as many revolutionaries have discovered, that you may throw out the baby with the bath.

Consider our conception of ourselves in the Christian metaphors with which we are all so familiar. We are the grateful children of a heavenly father; are we so busy that we have no time to say thank you? We are the obedient servants of a master; but have we not time to come for orders and directions? Or to use the most solemn metaphor of all, the church is the bride of Christ, but is she so busy do-gooding that she has not a moment in which to see her husband?

It is bad luck on the sheep when the shepherds are careless. And this particular shepherd, although he has a lot of good ideas, has, I must believe, been neglecting his Bible. From the first page to the last, and directly and indirectly, we are taught in the Bible to seek for God in praying, listening, learning, meditating. We are also taught by the experience of many Christians in many ages that God does work a miracle in the Christians who find that when they follow these practices they have time for their own daily work and for good works as well.

Many years ago I heard in a religious broadcast a story which I think may be a parable, of a poor, not very clever, not highly educated, man who went as a missionary to Africa. He worked or tried to work with an energetic but somewhat primitive tribe, and also with another tribe, their poor neighbours, who were called the coward men. He tried very hard to teach them about God and Christ, and he lived a very patient, earnest, self-sacrificing life.

But at last he got weary of the neglect and the mockery and the insults that were directed at him, and he was led, mistakenly many people would say, to challenge the ruler of the superior tribe by telling him that his God was powerful, and was the true God and would work a miracle. The missionary clearly had faith which encouraged him to believe that like Elijah he could call down fire from heaven. The tribal chief agreed to assemble the tribe and wait for the miracle on one condition, that if the miracle failed, the missionary would die. "Very well," said the missionary, he would. But he was confident that God would not fail him.

And so the appointed day came, and all the people gathered about, and the missionary knelt and prayed for the miracle which he named. Nothing happened. He prayed again, and nothing happened. He prayed again and nothing happened. He waited for a moment in doubt, and finally he acknowledged that he was defeated. The chief agreed and reminded him that his life was forfeited and ordered the execution to be carried out.

Then there was an interruption. Somebody came pressing through the crowd. It was one of the tribe of coward men, and coward man as he was he walked up to the chief and said, "Do not kill this man. He is a good man. He tells us about his God, and I think his God is good, too. Kill me instead."

There was a stunned silence for a moment, and then a voice came from the crowd, "But this *is* a miracle, when a coward man offers to die, that *is* a miracle. His God must be a true God." The king paused for a moment but he was both astute and intelligent, and finally he nodded his head. "Yes," he said, "If you can change a coward man into a man who will volunteer to die, you have worked a miracle. Your life is yours."

I have often thought of this story and of the implications. We may be very ignorant. We may be not very clever, but as the Bible clearly shows, we are not required to be either, and as Presbyterian teaching clearly shows, God rules human destinies, and He is prepared to use people of all kinds. This poor man was allowed to work a miracle, or a miracle was worked through him because he was not very clever, and his obvious mistake, his, we would say, unwarranted tempting of God, was in God's mercy used for his own good and for the good of the people whom he was trying to help.

In this centennial year, and looking into the next century, we must be grateful for all mercies, for our church, for our family, for our friends, for our material wealth. We also have much to regret, our selfishness, our laziness, the gloom of our religion, our narrow-mindedness, our lack of charity. But we do not have to apologize for our inheritance, for our tradition of feeding on the scripture, of being instant in prayer, and of assembling at church. We have to enjoy this inheritance and use it. And if we renew ourselves in humility, and in faith, the result in service to the community, in love and kindness to our neighbours, and in fellowship with all other Christians can be astonishing. To quote our Professor of Divinity, "Why should you go to church, again?" You go to church again to worship God with your fellow Christians, because the Bible, our own tradition, our own experience, shows very clearly that God has chosen to use this as a means whereby he can work His will in the world. If instead of neglecting that inheritance, we fully use it, and enjoy it, we can look forward to all the changes that are needed for the 20th and 21st centuries. Sometimes I think we know that a full commitment to our inheritance *would* change us, and this is what holds us back. To use a 20th-century expression, "We don't want to get involved." But our essential inheritance invites involvement, and total involvement, with God through Christ. It is perhaps not so much good work but fear of the consequences that keeps us from fully exploiting our inheritance. It may not be because we think there is nothing in our religion, but rather that there is too much — and we are afraid of it.[5]

LETTER TO KATE

133 Metcalfe Street
Ottawa
August 5, 1933

Dear Kate:

It was lovely to find your letter waiting for me when I got back this evening. I went out to get some supper and read it and one from Mother and one from G.W. — then onto the Archives to put away and organize my notes so that I can make a good start on Monday.

I will answer your letter in detail tomorrow, but there is one thing that weighs on my mind rather, so I think I will get if off tonight — re your not going to church much. I can't say that going to church always seems very profitable from the sermon point of view, but combined with what you said to me last fall I gather that your interest in matters religious is failing. I can say honestly that nothing in the world would give me so much pleasure as to know that you were trying to revive it. I know, on the surface, that sounds foolish, and as if I were trying to persuade you to fool yourself, but it is not so at all. The Roman Catholics had at least the right idea when they said that salvation was hard to come by. The Protestant reaction representing it as easy as magic is, I think, quite wrong. They may be right in stressing faith and not works, but they are wrong in saying or assuming that faith is easy because it is frightfully hard. It seems to me that it is not a gift, but an achievement — I do think that going to church even when the sermon is bad helps toward that achievement. The power of reaching God I suppose is like the power of reasoning. If you don't exercise it you lose it, but that is no proof that it never existed — I think a good deal about these things from being with the Burts and noticing how they bring up the children. You have no idea how awfully sad it is to see children growing up without any real religious sense, and therefore without any sense of duty. When you see . . . you will notice that their religious convictions have disappeared. I think their real happiness has gone too. That is no argument, I know, for trying to make yourself believe a comfortable fable, but after all Christianity is not very comfortable. It creates as many problems as it solves, but it has that quality of being alive which it is impossible to help associating with truth.

I hate arguing in a letter, and most of all about a thing that does not lend itself to argument, but I have been thinking of you almost all the time these last few days at Montreal, and taking a sort of miserable pleasure in going again to the places we went together. I cannot bear that you should not have what I think will make you happy, and that is why I ask you to try to get it. . . .[6]

Ever so much love,
Hilda

THE PROTESTANT CHURCH: A HISTORICAL ESSAY

I propose tonight to talk about the Protestant Church form the viewpoint of a Christian and a Protestant who has some historical information and who uses it in order to understand what Protestantism is about. I cannot offer a history of the Protestant Church for two reasons. One is that I have not enough time; the other is that I don't know enough. I am dividing what I want to say into three sections.

I. The Protestant Reformation; What Happened.
II. The Reformation: Inner Meaning.
III. The Reformation: What came of It.

I. THE PROTESTANT REFORMATION: WHAT HAPPENED

What happened was that there came to the surface in the sixteenth century in western Europe in a very striking fashion and with very remarkable results a kind of conflict inherent in the Christian faith, one of the great paradoxes of Christian belief. It is expressed in the words of St. Paul: "Work out your own salvation in fear and trembling, for it is God who worketh in you both to will and to do his good pleasure." There is no logical contradiction here but there is the expression of a paradox: a difficult truth expressed in apparently contradictory terms. "Do this because God does it for you."

The medieval Christian Church blended these two ideas. God works in man through the reconciling death of Christ. To have forgiveness of sin and to be saved from the power of sin, man must believe that he can be and that he will be reconciled to God through the merit of Christ in His death and in the power of His resurrection. But the matter does not end here: man must also earn and deserve his salvation through "good works" — through taking the sacraments, prayer and fasting and penance and deeds of self-denial and charity. He must appropriate Christ's merits in faith and must show in faith and love a merit of his own in order to win salvation.

It was this position that Martin Luther at first fully accepted and later came to challenge in Northern Germany nearly 450 years ago. You must understand that when Luther was born (1483) the Church was somewhat corrupt both in belief and in practice. Let us put the matter very simply and say that no fully developed system of belief can perhaps be entirely free from error; and faulty belief can help on faulty practice and vice versa, to such a degree that at times the Church has sunk very low indeed. This was one of those times. In particular, "good works" by which man earned his salvation were too often simply money payments to the Church; and too much of this money was ill-used by worldly priests and bishops who made a kind of trade of dispensing the sacraments — or who might even neglect their duties altogether. Some were good and devoted. Many led more or less scandalous lives and among them was very much ignorance and corruption even of the official doctrine of the Church of the day.

Luther grew up in this society with a strong, even a morbid sense of sin and a constant haunting doubt whether he had done enough to earn his salvation; whether it would not be his fate to go to the torments of hell about which the teaching of the Church was not ambiguous at all. Finally, he renounced a gay and genial life as a university student to go into a strict monastery where he endangered his health by rigorous asceticism. It was a wise and kindly superior (Staupitz) who advised him to use himself less harshly, and to turn to prayer and Bible study. At last he found the assurance he wanted. It came to him as a revelation in the much-quoted words, "The just shall live by faith." They need not and cannot do anything to assure salvation except to believe that it has been wholly secured for them, to accept the fact, and to live by it. Luther found infinite relief in this revelation. Later he was challenged: What about good works? Do you have faith and do as you please? His answer was "No" at least not in the sense in which the qustion was put. Salvation is secured by belief, by faith, but faith rewarded expresses itself in works of love and gratitude — and in necessary acts of self-discipline and self-denial. This became the Protestant interpretation of the paradox. You are enabled to work out your own salvation because God has worked and is working in you.

How did Luther's private anguish and belief produce Protestantism and Protestant churches? The story is very familiar. He had become a professor at the University of Wittenberg when his attention was drawn to the practice, very shocking to many beside himself of selling for money "indulgences" or certificates assuring remission of time spent in purgatory either for those who bought them or for their departed friends. Luther was particularly affronted by this practice. His new convictions would cause him to question the very existence of Purgatory. God's forgiveness would be as complete as Christ's sacrifice was sufficient. He would also of course question the securing of a spiritual benefit in this way or in any way but by simple acceptance. He wrote out a long, clear and very strongly worded protest. He published it. It was printed and distributed throughout Germany. It made a very profound impression. People stopped buying indulgences. This was annoying to the authorities. But Luther's protest also struck at the whole system of good works, at the special position of the priesthood and at church discipline.

After some discussion he was accused of heresy, ordered to recant, excommunicated. He refused to recant; he defied the whole power of the Church, which was not only all of religion, but in a sense of civilization. He did this on the strength of his reading of the Scriptures, his inner illumination, his reason. Notice these three, for they are the basis of Protestantism. In the strength of these he not only could, he *must* defy the whole organized power and learning of the church.

He survived, and this is remarkable, for, humanly speaking, it seemed very improbable that he would. His challenge to the universal church was sustained; and he founded or inspired a series of independent churches in Germany, Scandinavia and elsewhere that go by his name. It is from the German Lutheran movement that we get the word Protestant, meaning those who stand by a position firmly and clearly stated. ("I have a wife whom I protest I love.")

Historically there are perfectly good secular reasons for Luther's survival and for his success. In his day in Germany a rising feeling of nationalism resented the "Italian Church" with its centre at Rome; German princes also resented the overlordship of the strongly devout Emperor who was also King of Spain; wealthy merchants and many others not so wealthy resented the heavy taxes and fees and other financial exactions of Rome; and many a poor knight or rich merchant thought he would like to get his hands on the broad lands of the Church. It would not be difficult to tell the story of the birth of Protestantism as the secular revolt of Germany against a secularized church with its centre at Rome.

And yet, such an account, although perfectly true is only half the story. Luther's spiritual challenge found a response from many who, like him, did not feel that the external requirements of the Church fully met their need, or really dealt with their sense of sin. It was not that the medieval church denied the need of faith; not that it did not contain many who had truly appropriated to themselves the "full gospel." But to Luther and to the many who thought as he did the truth was overlaid and distorted by many false and corrupting influences. The "good works" of many had strayed out of their proper place and were corrupting in men's eyes the good and sufficient work of Christ. For their new revelation, and for their new freedom they were prepared to suffer and die as many did — but the movement as a whole prospered. Lutheran churches in North Germany and elsewhere were founded and protected by the states in which they were situated.

Many other Protestant Churches appeared, for many men were thinking as Luther and his friends thought, and finding their own way, with or without his help to a Protestant position. It may well be asked why there were many churches. The answer lies first in geography and in politics. In those days the church in men's minds was inextricably enmeshed with the whole social order. Once the authority of the universal and international church was challenged, the new churches adapted themselves to the varying conditions in the new national states which were appearing on the European scene. It was also a matter of dogma. The new churches all disagreed with Rome, but they did not all agree with each other. On the contrary, they disputed and fought with much bitterness.

Does Protestant then mean not Roman? Was there no agreement among the new churches? There was much agreement. Recall the fundamentals of Luther's position.

1. Study of the scriptures.
2. Use of Reason.
3. Inner Illumination.
4. Private Conviction — as a result of these three first.

These were all — more or less — marks of Protestantism, and they resulted in considerable areas of general agreement among the great Protestant groups: the Lutherans of Germany and Scandinavia; the Calvinists of Switzerland, France, Scotland, (England) and Hungary, the Anglicans of England, and the "sects" — even though persecuted by all — who appeared in Germany, the Netherlands, and England.

These all agreed on important matters:

1. *Authority* in the Church rested with the Scriptures of the Old and New Testaments and not with the Pope. This was perhaps the central belief of Protestantism.

2. *Interpretation* of Scriptures was individual and not imposed from without. This was hard, even impossible to maintain when Protestantism expressed itself in institutions. It may be true to say that no Protestant church completely denied it.

3. *Means of grace.* How should, how could man approach or be drawn to God?

Private study and prayer were emphasized rather than pilgrimages, invocation of the saints (forbidden) or elaborate forms and repetitions of set prayers. *Preaching of the word* was emphasized rather than the sacraments, which were reduced in number and somewhat altered in meaning. Here there was very great variation, from the Anglican Church, for example, to the radical sects, but the general tendency was to emphasize the word as power, and to see the sacrament always as a symbol and sometimes as not very much more.

Liturgy or form of public worship. It was simplified in all Protestant churches, vestments were largely eliminated, and the entire service was never in Latin, but always in the vernacular. The principle here was to appeal to individual reason and understanding, rather than to the collective evocation of a sense of mystery, awe and reverence.

II. THE PROTESTANT REFORMATION: INNER MEANING

The Protestant always objects to the interpretation of his belief and practice as being just not Roman Catholic and nothing more. This is indeed a natural impression, for Protestantism emerged as a result of a sharp controversy within the medieval church from which there resulted the Protestants, rather scattered and divided, and the Roman Catholics, more numerous, more united, better organized. The Protestant, however, insists that Protestantism is "not...a historical incident but...a permanent factor in the evolution of religion" (W.R. Inge, *Protestantism,* Nelson, 1935, pp 1-2).

Protestantism, it is suggested, is and must be, a permanent tendency in all true churches, a protest against the secularization that threatens every religious institution (including, and perhaps especially, Protestant churches!). "We find it claiming the right of immediate access to God without the intervention of a professional priesthood; we find it insisting on inward conviction in place of unquestioning obedience, docile acceptance, and surrender of private judgment. Protestantism usually asserts and emphasizes the absolute worth of the individual and rejects the extreme forms of institutional loyalty. . . " *(op. cit.,* 3-4).

"Protestantism," it is argued, according to this definition, appears with the Hebrew prophets who rebuked the priests, with the Christian Church itself emerging from Judaism, with many movements in the Christian Church of the Middle Ages — Waldenses, Albigenses, Wycliffites, Hussites — all of whom claimed they must search the Scriptures and see for themselves. that they could not ignore their inner light; that religion was an interior matter and not a question of external observances.

If this analysis of the inner meaning of Protestantism is accepted it is easy to see that it is likely to appear anywhere, and that it is constantly needed. Many a devout Roman Catholic is, unconsciously, in many respects, a very good Protestant; and many a faithful pew-occupier and envelope contributor in a so-called Protestant church is a very bad Protestant. He certainly is if he attributes the slightest merit to his pew occupancy and his envelope contributions; he certainly is if he is not constantly reminded of the Protestant privilege and claim:

the priesthood of all believers which means that no one can be a true believer who neglects his private priestly duties of study, prayer and intercession. Protestantism is not a church but a spirit; if the spirit grows feeble in a so-called Protestant Church the results are tragic indeed.

III. THE PROTESTANT REFORMATION: WHAT HAS COME OF IT

This brings me to the third question about the Protestant Reformation, What has come of it? In the first place, much difficulty and sorrow and danger has come of it to those who call themselves Protestants. What happened was not what they had planned. They did not want to make a new Church. To Luther the Church was one. Schism or division was a sin. He wanted to reform the Church, the Church he knew and loved. He had to choose between the old and loved institution and his new vision of the truth. As he said himself, he had to choose the second, but he did not do it willingly.

What was the result? It was, briefly, division, decay, and danger. Division for western Europe, as we have seen was divided into Roman Catholic warring on Protestant, and Protestants — groping wildly for some true and sound social expression of their new vision — warring on and persecuting each other. Decay, for when the inner vision faded, as it must at times in every individual a terrible apathy could succeed. The Protestant rejected many of the formalities of set prayers and religious observances, of ecclesiastical discipline, of the lavish use of symbols. He forgot, perhaps, that these things may be "the scaffolding of a simple and genuinely Christian faith" *(op. cit., p. 86)*. Danger, for when apathy and dryness set in there was a tendency to draw from the Bible a set of cold and dead rules more loveless and inhuman than the rules of the medival church. It was all very well to set the Bible in the place of the Pope, but in the hands of those who have lost the vision and the spirit of Christian love the Bible can be a terrible power. It is not, as Protestants have sometimes supposed, a magic formula, a mechanical answer to all questions.

What has saved the Protestant churches from self-destruction in this fashion has been the *positive spirit of Protestantism*. It has been obedience to the command to search the Scriptures with dedicated reason, as well as with humble faith, to wait for the inner light, to seek earnestly for personal conviction, not in arrogant self-assertion, but in humble seeking for divine guidance. This spirit has protected Protestants against the dangers of their own formalism through a series of periods of renewal or revival.

The English-speaking world is very familiar with many of these renewals. In the sixteenth and seventeenth centuries, the Puritans asserted against the formalism of the Church of England the need for personal piety, for private devotions, for family prayer, and for that simplicity of life which is the sign of inner peace and security. Puritanism itself became a formula, but in the eighteenth century there was another great renewal with the mass preachings, the study groups and the love feasts of the Methodists. They were followed in England by the Evangelicals; by the modern Protestant missionary movement, a spontaneous outpouring of love and loyalty marked by extraordinary individual sacrifices and achievements. This was accompanied and followed in the nineteenth century by great periods of "revival" in England and in Scotland. Protestantism is, indeed, a process of constant revival and renewal. Only through such a process can Protestant churches live.

In our own time, we are, perhaps, seeing such a renewal. It is taking two forms. One is called neo-orthodoxy, a reaction against the scientism which proved a terrible stumbling block to many Protestants because, appearing in many forms, from pure science to various forms of Biblical scholarship it seemed to take away many of the foundations of belief — faith in the Word as a living revelation of God. The neo-orthodoxy of the twentieth century strives to maintain the four Protestant principles, reverence for revelation in the Scriptures, the free use of reason, the waiting on the inner light, and the privilege and duty of private conviction.

The other great movement of the present day is the oecumenical movement. Protestants see now more clearly than ever what they have always known, that division of the Church is itself a sin; that as Christ is one, so all his followers should be one in Him. They cannot renounce what makes them Protestants: the right and duty of private judgment and conviction. But they are struggling to go below their differences to discern and reveal the true unity which makes them one in Christ. In this terrifying age in which we live, it may be that we shall yet see through Protestantism not only a true renewal, but a reunion of the Church of Christ.[7]

ADDRESS: ST. ANDREW'S COLLEGE DINNER, FEB. 17, 1956

I am indeed glad to be with you tonight on this very happy occasion. My recollections of the College and associations with it are very long and very pleasant. I recall when the present building was erected. I even recall the venerable rather barnlike structure which preceded it, although not on this site. And of course any member of the history department ought to recall the first Principal of this College, who was the first Professor of History in this University.

Talking of professors I must add that I am not only happy but surprised and grateful to find myself here. You listen to them all day. Have you not had enough? I almost wondered when I received the invitation whether you were not — most appropriately — carrying through what theologians call a work of supererogation — which I take to be a pious act that no reasonable person could really expect of you. Because of course in this age of open confession no professor has any illusions about himself. It is all too easy for him not to think of himself more highly than he ought. Formerly he was respected for his supposed knowledge — but nowadays who would be stupid enough to value that? Anyhow now they do not know very much. The last story I read was of the professor who got older and stupider, and older and stupider, and older and stupider — until at last, the professors noticed. And then there was the Oxford professor (Oxford of course) (in Mastermen) — a Fellow of New College. He met a colleague one day and observed him to be wearing one black shoe and one brown. "This," he said, "is strange." "Yes indeed," said the other, "I have worried about this problem all day and stranger still, much stranger, is the fact that I distinctly observed in my bedroom this morning another pair of which one was black and one was brown, too, I really cannot understand it at all."

However, in Saskatchewan there is hope. At last they become (even chronologically) 65, and retire to Victoria, where, as the Vancouver man said, he had once seen a dog chasing a cat — both walking.

It is, however, time for me to stop talking about myself and talk about you. The graduates who are honoured this evening have come to a critical period in their careers. I suppose that, strongly as I may support intellectual values in education, I ought as a Christian to acknowledge that the time has come, in a sense, for you to deny your learning. At least I am informed that you often do so. Just as the young B.A. proclaims with a joyous shout as he receives his diploma "And that's enough of that" so the newly made B.D. adjusting his hood may sometimes, I am told, be heard to murmur piously, "Thank God I am done with theology!"

And why not? Everyone knows that the best are not the most learned or even wisest. That applies, surely, to the pastors as well as the flock. The most faithful shepherds are not always to be found among the highbrows. The most convincing preachers are certainly not always in that class. And the foolishness of preaching can save. Will you forgive me if I say that I sometimes wish some preachers did not depend quite so much on that passage?

But this easy sloughing off of learning is not pure anti-intellectualism. Just as it was not love of learning chiefly that drew the young minister to his studies, so he may congratulate himself that, the tedious preliminaries being over, he can begin the true work of preacher and pastor among those who like him all the better for not being highbrow.

There is indeed a sense today in which the work of the minister seems to have become relatively easy. "There are no atheists in foxholes" it was said in the last war. We are still in foxholes. If only in desperation people are looking for religion. The fields are white. You may well say "Let's go out and reap. We don't need pagan learning. We can preach 'the simple gospel.' "

All this is true and sound. It is also, and at the same time, false and dangerous. The gospel is not simple in the sense of being easy and never has been except to the simple and humble who have special grace to receive it. But our age, though ignorant perhaps, is not simple and not humble. The insistence of the Church on secular intellectual attainments and on theological training is due not to snobbishness but — shall I say — to a kind of holy worldliness; to a conviction that only through long and patient study in a university or out of it can the gospel be preached in purity as well as in simplicity.

And, another thing: the need for religion in our day will be met, but not necessarily by the Christian religion. There are other gospels abroad, much more simple (and also far more flattering to the believer) than Christianity. There is Communism, there is racism, there are fascisms of every kind. There are infinite varieties of very simple and quite flattering "social gospels." People will look for religion and they will find it. They will not necessarily find the truth, the hidden wisdom, that is entrusted to you for their sakes.

The great intellectual problem in teaching, and I think in preaching, is not necessarily lethargy or opposition. It is often rather certain basic assumptions cherished by those who may be only half-conscious, or perhaps wholly unconscious of them. The assumption unexpressed and undefined, very often colours and transforms all that we hear and learn, and exercises a subtle influence over all our decisions and our actions. You cannot teach people unless you know and understand any assumptions they may harbour that are relevant to what you have to say. And if those assumptions run counter to you, you must bring them out into the open and deal with them, sooner or later.

It was not at one time, perhaps, so difficult to preach the simple gospel simply. The preacher might be addressing the complacent, the careless and the wicked, but he was generally speaking to those with certain moral and spiritual assumptions, assumptions derived from such profound simplicities as the Ten Commandments, the Twenty-third Psalm, the Creed or the Catechism. These assumptions so favourable to all he had to say were dormant perhaps. He will encounter no such readiness today. Today the Christian minister will encounter two assumptions which, far from favouring his work tend, humanly speaking, to stultify it completely. His task is to preach God to man. Modern scientific and psychological findings have — warrantably or otherwise — tended to produce widespread assumptions about God and man which essentially deny any true existence either to the one or to the other. Those who, not recognizing this, undertake to expound the Word may indeed seem to themselves to be beating the air.

I should like to examine those two assumptions very briefly. To deal with them the young preacher needs all his resources of learning, secular and sacred, as well as a double portion of the evangelical spirit.

1. The Elimination of God.

There is no need to remind you of the practical marvels of science or of the supposed pitfall of the theory of evolution. I am not going to speak of them. The falsity of this simple gospel is far more dangerous. It consists in the amazing revelations of truths undreamed of before. The immensity, the complexity — and the "manoeuvrability" of nature have been revealed by a race of patient, inspired, dedicated men, following their "method," humbly sharing their knowledge and building on each other's work. They have endured hardship and drudgery so great as to condemn them to something like a conventual life. For many of them the good is the true, and the true is what is revealed by their discipline. True there are perplexities and even terrors today for the scientist as he contemplates the work of his hands. But the work on which our food, shelter and health depend cannot stop. The devoted scientist points out that he and his colleagues work together in peace, that they produce plenty, and that they reveal truth, all by following their method. Shall we be medieval and say that they do these things by obeying their "Rule." If others would learn from them the world would be a better place to live in. Religious observances and ceremonies, church clubs and schools are very well on the fringe but Science will lead into the way of all truth. This conviction has ruled the lives of many devoted men; it is a deeply rooted *assumption* in the world which externally is dominated by science. This is what you will be preaching to. It's not bad: it is good. It is so good and so great that there doesn't seem much room for anything else. Therein lies its falsity and its danger.

2. The Destruction of Man.

Our current assumption concerning man is more simple and, in some ways more terrifying. Joseph C. Krutch in *The Measure of Man* quotes the Dean of Humanities at the Massachusetts Institute of Technology as saying at the Convocation of 1949 that scientists were contemplating their "approaching scientific ability to control men's thoughts with precision." Mr. Churchill (as he was then) who was present remarked, characteristically, that he would "be very content to be dead before that happens."

Mr. Churchill may be so fortunate, but a younger generation, unhappily aware of "brainwashing," cannot dismiss such prophecies from serious consideration. The truth is that our scientific insights, turned increasingly on ourselves, now suggest far more important conclusions than any implied by the Darwinian theory of evolution. Krutch in tracing the development of man's thought about himself remarks that two or three centuries ago Hobbes was proclaiming man to be an animal while Descartes was proving that an animal was a machine. Today we are prepared to assert that man is a machine and no more than a machine. The integrity of his reason and of his conscience, involving moral choice and the freedom of the will is tacitly denied. Scientifically his behaviour can be explained by other means which seem to render traditional explanations superfluous or misleading.

Of course few people are prepared completely to deny the humanity of man, but his distinctive character is being steadily whittled away by the unspoken assumptions which derive from the new scientific and psychological trends of thought. It is unfortunate that these assumptions are unspoken. If they were expressed in words some one would immediately retort: "It is no doubt true that man is conditioned by his inner drives and his external environment; but it is only part of the truth. It is equally true that he is a free, a responsible and a moral being. This human paradox has been recognized since man began to examine himself. Scientific findings have not revealed it. They have only defined it more sharply."

But the issue is seldom this clearly defined. Instead we vaguely and charitably assume that we are helpless and irresponsible. Every school teacher knows that the child is not fully responsible for anything that he does or does not do, is, or is not. All professors must have noted how engagingly frank young people are today in admitting their limitations and their errors (never of course vices or sins). There is no embarrassment; these are "symptoms" which may and should be discussed with detachment.

As Krutch points out, we thus establish the innocence of all men, so long as they admit their utter helplessness. They are rendered incapable of evil or of good. Their humanity is destroyed. And, he goes on, if you accept "today's thinking" you will have to say to the young man who seeks your advice:

> Some day the time will come when you will have an opportunity to murder your grandmother and to steal her purse. Do not, if that time comes, be foolish or unenlightened. In the first place, murdering one's grandmother is now called "anti-social conduct" — which doesn't sound so bad. But that is not the real point. The real point is that if you tried to resist temptation, even if you merely tried to summon prudence, you would only be calling on consciousness for aid which consciousness, being an epiphenomenon, is powerless to give. Be modern! Stand quietly by until the event informs you whether or not the unique economic, sociological, and psychological factors in your past history have determined that you will or will not hit the old lady over the head with an ax.

Krutch is being funny, of course, but not as funny as one would like to think. And what must we think of the Vancouver parents and citizens who, facing the undeniable facts of juvenile delinquency, proclaim with loud cheers that "there's nothing wrong with our adolescents," which leads one to suppose that what is wrong with Vancouver is too many adolescents of all ages. No wonder the young ones having no true sense of urgency are driven to destruction. Encouraged (albeit unconsciously) to assume that nothing is their fault and that therefore — obviously — they can do nothing about it — they alternate between apathy and indifference on the one hand, and violently anti-social performances on the other. Men who deny their freedom tend to destroy it by their very denial. But at bottom everyone — even the most irresponsible adolescent — knows that he *is* free and he *is* responsible and his most irresponsible actions are, in a sense, his assertion of the fact.

What does this mean to you in your calling? The Christian Church has the answer for this lost society at once arrogant and helpless, proud in its despair. What it needs is indeed the simple gospel: the gospel of God's love which has met man's helplessness, which does not condition him but redeems and renews him. It is simple enough but immensely difficult. You have to meet people where they are. You don't today just open the door and invite them in. You have to go on a lonely and difficult and dangerous track to find them. You have to penetrate a whole complex of assumptions which produce a mixture of apathy and complacency. I don't deny miracles of grace and I do expect manna from heaven, but may I return to my first principle? The Christian is told to put on his armour. Your education and the intellectual opportunities that are yours are surely given you for your work in the Providence of God, and through His grace. The Church in its mission of evangelism does not, perhaps, need learned and scholarly sermons. It needs learned and scholarly and dedicated men, who are in every way equipped to pierce through the perplexities and complexities of modern life and reveal the truth in all its sublime — and profound — simplicity.[8]

THE VITAMIN VIRTUE

The writer of the Epistle of St. James said, "My brothers what use is it for a man to say he has faith when he does nothing to show it? Can faith save him? Suppose a man a brother or a sister is in rags with not enough food for the day and one of you says, 'Good luck to you, keep yourselves warm and have plenty to eat.' But does nothing to supply their bodily needs, what is the good of that? So is faith; if it does not lead to action it is in itself a lifeless thing."

We would all agree with this. The everyday business of the Christian is to examine his behaviour to see if it consistently bears out his profession or if, to use the old cliché, any relationship between his Christianity and his conduct is purely coincidental. And Christians do this for the most part reasonably well. Especially in an age of decreasing faith they cannot be unconscious that if they don't others do. They try to practise the virtues.

There are virtues that are sometimes called the pagan virtues like honesty, industry, diligence, prudence, temperance, frugality, modesty, courage, fortitude, and so on; and then there are others that are more closely related to what we think of as the special Christian virtue of love, kindness, thoughtfulness, courtesy, generosity, unselfishness, patience. All of these virtues can be practised by non-Christians. Too often they are more evident in non-Christians than in some Christians. This is the mystery of the faith. It is the mystery referred to by Christ when during the Last Supper with his disciples he spoke of the uselessness for any purpose whatever of the Christian whose conduct does not show his Christianity. As he put it the Christian who bears no fruit. One might almost say it would be better to be a good pagan.

On the other hand, for those who do carefully practise the virtues there is another danger. As we anxiously cultivate our virtues we cannot help but cherish them and value them and this is very dangerous. The flower (to continue the metaphor) shrivels from our touch, the leaf wilts, the whole plant appears unlovely to everyone, except unfortunately to ourselves. How repulsive to others are the virtues on which we self-consciously plume ourselves — our generosity, our politeness, our patience, our honesty, our diligence. How they must feel and how they must long to say, "I do hate your smugness." And surely we must agree that they are right. The only virtues that we really possess are the ones we are unaware of. But yet we are supposed to work at them. How can you grow good fruit without knowing it?

The answer, I think, lies in what I am calling the vitamin virtue. It is, if it is genuine, invisible, silent, resulting in no positive word or action. As a rule it doesn't cause us to do anything at all. It does, however, preserve and enhance and strengthen all the other virtues. And in its truest form I think it is perhaps the most essentially Christian as well as the rarest of all virtues.

I am referring as you have no doubt guessed by this time to the virtue of humility. It has never been a popular virtue and I think one could say that now it is not only unpopular, it is even persecuted. This is not an age of self-abasement but of self-expression. The world is not looking for broken and empty vessels, but for mature and fully integrated personalities. The banishment of humility from polite society has gone so far that even courteous people avoid apologies because an apology shows that they have been wrong. To them it seems so undignified and unworthy to have been wrong that they are sure that you would rather they should not even mention it. Westerners used to make fun of orientals because they were so anxious to "save face" that they would not admit even obvious things but now we too are spending a great deal of our time trying to save face and sometimes these attempts exaggerate the importance of the thing that was originally wrong. We believe, however, that we must go to all lengths to preserve untarnished our public image. It is this tendency that makes us forget about the importance of humility. It makes us forget that humility is a virtue at all.

The reason for this attitude on our part is simple and understandable. The world too often confuses humility with humiliation and apology with unworthy self-abasement and lack of proper self-respect. And so it seems simpler in a kindly way for everybody to assume that nothing bad has happened and nobody has ever done anything they should not do. Unfortunately honest people know, if they have done wrong or injured their neighbours, that something *has* happened. The pride which makes a frank and humble acknowledgement of their fault impossible may produce a kind of outward confidence. At the same time it produces an inner insecurity because half-consciously one is hiding something that one is afraid of. Outwardly this fear may eventually show itself as real hostility. Today perhaps we overwork the expression "insecurity" but we are all aware of people who are bumptious, arrogant, even quite offensive because inwardly they are afraid of themselves. They have not had the courage to look at themselves frankly and take stock.

For this problem Christianity has a sure remedy because for the Christian, humility, that is an honest acknowledgement of the fact of goodness and of his own wrongdoing is basic.

I don't mean that the Christian should imitate the repulsive humility of Dickens's Uriah Heep who went about proclaiming that he was a very humble person, but all the while scheming to injure and cheat his neighbour as compensation for his servility. Servility is not humility. Humility, true humility, can only come from contemplation of a goodness which is not our own but which captivates us. Humility means forgetting ourselves in the contemplation of the goodness and the greatness of another person or persons.

This can often happen even in human relations. The complacent but honest individual sometimes has a flash of revelation in which he sees himself truly beside his neighbour and knows that this neighbour, whom he perhaps has despised or under-rated, is a better man than he is. From the moment that he is enabled to make this honest acknowledgement to himself, and to accept himself in this inferior role, he is in a mysterious way a better man. All his drooping virtues raise their heads and he is greater and (even if less self-satisfied) more fundamentally content with himself than he was before.

Moments like these, however, are likely to be passing. Only one Person can keep the Christian in true humility and that is the Person of Christ through whose sacrifice a man is reconciled to God. To put it in human terms the person who honestly admits daily that a good man had to die because he himself behaved badly is not likely to want to be bumptious and when the admission is made to God through Christ the grace of humility may be hoped for.

This grace does not come all at once. I said at the beginning that humility is the rarest of virtues although it is essential for the nourishment of all other virtues. And yet it should be no more difficult for the Christian if he is in any way consistent. He ought not to find it difficult to admit that he may not be very clever or very charming, or very handsome, or very popular because if he is consistent with his Christian profession he can say that he has offered himself just as he is to God and that, therefore, in a sense he has no more concern with himself. He may, in fact, simply forget himself and all his virtues, leaving them to look after themselves. You all know the saying "Love God and do as you please." If you love God you will contemplate Him, if you contemplate Him you cannot be anything but humble, and if you are truly humble in His presence the grace that is given you cannot but express itself in virtues that you desire. And so when someone like James encounters you he will have two evidences of faith.

First that you do exhibit the virtues he mentions, and second that you are quite unaware of the fact.[9]

THE PURE IN HEART

"Blessed are the pure in heart"
Therefore worship the Lord thy
God and Him only. . . .

The expression "the pure in heart" is not often used today, and one may wonder what the meaning is. James suggests it: "Purify your hearts, you men of double mind."

The pure in heart are the single-minded. They have heard the call: "Have no other gods before me." "Love the Lord thy God with heart and soul and strength and mind." And the commandment is added, "Love your neighbour as yourself." This is worth noting. The love of God does not prevent, it rather permits us to love other people, and even ourselves. This must be allowed, because it is used for the love for our neighbours. But only the "pure-hearted" can efficiently and intelligently love either himself or his neighbour.

Is the first commandment or the second often broken? Probably all the time, more obviously than any other commandment. But because we do not use the word "idol" or "idolatry" much, we hardly notice it.

When Gulliver fell into the hands of the Lilliputians, they were ordered by their king to get into his pockets to see if he carried any dangerous weapons. They reported that he had on him three things: a great carpet large enough to cover the hall of the palace (his handkerchief); a machine or engine with pillars in a row like those surrounding the palace (his comb); and another engine that made a sound like a waterfall, with a hard covering, but a covering that one could see through. It was reported that this might be an animal but more likely it was his god, because he consulted it so often. It was, of course, his watch.

Swift had some reason in his satire of man, the slave or idolator of time. But his definition of a god is simple and to the formally religious, startling. Your god is what you consult the most frequently. Your god is the one to whom you always pay attention. Your god is what your mind is fixed on. Your god is the one you desire and determine to obey.

Everyone knows the classic story of idolatry. The children of Israel had been brought out of Egypt, fed with manna, given water from the rock. At last they stand before the thunder from Sinai, in the presence of God, who speaks through Moses and makes with them his covenant: they are his people, redeemed from Egypt. He claims them and will provide for them, "His peculiar treasure" and "His Holy Nation." And they will obey him and in "purity of heart" keep faith with him. They promise "all that the Lord has spoken we will do." Then after the ten commandments and other commandments have been given, Moses goes up to the mountain to learn more of the law, and is absent for 48 days. The people become lonely and frightened, bored and restless. And, at their request, Aaron takes their jewellery and ear-rings, and makes the image of a golden calf. They feast and dance before it, heedless of God, Moses and the Covenant, until Moses returns to remind them that they have "corrupted them- selves" by forgetting the Covenant and have lost their "purity of heart," the single allegiance that they had pledged.

What is the character of this tempting calf, this classic idol?

First, it is produced because Moses is absent and God has not been heard from. In fact, as the story says, it was the people who asked Aaron to "make" a god, because Moses had vanished and probably would not return. And they said they must have something "to go before them."

In three thousand years we have not changed much. We have to have a god to consult. In this age, for many, "God is Dead," but we are a "do it yourself" people. We can make gods.

A lot of people have one single god that they follow with what they would call single-heartedness except that if it is true that there is but one God, he is the only being that can be followed with singleness of heart. But the world has very powerful gods, like money, the pay cheque; like prestige, to be first, the biggest, the best; in academics and social affairs, in sports, or perhaps in reverse to be the most eccentric or most far out, the one most capable of getting attention; and there is the even more powerful god of the 20th century, the god of power, in a power-hungry age. It is not just dictators who want power — everybody wants it. People want to be administrators, they want to be public relations men, they want to be organizers, they want to be operators, they want to be the boss. This is a more powerful and subtle idol even than money, prestige, or popularity.

These are the idols of the one-idol people. Those who are prepared to sacrifice everything single-mindedly for success. And it is right to remember that some kinds of one-idol people choose very fine idols, such as eminence in learning, in music, in painting, in literature, in science. These kinds of distinction or success are very fine, but not if idols, because the idol corrupts the heart.

Secondly, other people compensate for the absence of God by a bewildering variety of idols. These people do not have a very precise scale of values or a very clear hierarchy of idols. Many a young man must ask himself, if he stops to think about it long enough, which he values the most, his car, his current girl friend, his chance of making the team, his chance of getting a fellowship, or, if he happens to think of it, the likelihood of his keeping his health. One of the most difficult problems of the average person, and most of us are average, is to get our idols sorted out, and often failing to do so we run rather distractedly from one shrine to another. The people with many idols may perhaps be rather pleasanter than the single-idol men, but they are less dignified.

Thirdly, in the end, whether we are single or multiple idol people we all get the message: "These people have corrupted themselves."

Quite literally, idolatry does corrupt. You give yourself to your idol. And what you give, you do not have, in this world, and the idol to whom you give it cannot keep it in its integrity, because it is not meant for him.

The ancient prophets used to laugh at idols, meaning that they claimed for themselves, or men claimed for them what they could not do. It was the role of the prophet to warn man of the sure and terrible end of the idol and of those who worshipped them.

The prophets were right. The false god destroys. He does not save. Idolators do not always have the pitiful end of those worshippers of power, Hitler, Mussolini and Stalin. But they do cease to possess themselves. They are themselves possessed and driven.

If there were many gods, it would be rational to divide one's allegiance, but because God is one, man's heart, his essential self, must also be one or it will be corrupted. Being given wholly to God, however, man remains pure. He becomes more himself, and he is free, in God, to love and cherish his neighbour and himself.

What is the fate of the idolator, which we all are? God must forgive; he must also release, because the idolator is a slave. He releases through the terrible but enchanting vision of the one man who was wholly pure in heart, and who on the Cross was mocked and jeered at as if he were a fallen idol. But he remains to this day not a fallen idol, but the risen God who is ever able to rescue His brothers and sisters from the idols that they make for themselves.

Forgiven and rescued, we may be, we very often are, given back things like money and prestige and success, and power and learning and great gifts of all sorts. Being free we see them not as idols, not as things that we make or as things that we can worship, but as things which are given to us because they are indeed beautiful and useful in the service of God, and for the good of men.[10]

SERMON: THIRD AVENUE CHURCH, MAY 24, 1970

Scripture: *Romans* 5:1-11

Mark 9:23-24 "Jesus said unto him, if thou canst believe, all things are possible, to him that believeth. And straightway the father of the child cried out and said with tears, 'Lord, I believe; help thou mine unbelief.' "

Perhaps before speaking of "why I believe" I should say something of what I believe. It could be called "the simple gospel" but although it can be stated in a few words its meaning in human life is profound. The Christian belief, to the Christian, is the answer to one of man's oldest conscious needs. Almost as far back as we know there is evidence that man has cherished hopes, and has been haunted by fears. These have caused, or to speak cautiously, they have been connected with all kinds of religions, from the most primitive and crude to what we today call the higher religions. They all offer some kind of answer to questions which men have through the ages formulated for themselves: What am I? Where do I come from? Where am I going? What governs my fate here and hereafter? If man's basic conscious needs are for food, clothing and shelter, his emotional and spiritual needs have also been expressed in his customs and beliefs from very early times.

We believe also that man early associated character with conduct and identified the fact that even with his "given" character he had a choice; only though, in despair he might then sometimes think he had no choice. He arrived at the sense of sin, or something like it, and at the possibility of a release.

I am putting this in historical terms because these experiences are not confined to Christians. They represent man's sense of his own predicament, sometimes stated very crudely in religious terms but in higher civilizations with much sophistication. The historian Toynbee in . . . the higher religions and seeing much in common between them and the Judaic-Christian belief, reproaches Jews and Christians for their narrowness and suggests a kind of . . . oecumenicism, an enlightened syncretism which all enlighted people could share.

I do not find it possible to accept this because I think that Toynbee's syncretism denatures Christianity. Christians have a unique answer to the terror of the human predicament. What? Where? Why? How?

1. Man comes from God.
2. Man must return to God.
3. But he cannot; alienated by sin — by the wrong choice — he is lost, sick, destroyed, self-betraying.
4. But again, God early promised a plan for "finding" man, for saving, redeeming, restoring by re-creating him. It is this plan that we believe in.

God's Plan can be very simply stated. God loved for you. God's Son Jesus Christ died to get you out of your self-made prison. Now you are free and healthy. Be what you are, free, whole, united to God.

It can be put in more detailed and more complex form. God's love engaged Him in recreation of man who was using his freedom to destroy himself. In the person of His son He "came down." This does not mean he took a lower place only. He took on a new form, the form of alienated man. And in that form (C. S. Lewis almost cruelly says, imagine a man *choosing* to become a crab and to live among crabs.) In that form of alienated man Christ suffered total rejection from those whose humiliation he had been willing to share. It was through this total rejection that he released the great power of the Holy Spirit which can transform us so that united with Him, His Church, we now have the eternal life that will at last enable us to see Him and comprehend Him as He is. Even this remains a simplification. We cannot fully explain our belief, not because it is magic, because it is a mystery, just as human love, when it is real, retains its mystery.

WHY I BELIEVE THIS

1. One must here be practical and factual. I believe it first because I was taught it as a small child. I was taught it not only as a thing to be learned, but to be lived. It was quite obvious that those who taught me set a supreme value on their belief. This means, not that their conduct was always perfect or consistent, but rather that it was always ultimately under the power of belief as the needle of a compass, while wavering, will always pull toward the north. This belief is the child's belief, but even a child, using the means of grace, confirms his own faith.

2. Intelligent children and young people begin sooner or later to question their parent's infallibility. Sometimes the shock of finding them as they think wrong in one matter, leads them for a time to apparent total rejection. The more intimately the parents' religion is bound up with their lives, the more danger there is that the child's religion will be rejected during his rejecting phase. But our faith, as we believe, is not merely a matter of learning what we are and liking and respecting those who teach. An integral part of our belief is that the Holy Spirit in each one does individually overcome the alienation, re-create the person as a new being who on his own accepts what God has done, and is in spite of some appearance to the contrary a saved and a changed person. He has not got this from his parents, but from God. This is the "conversion" so much stressed by some churches, by others less emphasized, but necessarily, I suppose, implicit in Christian belief. If all have suffered alienation, all must recognize the fact and individually accept reconciliation and a new life. But no one can say how the Holy Spirit works, or when. Many good parents have perhaps unnecessarily harried themselves and their children by demanding specific accounts of changes which may be coming truly, but gradually and unselfconsciously.

3. But all individuals, sooner or later, have to face fundamental trials of faith. One is simple and obvious. In these days of almost universal education, trained in some measure to reason, to prove, to demonstrate all truths in scientific or logical fashion, what can we do about the mystery of the faith, about the gigantic improbability that the Creator and Ruler of all things would do what our Christian tradition and our Scriptures say He did do: become incarnate as an obscure man in an obscure part of the world, be executed for sedition and blasphemy, reappear in recognizable form to His followers, and create a divine institution in which His Presence we believe is as real as it was on the day of

Pentecost. As the Christian historian Butterfield points out, the historian by his discipline can say that a Jew called Jesus was executed under Pontius Pilate; but only as a Christian can he say by faith that this Man is the Saviour of the World, the answer to man's eternal dilemma.

Can one deal rationally with these rational doubts? Does one say if the Holy Spirit gives you no faith, argument is irrelevant? I think there are some very simple exercises in "apologetics" that may be helpful in all of us.

1. There is the tradition of the Church. Historians pay much more attention now to oral tradition than they did a generation or two ago. There is plenty of evidence that a group of people at Pentecost, apparently possessed, did really not just turn the western world upside down, but gave it a new and unique direction and shape. Some critics will say yes — but that Christianity has done more harm than good. The sins of "Christians," their horrifying inconsistency, their anger, cruelty and hypocrisy are too obvious. But historically we know most about their sins from the Christians who have deplored and condemned them. And the Christian church — very tardily and with the fearful backsliding of negro slavery — has done things unique in history — did free slaves, care for the sick, feed the hungry, proclaim equality and unity among all men. The western civilization of which it was the matrix was also uniquely responsible for the development of scientific principles and their application to technology. I say this only that we may remind ourselves that the faithful have not dodged or evaded "reason." On the contrary the only society to call itself "Christian" is the society which developed the scientific method and has done much to develop that scrupulous scholarly history which conveys to us all the sins and errors of the Church. Faith has cherished reason.

2. On a simpler level. Is the Bible "true"? Are the gospels "true"? One test is to read any one of them and then to try to imagine that someone invented the tale. That some romancer took a good man who had bad luck and made him God and the founder of a new religion. To many people it will be much *easier* to imagine that the gospels are born of a living, ineffaceable memory, a divinely sustained recollection of divine action preserved in amazing fashion, than to imagine by whom and how they could have been invented.

3. One other simple "apologetic." "Miracles" worry some who do not observe the "miracles" all about us. We tend to strain at gnats. If God really revealed himself to men in Christ as we believe — the "signs" he used are not hard to accept. . . .

All who truly believe do see [miracles] from day to day. I have in mind one now: a true change, a miracle which came to my attention in one I knew. I did not really think of it as anything but a passing phase in a lovable but unstable character. It has lasted now over the years. There can I believe be no doubt that there is now light and power and direction there where before there was darkness and confusion.

Belief is not easy. For those who have truly examined and tested the Christian faith I think unbelief may be more difficult still. And we have no choice but to *make* a choice. The world has not made a place for agnostics. The prayer for all of us in all our perplexities which are real in this apparently self-destroying world must be "Lord I believe. Help thou mine unbelief."

Loving Father increase our faith. Let us not be blind to the evidences of thy power. Let us not be unwilling to seek for the One who is also seeking for us. We pray in Christ's name. Amen.[11]

4 | *As Westerner*

Hilda used to enjoy saying that since she was a western academic woman, she was bound to be chosen whenever a commission or committee was searching for a board or panel or establishing a list. There was some self-depreciating truth in her statement, but only a little — there were others with those character- istics who could have been chosen. Hilda was chosen because she filled all three roles so well.

Despite her love of things English and refinement and civilization, Hilda was almost as much a westerner as she was a woman and an academic. Her brother Leslie thinks that she had not associated enough with the "riff-raff" to be a true westerner, but the first selection, her review of Edward McCourt's *Music at the Close,* shows her familiarity with the old west.

Hilda's west spanned the years 1906–1975. Her understanding of its character and development can best be seen in a speech "Some Western Canadian Paradoxes" delivered at some point in the 1950's to a group of academics whom she felt needed to be introduced to the reality around them. This is followed by "Address of Welcome," an address given to contemporary westerners, farmers and their wives, attending Farm and Home Week at the University of Saskatche- wan in January 1969. In this speech Hilda talked of the present and the future of the west to those who understood the area much more intimately than the visiting academics.

The final selection, from 1952, is a professional historian's approach to the question of local and regional, including western, history. Hilda was never only or even primarily a westerner. She usually managed to put most things in a broad context. At the same time, though, she remained conscious of the constituent parts of this context as her conclusion to the last selection shows.

REVIEW OF *MUSIC AT THE CLOSE,* BY E.A. McCOURT

The early part of this western story can best be appreciated by the true "westerner" — the one who has qualified by living year in, year out, on the open plain in the home-made shack furnished with a heater, a coal oil lamp, a water pail in the corner, and regular weather reports borne in on the blast through the front and only door. Such a one will find himself quite at home in the district of Pine Creek, situated thirty miles from a railroad, with rolling grass-covered hills studded in summer with brilliant prairie flowers, and broken by dark patches of bluff which lead back to the great Saskatchewan, grim and inscrutable. This Pine Creek country and the people, their homes and their ways are described with a bracing and optimistic realism that only one of the initiated could have achieved.

Outsiders, of course, might think Aunt Em's kitchen with its smoke-blackened saucepans and fly-spotted mirror a trifle squalid, but Mr. McCourt manages to convey that, while flies will be flies, and stoves will smoke, the aging Aunt Em is sound on essentials like custard pie and cream puffs. The school concert and dance, to a hostile observer, might seem to proceed from vulgarity through alcohol to a scene of sordid violence, but the author, with a little help from the admirable Mrs. Roebuck, leaves us assured of the essential decency of nearly all concerned. There is not too much glamour about the threshing scene; it is strenuous and noisy and the "golden grain" has been frozen. But it is full of life and vigour; things happen that way.

The district "characters" nearly all ring true: gentle Uncle Matt who "stopped work only as a concession to the weakness of horseflesh"; Old Man Hunter, over eighty, but "it had not yet occurred to him that he was mortal"; Mrs. Roebuck and her short way with inquisitive mounties; Jim Lowery who sucked in new ideas like a sponge, and who knew all the answers — for a while; and many others. The two remittance men, the district beauty, and the school teacher are less convincing.

The story covers the twenty odd years, from the close of one great war to the climax of the next. Western isolationism and preoccupation with economic affairs run through the tale from 1918, when Old Man Hunter hopes to retire in affluence if only the Huns will hold out two years longer, to 1939 when Neil Fraser solves both personal and economic problems in a recruiting office. Life in Pine Creek is never quite stable. In the 20's everyone hopes to make his pile and move out in style to the Coast; in the 30's they are moving out, but not to the Coast, and not in style.

The chief character is Neil Fraser, amiable, sensitive, and clever who spends his life dreaming dreams that do not come true, and going down before the crises of life through bungling, bad luck and something else. "You're a sucker, Neil. You always were," says his friend Gil Reardon, but Neil himself knows better. He is likeable, he means well, and he is no fool; the trouble is, he never achieves a real faith in anything. He envies reckless Gil who at last finds an ideal and dies for it. Neil drifts on. He thinks he is defeated by the bitter years of the thirties. He was really defeated long before, and is finally rescued from futility by a courageous death on a Normandy beach.

Some criticisms might be made. The story attempts, perhaps, to cover too much ground. With the picture of Pine Creek, the sketch of twenty hard years in the West, and the frustrations of Neil Fraser, it almost gives the feeling of three novels in one short book. Each theme suffers from overcrowding. The plot is loosely sketched, the main characters loosely drawn; both, at times, seem vague and unpredictable. In the midst of the closing scene the author approaches a profound philosophic problem, and settles it apparently, in a mood of black pessimism. Neil's death, it seems, is the only justification for his having lived at all, and there are millions like him, leading lives meaningless apart from the war which swept them away. This conclusion is, perhaps, not surprising in a cynical and despairing age. What is startling is the rapidity with which the author's romantic instincts enable him to pass us on to "a holy rest" and "music at the close."

Yet, these romantic instincts, always waging a successful war with brutal realism, are responsible for much of the charm of the book. They are happily combined with an easy, flexible style and a keen sense of humour. The dialogue is natural and engaging. The descriptions are admirable; some, like the one of the mining town riot, are amazingly vivid and forceful. This is a hard book to lay down. It is a rare pleasure in this age of dreary "compiling" to find an author who apparently cannot be dull.[1]

SOME WESTERN CANADIAN PARADOXES

It has been suggested that I should say something on the subject of Saskatchewan as a community. What sort of people are we, and why? The "why" is a tribute to my particular discipline. Historians think, or they used to think, that they can explain why things are as they are. It is a pleasant fiction. At least they have as much right to speculate as anyone else.

It is surprisingly difficult, though, for me to say what kind of people we are. Like many, indeed like most people of my age and older, I came to Saskatchewan from somewhere else. But I have lived here all my life, I know no other community as I know this one. It is not easy to stand back and describe it as it might appear to an intelligent man from Mars.

Some things however can be said. We are very new, we are very mixed, and (relatively), we are still very few. Along with our two neighbours, the other prairie provinces, we lie in the very heart of this large country, but we are not quite like the people who live to the east of us, or even like those to the west beyond the mountains. Prairie people, or "Westerners," as we often call ourselves, are a little different.

Perhaps the simplest way to explain Saskatchewan people is a series of paradoxes. The first one is, of course, familiar on this continent and particularly on the great central plains. We are an Anglo-Saxon community and yet we are also French, Scandinavian, German, Dutch, Pole, Ukrainian, Greek, Hungarian, Rumanian, Russian, Chinese, and North American Indian. Of these cultural minorities, some are in a peculiar position. The French-speaking groups are the first and oldest Canadians, representing one of the two chief cultures of this bilingual and bicultural country. In Saskatchewan at the moment they are in a small minority. The Indians, the earliest inhabitants, have lived and many do still live apart from the main stream of life. They have, however, achieved the status of citizens, and they are gradually taking a responsible place in the community.

As for the rest of us, we have assimilated ourselves into a blend which may be termed Anglo-Saxon. Fifty years ago you could have called at many a little prairie community and have found with difficulty one person to answer a question in English. That is not so today. Judging from language, laws and government, we are an Anglo-Saxon society, although the man from Mars confronted with the endless lists of Camerons, Wilsons and Moes in the telephone book might indeed be pardoned for supposing that we were a colony of the ancient Kingdom of Scotland.

There is another paradox. We are farmers, and rather dull dirt farmers. We cultivate the soil. We have only a few of those exciting and romantic farmers called ranchers. Our community has lived chiefly on the hard, dull, but occasionally profitable occupation of wheat-growing. But we have in our background strange memories of a wilder past. The whole of this province was once the domain of one of the famous chartered companies of the western world, the Hudson's Bay Company. But even before the Hudson's Bay Company made good its claim, our territory was crossed by a French trader from the St. Lawrence, La Verendrye. The French lost the St. Lawrence, and the English, or rather the Scots, took their place, but the traders from the Bay and the St. Lawrence still struggled as rivals over the fur trade. Here I must be allowed a complacent interjection. They struggled, but they did not as a rule fight. The Hudson's Bay Company men were instructed to stop short of violence and even to supply the wretched peddlers of Montreal with food as it was badly needed. Their efforts to keep the trade from the St. Lawrence men, however, resulted in the construction of one of their first up-country forts, in the present province of Saskatchewan, Fort Cumberland in 1774. Supplying this port with trading goods presented a delicate problem in logistics. The Hudson's Bay Company did not at that time use rum or brandy in the trade, but the day before trading began it was absolutely *de rigueur* to invite the Indians into the fort, and offer them suitable (but limited) entertainment. Unfortunately the previous liquids must be carried the long and exhausting way up the rivers to Cumberland by Indian boatmen. A distracted Hudson's Bay man explains how again and again his crew dropped their paddles and declared that they could go no further — meaning that they would go no further without a drink. The Hudson's Bay factor was torn between the absolute necessity of satisfying them and the fear that their requests would be so nicely timed that he would arrive at the port complete with crew but without a cargo.

It is a far cry from the hard and precarious life of the up-country trader to the equally hard and precarious life of the farmer struggling on the plains to the south with his 160 acres of government land, pushing the plough by day and sheltering at night in his little sod shack — a hut bought with a minimum of imported timber and a maximum of tough prairie sod. However, today we are forging new links with that old fur-trading country to the north. The trapper and the trader have always been there; they are now being joined by the prospector and the miner. The problem of transportation almost insuperable to the Hudson's Bay men has been partly solved by the bush pilot and the small plane on pontoons or sleighs, according to the season. Cities are growing where once there was only a waste of scrub trees, water and rock. The mid-twentieth century has brought together two halves of one history which once seemed utterly separate — the fur traders' Saskatchewan and the Saskatchewan of the prairie farmer.

Another paradox may be mentioned in passing. We are traditionally poor farmers but sometimes some of us are very rich. Farming has often been thought of as dull but safe. In Saskatchewan it may be dull. It is never safe. We concentrate on wheat and if we get a lot of wheat and can sell it we are very rich. But if we get little or no wheat, which can happen and this has happened when we have drought, hail, grasshoppers, or rust — or if we get wheat and can't sell it, which can also happen — we may be very poor. A very important aspect of our history has been the series of efforts by methods scientific, social and political to put up safeguards against the perils which beset the wheat farmer. These safeguards are elaborate and ingenious and all of them work sometimes, but ours are not quite the traditional farmers. They have been confused more freely with the prospector, the speculator or the gambler — these are exaggerations, but they give some insight into our character. We are an optimistic people — not carelessly, but rather stubbornly optimistic. We retain, perhaps, something of the flavour of the early Saskatchewan farmer who describes his experiences thus:

> (In 1885) we had only ten bushels (per acre) of very badly frosted wheat. I took some to Indian Head and traded it for flour, shorts, and bran. I had no money to pay expenses. . . . In 1886 we had 80 acres under crop. Not a drop of rain fell from the time it went in until it was harvested. I sowed 124 bushels and threshed 54. In 1888, we began to think we could not grow wheat in this country. I had now 120 to 125 acres under cultivation. We put in 25 acres of wheat, 10 to 15 acres of oats and let the rest go back into prairie. That year we got 35 bushels (of wheat) to the acre! So we went to work and ploughed up again. The next year wheat headed out two inches high. Not a drop of rain fell that whole season until fall. We summer fallowed that year (1889) for the first time, and, to show the optimism, we put in in 1890 every acre we could. We had wheat standing to the chin but on the 8th of July a hailstorm destroyed absolutely everything. My hair turned grey that night.

That man lived in very rich farming country where one good crop and a good price would atone for years of shortage.

Another paradox emerges from our interest in wheat. We are tucked into a remote part of Canada and yet we are keenly interested not only in national but in international affairs. This undoubtedly derives originally from our hope that foreign countries will buy our wheat and our insistence that our own government see to it that we are enabled to sell somewhere as expeditiously and as profitably as possible. And yet an interest that may have begun with our wheat, our alertness that may have originated with the profit motive do not necessarily end there. I remember being surprised and somewhat shocked when I went to live in a very large mid-western American city to find that the headlines on the front pages of daily papers almost always had to do with purely local matters. In Saskatchewan, by contrast, the larger papers almost invariably devote the front page to international and national news. This has become a community habit and it represents a typical outlook, and a typical way of life. Saskatchewan people travel as much as they can, and many of them having received their early education here study and work abroad for longer or shorter periods. In my young days the stock question (the weather having been disposed of) was "And where do you come from?" — those being the days when everyone came from somewhere else. Today to a young person it should rather be "Where are you going?" for they all seem to be on their way somewhere else, even though many will return to us.

Again, we represent an agrarian and therefore typically individualist tradition and yet we are the first socialist government in Canada. Admittedly our socialism is rather rose-coloured rather than red, but it is not what one would expect in a community of farmers who own their own land. I cannot undertake to explain the phenomenon but I can make some guesses.

I think — but this may be fancy — that the tradition goes back to our earliest government by the benevolently paternalistic Hudson's Bay Company. The H.B.C. was a capitalist company out to make profits, but its operations were on the whole far-seeing, shrewd and benevolent. Profits depended on the goodwill of the Indians. Much was expected of them but in different times in this hard country the Company did what it could to help the needy.

This tradition whether continuous or not appears also in the pioneer days. The federal government which took over from the Company had spent much money on a transcontinental railway and on surveying the land. It was important to get people onto the land and to keep them there. Although settlement here took place in the heyday of Canadian Liberalism, such was the difficulty of establishing and keeping settlers on isolated farms on a treeless and waterless plain that an inevitable tradition of government services (such as well-digging) and government help in emergencies grew up. Moreover, many of the early settlers from Britain came from Liberal-Labour groups that were even then laying the foundations of the present welfare state in Britain. They brought their mental baggage along with them and supported, or even initiated in Saskatchewan, numerous movements calling for confederative action, for government intervention or for government aid.

This tendency was strengthened in the days of droughts and depression when Saskatchewan as a wheat-growing province suffered with exceptional severity. First there was no sale for wheat; then there was no wheat for sale. Though people felt that they had received such a complete demonstration of unnecessary suffering caused by "too little had to late" that they were ready (as they thought) to turn their back on their old customs and to try a new way. My own reading of our history is rather different. As I have suggested, I think that one can trace something of the tradition of the welfare state long before the beginnings of our prairie community to the Hudson's Bay rule. I suggest that the very mildness and moderation of our socialism is due to the fact that it does not represent a revolutionary change but something that has belonged to our way of life and has appeared in some form under every government no matter what its name.

A final paradox that I must mention in our society is one that has a special interest for all of us. We have quite an extraordinary set of educational and cultural institutions costing very large sums of money, paid for almost entirely from public funds, and yet we have in our province relatively few people who could be said to belong to the intellectual classes. I would like to elaborate a little on this anomaly.

As I have said, our community is very young. A century ago almost no-one lived here — no one beyond a few fur traders. Three quarters of a century ago we were very few. Essentially as a community we belong to this century. And yet in the very early years there were three kinds of public building to be seen everywhere: the tin-rooted grain elevator, the typical red-brown railway station, and the one-roomed schoolhouse, a frame wooden building, usually painted white with a green trim.

Even more astonishing was the beginning of the provincial university, which will be 50 years old next year. This was a surprisingly precocious development even in relation to the growth of public schools. There were perhaps only something over 200 elementary schools in the province when the university was chartered. There were only between 300 and 400 when the first class graduated. High schools were still very few and far between.

Moreover, the university was not, like so many colleges of the early days in the United States, a senior agricultural school. The oldest college is the College of Arts, although a College of Agriculture was almost immediately associated with it. A community of farmers, many of them very poor, many of them illiterate, planned and paid for an institution of higher learning including and even granting a place of honour to the "unpractical" subjects while still lacking almost all of what are considered the amenities of life.

The explanation — or part of it — lies in the energy, ambition and intelligence of the leaders. Two men, each remarkable in his way, stand out in our early history. One was a lawyer of real keeness and ability, of English birth and Ontario education, shrewd and combative and ambitious for himself and for his community. He was the first premier of the old Territories before the formation of the present province. The other man, Walter Scott, who succeeded him as first premier of the newly formed province, had a very different background. He came from an Ontario farm, earnest, ambitious, of limited education, perhaps even of limited intellectual capacity, but with that intense desire for self-improvement typical of so many of his age and class. He made his way from type-setting to journalism and from journalism to politics, and he has the honour of approving, if he did not personally initiate, the planning and organization of the provincial university. He and his colleagues, representing the liberal and secular views of education current in their day, were no doubt hastened in their efforts by the knowledge that university charters were then being secured by theological colleges. There was a strong desire to forestall possible sectarian strife and to channel all provincial aid to one central non-sectarian institution.

Yet even with this incentive the achievement was a remarkable one. It must be explained, I think, by the kind of people, of all races and languages, who came to this province. They came, many of them, from Continental Europe, Great Britain, Ireland — But many were from the Maritimes, from Ontario, and from the American Middle West. A few were like Haultain and could value education because they had experienced it. There were 400 graduates in the prairies in 1909. Many were like Scott; education was a good thing that they had missed and they were determined, if they could not attend a university, that they would at least have the honour of founding one.

Our educational and cultural history is, I think, typical of this beginning — immense idealism, faith, ambition, confidence — a determination to create what we have not got. This has shown itself in many ways. For all our short history Saskatchewan was one of the first Canadian provinces to introduce adequate legislation and to provide adequate funds and staff for the preservation not only of public records, but also for the collection and preservation of historical manuscripts. Provision has also been made for the preservation of historic sites and of museum collections. Moreover, a Board sponsored by the government had given much independence of action, given aid . . . to the creative arts.

This development is, I think, astonishing not only in view of the short time in which it has taken place, but in view of the relatively few people who are able and willing to profit to the full by the facilities thus made available. That is, perhaps, the danger of our somewhat anomalous situation. Today as a province we are increasingly wealthy; we are very proud of what has been accomplished in days of relative poverty; we are confident of what we can do in the future.

There is some danger that, unchecked by the criticisms of a large and highly educated public, we may confuse professional and technical training with education; that we may become so concerned with the growth of "plant" and equipment as to forget rather what it's all about; that we may become over confident about the slow, difficult and even risky business of training and cultivating the mind. I think, however, that we are increasingly aware of these dangers and ready to try to guard against them.

I have been warned of the danger of offering you too rosy a picture. I am afraid that I may have fallen into it. I can only hope that you will be kind enough to forgive any patriotic excesses and to believe that we are most gratified when people are good enough to listen when we talk about ourselves.[2]

ADDRESS OF WELCOME:
FARM AND HOME WEEK, JANUARY 15, 1969

It is a great pleasure to be allowed to express the welcome of the University to those who are attending the annual Farm and Home Week Meetings. This is a venerable institution, and one which over the years has been the occasion of bringing together many old friends from different parts of the province, and of enabling those of us who work on the campus to engage in an annual renewal of friendship.

As we all know this great institute touches very many people who do not have other contacts with the campus. It was decided in the very early years of this university that we were not to be "a land college" with our interest chiefly directed to agriculture and related fields. The authorities of that day decided on a fully developed university with central academic interest. However a link with the farms and homes throughout the province has always been maintained and the services the university has been able to give and to receive have been perhaps even more valuable because we have on this campus a strong Arts and Science college with purely academic interests.

I have been warned that I am not to fall into the vice of the historian, which is to dwell so lovingly on the past that the present and the future are forgotten. I have in fact been instructed to think and speak of the future. Unfortunately, historians always like to avoid the future, insisting that history is not prophecy. However, one can of course plan, although here again I am embarrassed, for who am I to take this function from those who are so well qualified to perform it?

I could hazard some suggestions about changes that are taking place in the province, and that will inevitably affect all our institutions.

First, very many farm homes are now, as we all know, palaces compared with those that I and other old-timers knew when the prairie lands were being opened up. Instead of the endless labour required to maintain even minimum standards of food and warmth and cleanliness and comfort, farm homes now can have all the comforts that are available anywhere, and the homemaker, with water laid on, and modern kitchens and all electrical devices, knows nothing of the endless toil and even drudgery of her grandmother.

The big question then is what constructive use we are making of the increased comfort, the increased leisure, the infinitely better communications that we now enjoy. I suppose the obvious answer is that we now can see the possibility of a lively and active intellectual and cultural life which was difficult if not impossible to the early pioneers. The danger of the affluent age lies in the possibility that comfort and luxury may be valued too highly and the possibilities of what our Victorian great-grandfathers called "self-improvement" may be neglected. We cannot however afford to neglect them. What our world needs most today is better human beings.

Secondly, of course not all farm homes are luxurious, and many farmers, far from being wealthy are still poor. In this province we have, or we should have, a war against poverty, as strenuous as that which is going on in Toronto, Montreal or any other urban centre. The government does much, but one also reads much of the activities being carried on by private organizations including churches. It does seem to me that the members of this institution are already I know deeply concerned with our grey or black areas, [and] can look forward to the possibility of making great contributions towards the equalization of opportunities in Saskatchewan homes.

Thirdly, as for the farms, the trend to bigness and to scientific agriculture and to machinery has transformed completely the old typical quarter or half section farm. The farmer as we know faces with the possibility of increased wealth, greatly increased anxieties. All of us experienced that during the last fall when a large portion of the very large crop was being injured if not ruined. These anxieties do emphasize the need for what we have always had in Saskatchewan, close co-operation between individuals, voluntary societies and government, in dealing with the crises that seem to be part of our lives. There is however another matter that we obviously must bear in mind: as a vast food-producing province we have responsibilities not only to ourselves but to the whole world, in the face of the terrifying population explosion of today.

Finally, in connection with the future of Farm and Home Week, one must think also of the nature of the communities in our province. The new kind of farm has destroyed the isolated, sometimes narrow, but often pleasant and healthy little communities which centred in the schoolhouse and perhaps also in the church. The disappearance of this little rural community is not a new problem, and it has been much studied in Saskatchewan. The question of community life is, however, a continuing challenge to this particular group, representing farms and the farm homes. Experience has shown that the good life cannot be found by the solitary individual in a mass, but rather in families and in viable communities, preferably those with a firm and coherent tradition. Modern science and technology has conquered the old perils of isolation and has overthrown the barriers of distance. We still have, I think, to learn how to create the most favourable conditions for the active family and community life which young people today need so much.[3]

THE CANADIAN HISTORICAL ASSOCIATION, THE *CANADIAN HISTORICAL REVIEW*, AND LOCAL HISTORY: A SYMPOSIUM

Local history is a relative term. From the viewpoint of a national association chiefly concerned with the broad issues of national history, it means not only the history of somebody's village or school district, county or municipality. It must mean also provincial and regional history. Even in this very broad sense local history has not, I suggest, been sufficiently related to national history. Historically speaking, all Canada is divided into two parts: Central Canada, most of whose inhabitants live south of the 49th parallel; and the fringes, east, north, and west, those fringes which were garnered in by Central Canada for reasons perfectly well known to everyone.

In each part some attention has been paid to local history in the narrowest sense. In Central Canada only has provincial and regional history received full attention. It is well known that the inhabitants of this area, that is, Central Canada, are not completely homogeneous. Much of our national history has in fact been written to explain the occasional frictions resulting from this important fact. In comparison,therefore, with the extent of the work done on the regionalism of the Centre, the regional history of the fringe areas has, I believe, received relatively little attention. This is unfortunate. Regional history obviously has essential contributions to make to an understanding of national history. Moreover public interest in local and regional history, if properly developed and exploited, could be used as a means of support for the national association: support, that is, in the practical and sordid sense as well as in matters intellectual and cultural. These two matters — the importance of regional history in relation to national history, and the support which should accrue to the national association from active local and regional societies — are the ones that I should like to introduce as a preliminary to the morning's discussion.

The Massey Commission was frequently reminded throughout the fringe areas, and even at the centre, that national history has its roots in regional and local history. This statement needs little elaboration. Economic, social and sociological generalizations must rest on a knowledge of regional and local history; and sometimes the detailed history of very small areas may throw light on matters of national interest. It may be answered, of course, that the scholar who pursues broad national trends in a scholarly way will be led naturally to an examination of such material as he needs it. This answer is not quite adequate. The principle of disinterested scholarship operates here. Our scattered regions will not yield all their truth about our national history unless they are studied from their own viewpoint, and for their own sake.

For example, only through such a disinterested pursuit of regional and provincial history can we bring to light illuminating parallels and contrasts, many of which no doubt still lie buried. Some of these have already been studied. We have learned much of such parallels and contrasts between the American Middle West and the Canadian prairies. Some work has also been done on the life of various groups in Canada in relation to their ethnographic background. We have not so fully exploited the possibilities of parallel developments between various Canadian regions and provinces, and this may cause a serious loss of sympathy and understanding. The Ontario Historical Society in its brief to the Massey Commission, after speaking of the recent developments in local history in England and the United States, dealt with this matter. "In Canada no work similar has been attempted — at least on any directed and coordinated basis; yet our need of a national consciousness is greater because of geographical barriers and great racial division, and also because since 1867 the economic progress of our various provinces has been so unequal as to produce definite interprovincial antagonisms." To take an example from another field, the school texts of my youth implied, if they did not positively state, that the stupidity and ignorance displayed in Britain's dealings with the original Canadian provinces was inexplicable. But Canadians from the prairie portion of the fringe, looking at their history with regional eyes, and observing the somewhat limited knowledge and intelligence displayed by Central Canada as a colonial power, do not find even the British stupidity entirely inexplicable. The historical parallel enables them to contemplate the performances of both colonial powers with a certain philosophic detachment.

It is unnecessary to labour this point. Various works with special bearing on economic history, or sociological developments, and on politics have thrown much incidental light on regional and local history, as well as on national history. It seems reasonable to suppose that the converse would hold true. Work done from the regional viewpoint might well correct or clarify many currently accepted generalizations. This should hold true in the field of general national history as well as in particular interpretations of our economic and social development.

In short, it may be argued that in Canada, so far, half our history has been local history in the broadest sense. The other half often appears to consist of mysterious and possibly unholy transactions between the provincial capitals and Ottawa. Canada leaped into nationhood and even into a brisk participation in international affairs at a time when vast areas of the country were still at the pioneer stage, and relatively inaccessible from the centre. In such circumstances to be ignorant and careless of local and regional history is to renounce all hope of a true understanding of national history.

Turning away from this rather impersonal approach, it must be remembered that history is written and read by people. It will cease to be written when it is no longer read. As the commercial and professional value of historical studies is rated so very low, the preservation of national history must depend on maintaining the voluntary interest and support of the general public. I do not know how far that interest has been maintained in the past by formal instruction at school. It is clear, however, if present curriculum trends continue, that history will become a purely extra-curricular activity, or that at best academic instruction in "pure" history will be confined to the local scene. It may be necessary to build on the existing foundation, and experience seems to show that, in Canada at least, many who care for no other kind of history can be interested in the history of their locality or of their region.

Even if the historical enthusiasm of most of them begins and ends with local history, it may still serve more than one useful purpose. The Massey Commission heard much from local and from national bodies of the wastage of the historical sources through the deliberate or careless destruction of documents. Ultimately collection and preservation of these must be a responsibility of public authorities, but meanwhile destruction will go on until the public is sufficiently interested and informed to put a stop to it. If only one in ten thousand of the potential enthusiasts for local history has it in his power to save important material, the work of local historical societies is still of national importance. And in the subsequent preservation of the material the help of the same agencies can be enlisted. The British Columbia Historical Association, speaking of the want of adequate provincial archives, urged the Massey Commission to make representations to provincial authorities on the matter. Such representations were deemed outside the terms of reference of a federal commission. They would, however, come properly and forcefully from local, regional and national societies working simultaneously and in co-operation. The Canadian Historical Association in its brief, and in its oral testimony before the commission, spoke at length on the importance of finding and saving historical manuscripts. There is no evidence that the Association has recognized officially to what an extent this preservation must depend on purely local societies, and on the interest of people with little academic knowledge of history. Moreover, such societies, properly directed, should be able to develop in their members powers of appreciation and of criticism in historical matters, powers which will operate in any field of history. Recently two articles appeared in a national magazine on events of importance in our national history, and also in the regional history of the prairies. Written by one who professed to be a local authority they contained, along with many misleading statements, a quite unwarranted slur on a well-known national statesman of the nineteenth century. That the articles passed with little or no comment is not creditable, I think, to our interest either in national or in local history. If we had on the prairies an active regional society such abuses of our history would be much less likely to occur.

Finally, one can always hope that the interest aroused in local history will carry on to a broader field, and that local and regional societies may not only preserve historical materials and provide a critical spirit among their members, but that they may nourish future historians, and furnish the existing ones with discriminating readers. This attitude is perhaps too optimistic. Yet it is probably not too much to say that any general appreciation of, and support for, Canadian national history must come through local and regional activities.

The word "support" leads me to the practical and sordid part of the discussion to which I have already referred. The Canadian Historical Association in its present need of funds, must presumably seek them at least partly from the contributions of a much larger membership than it now comprises. Its membership should not be (and indeed is not) limited largely to those connected with universities. But, as has been stated, experience seems to show that public interest and support from provincial governments goes to local groups, and must be drawn to the national effort through them. The people and the government of Saskatchewan have shown in a very material way their interest in local history through the North-West Historical Association of some years ago, the Saskatchewan Historical Association, and now through the provincially supported Archives Board. The general significance of the facts is that in that province, which is relatively poor, and where one would not expect to find a strong sense of history, there has been generous support from public and private sources for the preservation of historical materials and for the writing of history. It is not unreasonable to suppose that private support at least would extend to the national field if the connection were to be made clear. It is certain that the local groups would welcome and would profit from the interest and co-operation of the national association.

This leads to a final and very important consideration. Much genuine and useful enthusiasm for history may be wasted on local efforts. As all historians know, the pursuit of local history is not without its dangers. It may, by over-emphasis on the trivial, the picturesque, and the pseudo-dramatic, produce the painful type of pedant who has so often been caricatured. Or, by way of reaction it may go to the other extreme and lead to endless and aimless counting and listing, sociological pedantry at its worst. Local history also nourishes the reminiscer. The editors of *Saskatchewan History* for example, know how much tact is required to maintain friendly relations with correspondents who have a natural desire to tell their stories and have them printed, but who lack discrimination in the selection of material, and experience in the verification of facts. And there is the chronic problem of the resentment of pioneers "who were there all the time" when young people who might be their grandchildren venture to question any of their statements. In all these matters groups could receive valuable help and support from a national association with a constant concern for scholarly standards.

Returning once more for a moment to the work of the Massey Commission, it was interesting to notice that local and regional societies in British Columbia, Saskatchewan, Manitoba, Ontario, Quebec, New Brunswick and Newfoundland had suggestions to make on matters of interest and importance to the national association: preservation of historical materials, training of archivists, preservation and marking of historic sites, and the proper policy to be pursued in relation to historical museums. Manitoba and Ontario spoke definitely of the need for close co-operation between local societies and a national organization, and Ontario had a definite suggestion to make. In the light of these facts it was remarkable that the brief of the Canadian Historical Association made no mention of local history or of the work of local societies, or of the suggestions that they made. In the circumstances this was, no doubt, unavoidable. The national brief was presented early in the proceedings. Nevertheless, it would perhaps have been possible to offer to the commission for transmission to the public through its report and in other ways a clearer picture of the situation and of the needs of the country in relation to the preservation of historical materials, the writing of history and the extension of historical studies had there been closer relations and more informal co-operation between the national group and the local or regional groups of which about a dozen in all presented briefs.

To sum up: it is now being increasingly recognized that local and regional history, apart from their intrinsic interest, have most important contributions to make to national historical studies. This is particularly true in Canada. In Canada also, it seems evident that general public interest in national history can most easily be developed through local organizations. There is ample evidence that those engaged in local history need and would welcome closer relations with the national association. I think that all will agree on the desirability of more effective co-operation.[4]

5 | *As Canadian*

Hilda could see the faults as well as the virtues of her English heritage, as the first selection, the conclusion of an encyclopedia article "The English in Canada" demonstrates, yet what England stood for was important to Hilda. As late as 1974 she wrote, "Canadians may read with that odd sort of pride reserved for mothers for which one can take no credit, that in Canada Britain brought into force the first constitution enacted by statute and the first comprehensive charter of religious liberty."[1]

Her love for things English interfered with a full appreciation of *les Canadiens*. The more Hilda learned of Canada, and the more she studied Quebec history, the more she came to appreciate the culture and religion of the French Canadians and their unique place in Canada and role in Canada's history. This appreciation developed from a vague feeling of *bienveillance* in the 1930's and 1940's to a belief that, with some difficulty, one culture could be developed in Canada, a view that she held at least subconsciously in the late 1940's and early 1950's. Her experience on the Massey Commission, especially her contact with Fr. Lévesque, brought her to a carefully structured position allowing more latitude for both cultures within one civilization. A short statement of this view was made in 1956:

> The obvious fact, that the English-Canadian existence stemmed from French-Canadian survival, and the French-Canadian survival has been made possible only by English-Canadian existence, seem to me to be the cardinal fact of Canadianism, known to everyone, but too often ignored. Since we are already products of each other, bound together by indissoluble ties of history, it seems absurd to talk of bi-culturalism as cultural co-operation. It would be truer surely to talk of better cultural circulation in what is and has for two centuries been one body. Canadianism is the nature of this body whose strange and romantic growth and development contrast oddly with its inadequate powers of articulation.[2]

The second selection "La Co-existence au Canada," is a fuller expression of Hilda's view in the late 1950's. Separatism in the 1960's at first enraged Hilda, but her continuing historical studies and her realism led her to a fuller understanding of *les Québecois*, as seen in the third selection, "Canadian Bi-Culturalism." Yet in private conversation there were undertones: we must appreciate them; recognize their culture, accept their differences, but not *vive la difference;* rather: they are not quite civilized, not quite moral. As she put it in the first selection in this chapter about the English attitude toward Europeans, they "are not barbarians and yet not 'one of us.' "

As for those in Canada who were neither English nor French, Hilda began by sharing the common Anglo-Canadian view that they should strive to become as English as possible. By the mid 1960's, as seen in the fourth selection, "Ethnic Groups: Assimilation or Integration," she was willing to allow the larger groups, except for Doukhobors, Hutterites, and Indians, to maintain their traditions.

She defended her stand on the grounds of education and level of civilization, but both parts reflect the influence of western Canada on Hilda's ideas. A letter to the Editor of the Saskatoon *Star-Phoenix* in 1969, which is the fifth selection, clearly gives priority to the English and the French.

As for the actual definition of Canada and Canadians, perhaps Hilda's most succinct statement of her fully developed view is found in the last selection, "Cultural Evolution," in words that she would use on a number of occasions: Canada originated with a series of rejected groups (French, Loyalists, Scots) who shared only their rejection and the "habitation of a vast, lonely and mysterious land." Though geographically isolated and culturally different, Canadians shared "a common determination to survive, a determination which has left its mark on a quiet, cautious, stubborn people" who have created "a national community with autonomous political institutions and an integrated economy."

THE ENGLISH IN CANADA

English influence may be seen in Canada through notable English institutions such as the Hudson's Bay Company and the Church of England; it may also be seen in the co-operative movements of the west, and to some degree in Canadian labour movements generally. It is much more difficult to estimate the contribution of Englishmen in general to our national life and our national character. It is hard, for example, to do more than guess at the immense influence of English non-conformity as distinguished from the sharply institutionalized Anglicanism. It is also difficult to fix on a distinctive English contribution in commerce, industry or agriculture, apart from the undeniable fact of the English provenance of almost all the best strains of livestock, and the plausible assumption that it is the Englishman's quiet and stubborn passion for flowers which has been chiefly responsible for creating a great gardening tradition even on the chilly windswept western plains.

In politics there is no doubt at all that if the English provided the machine they have been obliged for the most part to surrender the wheel in English-speaking Canada to the Scots. There are obvious reasons for this in an increasingly democratic society where it is hard for a man to win confidence unless he first inspires affection and sympathy. The Englishman does not assimilate as readily as the Irishman or the Scot. During the past century many Englishmen having, unlike their fellow immigrants, experience only of an urban industrial society found themselves initially at a disadvantage in a predominantly rural country.

Moreover the Englishman, unlike the Scot, is unable to work off his homesickness by any English equivalent of playing the bagpipes or parading the haggis. For him, like the Frenchman, homesickness may be a paralysing malady, rather than an invitation to indulge in sentimental songs. He requires some time to strike his roots into a new soil, and in the meantime his newly acquired country-men are likely to find his peculiarities irritating rather than endearing. His very virtues, it may be his evangelical zeal, or an occasional indication of a wish to resume the white man's burden, have often delayed his complete "socialization."

He may, too, be honestly puzzled by the perversity of Europeans who have emerged from a state of savagery without becoming Englishmen; those who are not barbarians and yet not "one of us" have constituted for him an enigma which he has never quite solved. These qualities may be inseparable from his greatness but they do not win him votes. With his own countrymen he has shown an unequalled genius for compromise; with primitive peoples, allowing for all his defects, an unequalled capacity for humane and intelligent government. With equals who are yet not quite at one with him he is often not very happy and not very popular. It is no wonder that democratic leadership falls more often to the Scot.

And yet in a curious subterranean fashion the Englishman has come into his own in Canadian public life. It is surely not without significance that Canada's late and justly celebrated prime minister whose life was consciously a tribute to his impulsive, dogmatic, intellectually argumentative Scottish grandfather, unconsciously displayed to an almost excessive degree those English qualities of tenacity, caution, compromise, a capacity for delay amounting to genius, and a political insight all the more effective for being hidden under a dull and unimaginative exterior. A consideration of this typical Canadian suggests that in Canada the English spirit is mighty yet.[3]

LA CO-EXISTENCE AU CANADA

En professeur d'histoire je réclame le droit de commencer par une toute petite conférence sur l'histoire canadienne. Le Canada est habité, d'abord par des gens qui parlent français — ce sont eux qui ont pénétré la région du St. Laurent pendant que leurs voisins anglais se sont etablis au sud sur la côte atlantique; et puis, il est habité par des gens qui parlent anglais, ou à peu près.

Or, tout le monde sait que la co-existence entre des tels groupes, anglais et français, ne se fait que difficilement depuis longtemps, depuis l'époque même de Guillaume le Conquérant. Produits d'une même civilisation, co-créateurs, on peut presque dire, de cette culture moderne, rationale, commerciale, qu'ils se sont forcés, en rivaux, bien entendu, d'étaler sur la terre, — malgré tout cela, Français et Anglais dans le passé n'ont jamais éprouvé de grande sympathie les uns pour les autres. On trouve souvent de l'admiration réciproque; l'amitié sincère et franche est beaucoup plus rare.

Et au Canada? Au Canada la chose est même plus compliqué. Au commencement de notre histoire on trouve les Français, les premiers Canadiens, faisant la pêche, faisant la traite, et s'efforçant difficilement de faire de la terre le long des rives du St. Laurent. Mais du point de vue des pieux le Canada était surtout une colonie missionaire, fondé par Dieu pour sa gloire et pour le salut des Indiens. Parmi ces premiers Canadiens étaient des héros, des saints, et des martyrs, dont on chérit la mémoire toujours.

En dix-sept cent soixante-trois venaient les Anglais, soldats et commerçants, qui n'étaient pas saints du tout, mais qui n'étaient pas diables non plus. Ils avaient le désir, sincère et bienveillant, de convertir, c'est-à-dire, d'angliciser les Canadiens; au cours des années cela devenait une idée fixe, toujours sincère mais quelquefois moins bienveillante. Anglais et Français au Canada se sont querellés, quelquefois durement. La disparition graduelle de l'autorité de la Grande Bretagne et de l'état coloniale a rendu ces querelles purement canadiennes. On aurait pu presque dire que le seul lien entre Canadiens, anglais et français, était la répugnance commune à se joindre aux Etats-Unis — qui, de sa part sentant son pouvoir et voulant bien taquiner un peu le lion britannique se montrait assez accueillant.

Disons alors que le Canada uni est né du dix-neuviéme siécle. Mais quel est ce Canada? Question difficile. Pour les Anglais, un endroit ou on parlait anglais et adorait le progrès — et souvent Dieu aussi; certes, on y trouvait des individus appelés "French-Canadians," mais on espèrait que bientôt le progrès changerait tout cela. Pour les Français, un endroit ou on parlait français, un endroit fait pour l'adoration de Dieu et la propagation de Sa culture française; certes, on se trouve entourés d'Anglais barbares, c'est-à-dire d'Américains et de soi-disant canadiens. Impossible de les oublier; il faut alors assurer à tout prix la survivance culturelle, tout en pour suivant la mission historique, catholique, et civilisatrice du Canada française.

Mais depuis la première grande guerre et même avant on voit un changement important. Ce que nous avons de mieux à faire au vingtième siècle, disent les hommes de bonne volonté, est d'oublier autant que possible les haines et les mépris du passé, et d'accepter le fait de notre co-existence, Canadiens anglais et français, deux communautés, deux cultures, dans un seul pays, en partageant la richesse et en y conservant le bon ordre. Nos deux jardins, dit-on, sont beaux; cultivons chacun le sien; admirez celui de votre voisin, profitez-en tant que vous le pouvez, mais laissez-le tranquille. Voilà le principe de co-existence, le vrai principe de la vie nationale canadienne.

Que doit-on dire de cette co-existence? Quand on pense à l'ignorance, au mépris, à la brutalité même de pensée et d'expression dont nous avons été coupables — je parle pour les anglais au moins — dans un passé pas très lointain, on est tenté d'accueillir avec enthousiasme un *modus vivendi* qui promet au moins la paix et la bienveillance. Mais, quand on se rappellez que nous vivons en 1957, au milieu d'une révolution peut-être sans exemple dans l'histoire de notre civilisation, il faut avouer que la co-existence n'est guère suffisante. La co-existence veut dire, je suppose, deux communautés qui ne se mêlent pas beaucoup excepté par le moyen des échanges culturels des hommes cultivés. Est-ce que cela est assez pour l'unité d'une nation moderne dans le monde d'aujourd'hui?

Moi, je ne veux pas tout simplement co-exister avec mes compatriotes de langue française. Je veux plutôt partager avec eux une vie commune, une vie nationale digne de la grande civilisation de l'ouest qui est la nôtre et qui est aujourd'hui en peril.

Je sais bien que mes compatriotes de langue française, fiers de la survivance presque miraculeuse de leur race et de leur culture, craignent des rapports trop intimes avec les Canadiens de langue anglaise. Cela se comprend, car ceux-ci ne sont qu'une petite partie du vaste royaume anglo-saxon qui s'étale sur notre continent. D'ailleurs, il y a parmi les Canadiens de langue anglaise quelques-uns qui entretiennent encore le désir d'assimiler la culture canadienne-française à la leur. Se mêler librement avec les anglo-saxons dans toutes les affaires de la vie serait alors un acte de foi et de courage exceptionnel.

Mais l'histoire canadienne-française offre à nous tous une tradition glorieuse de foi et de courage. Nous en avons grand besoin dans le crise actuelle. Le co-existence, je le répète, est nécessaire, mais elle n'est pas suffisante. Selon moi, nous devrions oublier cette expression un peu froide et négative et apprendre à faire une vie commune. Bien entendu, on peut prévoir des dangers de toute sorte. La pureté des deux langues, par example, serait menacée. Mais, mise en face de grands périls, on perd de vue les moins grands. Nos descendants de l'avenir — dans trois siècles, deux, un même — parleront-ils français, anglais, ou un mélange des deux, relevé peut-être d'un tout petit peu de russe et de chinois? Je dirai même que cela ne fait rien s' ils parlent encore la langue de la vérité et de l'amitié, de la liberté et de la justice. En temps de peril on revient aux sources mêmes de la vie humaine.[4]

CANADIAN BI-CULTURALISM

Canadian "bi-culturalism" has a complicated historical origin which has had much influence on the peculiar development of the current situation. From the early 17th century French traders were settling on the St. Lawrence as English-men spread along the Atlantic seaboard and up the Hudson. Both were interested in the Hudson's Bay, but early in the 18th century the English had made good their claim against the French. The two countries, intellectual leaders of the world, and intellectually each admiring the achievements of the other, became locked in a cutthroat competition for markets, which included colonies. In the course of the struggle the English conquered the St. Lawrence colony and eliminated the French Empire from the North American mainland.

If this colony of some 75,000 people, with relatively few educated members and very few rich ones, had been immediately swamped with English farmers and artisans there might be no bi-culturalism today. But geography and economics were opposed. There was farming land elsewhere, better and more accessible. The English who came in replaced only the French who had left: top civil servants and soldiers and big businessmen who took over the long-range fur trade.

A second "if": if the Americans who revolted only 15 years after this colony was conquered had been more unanimous and more competent in a military sense, they might have taken over the colony and excluded Great Britain from the continent, and ultimately there might have been no bi-culturalism. But the Americans were not strong enough to take over the northern area. Instead after the revolution only a very small minority came north to settle on the Upper St. Lawrence, along the lower Lakes and in the Maritimes.

This produced in what is eastern Canada today two groups who wanted to be themselves, the French-Canadians and the United Empire Loyalists. In the long run each decided that as they had most to fear from the United States, and as their most profitable trade connections were with Britain, they should cling to protection from Britain with a hope in the future for autonomy. It was the French who first exhibited their own racial-cultural nationalism, early in the nineteenth century, — "Notre religion, notre language, nos lois" — against British officials and English-speaking Canadians, both of whom thought Canadians should all be "English." It was English-speaking Canadians who first and strongly envisaged a united Canadian (French and English) nation with autonomy and eventually independence from Great Britain. Leaders of each group have helped to make this a reality.

The French-speaking Canadian has, however, often been dubious. Would not the united nation be an English one? The fact that for a long time there was not much communication with France (revolutionary, Napoleonic and anti-clerical), and that English immigration was very large, and that American immigration to say nothing of the American nation, was also very large increased this fear. The slow immigration and the very large French-Canadian birth-rate eased the tension early in the century. It seems likely that the recent influx of immigrants who speak or who will speak English, along with the decreased French birth-rate, may be in part responsible for the increased tension today.

What is the legal relation of the French and English-speaking groups? Contrary to a belief very widespread among French-speaking Canadians, there is no legal or constitutional recognition of these two groups as such in the Canadian federation. There is a recognition of provincial rights, and of the rights of certain religious minorities which certainly has reference to the two groups; and there is the explicit provision that French equally with English is recognized as a language of debate and of record in the Canadian parliament. That is all. The provinces, as provinces, make their own arrangements about language with the result that, officially, Quebec is French-speaking and all the others are English-speaking.

So much for the legal facts. The political and practical situation is different. On the one hand, the French have less than one might expect from the letter of the law. In national affairs French legally has equal rights with English, but nothing is so difficult to regulate by law as language. Communication is basically and literally democratic. The will of the majority will prevail and in Canada the English majority is fortified not only by being an overwhelming majority over most parts of the country but also by the enormous cultural support at every level from the vast, wealthy, English-speaking United States.

But the French-speaking Canadians in practice on the national scene claim much more than strict law would give them. The little French-speaking colony which for various reasons prospered very greatly under British rule in the eighteenth century, in the nineteenth bent its surplus energy to a remarkable expression of the nationalism that was so strong a moral force in contemporary Europe. This nationalism was fed and nourished on history, the glorious history of the French Empire in North America, and on the legend (both true and false) of French betrayal and English brutality. Nationalists resented "colonialism" in the sense both of subjection to Britain and to the English-speaking majority, which was only another kind of colonialism. This nationalism grew and flourished with the relatively undivided support of French-speaking Canadians. English-speaking Canadians meanwhile were rather deeply divided: about their link with Great Britain, their relations to the United States, and, sectionally, about their relations to each other. French-Canadian nationalism in a separatist sense has been fed in the twentieth century by two wars in which the French had less interest than the English-speaking Canadians because all their loyalty was rooted in Quebec, which as a community had not yet achieved a world outlook. And the development of this was not helped by bitter reproaches from English-speaking Canada on their failure to bear their share of the sacrifices of war.

The result is that today French-speaking nationalism has developed into a national statism: not just two languages, cultures, races in one state, but two states. This is their answer to the current trend in Canada as elsewhere, away from local autonomy toward a strong central government. If this must be so, the strong government, say some, must be in Quebec. Quebec must be completely independent, say the extremists; with a nominal link, say those less extreme; with much greater autonomy than at present, say the most moderate. These last add to their requirements much greater concessions on the part of the other provinces to French-speaking communities. Naturally the extremists, demanding independence, can make no such claim. It follows from this last that the contemporary cultural picture, as distinct from the political one, is confused. The people of Quebec strive to maintain cultural and religious ties with all French-speaking North Americans, in the United States as in the other Canadian provinces. As an independent or semi-independent state Quebec could do less for other French-speaking Canadians than she may do today. She may do less, for if Quebec were to go to the extreme of political independence the result might be the absorption of most other Canadian provinces into the American union, leaving Quebec in a difficult and embarrassing isolation and (almost certainly) a prey to serious internal divisions. Thus it is probable that those in Quebec whose concern for the cultural values of the nation is greatest are those opposed to independence in any extreme form.

This is a mere sketch of the origin and nature of the separatist tendencies in our country today. The French-speaking Canadians are conscious of these tendencies as most of the English are not. Too many English have the comfortable feeling that, in a general way they have "taken over" the French. The French on the other hand, acutely sensitive to this feeling, think of nothing so much as that they have not been and will not be "taken over." That is why the English have readily and happily taken the heroes of New France into their national Pantheon, while the French for the most part are unaware of, or at least entirely uninterested in, the history of non French-speaking Canada. They adopt the stirring and dangerous slogan "notre maître le passé" but it is inevitably the past of French-speaking Canada, for they have no real sense of union with any other.

The reasons for this exclusiveness are sufficient and entirely comprehensible: the constant sense that English-speaking Canada is really taking over them; and the all-pervading sense of the nearness and might of the English-speaking United States. They are isolated in an English speaking continent; they are constantly menaced by "manifest destiny."

The Anglo-Saxon looking at this situation, if he is a good Anglo-Saxon, is likely to pull himself together and consider not the history of the issue, but what is to be done, what can be done. This matter is now under consideration by a Royal Commission which may well find the problem broader than its terms of reference. The centennial of confederation, a year which makes a deep appeal to most English-speaking Canadians, sees among many, we do not know how many, French-speaking Canadians a demand for the recognition of the two nations and even the two states. In its extreme form, this demand is simply not viable. Better, if such a thing must come, a complete and friendly separation from Quebec, with the necessary agreements for handling joint affairs such as we have with the United States. There is no doubt that many French-speaking Canadians do not wish for this, for reasons already suggested.

The extremists derive their strength from the gulf which does exist between these two peoples engaged in a kind of cold war within a single state. If we are to find any humane and civilized way out of the unhappy situation in which we are placed, we must bridge this gulf. As no personal sacrifice is too great for such an end, so no personal effort is too small to be worthwhile.

First, in English-speaking Canada we should get over our indifference and our laziness and see to it that all educated people, or at least all leading people in professions, business and government services can read and speak French easily, accurately, fluently. This is not easy. It is not as easy as many of our French-speaking countrymen who live in a completely bilingual atmosphere believe. But it is quite possible. Modern teaching devices make the task much less difficult, and modern communication — radio, television, "paperbacks" and rapid travel — mean that linguistic barriers would really go down like the wall of Jericho if only English-speaking people were prepared to do a little hard work (the Israelites did have to walk round the city thirteen times) and then give a great shout, in French.

If the people in English-speaking Canada were fully competent in French, a second aim could be achieved eventually. Anyone should be able to enter a federal office or institution, or corporation, anywhere in Canada and feel free to speak in his own language because he is sure of being understood. Those who speak the language of a majority can have only a slight idea of the sense of humiliation and frustration experienced by the person forced always to express himself in a language not his own. Certainly if we are to be bi-lingual some of us must always be doing this, but let us take turns fairly. When a national committee meets today, English-speaking Canadians are always associated with French-speaking colleagues. What language do they use? English — and probably the French-speaking Canadian would not have been chosen unless he could speak English, although none of his English-speaking colleagues may be able to speak French. As a result they speak English all day until by evening the French-speaking member may be too exhausted even to think in French, let alone explain the intricacies of his point of view in comprehensible English. And so, perhaps, he says nothing and goes home to Quebec from the foreign city that is Ottawa with a sense of great relief. This is stating the case strongly, but this kind of thing happens much too often. It would be most helpful if it could happen at least once to every English-speaking Canadian.

Once we have learned and are using the French language we can understand and value French and French-Canadian culture: music, art, literature, religion, social values. We can stop looking at them as un-Canadian, or quaint or foreign. We can see them as our own to be valued and cherished as part of our common life.

This does not mean English-speaking Canadians need scorn their values or call themselves barbarians. The more we know each other the more we realize that each can find much to admire in the other. Looking at each culture at its best, the English have much to learn from Quebec on appreciation of intellectual and artistic values, of general culture as distinguished from specialization, of the value of family ties, of a community as well as an individual expression of religious belief. On the other hand, we (at our best) perhaps show excellence in civic virtue, in a sense of public duty, in strict integrity with public as well as private funds, in co-operation and compromise in the interests of joint action, and in a willingness to endure the discipline of long professional and technical training, in an insistence on universal education, dull virtues, but useful. All these efforts to bridge the gap between our two languages and cultures should have been under-taken long ago. Unfortunately, in the first blush of nationalism after 1867 English Canadians, as their writings show, saw Canada as Ontario writ large; and unfortunately, except that some of us criticize Toronto, we have not changed much. Now, a hundred years after Confederation it is easy to believe that it is too late to do anything.

To this pessimistic view one answer is obvious. It is never too late to do the wise, the generous and the just action. And it is not only wise and generous, it is just to recognize our other language and our other culture. If the English would only "take over" by seeking to learn rather than to dominate they would be right, where now in so many ways they are clearly wrong.

Moreover if our Canadian state cannot last (and nothing is too bad to happen), we had better learn as soon as we can to understand and communicate with our Quebec neighbours even if they are fellow-citizens only in a nominal fashion, even if to us they are to be "foreigners." Incidentally, without Quebec, we still have a large French-speaking population.

Finally, these efforts that we might make for the common good, let us remind ourselves, are for us as individuals pure gain. What a pity it is that we have lost the fine tradition which taught that educated people learned at least Latin and French as an essential part of their cultural heritage. It is a curious comment on the mentality of English-speaking Canadians if they have lost the ancient English admiration for the achievements of "that sweet enemy France." And it does us Canadians small credit as a "middle nation" defending the values of the western world if we do not consider it pure gain to be invited to take possession of the keys of a culture whose greatness will not be forgotten while western civilization remains. It is a pity that a country endowed with two such languages and two such cultures should find bi-lingualism and bi-culturalism a problem rather than an opportunity.[5]

ETHNIC GROUPS: ASSIMILATION OR INTEGRATION?

I have been asked to spend no more than 10 - 15 minutes suggesting questions that should be considered in dealing with this problem.

First, we might remind ourselves of what we all know: Canadians contrast themselves with Americans: they (we say), prefer assimilation; we choose integration.

There is, no doubt, some truth in this, and some reasons for it are clear. The American colonies received many non-Anglo-Saxon groups in the eighteenth century before the days of romantic nationalism. No one bothered much about the issue at all. After the Revolution it was natural that a new republic in a still largely monarchical western world should press its political, constitutional and equalitarian views on newcomers from Europe — and those newcomers who were political refugees were often happy to receive them.

The Canadian situation was different. First, romantic nationalism was in its first youth only a few decades after Conquest and the American Revolution brought together two groups whose religious differences accentuated the distinction between two cultures which after all did have much in common. English Canada made a virtue of necessity and renounced by the mid-nineteenth century the impossible task of assimilating the French.

Second, when Canadian immigration authorities half a century and more ago were intent on making the twentieth Canada's century by filling the west, they encouraged mass migrations by promising a certain groups (for example, the Doukhobors) freedom to follow their own community life.

Circumstances, then, have led us to repudiate the need of, or the benefit of, assimilation and to concentrate on the advantages of a society that cherishes peoples of diverse cultures, working together to a common end.

The conception is a fine one and the results may be most advantageous to society — on certain conditions. First, there must be a rough "equality" in the cultures preserved — equality of esteem. Men should be encouraged to value what in their heritage is good. To retain what is clearly bad, or inappropriate in the modern world *because* it is yours, is to lose the respect of others and your own self-respect. Moreover modern conditions may make it impossible. The very serious problem of the Doukhobors is a case in point. A less serious problem, but a real one, is that of the Hutterites. Have the parents (as a group) the right to rear their children under such conditions as may make it increasingly difficult for them to adapt to a rapidly-changing and increasingly centralized and urbanized society? (I do not suggest how they can be prevented; I only mention this as an instance where the integration has failed and (perhaps) one can only hope for ultimate assimilation).

The Indians — We hear much from champions of the poor Indian. It seems to me that many expend more energy on righteous indignation over sins of the past than in working to ameliorate conditions in the present. Moreover, what one does *not* hear from these vocal individuals is what our policy should be. Bluntly, it is a fact of history that Indians were not numerous enough, and their culture not sufficiently advanced, to cope with the vastly more sophisticated western European. Moreover, the ways of life of the various Indian tribes cannot possibly be perpetuated in the modern world. Should not someone have the courage to say openly that the best hope for the Indian is to aim at assimilation? His group cannot compete on a sufficiently modern level to make integration possible.

Where ethnic groups can compete fairly — that is, where a group can preserve its own traditions of art, music, literature, family life, ethics, religion, and still co-operate adequately with other groups, no one could wish for assimilation. Nothing could serve so well to protect us from the hideous tyranny of a completely centralized, computerized, mass-advertised society. But such a preservation of group values must depend on true taste and real conviction. Otherwise it can easily degenerate into worshipping one's ancestors, and despising, or even hating, one's neighbours.[6]

LETTER TO THE EDITOR, SASKATOON *STAR-PHOENIX* 1969

Sir: I have read your editorial of Dec. 20 with much concern.

Your attempt to moderate between the claims of various groups to cultural recognition and support is obviously well intended. Unfortunately it is regrettably ill-informed.

French-speaking Canadians are not and never have been merely one among many "ethnic minorities." It is culpable ignorance of Canadian history which prompts such a suggestion — a suggestion that understandably exasperates all Canadians of French origins and speech, and is one cause of the extreme nationalist attitudes which are such a threat to Canadian unity.

New France was occupied by British troops in 1760 and was formally ceded by France to Britain in 1763. This was "the Conquest." But, as rulers of all great empires have realized, conquest is not enough. Ultimately all peaceable and civilized government rests on the consent of the governed. British statesmen for various reasons, more or less worthy, devoted themselves to securing the consent of the governed. For almost a century the majority of the governed were French-speaking, and these constituted by far the oldest and most closely knit of all the communities that ultimately made up the Dominion of Canada in 1867.

One finds many ill-informed statements about the pact of confederation and the terms of the BNA Act. This much, however, is clear. Whatever the legal position, the communities which by their own consent were united by the Act all accepted, even if unwillingly, the fact of an ancient French-speaking community which was proud of its own history and traditions, and determined to maintain them in their integrity.

Other ethnic groups which have since that time chosen to come to this country have done so, it must be presumed, knowing these historic and constitutional facts, and prepared to accept them. In a fully democratic society these ethnic groups have every right, as citizens, to promote such changes as they think fit in our society and government. But for English-speaking Canadians to attempt to lump French-speaking and other minorities together as "ethnic groups" equally significant in the tradition of "Canadianism" is to ignore our entire history.

The original Canadians were French-speaking Roman Catholics, members of a closely knit community and preserving a very special historical tradition. They were surrounded and ultimately outnumbered by English-speaking immigrants. These two peoples have founded our nation, if indeed we are one nation.

We are deeply indebted to the many others who have joined their lot to ours and who are enriching our common life. But to confuse them with the original founders of the country is to deny the facts of history, and to promote that future punishment which must come to those who wilfully misunderstand the past.[7]

Hilda Neatby

CULTURAL EVOLUTION

This title covers such a wide and ill-defined area that it seems necessary to ask, first, what it means. I suppose that a study of our cultural evolution really calls for an examination of the nature and influence of those forces which have been calculated to keep alive and to develop in us what is essentially human in face of the deadening impact of the forces of materialistic democracy which have been so powerful in the western world and particularly on our continent during the whole period of our national life. Material wealth and a moral urge toward social equality have their dangers for the good life. An American writer presenting this view asks whether the "good is always the friend of the best," or whether "excellence is not more likely to lose out to mediocrity than it is to mere ignorance or nullity." And in a well-known Canadian play an artist emerging from an unhappy encounter with some professional uplifters remarks: "The educated like my work, and the uneducated like it. As for the half-educated — well, we can only pray for them in Canada as elsewhere."

It is the half-educated that are hostile to the creative artist for they tend to be happiest with the mediocre. Not only have they confused quality with quantity; they tend to blur the terms "creative work" and "self-expression" in such fashion that all self-expression somehow rates as creative work — or as something just as good. It seems therefore desirable in a brief survey of this broad subject to go directly to the heart of it, which is the creative artist and his work, and to ask exactly what he does and why his work has value.

The role of the artist in society is simple and essential. Art is communication, the communication of the artist's experience. Art is also creation because the experience communicated is created or brought alive by the artist. Experience, it has been said, consists not in impressions but in making sense. It is the artist's job to make sense, "to render actual new sectors of the inexhaustible field of potential experience." This does not, of course, mean that artists are a race apart or that it is easy or even possible always to identify the original experience of the creative artist. It does mean that civilization lives on the communication of valid experience by the honest artist. Without such communication we may exist but we do not live. We are confined to the objective truth which is the truth of a moment. We fail to enter into our human inheritance.

It is often said that artists have a bad time in Canada, but in the twentieth century artists have a bad time everywhere. The chief cause of their frustration lies far deeper than persecution or neglect. Civilized societies live, or have lived, on a general agreement on "the valid morality of experience." A loosening of accepted patterns may for a time stimulate activity and inspire a vigorous period of art. But when the whole pattern is lost in confusion and uncertainty the artist himself is at a loss. He must have liberty, but he must also have a frame of reference. The dilemma of the artist in the twentieth century is that he lives in an age of widespread doubt about the very existence of ultimate truth. If such doubt became certainty the artist would presumably have nothing to say. Even the doubt affects profoundly the capacity to communicate experience. The artists of no other country, perhaps, have been so much affected as those of Canada, for Canadian cultural development has in time paralleled the loosening of patterns, the dissolution of foundations, the general disappearance of the overriding sense of ultimate truth and of any commonly accepted symbols through which the artists' sense of the truth could be conveyed. Artists in older countries had their schools and their traditions founded in an age of greater spiritual and moral security. The Canadian artist began to raise his individual voice against the background of a western world in process of dissolving its standards and discarding its values. The First World War, for example, so critical in our national and cultural development, has rightly been referred to as "an episode" in "the general breakdown of liberal humanist culture." The general background of our cultural development has not been favourable to a clear and vigorous creative expression.

Against this intellectual and philosophic background must be set the familiar material conditions of Canadian life and development. We have had, and we still have, a small population in a very large country. The population is neither concentrated in one part nor evenly distributed over the whole. Rather there is, as the geologists say, a series of deposits of people — one very large one in the area of the Great Lakes and St. Lawrence Valley, and smaller ones in the Maritimes, on the prairies and on the Pacific coast. Moreover, the one large block, although united geographically, is divided within itself by differences of language and of tradition. The artist in Canada, in any communicating of experience to the country as a whole, has encountered not only physical obstacles of space but also more subtle forces of separation: language and modes of thought. The physical obstacles have been overcome in part; other divisive forces have resolved themselves in the growth of two cultural groups each with its own accumulated wealth of inherited experience, each one more or less ready to listen to its own artists but too often unwilling or unable to learn much from those of the other group. It is polite to say that Canada is richer for her two cultures. If we bear in mind that the essence of cultural development is the enrichment of human life by a general appropriation of artistic experience, it must be obvious that no country is the richer only because one-half of the population cannot appropriate the experience of one-half of the artists: a crude mathematical expression of a truth too often ignored. This is not, of course, the whole truth, but it does represent an essential condition of our present situation.

There is one other important condition of Canadian cultural development. Each deposit of population along the Canadian border lives in close and constant contact with communities in the corresponding geographic area of the United States. For English-speaking Canadians the obvious destiny would seem to be to blend their cultural lives with those of neighbours of common language and tradition. To a large extent English-speaking Canadians do do this. That they do not do so altogether is part of the whole paradox of Canadian survival as a national entity.

Canada, it has been suggested, originated with a series of rejected groups: French cut off from France, Loyalists from the former American Colonies, Scots from the Highlands. These groups, without having much in common beyond their rejection and their joint habitation of a vast, lonely and mysterious land, have together created, though doubtfully enough and slowly, a national community with autonomous political institutions and an integrated economy. The different groups may be geographically isolated or culturally distinct or both. With all their divisions, however, they have been thrown together by a common determination to survive, a determination which has left its mark on a quiet, cautious, stubborn people. . . .

When one is asked to peer fifty years into the future the instinct is first to look back fifty years into the past.

The last half-century with two major wars, the unexampled period of the depression, and the present unexampled accession of power and prosperity have seen an amazingly rapid rate of economic and constitutional development. In intellectual and cultural matters there has also been remarkable growth. It could hardly be otherwise in a period during which not only has Canadian destiny but the destiny of our whole world seemed often in doubt. Only a completely insensitive people could fail to be moved by the universal sense of crisis. The First

World War was followed in Canada by a self-conscious effort at national self-expression. The second one has been followed by a more mature self-examination. Have we anything to say, and how are we saying it? This has led to important considerations on the difficult lot of the artist and of the scholar, their need for help, the proper means of securing it, and the inevitable suggestions that artists and their like be allowed to find their own level.

Our concern, kindly or patronizing or critical, with the future of the artist may in more ways than one provide the key to an understanding of our future. We should ask, not so much what we are going to do with the artist, but what we are going to do with ourselves. The true artist has vision and insight; by definition he is a seer. He conveys the truth by which, literally, men and nations live. He shows what life is in all its aspects. Man cannot exercise his faculty of refusing the evil and of choosing the good unless he knows, and that means unless he has been shown, what these are. It is not a question of what we are to do with struggling artists, a question asked in the same tone as we ask what we are to do with the victims of poverty, disease and vice. It is a question of what we want to do, of what we should do, with and for ourselves. Do we want to get below the surface of the obvious and the material in order to penetrate into those mysteries which, even though they may sometimes be dark and difficult, yield life as distinguished from existence? Or do we want rather to use the wealth which we have gained from the achievements of reason and the fruits of toil to bury ourselves in material satisfactions?

We have the elements of a national culture in those who have given themselves over to the values of religion, philosophy, scholarship, art, music, literature, but we have not a coherent whole. Cultural evolution is not organic evolution. In a democratic society it must represent a conscious dedication to the good life, a genuine worship of the truth that makes the good life for the community. If in Canada we can secure that dedication and worship, there is every hope that we shall not lack artists, philosophers, and scholars to interpret to us in their various ways the aspects of truth that they have seen. If on the other hand we refuse to give to our hearts and minds the thought and care that we lavish on our physical needs we may very easily use our wealth only to demonstrate a premature decadence and a relapse into barbarism.[8]

While each of the chapters in Part Two and Three of this book reflects one aspect of Hilda's thoughts, few of the selections were written before Hilda was forty. This chapter is the exception. Hilda wrote two sets of letters to her sister Kate, the first in 1924–25, while she was in Paris, and the other between 1932 and 1935, while she was a graduate student in Minneapolis and a teacher at Regina College. A number from the second set have been reproduced in this chapter to show Hilda both as a letter writer, something she excelled at, and as a graduate student. In the process it is possible to obtain a picture of what life was like for most graduate students in the 1930's.

Most of what remains of Hilda's writing is of a formal nature. Even her extant letters are mostly concerned with professional matters. The letters in this chapter are different. They reveal Hilda's charm, her femininity, her need for sleep, her interest in clothes, her love for her sister, and her concern for her mother. They may surprise those who knew Hilda only through her writing or in a professional relationship. Those who knew her personally will recognize her humanity breaking through her standards, her ups and downs, her sense of humour, her concern for others as well as her persistence and intelligence.

At the time these letters were written, Kate was in England, first studying and then working. Mr. Neatby died in 1932 before the letters begin. During the years covered by the letters, Mrs. Neatby was working at a Bible Institute in Manitoba. After Hilda moved to Regina, her mother joined her. Her brother Kenneth, referred to in the letters, went to England to study in 1933. Her brother Leslie, also mentioned, was a school principal in Shellbrook, Saskatchewan, during the 1930's.

1427 Raymond Ave.,
St. Paul, Minn.,
U.S.A.
Nov. 20, 1932

Dear Kate,

Thank you for the letter which I did not receive this week, but which I charitably assume that you wrote. With reference to the complaint in your last about paying 3d. on your stockings, I should like you to know that I had to pay *fifteen* cents on the rouge, it being apparently a *parcel* within the meaning of the act.

I have just been smoking a cigarette with Kay Dietrich and discussing problems of courtship and marriage. Either we are naturally sexless, or we were brought up in a very sexless way, for it is quite amazing to me what a large part that sort of thing seems to play in the average unmarried woman's life. I can understand a craving to be married to a particular person, but I think the general urge to marriage is rather a tragedy, and yet when you think about it it seems to be almost universal. Kay is an extremely normal person but she has a special problem on her hands just now which accounts for her interest in the subject. Unfortunately she is also reading for her prelim. & it makes a bad combination.

As usual I started this week with good intentions which hardly materialized. On Monday I went to the tea I told you of, and being one of the first two ladies to arrive Miss Nute asked me to pour the coffee. It was not a very large tea and was quite informal. I had a very good time, because I saw everyone and was able to talk to them a little but not too much. Miss N. was very nice. I am sorry if I ever said anything agin her.

On Tuesday we went home (Ronnie Lee, Miss Thompson & I) with Mr. Burt for our weekly tea meeting. They asked me to stay to supper as they generally do and afterwards they took me to *Grand Hotel* — rather against my conscience but I enjoyed it. On Wednesday I did study & also on Thursday, Friday and Saturday. Yesterday evening I asked Mary Burt to come to supper with me at the Farm Campus Cafeteria. They always have waffles on Saturday night and as these are her favourite food I thought it was a good chance to pay back some of the hospitality I owe. I think she enjoyed it, because when I suggested another order of waffles she hinted most delicately that it might be better to come again another time than to have a double quantity on one night. We went back to my room to talk for a few minutes and we too discussed problems of courtship & marriage although not in quite the same strain as Kay & I do. Mary is rather romantically inclined and she shows a most flattering curiosity as to why I am still unmarried. I don't know whether she has provided me with an unburied flower or not. I gather that she has no intention of living a single life.

To-night the Pet Idea Club has a supper meeting chez Mrs. Tyler by special invitation. I don't know who is to hold forth. So far the thing is most popular. We are still airing our views jointly and severally as to what history is. We shall probably continue to do so all year, but it is quite entertaining.

The cut which threatened for a time is an accomplished fact. We each have 1.25 deducted from the next ten cheques. It doesn't sound much but 2.50 a month can make all the difference between penury & plenty. Still it might have been worse.

I enclose a letter from Mother which should have been forwarded early this week, but I held it over for a day expecting a letter from you, and then I must confess I forgot it. I don't think it makes so much difference because I reckoned that if she wrote when she said she would you would hear from her first anyway, but still I am sorry to have held it up.

The Burts have a mad idea of going to Toronto for Christmas by motor, as Mr. Burt has to go anyway to the American Historical. They will be away about 3 weeks — we have long holidays this year — and they are suggesting that Norma & another Holyoake girl & I when I am here, come & live in the house in their absence. I should like it very much because although I want to be with Mother as long as I can I feel that I must give about half my holidays to studying & the prospect of coming back to that is a lot pleasanter than that of working here alone in my room. I hope you won't feel that I am neglecting Mother by only staying part of the time at Winnipeg. If she were unhappy I should stay there and try to study at odd times, but as you know, that is not an easy thing to do, and she does seem so much happier now that it will not be so hard to leave her. I feel I must study as regularly as I can, because I find I can't manage as long hours as I did last year. I feel perfectly well, but if I work too long I am apt to lie awake at night which is really no help. I got over nine hours last night though which accounts for the cheerful strain in which I now address you.

Thanksgiving comes on Thursday and I am asked to the Burts along with Hope & a crowd of homeless assistants. I was at lunch there yesterday and had some of the cranberry sauce made that morning & heard the pumpkins being mashed by Emily (daily maid) so I can echo Marion's classic sentiment. Emily is not coming on Thursday so I am going down early in the morning to help as about fourteen are coming to the dinner.

I must write to Mother now. If it isn't too late when I come in this evening I will add something to this.

Later — A damsel held forth on the theme "History should be nothing if not amusing" and tried to show by illustration how to make it amusing but I didn't think she was awfully successful. I think the amusing part has to be a by-product. I saw Norma and told her Mrs. Burt's plan which she more or less knocked on the head. She wants to spend the holidays in the Minneapolis Public Library which is too far away from here. Also one of the men dashed my spirits by telling me all the reading he is going to do in Ec. history & I can't do half as much. Don't imagine from this that I didn't enjoy myself, because I did. It is a beautiful house and the supper was beyond praise. All I need now is nature's sweet restorer.

If I don't hear from you shortly I shall be extremely annoyed. Your last came a week ago Thursday.

Yours expectantly,
Hilda.

This is the last of my good writing paper. It will probably be years before you get a letter from me on anything so superior.

1427 Raymond Ave.
St. Paul, Minn.
U.S.A.
Dec. 11, 1932

Dear Kate. . . .

To change the note — I am glad that the dentist has dismissed you at last, and glad that you are getting a taste for English history. It is beginning to pall on me ever so slightly but only because I am suffering from a surfeit. I still know that there is no more delightful pursuit even though at present I can't enjoy it as I should. What you should use for your purposes is either *The Political History of England* — edited by Hunt & Poole — in 12 volumes by different authors — or a shorter series edited by Oman. I am not suggesting that you read them through but they are the two standard long histories and the only ones — I should think — where you could be almost sure of running down any literary reference. For a general survey Trevelyan has a very charming history that you could read in a short time. I don't know the dates of the chronicle plays but I should like to hint in the most delicate manner in the world that as Macaulay does not start until some time after 1660 he probably would not be much use to you. Froude covers the period 1509–1588.

Talking of books I asked Mr. Burt to-night to lend me one each out of the two series I just mentioned in order to get up James I whom we discuss next day. He insisted on my taking as well 5 volumes of J.R. Gardiner of whom you may have heard. He isn't the least bit like father but sometimes he reminds me quite painfully of him, especially when he gets up even in the middle of a meal and dashes into his study to look things up. With regard to Gardiner I gently suggested that I couldn't hope to read the 5 volumes, which he admitted, but advised selections which he evidently thought should be as full as possible. . . .

I can get to Winnipeg and back for $15.90 which pleases me vastly. I intend to go just for the week. I may have told you this before. If the Burts go to Toronto Norma & I and Elizabeth Warner — another Holyoake girl who is doing zoology — are to keep house for them. N. & I will be away part of the time but E.W. will be here right through. Elizabeth's friend Gertrude Ward is in history and is in all of my three classes. I may have mentioned her before. She is pretty and nice and dresses beautifully. I spend some very pleasant hours in Canadian history contemplating her shoes. Her father is a New York business man and apparently very solvent. She was at the Burts to-night and when the talk turned on bathrooms mentioned quite casually that when they built their house their mother let them each choose what coloured tiles they wanted in their bath-rooms (3 children). I hope it is not snobbish but I find it curiously restful to associate with people who simply do not know what money worries are. G. is anything but objectionably rich — she is evidently so accustomed to it that she takes it for granted. I should think her people are very nice.

This week the learned Lipson gave three public lectures and talked to our seminar, and also at a banquet attended by faculty and graduate students. I liked him very much, although some of his lectures were a bit too boiled down, so that most of the original parts were eliminated. . . .

I can't think of anything else that is really important to tell — Exams start next Saturday. I only have one — on Tuesday — but I am unreasonably annoyed, because I hoped not to have any — our finals cover everything & we hoped not have any now. However it may be just as well in the long run. I am not particularly worried about it, though I wish I had not lost my notes.

As I rose this morning at 10.30 just in time to dress and dash out to church my bed is still unmade, and it is after eleven now. To-morrow will be here regrettably soon and I therefore bid you farewell,

Hilda.

I gave Norma your address the other day — She is sending you, I believe, an introduction to a friend of hers who seems to be a remarkably good sort. Apart from that I think you would find it interesting to get acquainted with a type of American different from those we usually encountered in Sask.

January 22, 1933

Dear Kate,

Don't think I have an economical streak, but I am writing from the Burts & this is supplied as being the most suitable for a long letter.

Having received two letters from you last week I got none this week, but I had none the week before, so you are one in arrears. I think you English people might arrange something better than a fortnightly service.

I got the application forms for the R.S. fellowships on Friday & broached the matter with Mr. B. yesterday. He knew about them & I think had been inquiring when he was at Toronto. Why he had said nothing to me I don't know. Perhaps he thought that under the family circs. I would only be interested in a job. I wouldn't hesitate if there was a chance of a real job but that's the difficulty. Anyhow Mr. Burt admitted somewhat tentatively that it might be all right to apply, and as he had to go out yesterday afternoon said he would discuss it with me to-day. I was here at lunch and he didn't say anything. They are all out to tea but I am staying here because Norma Adams is coming later to tea here with me. I shall see him later this evening & hope he may bring it up. If he doesn't I shall have to, for my application must be in by Feb. 1, and I shall have to write for recommendations. The fellowships are $1500 for research only, and may be held anywhere outside Canada. There is work that I could do quite well either in London or the Eastern States, but in view of the exchange I suppose London would not cost much more. They don't say when the awards are announced, which is unfortunate.

There is great excitement in the history department just now, because Mrs. (Professor) Deutsch has produced twin boys. They already have two daughters aged about six and eight, so that a boy was badly wanted, but she has gone one better so to speak. Mr. Deutsch is a great bargain hunter, so Mrs. Burt says she is going to tease him about his one-cent sale purchase. Everyone is very delighted because Mrs. D. had flu badly about Christmas and has hardly been out of bed for five weeks. She is so weak now that they won't let her see the babies for a week — excuse all the repetition — but apparently she and the babies will be all right.

This week I bought a pair of breeches (2.95) — khaki whipcord, mostly if not entirely cotton, but they look quite smart. I had to buy them having promised to go skiing with Renata Picenouski. When we arrived at the spot everything was covered with clear ice, for it has been thawing, freezing and raining by turns for the last fortnight. In view of the fact that we are neither of us experts, and that the ski man who had just been out said he could hardly keep his feet, we decided that a toboggan would be more prudent. We had a splendid time. The ice enabled us to make marvellous speed, and we were in a very pretty place — the same where the Kreys had their toboggan party last year. It is on the University Golf course, about half a mile from the dormitory where I live. R. came back to supper with me, after which she went home and I studied.

All this frivolity is calculated, because I still find it hard to sleep as much as I want to. I get quite enough to keep me going, but I think if I got a little more my mighty brain might function more efficiently which is rather necessary.

I have been wondering whether, if I get an R.S. fellowship we could get Mother over to England next year. Mine certainly wouldn't be enough to keep us both, but I could help with her fare if she could stay with friends in England. I wouldn't dream of applying if there were any chance of getting a decent job and making a home for her, but that seems hopeless. Of course if I got a prospect, no doubt I could give up the fellowship. . . .

11.00 p.m. — I had a very nice tea with Norma and we stayed and talked for a while after the Burts came home. I am completely at sea about what Mr. B. wants me to do about the R.S. thing. He said yesterday he would talk to me about it to-day, and Mrs. B. referred to it in his presence after lunch, but he said nothing about it then or this evening. I don't feel I can do anything more for a day or two because he knows this application has to be in by Feb. 1. I am not worrying at all, because he isn't the kind of man to neglect a thing like that and no doubt he has his reasons for whatever he does, but my present feeling is that as I have asked his advice he ought to give it without keeping me hanging about.

Ever so much love,
Hilda.

Dormitory.
March 12, 1933.

Dear Kate:

I got your letter on Thursday this week again. We seem to be getting into our stride just as the year draws to a close. It is difficult to keep up an intelligent correspondence at such long range. I note that you approve of an explanation I offered of Mary's behaviour. I am pleased to hear it, but I have no recollection of what the explanation was. . . .

I hate to think of you being cold. Cold is a thing I cannot endure with any fortitude. I speak feelingly because Mr. Burt is a fresh air fiend & he nearly froze us for two hours yesterday when we met for our weekly session in his office. I trust you are warmer now. Talking of Mr. Burt's class, apart from the cold we had a bitter session yesterday. The third girl (the important ones being Gertrude Ward & myself) held the floor & as her subject coincided with part of her thesis she brought that in to read. She is one of those fearfully solid people — every fact is equally precious in her sight. She had threatened to be rather long, so Gertrude & I some days previously got her into a corner & warned her with imprecations not to exceed forty minutes. She read for one hour & twenty minutes. Poor Mr. B. who does not enjoy her productions any more than we do remarked at the end, as he always does — "Very good" — and added somewhat feelingly "plenty of it, too" — Then he felt he had been unkind & hastily tried to back out. What I really started to explain was that a problem of etiquette came up in the course of the agony. Betty (the girl) rashly includes in her productions long words which she cannot pronounce. On this occasion after tripping over a number of them she was completely floored by *contumeliously*. Gertrude and I giggled — G. with such force that she let loose a hairpin (she is growing her hair) which bounced off a chair & clattered gaily to the floor. Now Mr. B. prides himself on being correct in all things so I watched to see what he would do & saw a mental struggle going on: when a lady drops a hairpin does it come in the handkerchief-glove class which a gentlemen retrieves for her, or is it one of those female disasters of the sliding stocking type which he tactfully ignores? He evidently decided that it belonged to the latter type & G. inconspicuously retrieved her own hairpin at the close of the class.

The time I have devoted to this incident is an indication of the barrenness of this week so far as news goes. On Monday I talked to the Pet Idea Club & got on better than I had dared to hope. Everyone was extremely kind, & one of the men, who is very clever, but sometimes more than a little patronizing, assured me that any one who could produce such an idea ought not to hesitate to take a preliminary immediately. I feel that there is a flaw in the reasoning somewhere, although I appreciated the kind words. We have two men coming up for orals (one a repeat) this week & another is taking the writtens which precede the oral, so we are not without our academic excitements. I have got to the paralysis stage. Knowing that I cannot possibly get through what I should by the middle of April I simply don't know where to start. I feel as if I were running round after my own tail. Don't let your tender heart bleed for me. I am not in the least depressed, appearances to the contrary notwithstanding, and when I can get some work done I still enjoy it. . . .

Spring appears to have come here — I have held a financial session with myself & determined to commit the extravagance of having both my coat and hat dry cleaned, which will cost me a dollar and a quarter. Last week I committed a terrible extravagance & paid $1.10 for a jar of Yardley's complexion cream which was recommended to me as a foundation. It seems very good & comes in a large & very beautiful cream coloured pot with a lid the shape of a daisy, & no vulgar lettering or label of any sort on it. However, what I was about to explain was that I had done all that & bought my food for over two weeks with 12 dollars, & I still expect a balance by the time the next check comes. It's due more to good friends than good management, for I certainly get plenty of free meals.

It's getting late and as I beat my record last night I must get to bed now.

Much love,
Hilda.

Dormitory
April 24, 1933.

Dear Kate

I must admit you did nobly. I was all prepared for the p.c.'s and was delighted to get a real letter and a very interesting one — only *profession* is written so, with one f, not two. However, not to carp, I gather from your very vivid description that the w.t. is being a success, and that both weather & scenery meet your approval. I am very sorry that one of the members is not compatible. It is amazing what a lot of damage a trifle like manners & personality can do on a holiday. Do you remember Edison and the Banff trip?

You may have guessed from the complacent style which breathes through this letter that I have passed my preliminary and am now accepted as a candidate for the Ph.D. Degree (see Graduate Bulletin). It really was not bad at all because most fortunately the majority of the committee confined their questions to arguable propositions so that I felt quite at home. When one or two inconsiderately demanded cold hard facts the going became rather heavy. Mr. White who I may have mentioned last week gave me a very long paper & whom I punished by a proportionately long answer, remarked bitterly and, as I realized later, sarcastically, when his turn came, that as I had written "a small volume of 92 pages" no doubt questions were purely a matter of form. He then, with 1400 odd years to choose from selected a period of 11 years & in spite of my honest efforts to convince him immediately of my complete ignorance he concentrated on that for 10 minutes. Then, with the air of being generous & giving me another chance he moved to Henry II & wanted to know the contemporary sources for the history of his period. I knew those tolerably, although not considering them in any way essential I had made no effort to prepare them, so he left it at that. I rather think there is a slight feeling between him & Mr. Burt for various reasons. They differ radically on their viewpoints and it might be suspected that Mr. W. did not object to showing up a student of Mr. Burt's. That is probably a very mean thing to say, because Mr. White is such a nice man that it is hard to believe he would be intentionally ill-natured. I think he tends to be nervous on exams. However, I was particularly sorry to go down on his field because for reasons explained above, that is naturally the one that Mr. Burt would have liked me to do well in. I am afraid he was a bit disappointed on that account, although he was ever so nice & repeated a very flattering remark of one of the committee — I am consumed with curiosity to know which, but I never shall.

An oral exam with a fairly large committee — I had eight, which is about the average — is a very curious thing. It's rather like a speech in the way that you know instinctively when you are going over well and that helps you to go over better still. My biggest helps were Mr. Shiffer who when he is present merely as a spectator, as in my case, has the reputation of putting all his moral psychic force at the disposal of the candidate so to speak, and Mr. Heaton. Mr. H. is the only living person, so far as I know, who really approves of my style both written & spoken. It's quite a new experience for me, and I enjoy it very much. Mr. Burt, I gather, considers it pretty foul. That is a favourite expression of Gertrude Ward, and I think it's quite effective. Anyhow, Mr. Heaton provided a very inspiring audience even when he was questioning me himself. By the way either by accident or design he ignored most of the questions he might have been expected to ask and we spent most of the time discussing social & economic problems of the nineteenth century. That was quite all right because I had boned it up for classes in Sask. & remembered it quite well in spite of the lapse of time, but I hate to think of all the time I wasted learning the other stuff. Mr. Heaton by the way has a charming way of receiving a wrong answer which I would commend to all examiners. I mentioned a piece of recent research and carelessly referred to the man as "he" — "Who do you mean by he?" — I hadn't the faintest idea but I associated modern research in English agriculture with one Gray so I tried that out. "Oh well, Gray or Gay, it's easy to mix them up; and they both worked in the same field!" That, darling, as Mother would say, shows the true gentleman.

Before I quit this absorbing subject, Mr. Burt told me rather a good Oxford examination story. The examiner: "What was Clarendon's name?" — "Hyde." — "What was his first name?" — "I don't know. I was more interested in his policy." Apart from the exam I had quite a hilarious week. On Thursday Norma & I took a walk in the afternoon & we went with Gertrude to a show in the evening, *Be Mine To-night*. I admit the title is sloppy, but the show is not. It is English, scene in Switzerland, and the hero is a tenor who has done grand opera & doesn't hide his light under a bushel. They worked in sections of Rigoletto and La Bohême. Friday morning was my big event. Afterwards five of us went to celebrate by lunch at the Yellow Lantern. You may remember it was recommended to me by Bunny Usbarne. Four sympathetic friends waited for me outside the door and Mr. Shiffer who had been out to a class & returned to be in at the finish referred to them as the salvage corps, and cheerfully recommended them to fetch a stretcher. Anyhow, we had a very nice lunch. In the evening we (N. & I) attended the last symphony concert. On Saturday Gertrude Ward took me to the university play — *Berkeley Square* — rather spooky but most extraordinarily well done. I would never have believed unless I had heard it, that a cast of middle westerners could give an English play with an accent English enough not to jar you in the least. The acting was frightfully good, too. I spent the night with G.W. in the apartment she shares with a couple of others, spent most of Sunday with her, & arrived home in the evening. To-day I have been getting started at my thesis again. I haven't done much but I don't care particularly. I want to work steadily, but I have decided that if my thesis is going to be any good I had better do some systematic loafing occasionally as well. Considering that I have worked practically without a break for eighteen months & that this exam has been a small scale nightmare ever since last fall I really feel awfully well and not half as flat as I expected to, but although it will certainly be all I can do to get through this summer I don't intend to rush much for a while.

By the way, I have sent Mother 3.50 from you for a blouse. You did not name an amount, but buying one here seemed out of the question as they were all too expensive, and I thought that would be about right for the material. She tells me she has bought shoes & a hat. I think what she needs now is undies, so I will send her some for Mother's Day.

I have now started a new page, but I think my news is exhausted. I forgot to say that I bought quite a fetching pair of two-toned rubber-soled low-heeled walking shoes on Monday. They wear them here with sports clothes & summer dresses. I wore them to my prelim. with the green suit and Mother's little sweater, & a finger wave. Norma was very particular about my costume because, as she remarked, with an entirely male committee, that was important. She was quite satisfied and the result seemed to justify the effort. To get back to the shoes, they only cost four dollars, which I thought very reasonable.

There seems nothing more at the moment and it is twenty to twelve, so au revoir.

Much love,
Hilda.

Dormitory,
May 6, 1933.

Dear Kate,

Prepare for a disappointment. I didn't get a Royal Society Fellowship. If you are in London next year as I hope you will be, this will be harder for you than for me, but I know you won't let yourself be lonely. My great hope now is that Kenneth will be over there. I am not seriously disappointed, although perhaps I had been thinking about it more than I had realized, and more than was wise. It is too bad to think of all the good times we might have had and won't, but we still have the future before us. I heard yesterday and I haven't told the Burts yet. I don't think they expected much so they won't be so disappointed. I am just hoping now that the Department of Education will be reasonable about my certificate. I wrote to them a week ago, so I should hear soon.

I am sending you a blouse with some fear and trembling. It is somewhat snug for me and not at all becoming, but I rather thought that neck would suit you and would look very well under a suit. It cost two dollars. I didn't like to risk more in view of the duty etc., but of course I could do better for a bit more. Don't bank on my rash promises but I might get ambitious and make you one. I have the pattern of my plaid one which is easy to make and looks very well under a suit. It's taken nearly half an hour to type this, so I must leave you for a time and do some thesis.

Sunday — I am reading your letter to see which if any of your bright remarks require comment. Thank you for concentrating on me. It was evidently effective. The final ordeal was completed the day before you wrote. I am so glad that you got in another week at Bungay. It seems to be a highly [word missing] place. I am also glad your foot is all right, although I didn't worry about it seriously after I knew you were in London. I hope cutting it open didn't hurt too much. It would be lovely if Aunt Edythe could come to London while you are still there. You would love going round with her. I haven't wearied of the typewriter, but it is getting a bit late, and I am afraid my neighbours may have.

I have spent another light and frivolous week. I don't say that I have done no work, but there is no doubt that I do need a prick to stir the sides of my intent. On Wednesday Gertrude Ward and I went down to help Norma Adams buy a hat. N. said two dollars was her limit so we strolled around the bargain basements — neatly referred to here as "our downstairs store." We also visited a number of one-price shops — the one price being $1.88. It was at one of these that we finally located a very nice little navy blue straw with a white organdy band & bow. Like all modern hats it would have staggered us a few years ago but it looks very chic now. Norma had to depart about 3.30 to do some work in the downtown library & G. being amenable we strolled around to price some hats for me. I tried on a summer felt — light tan with a brown band & just a spot of colour in front — and she insisted that it was exactly right, so I bought it — $3.00. I don't think it will give me the wear that the other one has but there is no doubt that the brim has some quite fetching curves. We got your blouse the same afternoon, and also a birthday present — costume jewelry — for Gertrude's sister.

On Thursday I went downtown to dinner with G.W. by invitation — apparently on acknowledgement of the fact that I went to see her when her foot was bad & scolded her regularly for not looking after it better. She had two bleeding heels for several days & went around on them, but she was more lucky than you in escaping infection. Anyway she took me to Mrs. Jones' tea room which is a period room & the period is ? — *Mid-Victorian* — I should love to take Mother there — she would get a real thrill. They have prints & engravings on the walls & red curtains & glass ornaments & wax fruit under glass covers. They have the stuff quite carefully picked and the general effect is most pleasing. We had a very good dinner — lamb, potatoes, beets, pickle, coffee & pineapple ice — and a salad, but it cost 75 cents each so I am glad that G.'s father is fairly solvent. He is a real estate man in New York. She did remark cheerfully that very evening that land was a poor thing to have money in, and that he might go broke at any time. However the general impression is that they expect to have enough to keep the wolf from the door.

To come to my more serious activities, I purchased a box — about 6″ by 24″ — G.W. rather unkindly calls it my shoe box — Anyhow it is designed to hold notes & it is holding my thesis notes at present with the help of some neat little orange index cards. It looks terribly professional. I also bought some mucilage & stuck together the sheets you so kindly typed for me last fall & I hope to display them to Mr. B. shortly. I spent yesterday evening going over some of my stuff with him and have succeeded in convincing him that the subject is not so simple as it sounds. My opinion of his intellect goes up, however, because he is remarkably quick at getting remarkably intricate things. He is going to be all through with his book this summer & is apparently enough interested in my thesis to be anxious to go through some of the stuff with me himself. He said he thought he would go down to Montreal & go over some of the records there with me. There is no doubt that with his help I can finish more quickly & more satisfactorily than without, and it is far more fun working with someone than working alone, but I am not quite sure that it is a good idea. I am not afraid of the thesis being mine, because I have my ideas pretty well worked out, but if Mr. Burt works with me much, I don't know how many people will believe that it is mine.

I told the Burts about the R.S. last night. I think perhaps they had rather hoped I would get it, and were therefore disappointed. They didn't say much, there not being very much to say, but they were very nice. I think they feel that my prospects of ever getting any university work are pretty vile, and they naturally feel rather sorry. The regrettable fact is that as the U's here are not going into any new lines, & those at home are pretty well on the rocks, a Ph.D. in Canadian history is practically an unsaleable article, and when it is saddled with the wrong sex things are even worse. However I am not worrying, and I think I could be quite happy in a Sask. high school even though I hadn't planned on it.

We had our final history tea to-day. A vile day it has been too — we have had a fearfully cold spring and to-day it has been raining hard. I hope it may warm up after this.

I am expecting every letter to get news of Kenneth. Until your plans are settled it is hard to know whether Mother should go with him. I think what you say about her being happier with regular work is very much to the point.

I must stop now. I will send along your blouse in a day or two.

Very much love,
Hilda.

Public Archives, Ottawa,
July 1, 1933

Dear Kate,

I have two letters to answer — yours of June 16 arrived last Tuesday which is pretty good considering it had to be forwarded from Minn. To take serious matters first: I am terribly sorry you still have no prospect, and although I keep on hoping something will turn up, it is certainly necessary to consider alternatives. If you must come back here, why go to Sask. to take Education? There is no money in Sask. and that, at the moment, is what you want. It would cost a bit more to take education at Toronto, but I think it would be far more worthwhile. In these hard times you have to exploit what you have got and you will find more people in the East to pay you for an English accent and a year abroad than you will in the West. I think this would apply to ordinary high schools as well as private schools. The money is a problem, but we should be able to raise it somehow. I have heard from Leader that there is nothing doing. I had written to hint that I would modify my salary demands on Leslie's suggestion, and in answer to that, they informed me that principals in Sask. were now getting from $900 to $1000. I am almost glad I didn't get the job. To be principal of the school & to teach half the high school subjects to all the grades would I feel sure have endangered my reason which, at the moment, I value more than $900 a year. How long I shall be able to maintain that lofty attitude remains to be seen.

At the moment I am a bidder for a position at Kennedy — grades 7, 8 & 9 at $750 a year which to me sounds much more attractive than Leader. Walter spoke to the chairman about it — a Dr. Hilts whose son was at Sask. Dr. Hilts politely remarked that he hadn't supposed I would be interested, but if I was, would I apply at once? — which sounds hopeful. I applied a few days ago. If I get that I should be able to help you a little, although I am afraid not much, but Leslie would also help, and I think he should. At present he is in a pained mood because I disregarded his advice about going to interview the Leader people and came to Ottawa instead. I am ever so glad I did now, for he evidently greatly overrated my chances there. Of course you don't want to borrow from him unnecessarily, but I shouldn't have any compunction about doing it if it was necessary. . . .

I have been thinking about you in the Lake country this week. I do hope you had a good time, and that you did not let your worries spoil it. After all we can both get a living job sometime and it is foolish to let our ambitions spoil things. I don't think you do — that is my vice.

The Burts drove up from Toronto on Thursday & Mr. B. & Forrie appeared at the Archives yesterday. They didn't stay long as they had much shopping to do, but they asked me to go out to-day (Saturday) for the week-end. He offered to come in for me, but I said I would go out by train. I leave at 1.45 — I am now at the Archives, ostensibly to get in a half-day's work, but really as you observe, to deal with my week-end correspondence. I am going to close this interesting epistle shortly and do about an hour's work before I [go] back to the Y. for dinner and my bag. It is looking very like rain now, and as this is July 1, and everyone wants it to be fine, I suppose rain is exceedingly probable.

I have had quite a profitable week from the thesis point of view although I don't know about getting through this summer. There is one wonderful thing that applies at least to collecting material — I don't know about writing — and that is that you can do it when you would be much too tired for ordinary study. I can put in longer hours here with less trouble than I can at Minn. . . .

Ever so much love,
Hilda.

212 Walnut St.,
Minneapolis S.E.
Nov. 13, 1933

Dear Kate:

The above is a lie. I am at present in Falwell Hall "proctoring" as we say here, an exam. for Bernice who is more busy doing a paper for to-morrow. She is very much over-worked this year and is in no condition to stand overwork.

Your letter this week was most interesting. Am I right in supposing that you are weakening? From the viewpoint of an outsider I don't think you would make much mistake if you did. A modest man, nowadays is a rare item, and a man who thinks himself unworthy of you must be the last surviving specimen of his kind. Also, I don't quite agree with you that that is an undesirable attitude. I believe there was a time when all nice men had it — purely temporarily no doubt — but even in Ted's case I shouldn't think it would be permanent. I think his resolution to wait for you to make the next move is certainly awkward, but it probably won't hold. I need not say that I am waiting most anxiously for news.

I must confess that this week has been an off one for me — mainly through my own fault, but that doesn't help much. My thesis has got to the awkward stage where what I really need is some intelligent person to whom I can confide my difficulties, even though no one can really solve them but myself. This is the place for Mr. Burt to step into the breach but he doesn't. Like so many men he enjoys a sense of omniscience, and although he would never admit it, it worries him to have to admit that there is anything he doesn't know. I realize this, but I haven't the strength of mind to act accordingly, and I still go to him in the hope of getting some encouragement at least, if not any help. — Anyway, to make a long story short since I got back here he has never betrayed the slightest interest in my thesis, has never even asked when I expected to get it done. The week before last I tried twice to see him, and was twice put off without any expression of regret. I did see him on Monday and we didn't get along together very well — I admit that was as much my fault as his. I argued too much. At the end, I asked him as a favour, if he would let me come to him from time to time & read through what I had written to see if the general contents were satisfactory. As this would save one re-typing it would mean quite a lot to me. He agreed, but I thought most unwillingly, so I went back the next day on some other pretext, and offered to release him, and he jumped at the proposal, saying he didn't think the thing would need much alteration anyway. I cut his class that afternoon because I didn't want to see him again, lay awake until 4.30 that morning, and haven't written at all on my thesis since. I know that is absurd but as you know writing a thesis doesn't depend entirely on your will power. I really am tired of mine, and professionally neither it nor my degree can mean anything to me. I think that unconsciously I have been spurring myself on with the idea that Mr. B. was really interested in it and that he would be so pleased when it was done, especially if he thought it was good. Now that is all off, and I am more or less collapsed mentally speaking. I have no doubt that if and when I do finish it he will be pleased, but that won't make any difference. After helping me more than I ever expected he has let me down flat when I depended on him, so now I don't care whether he is pleased or not. I know all this is due to a semi-psychopathic condition caused by too much concentration on one thing, but just what the remedy is I can't quite see. If I could get it off my chest by telling Mr. Burt exactly what I have told you it might help, but I am afraid there is no prospect of that. I went out there yesterday (Sunday) to church & went home to lunch with Mrs. B. as I expected, not because I wanted to, but because I had no good excuse for staying away. Mr. Burt wasn't particularly talkative at first — I think he felt injured at my having cut his class for what he would consider no reason at all. However, later he warmed up & made conversation assiduously all day — asked me how I liked the Art Institute, whether I had been to various lectures — in fact he asked me about everything except my thesis. He also told me I looked tired and asked if I were sleeping well. The result is that outwardly we are extremely friendly and inwardly I am as a ravening wolf. I realize that all this is very silly, and I shouldn't have mentioned it at all, even to you if it weren't that when I don't mention what is on my mind I can't write you much of a letter. As I don't feel like writing on my thesis at present I am putting in the time typing what is already done, and I am getting on really quite well. . . .

Much love,
Hilda.

Dormitory,
April 30, 1934

Dear Kate. . . .

Thanks very much for the henna tip. I will try it out, for my hair is pretty bad. Dr. Garnin is no relation to Edison — quite a superior species. He has never sent me an account, and I don't quite know what to do. I asked Mother to call his girl about it, but she doesn't seem to have done anything definite. I am very sorry I did not pay at the time, but my cash had run rather low, as I had not expected to get the thing done.

As usual my news is largely confined to the thesis. Mr. Burt and I after weeks of skirmishing had a final bout over the conclusion on Wednesday which culminated in his telling me to go home & think it over, and to try not to be obstinate. Truth compels me to admit that the remark was entirely called-for, but I don't know that it came so well from him, he being worse than the proverbial mule. On this occasion I came to the conclusion that he was right on the main issue, although I still disapprove of his method of attack. I re-wrote the thing and brought it back on Friday along with a lot of other stuff we had to go over. He, also, was in a chastened mood. We did everything else, and then he asked rather nervously if there was anything more. I produced the bone of contention which he read and approved, but he firmly declined to retract his Wednesday's statement, or rather his Wednesday's implication. On the whole I think we got through the thing very well. Mr. Burt's alterations have greatly improved it, and now that it is done I suppose they were worth while.

The typing has been held up a bit. I think Betty is getting rather exhausted, and I don't know that I blame her. However she assures me it will be done by Monday when it has to be filed. I don't know how much it will cost, but I am afraid not less than seventy dollars. I hate to think of all the other things I could do with the money, but such is life.

The weather at present is like we had in Sask. 3 years ago. You may remember it; it was horrible. We had a few spots of rain to-night but it seems to have stopped now. We had practically no snow this winter and no rain since, so things are absolutely parched already.

This isn't a cheery letter, but my spirits are excellent only like you I haven't much news. Lots of love,

Hilda.

Dormitory
May 28, 1934.

Dear Kate,

The Royal Society fellowships are announced, and I have not been given one. I don't know that there is any comment to make. I am relieved to know definitely, and I feel sure you will be too. What I feel about knowing for certain that our reunion is indefinitely postponed, I need not say. I feel sure that it really is for the best. Perhaps I am going to get the Illinois job, and if so, I think I should have had to turn down the R.S. anyway. If I get a job at any reasonable salary I shall feel sure it was better not to get the fellowship. . . .

I enjoyed your letter greatly, especially the gossip from Saskatoon. It is dreadful about Dr. Ferguson. I suppose his practice was falling off because of the hard times, and he felt he just had to do something to make ends meet. Evidently the Dental Association wants to force him to leave Saskatoon, but does not want to ruin him for life.

I think your suede coat sounds lovely. I am so glad you have one, and it should be just the thing for your walks. Theses are really quite productive things. My modest effort bought a car for the Beesons — or at least went a long way towards it. I feel that your summer wardrobe must be attended to. When Mother and I get together this summer we must see what can be done. I very much approve of your present to Mildred — at least of its description. I would like very much to get her something, but financially I am all at sea just now.

I must not omit the important news that I have passed my final examination. All I have to do now is to pay ten dollars graduation fee, six dollars rent for a cap and gown and hood, and then I shall be the thing that I have always despised — an American Ph.D. I admit that since coming here my opinions have partly changed, but it amuses me to think how scornful I used to be about them.

I don't know if I told you that I did not think I should give the usual bond of a hundred dollars to publish my thesis within a year. It is extremely difficult to get a history thesis published because it has to be done in book form, and there is little or no prospect of its ever paying expenses. I told Mr. Burt this on the way over to the graduate office after the exam because I knew they would produce the bond when we got there, and it is customary for your adviser to sign it. I said I thought I had better postpone taking my degree until my financial prospects were a little more stable or words to that effect. When we got to the office the female produced the bond and told him it was customary for the adviser to sign it, which naturally gave him pause as he realized what a broken reed he was asked to be financial prop to. However he went in to see Dean Ford who soothed his alarms and explained that in these hard times they couldn't insist on an exact observance of the rule, or their staff would be ruined. The upshot was that he said he thought we had better sign it. He then remarked in his benevolent way that now I could get my degree. I didn't like to spoil his pleasure by telling him that I would gladly be relieved of the honour since it is costing me sixteen dollars and ten days extra in Minn. waiting for Commencement. However Mr. B. now has a real incentive to get my thesis published, if he needed one.

I haven't much extra news except that I saw the University Singers put on *The Student Prince* on Saturday afternoon. It was very well done, and I think the play itself is much better tied together than the average musical comedy. The only disappointment was the men's chorus which I thought a little feeble.

Ever so much love,
Hilda.

— Don't be too disappointed — you don't know how I want to see you, but things might be so much worse. I am so glad you have Ted.

Renown, Sask.
June 29, 1934.

Dear Kate:

I have two letters to answer, but perhaps I had better begin with the bad news that the Knox job has fallen through. There was a letter waiting for me here to say that they had appointed one of their own graduates who was, I think, an assistant at Minnesota before I went there. I may be slandering him but I don't think he had his Ph.D or anything near it. I suppose his sex, and possibly some personal influence did the thing. They have a perfect right to appoint whom they please, but as they must have known about this man all along, I don't know why they had to bother me to apply, and keep me on the string for two months. From the beginning they have been very casual and not very polite. It is a bit mysterious, but the only thing to do is to forget about it. . . .

Ever so much love,
Hilda.

Renown, Sask.
July 22, 1934

Dear Kate,

I have no letter of yours to answer, but that does not surprise me, as I had two last week. Anyhow we have had no mail since Wednesday.

I have no job news I am afraid — at least none good. I had a nice letter from Dr. Murray about the Regina College job — He said they had hesitated somewhat, but had finally decided to keep the other chappie on — Clara evidently heard a false rumour. He said he would be glad to do anything he could in the way of letting me know about jobs etc. but they seem to be a minus quantity. My numerous applications have brought no response.

Since last I wrote Mother and I have moved up to Edith's. The family here are all well and cheerful except that Edith herself has been suffering from a bad cold. I had one myself a week ago — in fact I spent last Sunday in bed with it — but it left me quickly. Edith's is more obstinate, but she seems to be recovering.

The family here are all very nice and tolerably cheerful although the elder boys seem to be somewhat depressed by the general outlook, which is hardly surprising. William has decided to take up teaching as a profession, and with that end, he intends to take the Bachelor of Education degree. I think that from the academic viewpoint he is probably quite wise, but I am sorry he should be obliged to imperil his sanity by submitting to a course of instruction by Drs. Laycock and Quantz [sic]. Mr. Burt told me that Dr. Laycock had had a job in Alberta and that they were only too thankful to unload him onto Saskatchewan. Of course, that isn't as bad as it sounds, for I believe he did do his work at London in between.

This week I have been reading through Strachey's Queen Victoria. It is very interesting but as a historian I should call him distinctly shallow. I believe that has already been said about a thousand times, but I can honestly confirm it.

I have also knitted and cross-stitched a decoration for a cream linen purse cover. I bought a summer purse in Minn. that can be used with any cover, and the one I have just made is, I think, a great improvement on the one I bought. . . .

Ever so much love,
Hilda.

Teachers' Hostel
Sept 10, 1934.

Dear Kate,

I have a real job at last. I am to teach history at Regina College at $100 a month (for ten months I think) and my board. It is not a huge salary but it is just $75 a month more than I am getting now.

As I said in the letter posted this morning, I have quite given up Kentucky and was endeavouring to resign myself and succeeding pretty well I think. This morning I got a call from Dr. Murray asking me to come and see him this afternoon, which I did. It appears that Matheson is to be sent to Regina to teach English, and that one Mr. Smith who has been doing the history and English was to stay on and assist him — not because he knows any history or English but because he has a wife and child and they didn't like to throw him out. He was the man that Clara thought was to be fired. The present arrangement is that Jean Murray should be away this year (as Prof. Morton is coming back). This leaves the history correspondence courses with no one to do them. They are therefore to be combined with the University classes at Regina & the Grade 12 history if I want to do it, which, with other oddments makes a full-time job. I am to see Mr. Simpson & get details, but I shall be teaching a university course at Regina College & Luther College. Dr. Murray is writing to Moose Jaw to say that I will give the same course there if they will pay my bus fare twice a week. He also wants me to get into touch with Sacred Heart to see what they will let me do there. Also, if I like, after Xmas I may give a half class carrying credit to city teachers on anything I like.

I will give more details when I get them. I would have cabled you but I thought by counting my pennies I might get along without borrowing. I get my first cheque at the end of Sept. Dr. Murray offered me an advance, but I thought it not necessary. I hoped to save going onto another page, but I forgot to tell you that Dr. M. asked most kindly after you and Ted and all the family — I think the whole situation is very queer. When I went into the office Mrs. Cameron was there. I prepared a friendly greeting, and she responded politely but most limply, and immediately went on typing. Then she seemed to recollect herself and asked after you and Mother, still rather limply. She finally hazarded the remark that I had been in the States, to which I assented. She then asked if I had my Ph.D. etc. I thought her manner betrayed an indifference tempered with dislike, not wholly to be accounted for by the fact that I gave her daughter a B in history.

Then Dr. Murray appeared. His manner was as curious as Mrs. Cameron's. He said "how do you do" somewhat coldly, then recollected himself, shook hands and said he was glad to see me, but in rather an absent way. I didn't expect or want him to gush, but I felt the occasion really did call for some slight show of enthusiasm.

When he began to discuss business he was at first perfectly formal, but also quite nice. He seemed apologetic about the salary, and asked me if it would satisfy me. I imagine it is less than the others are getting, although it may not be. However I am in no position to haggle, even if I thought it good policy, which I don't. It was probably a strain to find the money anyhow. After a time Dr. M. warmed up — he asked me about all the family individually, but first and specially about you and Ted who was, he said, a very nice boy. He also asked about my thesis, whether it would be published etc. I can't understand his curious manner at first except that he looked dead tired & very worried. I really am awfully sorry for him.

Lots of love,
Hilda.

Please excuse this awful mess — there must have been cocoa on the common room table where I wrote right after evening lunch.

7 | *As Teacher*

On occasion, Hilda reflected in general terms on what it meant to be a teacher, as in the first selection in this chapter, "The Art of Teaching: Reflections of an Amateur," and the second, "The Obligation of the Teacher." What stands out is her love for teaching, which included love for both knowledge and students. Both of these were originally talks: the first given in 1962 reflects concerns of the 1950's; the second from 1970 shows how Hilda was adapting to a changed world. Neither was ever revised for written presentation and deciphering and determining the correct placement of handwritten additions both presented more than the usual difficulties.

When Hilda was asked to speak or write about her role as a teacher, she did not simply whip out some preserved stock phrases. On one such occasion in 1962 she described her goal as a teacher, and revealed just how far the world was from what she wanted:

> My job in teaching is to cultivate intellectuals or at least to teach respect for intellectual values. I have worked hard over many years with freshmen and undergraduates. Many, I think, fail to see what it is all about, not for lack of capacity or goodwill, but only because it is too late. Too late to learn to read, too late to learn to write, too late even to commit to memory the great passages in prose and verse in their own and other literatures which would constantly nourish and form their thought and expression.
>
> That is why I regret the inflated prestige of the university in North America. It partly conceals the fact that education is probably given in the secondary school or not at all. And when I say this I am not thinking of "drop outs" or those who don't go to university. I am thinking much more of the hundreds, even thousands of M.A.'s and Ph.D.'s who might have been intellectuals and are not.[1]

The third selection, "History Teaching: Hope or Menace?" appeared in the Prince Albert *Daily Herald* in 1968. In a short space Hilda spelled out both the importance and the dangers of the teaching of history in the high schools. Through the use of imagination, the teacher must save himself and his students "from falling into the captivity of the dead past, an inert and sometimes even a malignant deity, capable of controlling the present and destroying the future."

THE ART OF TEACHING:
REFLECTIONS OF AN AMATEUR

The title of this talk is not as modest as it sounds. An examination of the root meaning of the word amateur shows how much it is abused by correct usage. "Amateur" is generally used in the sense of one who is not a professional because of inadequate experience, training or skill or pertinacity, — or from want of all of these. The word has become fitted to the customs of our age, when everyone has an occupation or calling and when preparation for any and all callings is highly developed and organized and known all too often — alas! — as "education."

But amateur came into the language in a different age and originally it had a meaning which now we have almost lost. There was a time when most men worked, many toiled to an excessive even unbearable degree, and a small but very important and highly respectable section of society was not "gainfully employed" but lived on unearned income instead of salary. (This is still true today but those living entirely on unearned income are much less important and often less respectable.) Those who did not work from nine to five were not, however, idle. They constituted an important part of the "growing edge" of civilization. They were the ruling class; they were also the "chief consumers" of knowledge, of science, art, literature, architecture, music. They might engage in scholarly, scientific literary and artistic pursuits themselves, but for love, not for money. They were the "amateurs," the "lovers."

It is thus only in modern times that the proper adjective for "amateur" is "clumsy." Originally the amateur is the man great or small, skilled or unskilled, languid or fanatic who loves what he does, who works for the joy of working, who pursues his ideal for its own sake.

In this sense all the best workers and the greatest must be amateurs at heart. Our own society is different and potentially better, far better than the aristocratic one that I have described. There is, however, some danger in our enthusiasm about professionalism — that we may forget not only what "amateur" originally meant, but also what an important social and moral value this meaning represented. Whatever we may claim as material reward, and however much (quite properly) we appreciate it, however intensive may be our professional training and skill, the true value of what we do in most callings (and especially in those we call "professions") depends on our maintaining the soul of the amateur.

There is a test that we should perhaps apply from time to time to determine our amateur status. Would you continue to do your daily work if you could earn (a) almost as much, (b) quite as much, (c) *more*, without doing it? This tests one's rank as an amateur in the highest and best sense. It is a difficult test and perhaps even those of us who feel that we are amateurs may be thankful for a little economic pressure to keep us steadily on the course. Personally I claim, in a modest sense, to be an amateur because I cannot imagine myself wanting to be not teaching (even though I welcome the end of the term as enthusiastically as anyone can). My confidence in my amateur status is reinforced by the administrative jobs that come my way — not without their interest but dull and dead, if not utterly frustrating, in comparison. (It may be urged that teachers like doctors can, in a sense, do what administrators cannot do, bury their mistakes. It is quite true and is something that we can't forget: we do not really know the harm we may do or the opportunities we may lose.)

This brings me to another question and I think a very important one: the motive of the amateur teacher. It is possible to believe oneself to be an amateur but to be a complete phoney because the love, if one can call it that, is for the wrong reasons. We may be loving the wrong things. Some people I believe really do like teaching because they like to dominate, they like to be always right (or to seem so); they like, in their insecurity, to mingle with the immature and the ignorant or even, they may imagine, they like a job with short hours and long holidays. All these motives are for some people, perhaps for almost everyone occasionally, temptations. They are not valid motives, they are not healthy incentives. They are not true love and they can make really good teaching impossible.

The real amateur is the one capable of true love. This love may vary somewhat in its object and nature. Teaching is communication. I am using a broad word here. It is, more specifically, deliberate instruction about something we know, addressed to someone who does not know. We all (including the teacher) communicate unconsciously as well as consciously to everyone we meet. But the teacher instructs deliberately and with a purpose, having in view the condition of those he instructs. Today I am not instructing or teaching; I am communicating. I am offering you my reflections and ideas on teaching, not as instruction because many of you already know all I am saying and agree with it; and many others also know it and disagree. But true teaching in my view is communication from those who do know to those who do not. This is an heretical view in modern times. I would be prepared to defend it even though there may be powerful arguments on the other side. I think neglect of the fact has done much to undermine learning and cause it to collapse into the bottomless morass of so-called "education" — a word which, so far, I have been able to avoid except for once at the very beginning.

I will return to the true love of the amateur which expresses itself in two ways: love of the persons whom we teach; love of the things that we teach. Both these loves are necessary or at least highly desirable. Lacking either one it is hardly possible to be a true amateur, and therefore, if my definition is sound, it is not possible to be a great teacher. The first love is more necessary to those who teach younger people. You can do little but harm if you don't love them. The other is more necessary for advanced instruction. If you don't really love your subject you will not submit yourself to the drudgery necessary for mastering it, or if you do, you will probably dislike it and convey the dislike to your students.

Most people begin with one love or the other. Those who love people, who have ready sympathy and patience, who want to understand the problems of children and very young people (and who, one hopes, are blessed with a tough and enduring physique) — these want to communicate and delight in communicating all that is essential to the well-being and usefulness and happiness of the children. I have slipped back here to the word "communicate." Obviously, in the teaching of the very young, while carefully planned direct instruction is of the first importance, indirect communication may have an even greater impact, a more dangerous one or a more valuable one as the case may be. That is why without undervaluing learning for anyone I cannot agree that advanced academic qualifications should be as essential for the lower grades as for the higher. I would like to see all teachers equally gifted and developed in personality, character and mind, but as this is impossible I would put the best minds in the senior groups and the best people in the junior ones.

It is in the senior groups that those who love learning first are likely to be happiest and most useful. Many people with a passionate love of knowledge want to teach or to communicate in some way. There are, of course, exceptions. Historians remember the great nineteenth-century exponent of freedom, Lord Acton. A man of enormous industry and very great mental gifts he devoted a lifetime to research and left behind him at his death one or two collections of lectures delivered to university students and a vast, an overwhelming mass of tens of thousands of slips of paper on which he had jotted down data and ideas for his life work which was to be a history of liberty. His colleagues had implored him to publish something, but until he knew everything he was unwilling to communicate anything, and so he died, a warning to the perfectionist.

But there are many at the opposite end of the scale from Acton. They are in love with their learning and they have the true evangelist's urge to convert. Or they have in a curious but very real way a sense that their own knowledge really comes to life only when it is given to others. Teaching and learning may be with them a continuous circular process. It may be objected (it almost certainly will be!) that these are not good teachers. They are egoists, eggheads ignoring their social function in a selfish desire for self-expression. This may sound like a fair judgment, but it is quite wrong. Especially on a senior level these may be inspired teachers. They are not real egoists for they are dedicated to a pursuit beyond themselves and in their unconscious enthusiasm they will enlist their students in the same self-forgetting pursuit of knowledge. Here, too, conscious teaching is inevitably and most helpfully related to unconscious communication. They cannot help communicating their passionate zeal for knowledge, and in later years their students forget neither them nor what they have taught.

Gilbert Highet, emphasizing the need for clarity and ease of communication in the early stages, argues that for senior students this is less necessary than the infectious devotion to his subject which may be present in those whose teaching techniques are very far from perfect.

And this brings me at last to what I am supposed to talk about: the art of the teacher. Really I have already talked about it. What you can do and how you do it is determined by what you are. A true amateur — a lover of people and a lover of learning can and should teach well. Can he teach without "professional training"? Well, probably not. If he is going to teach people, he had better know what science can teach him of their make-up even though an artist's perceptiveness can and will teach him much. More important, he had better know what philosophers have said and are saying about man, his nature and his destiny. And if he does his teaching in a certain political-social-moral-economic society, he can only do so intelligently if he has a precise and scholarly and analytical knowledge of that society as well as a personal one. And as he will use a building, equipment, text books and innumerable other teaching aids, he had better know something of them, and of the army of administrators who produce and maintain them and who organize him and fellows. For all these things (and others) good "professional" training is necessary or at least highly desirable.

What about "methods"? Can you really teach him how to teach? Only to a very limited extent. For the true amateur, loving his knowledge and those whom he is teaching, methods cannot be dictated — not even by himself. He is always trying new ways, learning, adapting, inventing. This does not mean that there may not be one best method in some subjects at some stages, although this is doubtful. (Recall Hedley and *the* method of teaching the number "two".) But even if there is, many of the best teachers cannot accept it automatically. They are not teaching machines. Cut-and-dried methods may be the best for the competent but uninspired professionals who are not amateurs. (And these apparently uninspired professionals may indeed be very good. They may have certain merits that the free-wheeler who remains an amateur at heart does not possess.) But the inspired amateur may break all rules and yet achieve his end. And if he is worried and bothered overmuch about rules, he may achieve nothing.

A superintendent of schools from British Columbia whom I met at the Canadian Conference on Education last spring told me that his advice on methods to any teacher would be no more than, "This has worked for me. Try it if you think it worthwhile." No doubt this is true of most good superintendents. (It certainly is all that I would want to say to anyone. I have suggested to people what I thought were deficiencies or limitations but have urged them to be careful in correcting their faults not to lose their virtues for this is all too easy to do.)

There is not much time left to talk about what the teacher teaches, but I want to say something. I have avoided the word education. This is only the third time I have used it. Education has become so wide and so deep. It covers the whole length of life and includes the whole vast range of human activities. Far more, it penetrates the innermost secrets of body, mind and soul. It is (if one believes all one reads) limitless and therefore indefinable. But teaching (as I have said) is something else. It is instruction of the ignorant and untrained in something they need to know and to do. What should we teach?

There is one central responsibility of all teachers at every stage. We all neglect it, because the task seems almost beyond us. I mean the teaching of reading and of writing. I think it fair to say that our students on the whole are deficient in the power of *reading* and *retaining* material that is well within their comprehension. Reading lags behind understanding instead of serving to stimulate and develop it.

And our students are also incapable of expressing correctly and clearly even in their own language what they know and understand. The danger of this reading-writing lag is very great because to some degree in an audio-visual age one can dispense with both without discomfort, but not without danger. The avant-garde cranks who argue that because many happy people didn't read in the middle ages they needn't read now simply don't understand the conditions in an over-crowded world existing through applied science. Children must be *taught* to read. They should be read aloud to a great deal. And they should read aloud.

One very good reason for being read aloud to and for reading aloud is that it helps appreciation of the rhythm and even of the structure of the language and so helps them learn to write. And why should they learn to write? For one reason (there are several, including the usefulness of communication), it is one very good way of developing logical methods of thought. The writer looks back at what he has written, he analyses, corrects, amends in order not only to express but to clarify in his own mind what he sees, thinks, knows. In the primitive ages of poetry, writing was less important. The language was oral and poets who had mastered speech rhythms could convey impressions and emotions truly and powerfully in poems that were never written down. But the age of science and of the planned society is also an age of reason and of prose.

The technique, the art, and habit of learning through reading and communicating through writing can only be developed in most people by conscious instruction and by arduous practice. Perhaps formerly it was imposed too soon and too heavily. But now I think we are leaving it too late. I do not want to roll off the burden of responsibility which the university must certainly bear for releasing graduates who cannot write even passably well. I think we also bear a responsibility for speech. . . . But I am beginning to wonder whether writing like music must not be taught methodically early if it is to be learned at all. Some of the people whom I meet seem to be literally muscle-bound. They *do* know and understand, but they can't put it on paper.

This essential training central to all other instruction, and without which education becomes an undifferentiated mass of "experiences" does indeed require the love, the patience and the dedication of the true amateur. But unless we *all* at every *stage* keep central the training in learning through reading and communicating through writing, we are cheating our students of the means to intellectual life and betraying the learning that is entrusted to us.

I have contrived to ride several hobby horses. The title "Reflections" allows latitude. Can I conclude with some statement of the art of teaching? Yes — teaching *is* an art; no one can reach the highest levels unless he subjects himself intelligently to all *necessary* professional training (including and especially training in his subject), and also contrives to retain through it all, as a true artist should, the single-minded enthusiasm of the amateur.[2]

THE OBLIGATION OF THE TEACHER

I have been invited here to give informally my ideas . . . on the opportunity and obligation of the teacher as determined by the function of the school in society . . . . Of one thing I am fairly sure. I think that the good teacher does much more than convey facts or see to it that they are conveyed, trying at the same time to ensure that they are also received, consumed, assimilated in such fashion as to enlarge and clarify the understanding of the pupil. He should do that, but he should do much more. But I do not feel that teachers have a special claim to guide society . . . . I think this proposition is too broad, too vague, and — this is important — I think it requires teachers to undertake far more than they — or any large professional group, however well-trained and well-intentioned, can do. Laying claim to too much responsibility, to too much power, we can mislead ourselves and perhaps society. (Or perhaps society won't be fooled.)

One reason why I am suspicious of these and many other wide claims that I have read, is that they ask the teachers to play God to society [by stating that they are primary agents of change in our culture]. . . . I shall deal with two separate ideas here that do suggest that the teacher is called to be, if not God, at least Moses or a major prophet to lead people to a better land and better lives.

First, society or culture does not need to be changed. It is changing, as every living thing changes. Neither the individual nor society ever stands still — nor can either be put in the deep freeze. Change is the fundamental *fact* in this life. It needs no agents for it is, in fact, self-operating. What the responsible adult citizen needs to do is to ask; what changes *are* occurring? Are we moving in the right direction? Should we accelerate, slow down, even occasionally, reverse?

The analogy is not perhaps a good one. Let's go to the field of medicine. The doctor is summoned to the patient. *Change is now going on* physically and will while life lasts. Does he arrest or accelerate, or deal in one fashion with one symptom and in another way with another? And unless he is pretty good, is he not in danger of applying treatment that does what he wants in the immediate future but may also have all kinds of unforeseen and undesired effects later on? In my young days they loved to use x-ray machines. They were the "in thing" — and they had their uses — but they are much less in evidence today. Sometimes the best thing a doctor can do is to play the nurse — by care, kindness and caution — give healing nature a chance.

A second point . . . is [that there is an implication that it is] a teacher's duty to make a judgment [on] public and apparently moral issues and convey these to the pupils. I think this is dangerous. Some issues are far too difficult for the average, or even for the extraordinarily competent teacher. If on any important issue the teachers make a pronouncement — *ex cathedra* — it may differ from that of the parent, the clergyman, the extremely knowledgeable family friend, the trusted political leader, and all of whom also may claim and receive the loyalty of the child and here, of course, the parent is in a unique position. It seems to me of the first importance that, during most of the school period at least, the teacher should see himself as supplementing but in no sense offering a substitute for the functions of the parent. I know there are bad, deficient, ignorant, neglectful parents, but it has always seemed to me foolish and most dangerous from the viewpoint of society for the teacher to assume that he can move in and take over. He is honoured in being a junior partner in this difficult job — a part-time expert.

I come back to the point I have wandered away from: I don't want the teacher to play God. Here I may perhaps explain my personal views. I don't want to impose them on you, but only show you, if I can, why I think as I do. I happen to believe that there is a God, a good God, deeply concerned and utterly powerful, operating in and for our society. I admit that appearance sometimes seems to contradict this belief and that many historians would say, "You had better have a strong faith for you certainly do not have much evidence." I accept that, and yet I think there is an answer: the sum of human selfishness, greed, cruelty, violence, is so great that without a very strong operation in men and women of a counter-acting spirit of love, humility and self-sacrifice, we would have destroyed ourselves and our world long ago. Believing this, I cannot in considering my role as a teacher, dismiss from my mind my belief in the overruling providence of God and his equal call to all men to serve Him by serving their fellowmen, although in different capacities. I respect, indeed I reverence, my work. I believe that, as a teacher I can do incalculable good or harm. But I don't see myself as one of a group of islands in the sea of humanity to which the lost, and bewildered, and so forth make their way. If I am a really good teacher, I may have a wider and apparently more valuable impact than a really good butcher, baker, candlestick maker — or janitor, policeman or journalist, but I don't know, and I don't think any one of us has any exclusive responsibility to guide and inspire humanity. I think that each of us has a particular and an important job to do with all the power that is given to us. . . .

What then do I think is my job as a teacher and especially if I happen to teach younger people? Primarily the schools (I think) exist *not* to preach or inculcate change, but to help children develop a total awareness of what is going on about them, of what they have been given, and of what may reasonably be expected of them as members of the community. It order to do this, the children must master the arts of communication and especially of reading and writing. This will help the teacher in his fundamental task of making them aware, in an orderly, planned, rational manner (different from, and supplementary to the less formal more spontaneous communications of the home, for example) of the nature, principles, purposes and problems of the society of which they, the pupils and the teacher, are a part. [Teachers] are *not* islands; we are in the sea struggling with the rest of humanity. How does one make children aware? Through what are, perhaps unhappily, called "disciplines": the languages or media of art, music, literature, the reflections of historians, economists, political theorists, moralists, on the experiences of mankind.... A great Greek [for example] after much pondering on the duty of a good citizen, admitted sincerely, if reluctantly, that the greatest service he could render to his country *might* be disobedience with voluntary acceptance and suffering of the penalty of that disobedience in order to communicate as clearly and unambiguously as possible what he believed to be the truth. There are young Americans today in prison doing just that. But it was no part of their teacher's duty to tell them whether the war in Vietnam was right or wrong; only to give them the knowledge and to help them develop the principles that would make them able and willing to judge rightly and act for themselves. [To suggest] that we ought to indoctrinate pupils ... is, in fact, inviting us to do exactly what ... we should not do — "merely to serve a utilitarian society." What can be more utilitarian than to spend my time trying to supply children with what I think are the right solutions to contemporary problems which (however agonizing they may be at the moment) will be half-forgotten before most of them are men and women? What can be more utilitarian than programming little human computers to give the right answers? What can be more "relevant" than opening windows on the world of human experience and inviting pupils to accept the discipline of examination, criticisms, thought in order that confronted by all sorts of future unknown questions they will be able themselves to judge, choose and act — perhaps do what you would have advised — but you are a teacher not a dictator.

I do not, in fact, think of teachers as creative leaders in mind or in morals. They are, surely, rather the guardians of what we have, the honest, faithful, self-sacrificing trustees, who prepare the young wisely to receive, use and respect the new things that will be undoubtedly offered them by artists, poets, prophets *and* politicians. It is not my job to be any of these. It is my job I think to do three things:

[First, to] show my students *in action* a person who is more willing to be underpaid than overpaid — not that pay should not be adequate (and I have never refused a raise), but is it not an urgent responsibility to try to be worth more than you are paid than to be worth less? When you retire, would you not be happier if some imaginary all-knowing person could say "Well you have always explained more than you were paid (or at least "you have tried to")?

[Secondly, to] show my students a person who is never content to do his duty by them as a group — but who always meets them as persons and with love — and if I may borrow again from "the Greek Disciplines" this means agape, the love which gives to (and perhaps receives from) but never uses or exploits other.... Our work goes far beyond our "discipline." I ought always to leave with my students the belief that however much pride and pleasure I may take in their achievements for example, in history, their total well-being, their health, their happiness, their power . . . is of far more importance to me because I ought to see them first as people and second as budding historians.

[Finally,] I give them what I have to give, and I enable them (if I do) to help to change, preserve or improve their society, *not above and beyond,* but *through and by the way* I teach them (to the best of my power) the precise matters that their parents and society have trusted me to teach, arithmetic, spelling, the Quebec Act, or Plato's *Republic.*[3]

HISTORY TEACHING; HOPE OR MENACE?

Is history the deadest and dullest subject taught in the schools, or is it as someone has suggested, along with other social studies, "the hope of the future"? I find the one view too pessimistic and the other much too optimistic. It does seem clear that if something is not done to give us all a more intelligent understanding of the society we live in, there may be no future at all for the human race. Here the work of the schools is indispensable. We need not argue about which subject is the most important, for each is in its own way essential, and failure in any one area could be fatal, but in no area is the war against ignorance, neglect, misunderstanding and falsification more difficult to win than in the teaching of history.

During the course of human history men in society often have been harassed by two opposing evils: on the one hand, the danger of anarchy where, without law and government, the weak became the prey of the strong; on the other, the constant threats of that personal lust for power, always latent in some men which, unguarded, can lead to despotism and tyranny.

In recent times the old personal lust for power has been sublimated into collective lusts in entities that we call nations. In Europe the power-hungry individual representing the power-hungry nation has become familiar to us in the persons of Napoleon, Bismarck, Mussolini and Hitler. The desire for dominance grows out of private and collective frustrations in a search for security. The process is understandable, but the will to power is always a danger to the security of others.

In recent times another kind of danger has appeared. The world is divided into nations very rich and very poor; into people preoccupied with the problems of obesity, and people who lie down hungry every night and struggle every day with weakness caused by deficiency diseases. There have indeed always been contrasts between the too rich and the too poor among individuals and nations, but today the social effects are intensified. The fantastic speed in the improvement of communications enables us to transport men, goods, ideas and feelings and convictions as we never have done before. We face the consequences of airplanes, mass media and universal literacy, utilized it may be through propaganda, subliminal impressions and brainwashing. These are the facts of the present age, and responsible people have to accept them and work with them.

Our situation can be described briefly and all too clearly. On the one hand, science, the unique child of western civilization, has given western nations an affluence undreamed of in past centuries. On the other hand, unbelievably poverty-stricken peoples in our shrinking world are now our very near neighbours. As a result, with a booming population, and a criminal wasting of the world's resources, there is a possibility of the whole race perishing at last from want. This, however, may not occur because there sometimes seems to be an even greater possibility of rapid or gradual physical destruction from nuclear warfare. And yet, as no one can measure; or no one ever has measured, the possibilities of human ingenuity in discovering fresh resources, or the potential capacity of individuals in society to overcome moral weaknesses, no one can say that disaster is inevitable.

It might be argued that the historian has nothing to say about this and that the problems of the so-called New Age must be turned over to the psychologist and the sociologist, the geographer and the scientist, who with the aid of computers will tell us what we must do. To say this, however, is to ignore one very important fact — the mental and emotional make-up of men in the western world, including psychologists, sociologists, geographers, scientists and the rest. We must reckon with the way in which men and women in our world do actually think and feel. Our minds were formed by the western civilization that we call Christian, a civilization which, absorbing and transmitting the Graeco-Roman heritage, has left even in this post-Christian age the stamp of its own values. Christianity is an historical religion and those bred in the Christian tradition think and feel historically. Whether they know it or not, they are dominated by a certain approach to the past. Whether or not this is good or bad, it is a mode of being so involved in our deepest emotions that we cannot free ourselves from it.

Therefore those concerned with history and the teaching of history see three facts which must always be borne in mind. Nearly all of us have an awareness of the past which suggests appropriate attitudes and actions for the present. But the historical convictions that move us may be based on a mistaken or even a wholly erroneous understanding of historical fact. Finally, most people who feel historically tend never to question the dictates of history, but rather are willing to give them unquestioning obedience.

In the twentieth century there have been many terrifying examples of the power of the historical legend. Few historians accept literally Marx's interpretation of history as a series of struggles with the minority of the haves being periodically overthrown by the majority have-nots, or his final conclusion that the bourgeoisie must in the end yield to the working classes who will create a classless state. It is important to note the subtle combination of reason and emotion that led up to the conclusion of the famous manifesto, "Working men of the world, unite. You have a world to gain, you have nothing to lose but your claims." The historical argument is this: first, the working classes must prevail over the bourgeoisie; second, the working class ought to prevail over the bourgeoisie. The first of these propositions is dubious, and the second rests on no foundation at all. Because a general has waged two or three successful compaigns, it does not necessarily follow that he will be successful in another, and it does not follow at all that he ought to be successful, or that his success is something that good men should desire and work for. And yet, in the last century or so when history has become a universal study, frequently historical arguments of this kind have been used, and used successfully, as a moral defence of procedures sometimes most immoral.

For example, late in the last century the historian John Seeley, in a series of brilliant essays on the British Empire, remarked that Britain had conquered half the world in a fit of absence of mind. Whatever Seeley meant, the remark was quoted and was used to suggest that this must have been an admirable thing. Destiny led to the conquest, and the conquest therefore was right and good. Without arguing over the morality of imperialism, the historian must still ask first whether these conquests were inevitable in some mysterious historical process; second, if they were, whether they were right; and finally, if they were right, whether absent-mindedness could be offered as an excuse for doing a wrong thing. Similarly, the theory of manifest destiny convinced many Americans that because they had taken over so much of the North American continent not only could they but they ought to take in Canada as well. The Canadian might say, "But why 'ought'? Haven't you already enough?" The fact that the teacher and every intelligent citizen must remember is that historical arguments are presented in this way, and, because of special circumstances, they are extraordinarily persuasive and convincing. Hitler frequently used them, pointing out that a thousand years of German history required Germans to go on and impose themselves on all of Europe. It can be argued that this was only a rationalization of Hitler's personal ambition. But as he thought it worthwhile constantly to reiterate the historical argument, he must have found that it was convincing to many.

Every teacher of history in the classroom is confronted by these alarming but also stimulating facts. The teacher faces young people who instinctively feel, even if they do not consciously think, historically. They are therefore, potentially, the helpless victims of any powerful emotional appeal from those who, whether sincerely or cynically, offer distorted interpretations of history in order to persuade them to actions which the speakers feel to be appropriate.

One must add that bad history is insidious, just because it is so easy and so satisfying. How many people have heard the orator who says, "All history goes to prove . . ." something or other, whatever he wants to prove at the moment? Few realize how very difficult it is for an honest historian to get up and answer him, because if he is honest he has to say something like this: "A casual reading of history certainly suggests that you are right. There are several events which seem to bear you out. You must however remember that not all of these supposed events are well authenticated; some of them have been recently proved to be exaggerated and distorted. Moreover, taking into consideration all the evidence, it is possible to put an entirely different interpretation upon it .... " By this time, of course, the audience will have gone home, leaving the historian to talk to an empty hall, and entirely convinced that his oratorical opponent was right. This is understandable. Sweeping statements are emotionally satisfying and seem to justify unqualified consent and action. The scholar who carefully examines evidence invites and compels people to think (and thinking is painful), and may yield no clear conclusion or invite to no definite course of action. To the young and energetic this is frustrating.

These social facts confront the teacher of history. He may do much positive good. Indeed there is no doubt that he can do much positive good by sound historical instruction. But, and this is even more important, he can try in advance to guard his pupils from the many historical legends and distortions which they are certain to meet in the course of their lives. They will have no armour except what they receive from him. As a sound historical scholar he can teach them some good history and he can show them something of the modes of historical thought.

To do this is not easy. I think no one has a harder task than the teacher of history. The student of history requires not only powers of thought and imagination, but also a certain measure of social experience, which many young people do not have. The teacher's problem is made still more difficult because many administrators who know no history think that it is very easy to teach. As a result they may be less demanding in the matter of qualifications for history teachers and less generous in their allowance of time for preparation and in the granting of special facilities to the history department. The result of all this is that in many schools history is beyond all question the worst subject taught.

In recent years, however, many encouraging things have happened. Various devices have made it possible to project onto a screen in the classroom, maps, illustrations, tables, and so forth, which not only make it easier for the student to absorb information, but serve to show them the importance of a precise mastery of the facts in order to arrive at valid conclusions. Moreover, the increasing wealth of Canada has made it possible for Canadian publishers to produce much useful material on Canadian history, a field which until twenty or thirty years ago was almost closed except to the scholar with a rare and expensive library.

Another encouraging development, and this applies to the teaching of all history, is the constantly higher standards of qualification which are sought by teachers and are demanded of them by those who engage them. It would be too much to say that no one now believes that anybody can teach history if he has the textbook, but there is an increasing awareness on all sides of the need for longer and more intensive study and preparation.

It is however important that all who are interested in the dissemination of good history should remember that history teachers cannot be polished off with an advanced degree and then sent into the classroom to perform for the rest of their professional lives as if they were self-winding watches. A teacher may be excellent in his first year or so and thereafter steadily deteriorate unless he receives due care and cultivation.

The good teacher must first be sustained. He must have adequate time for preparation. If he is to convey to his classes a vision of the past, he must have the opportunity to renew his own vision. Our historical knowledge, no matter how precise, is a fragile thing, always ready to fall back into a pile of dry bones, dry bones being the original material that the research historian has to work with. The vision needs constant recreation by fresh reading, by contacts with his colleagues, by lectures from specialists who have had leisure to give themselves to one particular field. If it is impossible for collegiate teachers to attend the meetings of the Canadian Historical Association, they should have a professional organization of their own where they can meet from time to time and exchange ideas and information, to learn what new areas of history are being opened up, what new theories are being developed. Admirable work is being done in our own province by a provincial association. More should be done on the provincial and the national level.

Along with opportunities for leisure and for refreshment, every history teacher should of course be provided with an adequate reference library, appropriate to any course that he is asked to give. At least one year before any new history course is authorized, all necessary reference material should be in the hands of everyone who is to teach the course, so far as these are known. I am constantly startled to find that teachers even in elementary schools are asked to give instruction on all manner of topics on which the material, probably available only in a good reference library, is likely to be scanty and scattered. No one should be allowed to decree that something must be taught in the schools just because he thinks it would be good for the children to know it. He should first make sure that adequate information on the subject exists and that it can be made completely available to the teacher and in a certain degree to the pupils also. It is not only wrong, it is silly, to ask people to make bricks without straw.

When the French writer Flaubert was asked to suggest certain rules of style he is supposed to have answered that he had just three: "De la clarté, encore de la clarté, et toujours de la clarté" — clarity, more clarity, and still more clarity. In teaching history, I think I would say: imagination, more imagination, and still more imagination. Our fundamental task is to resurrect the dead past. It is dead until we resurrect it; and it is more dangerous dead than alive. The dead hand of the past will not let go. The slogan "nôtre maître le passé" to my mind elevates a dead god. The living past is like a living person. It can be freshly understood and freshly interpreted with our own growing knowledge and experience. Nothing can be done until the pupils see the men and women of the past as people like themselves, living in the world they live in, meeting the same kind of troubles and triumphs that they meet. All that differs, and this all is very much, is that they have met their problems with different emotional attitudes, different pre-conceived ideas, and, often, much less adequate information.

Most people think, and naturally, that the first thing the historian needs is a command of the so-called facts. It may seem wrong, and even scandalous, to suggest that he needs imagination first. The historian's imagination, however, is not fancy, and it does not justify invention. He must create an imaginative picture, but as he does so, he must govern himself by definite rules. In the first place, he must not invent anything. Second, he must not deliberately or carelessly discard any relevant facts as he constructs his picture. Finally, his imaginative reconstruction must not include anything inconsistent with the established facts which are at his disposal.

It is the responsibility of the teacher of history to use his imagination in this way, and to stimulate his pupils to do the same. Only so can they encounter and use the living past as an essential part of themselves. Only so can they be saved from falling into the captivity of the dead past, an inert and sometimes even a malignant deity, capable of controlling the present and destroying the future.[4]

Whatever else Hilda was and however else she will be remembered, it is as a historian that she would wish to be known. For Hilda a true historian was a person committed to a special period or special topic who had breadth of vision, depth of learning, and basic guiding principles. She was a historian of Canada, interested in all of western civilization, who, because of circumstances, (including necessity as well as interest) did most of her research, as distinct from reading, in eighteenth-century Quebec history. She often expressed a feeling of inadequacy about the breadth of her wisdom and the depth of her learning. Every good historian has that feeling. She had no doubts about her principles.

Hilda wrote more on and about history than any other subject. But it was not just a matter of quantity. As the years went by Hilda became more tolerant in religion, more interesting as a teacher, more accepting as a Canadian, and more cosmopolitan as a westerner, but her real development came as a historian, and that development can be traced in her work.

Hilda does not figure importantly in the one book that has been written on Canadian historians.[1] This may be because she was not involved in the production of Ph. D.'s and for many years wrote on a wide variety of topics, or because there is an imbalance in the book. Perhaps her articles on Quebec in the 1960's and 1970's, and her last two major books, *Quebec, The Revolutionary Age, 1760–1791* (1966) and *Queen's University, 1841–1917: And Not to Yield* (1978), have earned her an honourable place in Canadian historiography. In the first she discussed an important, complex, and controversial period in history with attention both to detail and context and in a style that is attractive. She did this well enough to please many of her colleagues, though by no means all. Mason Wade called it "apologetic, imperial history of the old Oxford School."[2] In the second book she managed to write interestingly and well about the history of a university; something that few historians have been able to do. Furthermore, she gave a much more realistic picture of the functioning of a university within its province and country and within its own walls than any other Canadian historian has done. Since both books are readily available no selections from them are printed here. Both Chapter 10 of the Queen's book and Chapter 16 of *Quebec* would serve as excellent examples of Hilda as a mature historian. Chapter 11 of the Queen's book shows Hilda's originality as a university historian — she had a genuine interest in the students. Chapter 6 from the Quebec book shows that, contrary to received opinion, Hilda could handle economic history. Chapter 9 on the Quebec Act is quintessential Hilda, but her last words on that subject came in *The Quebec Act: Protest and Policy* published in 1972. These words are reprinted in the next chapter.

Chapter 9 contains Hilda's work on Canadian history as such. The selections in the present chapter, divided into two sections, illustrate her development as a historian both in the technical sense — as a researcher and writer — and in the broader sense — as a human being reflecting on history and its place in the scheme of things.

The earliest extant piece of historical writing by Hilda is her honours essay written for A.S. Morton in 1924, a bibliographical survey of the reign of Louis XIV written in French. Her master's thesis of 1927, "Imperial Sentiment in Canada (1867–1896)," is the next available piece of historical work. A few pages are reproduced here as the first selection in the first section of this chapter. The approach was clumsy, many of her attitudes came from the nineteenth century, but the principles, some of the style, and a strong concern for Canada were already present. Both the unpublished and the published versions of her doctoral thesis, *The Administration of Justice under the Quebec Act,* show that by the mid-1930's Hilda had learned how to integrate many strands into one narrative. However, in accordance with custom, she had severely limited her topic. One positive result of this was that her book remains the definitive treatment of the subject.

Hilda reviewed many books on both education and history. The reviews of historical works read in chronological order reveal her development. Her first review was written when she was over forty and had already published a book and several articles — a significant part of her development had already taken place. However, her reviews show that she continued to develop.

Three reviews are reprinted in this chapter as the second selection. Her first scholarly review, from 1944, shows the same concentration on detail that had appeared in her first book. The second shows how she handled a scholarly book for a popular audience. This review of the second volume of Creighton's biography of John A. Macdonald was one of many that Hilda delivered over the radio in the 1950's. The opening and closing sections of her review of Fernand Ouellet's book, *Histoire économique et sociale du Québec 1760–1850,* which appeared in 1967, show Hilda at the height of her development as an historian, once again primarily interested in Quebec. The editors of *Revue du centre d'étude du Québec* scored a coup by following this review immediately with a review by Ouellet of *Quebec: The Revolutionary Age.* His conclusion, after criticism because of lack of attention to the "réalités de base(économiques, démographiques, sociales)," was:

> Written from a traditional approach, utilizing especially official sources and diplomatic sources, Mme. Neatby because of her prospecting in other series of documents and because of her rigorous investigation, has not only done something new in comparison with her predecessors but she has created new questions. Such is, it seems to us, the great merit of this fundamental contribution, which constitutes, it must be said, an invitation to go further.[3]

Hilda's informal reviews, found in her letters, were often more direct and biting than the ones she published or broadcast. Compare, for example, her public reviews of Donald Creighton's work on Macdonald with her comment to Frank Underhill in 1957, "He [Creighton] finds it hard to approve the old chieftain except as a faithful clansman and he must have his knife into every enemy of the clan."[4] A year later she wrote again about Creighton's Macdonald: "There is a great deal of bad taste as well as bad history — and yet it is a blessing to have such a generally useful and readable book."[5] A longer example, also in a letter to Underhill, is, in effect, a review of A.R.M. Lower's book *Colony to Nation*. This is the third selection. The last selection in this section is in a sense a review, and is also in the form of a letter, but the approach, this time to an article by Roger Graham is quite different.

The second group of selections in this chapter, showing Hilda concerned with the nature of history, come from the years between the two theses and the book on Queen's. The first selection "The Quebec Act: Protest and Policy" is a general statement of method applied to the problem of the interpretation of the Quebec Act. In addition to the theme of the article — historians are affected by their environment but must strive to overcome it — there is another idea mentioned only in passing but of great importance in understanding Hilda's historical thought: historians use the judicial method (which includes but goes beyond the scientific method) of constant questioning, constant reference to reality, and constant concern for personality and circumstance.[6]

Hilda would continue to describe herself as a historian during the years that she was involved in the problems of contemporary Canada through her work on the Massey Commission and her interest in education. The need to speak and write about these issues (evident in the other chapters) combined with the necessity of teaching a variety of courses made it impossible for her to become a historian of Saskatchewan. She had planned to do this in order that she might have ready access to original sources. However, the demands that kept her from the history of her province led her to return to a study of the broad outlines of European civilization and to consider the nature of history. Her picture of European history tended to remain "old fashioned," except that the rise of Nazism destroyed her belief in continual progress of western civilization:

> As I picked up a paper in March of 1933 and read of the outrages perpetrated on Jews in Berlin I remember that my instinctive reaction was, "But the Germans are a civilized people. This can't be happening there." At that moment the comfortable assumptions of nearly thirty years of the life that I lived in an apparently increasingly civilized society began to crumble away. At that moment my own approach to history began to change.[7]

For the most part Hilda's ideas on the nature of history were the usual ones for the time. She moved from a fascination with pattern, especially Toynbee's, and a concern for the place of religion, as in Butterfield and Dawson, to an interest in the new methodologies. What separated Hilda from most other historians was a triple combination of a nineteenth-century liberal appreciation of the past tempered by a Presbyterian understanding of depravity, a willingness to consider new methods, and a radical insistence on the importance of Christianity.

The second selection of the second group is an excerpt from a 1970 speech "History and the Computer" which, while accepting new methods and tools, discusses history as an independent subject. This is followed by an undated piece, "Christ the Centre of History," probably a sermon, that questions the view of many Christians that history should serve Christianity. This was a crucial problem for Hilda. The result of her reflection in a scholarly context can be found in an article published in 1958, after it had been written and rewritten for four years: " 'Christian' Views of History: Toynbee and Butterfield."[8] For Hilda, Christianity served history while remaining independent, transcendant, and yet involved. She expressed this succinctly in " 'Neutralism': Is It Possible for a Christian?"

> Would I, as a Christian, observe the law of love by presenting human history in this "neutral" university as centering in the supreme revelation of God in Christ? No — even though I believe that to be so — because I have under-taken to show how far we can go in explaining the mystery of man's past and present by purely rational methods. I am not "neutral"; I am only accepting a necessary means of achieving an end which I do believe to be according to the will of God and a fulfilment of the law of love.[9]

As mentioned earlier, Hilda believed that historians should use the judicial method. Under the influence of William Dray she consciously accepted what she had actually been doing, not only using the judicial method but also judging. This led to a new aspect of the problem of the relationship of belief and history:

> If it is right to make history and if this necessarily involves value judgements then it is clearly right to make value judgements in history. But does not this mean that history can be satisfactorily "made" only on the basis of a common belief about man's nature and destiny? . . . Failing a common background, must not each historian open his work with a kind of confession of faith or statement of the language in which he is going to write, or else labour under the fear that he may not be playing quite fair?
>
> Surely it was partly such conscientious scruples that inspired the experi-ment of scientific history. Trevelyan is unembarrassed because of his complete faith in rational humanism but have you noticed that D.G. Creighton, who had made such a tremendous contribution to Canadian history, when he gets away from economic explanation tends (as in Macdonald) to waver between the sentimental and the cynical?
>
> I notice that you refer to the Nazi policy toward the Jews as "a monument of human depravity." I agree, of course. We can't consider history without such judgements and this one would surely receive almost universal rational acceptance. But how few in these days could be made with equal confidence.[10]

Hilda had hit upon a problem which would concern her more and more in the last years of her life, as can be seen especially in her speeches to student audiences: as commonly accepted standards disappeared, civilization became impossible.

> The secular historian cannot now by any rational means open to him offer any optimistic prognosis of our present condition. Historians avoid prophecy. But they will say that *in the past* societies where individuals have renounced all fundamental beliefs, all healing obligations, recognizing only the duty or the right to "do their own thing," expending their moral fervour rather in inveighing against the bad than working for the good is on the way out as a society, likely to be submerged by others more vigorous or to fall into revolutionary anarchy followed by a rigorous but not necessarily righteous dictatorship.[11]

But Hilda had hope:

> As Augustine contemplating with the fall of Rome the loss of all secular good felt compelled to construct a theology of history, so historians today, who though Christians, have pursued history as a secular calling ask themselves whether the two may not be brought into relationship. It is not that the historian can ever *prove* from history the fact of the hope that is in him. As Butterfield has said, the historian is satisfied that a man called Jesus was crucified about 30 A.D. and that his followers laid the foundation of one of the world's great religions. But only the believer, not the historian, can say, in faith that this Jesus was God Incarnate, the direct intervention of God in human history, the fulfilment of the divine plan. What the man who has said this by faith may do, however, is to look out of his history with new eyes, to seek not for proofs, but for evidence of the working out of God's plan. History alone can neither prove nor disprove it, but a historian I think might say, looking at the tragedy, the grandeur, the pettiness, the horror of man's past — there is *no* explanation which gives hope except the Christian one: the full expression and permanent intervention of divine love in the affairs of man.[12]

IMPERIAL SENTIMENT IN CANADA
(1867–1896)

Sixty years ago next July an act was passed by the Parliament of Great Britain which united four of the provinces of British North America into a single federal state, under the name of Canada. This act has proved to be one of the most important, not only in the history of Canada, but in that of the British Empire.

In Canada, the act is looked upon as symbolizing the birth of the nation. Obscured as the event is by various issues and by the modifications called for by the needs of the moment, there is no doubt that the British North America Act is a concrete expression of the national aspirations, which, in North America as in Europe, were one of the greatest moral forces of the century. The enthusiasm evoked by the idea of a united Canadian nation spreading itself over the whole of the northern half of the continent was sufficiently powerful to overcome not only the defects of the scheme itself, but also the enormous difficulties involved in carrying it out. The manifestation of such a spirit for the first time may well be looked upon as the greatest event in the history of any country.

However, the unique characteristic of the British North America Act, and that which gives it its place of importance in the history of the British Empire, is the expression of an imperial sentiment hand in hand with the national sentiment instead of, as is usually the case, antagonistic to it. In 1867 Canada assumed the position of an almost completely self-governing community — a potential nation — but a nation within the Empire. This does not seem peculiar to-day, because custom if not reason, has sanctioned it, but in 1867 it was an entirely new departure in colonial development. National sentiment was understood, but an "imperial sentiment" which involved no particular duties or obligations to imperial authorities was a thing for the most part neither understood nor approved of by the statesmen of the mother country. It was the work of Canadian statesmen, born, as will be shown, not of reason, but of the necessity of the moment, instinctive rather than logical. It is with the factors which lay beneath this sentiment, and the circumstances which formed and developed it, that this study is concerned. . . .

Macdonald's views differ from those which have just been discussed in that while theirs represent definite schemes of a practical nature, his represent simply an attitude and an ideal. The first group had seemed to desire a continuation of the colonial status and colonial privilege. The second group realizing that this was impossible, desired a development of imperial relations, at the expense, if necessary, of national development. The third group put national development first, and were prepared, although with regret, to see the final severance of the imperial tie. Macdonald, and he represents the vast majority of the Canadian legislature of that time, left the future to take care of itself, and considered only existing conditions. He saw that Canada's national future depended on the maintenance of the British connection, and he therefore bent all his energies to securing this end, concealing his lack of constructive ideas by drawing an imaginary picture of an empire as ideal as it was vague. His followers reflected his attitude perfectly, and indeed nine-tenths of the men who spoke on imperial relations followed his lead. They said in the same breath that Confederation would further the cause of

Canadian nationality and strengthen the British connection, but it cannot be said that the constitutional aspect of the question was seriously considered by them.

An examination, then, of the Confederation Debates leads to the following important conclusions. In 1865 the Canadian provinces had, almost for the first time, been brought seriously to consider their ultimate political destiny. They had decided, partly from traditional habits of thought, and partly from an instinct of self-preservation, that the bond with the Mother Country must be maintained. The few suggestions as to the development of imperial relations were of no practical use in that they ignored the national factor, although two of them — those of Dunkin and Scoble, were destined to reappear in another form in connection with the Imperial Federation movement. On the other hand the large group who realized the importance of the national sentiment failed to make any suggestions as to the manner in which it was to be reconciled to the imperial system.

This failure is not surprising when it is remembered that as yet the British North American provinces were only colonies and that the hope of a Canadian nation was a hope and nothing more. A genuine revival of national sentiment was required before the people as a whole could be brought seriously to consider their destiny. This national revival, which came with what is known as the "Canada First" movement, was destined to bring about a serious consideration not only of imperial relations, but also of Canada's other two possible futures — Independence and Annexation to the United States.

THE "CANADA FIRST" MOVEMENT

The fusion of local and provincial sentiments into a common national feeling which went on rapidly during the years which followed Confederation forms one of the most interesting passages in Canadian history. In every nation the development of a national spirit is a slow intangible process, very difficult to analyse or define, and making its presence felt more or less indirectly. Usually, however, there is some more or less definite movement or event connected with this development which is considered as typical and representative of the whole process. Canadian history is no exception to this general rule. We find our "Young Canada" in the "Canada First" movement — a movement important not only on account of the work of its originators, but because it represents the spirit of Canadian nationalism, appearing then, almost for the first time, and working, although slowly, ever since. A study of this movement, its organization, theories, and the events to which it owed its inception is essential to an understanding of Canada's later external development.

Colonel George T. Denison, one of the founders of the movement, has left an interesting account of its origin in the spring of 1868. He tells how he and William A. Foster, obliged to spend a few weeks at Ottawa, were introduced by their friend Morgan to Charles Mair of Lanark and R.J. Haliburton of Halifax. The five young men saw a great deal of each other and soon became firm friends. Being all of them sincerely and intelligently patriotic, their conversation naturally turned to the future of the new Dominion, then not a year old. As Denison says: "Nothing could show more clearly the hold that Confederation had taken of the imagination of young Canadians than the fact that, night after night, five young men should give up their time and their thoughts to discussing the higher interests of their country, and it ended in our making a solemn pledge to each other that we would do all we could to advance the interests of our native land; that we would put our country first, before all personal, or political, or party considerations; that we would change our party affiliations as often as the interests of Canada required it. Some years afterwards we adopted the name "Canada First" meaning that the true interest of Canada was to be first in our minds on every occasion."

This little group and others who joined them worked together steadily for three or four years, with one single object in view, — the creation of a Canadian national spirit. They worked first by means of lectures. Various members of the group prepared and delivered in different parts of the country lectures calculated to arouse in Canadians a sense of their existence as a nation and of the duties which they owed to each other and to the world at large. Besides this, in any event of public interest, such as the Red River Rebellion, the members of Canada First, having made up their minds in which direction the true interest of Canada lay, worked steadily to secure them, pitting the forces of public opinion against those of party interest which too often carried the day.[13]

REVIEW OF *DOMINION OF THE NORTH,* BY D.G. CREIGHTON

Dominion of the North, we are told, was written for the American reader. It should, however, receive a welcome from many Canadian readers, as a new and stimulating interpretation of the history of their country.

The early chapters are concerned with the French Empire, when the original search for gold and silver yielded to the pursuit of fish and furs which led through the St. Lawrence to the heart of the continent. The overthrow of the French power on the St. Lawrence was immediately succeeded by the challenge of the thirteen colonies to the imperial power of Britain. The fate of the northern colonies — Quebec and Nova Scotia — remained in doubt for a time, but French institutions kept them aloof from their southern neighbours and the monopolistic nature of the fur trade bound them to Europe.

Settlement was fatal to the fur trade which became concentrated in the Hudson's Bay. While British North America was finding new economic bases in lumber and agriculture, radical immigration from Britain as well as the influence of the Jacksonian democracy of the south caused political agitation. Meanwhile Manchester School sentiment in Britain was undermining the Old Colonial System. The result was free trade, a fearful shock to the dependent colonial economy, accompanied by "responsible government" or local autonomy in 1849.

During the fifties and sixties railway development, expansionist ambitions, political friction, and sectional jealousy stimulated and distracted the half emancipated colonies. Always a prime factor in their testing was the influence of the two great English-speaking nations, the United States and Great Britain, the one passing from civil war to imperialism, the other anxious to throw off imperial responsibilities for the sake of industrial expansion; each was half hostile to the other. Against such a background the new Canadian nation was born in the federal union of 1867. Canadians alone appreciated the significance of the event. " . . . Canada started off on its career without arousing the slightest enthusiasm or winning more than perfunctory goodwill. The attitude of even Great Britain and the United States, the two English-speaking countries with which the provinces had always been most closely associated, was an attitude of complete indifference, qualified on the one side by a bored sense of obligation, and on the other by an unmistakable feeling of hostility."

In this first part of the book which ends with the creation of the Dominion, the author resolutely parts from the traditional pattern of Canadian history. For the heroic achievements and picturesque personalities of the fur-trading era, degenerating into a dreary succession of racial and political squabbles as settlement and civilization creep on, he substitutes a definite, if not exclusive, economic determinism. Professor Creighton's selection and interpretation of facts may occasionally suffer from this approach. He is not happy in dealing with the church in New France; he does not manage to explain the enduring qualities which he notices in French-Canadian civilization; he perhaps does less than justice to the constitutional and political interest of the period preceding the admission of responsible government. At the same time his whole approach offers a very necessary correction to the false emphasis of the past which threw an air of unreality over even the genuine heroics of Canadian history. The reader feels that living history is replacing a somewhat faded romance.

By way of contrast, in the latter part of the book, the author himself seems to be gripped by a sense of romance as he describes how the feeble settlements, isolated in the wilderness of the north, struggled towards unity and strength. Economic factors are not neglected, but they are somewhat subordinated to the general theme of Canadian national growth which centres in the personalities and policies of those two great statesmen of the Dominion, Sir John A. Macdonald and Sir Wilfrid Laurier. The former had to cope with problems of economic depression, and racial and religious sectionalism; the latter profited by the boom accompanying the opening of the West, but had to meet the difficult imperial and international problems of the twentieth century. The closing chapter is a most interesting account of problems and politics between wars.

An admirable quality of the book is the clear and consistent approach to the subject as a whole. Mr. Creighton avoids the easy old method of a series of sectional histories, and concentrates on a description and analysis of the forces which at last created a true unity from the strange diversity of British North American communities.[14]

REVIEW OF *JOHN A. MACDONALD: THE OLD CHIEFTAIN,* BY DONALD CREIGHTON

This is an enchanting book. Many Canadians have been waiting eagerly for *The Old Chieftain* ever since the time, some two years ago, when they turned the last page of *The Young Politician*. They will not be disappointed. It is not often that distinguished Canadians achieve distinguished biographies, but this life of Canada's first prime minister is great by any standards.

In this second volume Professor Creighton has been free from certain difficulties which may have embarrassed him a little in writing the first. *The Young Politician* held no very secure position in politics, and left behind him no super-abundance of historical evidence. With *The Old Chieftain* it is a different story. The materials are more ample and varied, and the hero occupies without question the centre of a new and larger stage provided by the new Dominion of Canada. These advantages raise their own problems no doubt; but Professor Creighton handles a wealth of material with apparent ease, and in spite of all temptation, he refuses to allow Macdonald's personal story to be dissolved in national politics.

And yet no one can read this book without being impressed by the fact that Macdonald's life was indeed almost identified with the history of Canada for nearly a quarter of a century after 1867. Professor Creighton presents here again the three-fold national policy that he has already set forth so lucidly elsewhere. From the time that he lent himself to the Confederation scheme Macdonald was putting together in his own mind his great design: British North America was to be no longer a group of small, scattered, impotent colonies, but a nation, an "auxiliary nation" certainly, but still a nation capable of dealing with its own affairs, and, ultimately, of meeting its two great neighbours in the North Atlantic Triangle on something like equal terms.

The end was clear. The details of the design gradually became clear also. By one means or another he must draw in the reluctant fragments: Newfoundland, Prince Edward Island, British Columbia; he must secure the vast North-West claimed by so many Canadians as theirs by manifest destiny. Having done this he must bind all together by a railway, a material bond of union for the provinces, and a great imperial link between the Atlantic and Pacific Oceans. This railway would fill the empty North-West, and by filling the empty North-West would pay for itself. And, finally, the east-west traffic essential to the whole scheme could be secured from American depredations by a national tariff wall. This immense and complex design, each element dependent on the others, was undertaken in the face of commercial depression, external hostility, and cultural and sectional strife. It was, moreover, towards the end, carried through almost single-handed for Macdonald especially in his later years after the death of Cartier and the departure of Tupper found no *alter ego* in his cabinets. The common pretext that he could not retire because no one could take his place was no pretext; it was a conviction shared even by those who were not whole-hearted admirers.

Perhaps no part of Macdonald's design required so much patience and skill and such untiring vigilance as the maintenence of fair and friendly relations with Great Britain and the United States. In the conduct of these relations Macdonald showed constant patience, untiring vigilance, and a high degree of diplomatic skill. Professor Creighton has to go over familiar ground here as in the story of the Canadian Pacific Railway. He always contrives to give his stories as much freshness and vigour as if they had never been told before — and, indeed, much of this story never has been told before. The chapter on the Washington Treaty — I liked it the best of all — shows Macdonald, who could lose his temper completely and disastrously, exhibiting patience, tenacity, good humour — and humour — to a remarkable degree under strange and most trying circumstances.

In this volume as in the first we learn much of Macdonald's personal story — the great happiness of his second marriage, marred as it was by tragedy, his nagging financial worries, his courageous battle with ill-health. Most interesting of all are first-hand impressions of him by many well-known people. We begin with his wife: "I tell him his good heart and amiable temper are the great secrets of his success" — a judgement which, it seems, she never retracted although in the extracts from her personal diary which add so much to the interest of the early chapters she does give shading as well as colouring to this flatly respectable picture.

The evidence of a wife goes for nothing, of course, but Macdonald charmed his Governors-General also. Lord Dufferin, who might well have been critical of this petty colonial, found him "charming in conversation, gentlemanlike, with excellent manners, quick apprehension ... good-natured, placable and magnanimous" with "a great faculty for managing people." Even though Macdonald is "gentlemanlike" rather than a "gentleman," this is high praise. Lord Lansdowne expressed the most sincere liking and respect for him. And going beyond Governors-General, the great Disraeli — like Dufferin — found him "gentlemanlike, agreeable and very intelligent ... a considerable man." And Lord Kimberley, the Colonial Secretary, noting with mingled horror and admiration the details of what Dufferin called "a transient weakness" and the *Globe* "simply drunk" genially remarked that he belonged with the great two-bottle men of the 18th century. As for Canadians whom "he knew ... better than anybody had ever known them before — and better than anyone would ever know them again" they showed what they thought of him time and again, in good days and in bad.

It would be easy to go on quoting and praising, but time is short, and a reviewer must maintain his reputation by at least a few carping criticisms.

I began by saying that the book is enchanting and I believe that most readers will happily and wisely resign themselves to the enchantment. But perhaps the student of history, the earnest seeker after truth, should if only for a brief moment resist the enchantment and ask himself and the author a few earnest questions. First, a representative of those whom Macdonald called the "wild people" of the West might wish for a little more light on Macdonald's concern with the two western rebellions, disasters which (as Professor Creighton shows) might well have wrecked his national plans. Assuming that McDougall's appointment as Lieutenant-Gôvernor was the crowning blunder in the first rebellion, is the second to be attributed purely to the wickedness of Riel, the wildness of the West, and bad luck?

The tragedy of McDougall raises another question: What were Macdonald's relations with those who worked with him and for him in building the Dominion? We hear of the devoted Campbell, the stalwart Tupper, the indispensable Cartier, the faithful Langevin, of Rose, of Galt, and of Stephen. But (apart from an unqualified tribute to Stephen's financial genius and a brief appreciation of Tupper) we hear of these men chiefly when they are being patronized or criticized. Did Macdonald almost always fail to attract to his leadership first-class men, or has his biographer unconsciously belittled his colleagues?

In one other matter I find this book is a little less than satisfying. We see Macdonald always in the centre of the stage. We are given a wealth of background detail and many close-ups. We do not really get into the man's mind, and for a curious reason. Professor Creighton is constantly opening the door, but having done so he stands in the way and blocks the view. And we hear a voice, but we are not quite sure whether it is Macdonald or Creighton who speaks. Is it, for example, Macdonald or his biographer who defends the gerrymander of 1885 as essential for the winning of the election? This method, used thoughout the book, of blending his voice with the voice of his subject prevents Mr. Creighton from offering the mature and informed judgements on Macdonald that he is so abundantly qualified to make. Macdonald is never called to account on any matter of consistency or principle, and yet this cannot be attributed to scholarly detachment for the errors and follies of Macdonald's opponents are frequently greeted with outbursts of righteous indignation.

It is, however, ungracious to look about for those things which Mr. Creighton has not done when he has done so much and done it so magnificently. This is a great biography of one who was beyond all question a great and remarkable man.

As a colleague of mine has said: "All literate Canadians should read this book; all solvent Canadians should buy it."[15]

REVIEW OF *HISTOIRE ECONOMIQUE ET SOCIALE DU QUEBEC 1760–1850,* BY FERNAND OUELLET

All who know Professor Ouellet's work will have been expecting to find in his most recent book a fresh view of the province of Quebec. They will not be disappointed. This is no straightforward narrative of how men earned their daily bread and what they did in their spare time. M. Ouellet has set himself the task of applying to this critical century following the conquest insights derived from quantitative measurements. From an examination of available statistics on prices, volume and value of imports and exports, levels of production, immigration, emigration and so forth, he has prepared a series of charts which, as he says, make it possible to view within a chronological framework "the different series of phenomena (separated not in reality but only by the exigencies of narrative history) in order to elicit from these series set down in graphic form, relationships which former methods of exposition have failed to make clear" (p.33). M. Ouellet thus seeks to examine the impact on social, political and even mental structures of economic crises; or rather he considers statistical evidence for signs of economic crises and mutations, at the same time considering the social and political scene. . . .

This is an enormously interesting work. No one can read it without being excited and stimulated or possibly shocked and revolted. In his treatment of the early period M. Ouellet hardly allows himself to use the names French or English and the reader yields himself unsuspiciously to this unusually peaceful and benign approach. He is awakened with a shock as the work moves into the nineteenth century. Papineau gets rough treatment, but not so rough as that meted out to patriotic historians who have waxed eloquent over the divine destiny which summoned Canadians to seek happiness with virtue on the exhausted soil of an overpopulated seigneury. Quantitative history seems to be almost as provocative as qualitative.

This M. Ouellet would say is unimportant if it is true. Can we accept without reservations findings dependent on quantitative methods? One of the contemporary French historians whose work is noted by M. Ouellet, Frédéric Mauro, has suggested in a recent review that on this matter there is still a measure of doubt and disagreement as to how far quantitative descriptions of economic entities can be depended on for modern as distinguished from contemporary history. Certainly some doubts may be raised about the prices cited for Quebec and

Montreal before 1791 if they are to be taken as any precise indication of the total economic condition of the community. The impression given by qualitative sources is that one of the chief problems of the merchants was that there was no clear "price" in an isolated area where communications were very poor, where at least three different currencies were used, where much trade was carried on by barter. It is even possible that recorded prices for wheat may have been, not reflections of an almost non-existent "market," but bookkeeping devices of the seminaries whose rents were paid in wheat.

But M. Ouellet's most important conclusions are not drawn from this early period where, as he acknowledges, statistical material is not as plentiful as he could wish. Moreover his important conclusions about the economic situation of the *habitant* are based less on precise local price levels than by what he has been able to determine of the actual quantity of wheat produced in relation to the population. Nor does he profess to depend entirely on quantitative material. He does not profess, if I understood his work correctly, that quantitative history is autonomous, but that it provides fresh insights into, and perhaps requires a total revaluation of qualitative material.

M. Ouellet's thesis invites historians to forget about racial and cultural considerations and to view the intense political struggles culminating in 1837 as the clashing of socio-economic groups, the French compensating for economic weakness by the use of their majority vote, and for lack of true social solidarity by the emotional nationalism which united and moved the scattered farms and parishes to a passionate sense of unity.

One way of testing this persuasive thesis is to ask whether the phenomena which M. Ouellet explains in terms of the agricultural crisis existed during the previous period of prosperity or the still earlier one of stability. The answer is that some, at least, did. To take a very simple example, the *habitant* was apparently manufacturing most of his own clothing long before the reduction of wheat sales compelled him to limit his purchases abroad. *L'étoffe du pays* clothed him and his wife and was also sent up from the lower district to furnish grain and flour sacks for Montreal. Moving from economic realities to social abstractions, it cannot have been the growth of the liberal bourgeoisie in the 1790's that dislodged the seigneurs "de la vielle souche" from their position as social leaders. It seems quite clear that at least after 1760 the seigneurs aspired to a social leadership which they did not possess. Carleton found them almost useless for his purposes in 1775–6. The *Montreal Gazette* gives ample evidence of the hatred and contempt that they excited after 1785 (the priests find some defenders in this radical journal, but not the seigneurs) and there is other evidence that their sedulous support in Council of the militia act, which in practice affected only Canadians, alienated the *habitants*.

Again, during the period 1760–91 M. Ouellet consistently refers to the merchants, Canadian and English as a single group, assuming that there was no real division of interest between them. Although this represents a much needed revision of the old French v. English thesis, it probably assumes rather too much. Repeatedly during these years merchants conscious of their common interests and of their comparative alienation from seigneurs and officials, tried to send joint petitions to Britain but without success (although during the years previous to 1791 they did maintain in London a common agent, Adam Lymburner). And on the eve of the Constitutional Act a knowledgeable member of the merchants' party urged that there be no representative assembly in Quebec unless English domination could be assured.

These minor comments suggest that the social cleavages in Quebec society may have been of longer standing, more complex, and rooted in a greater variety of causes than M. Ouellet's socio-economic theory would suggest. They suggest that cultural and national self-consciousness of a kind was developed before 1791. They do not, I think, in any way invalidate his view that the shock and resulting antagonisms of the conquest have been greatly overrated.

Nor do they qualify the enthusiasm of this reviewer for the splendid fruits of M. Ouellet's quantitative labours. He himself expresses the hope that for his work "vieillissement viendra vite." This does not seem likely except in the sense that he has opened a road along which historians of the future may travel even farther than he may hope, continuing to shed as he has more light with less heat.[16]

INFORMAL REVIEW OF *COLONY TO NATION*, BY A.R.M. LOWER

University of Saskatchewan,
Saskatoon.
September 9, 1947

Dear Mr. Underhill,

I am reading A.R.M. Lower's book with much pleasure and interest. In many ways, it is even better than I expected, and I expected a good deal.

I have just seen your review in the *Canadian Forum*. I do see that the term "philosopher historian" is appropriate as I suppose he is the first person to attempt a philosophic analysis of the Canadian past. At the same time, for a philosopher, Mr. Lower seems to me to allow himself an extraordinary amount of vagueness and inconsistency. His sentimentalizing at one moment over the self-contained parochial communities of Quebec, and the next over the rugged individualism of the frontier is one example. I can sympathize emotionally, but I don't see how any one can — as a philosopher — admire both so much at the same time.

Then, in the midst of bitter attacks on aristocracy, privilege, and commercialism, he pauses for a splendid eulogy of Durham and his report, which he attributes to the "great English Whig tradition," without mentioning that this tradition grew up, not among the fresh breezes of the frontier, but in the very soil of aristrocratic commercialism. Then he forgets all about Durham and closes his remarks on responsible government by saying that some fresh frontier breezes had blown into Upper Canada, but not enough. One could almost say that many of his interpretations have just enough truth in them to be thoroughly dishonest.

I don't think that one or two instances of this kind are important, but I feel constantly in the post-Confederation section which I am now reading, that he lets his judgements be warped by his enthusiasm for a Canadian nationalism. I can sympathize entirely, and I feel that this enthusiasm adds tremendously to the interest of the book, but I think he betrays his responsibilities as an historian. If he would take an extreme postition and give a reasoned defence of it, it wouldn't be so bad, but he seems to get his effect by slightly shifting his ground, by assumptions not stated or proved, and by other devices which are not even honest, much less philosophic. After all why was Mackenzie right in standing up for his local rights, if Home and Tilley were wrong in defending theirs? And even more, if Mackenzie is a crusader, why is Riel a rebel or a murderer, and nothing more? I like Mackenzie myself, but I think, particularly in terms of Lower's own frontier democracy, that Riel has quite a case. And, apparently, British institutions aren't much good until they serve the Dominion of Canada, and then they are wonderful.

I think I may be emotionally biased, but even when I am most enjoying the book I am bothered by a sense of intellectual vagueness, or even a want of intellectual integrity. I know I have put the case in extreme terms, but I would be interested to know if you think there is anything in it.

Sincerely yours,
Hilda Neatby.[17]

COMMENTS ON "ARTHUR MEIGHEN AND THE CONSERVATIVE PARTY IN QUEBEC: THE ELECTION OF 1925", BY ROGER GRAHAM

Department of History

May 16, 1955
Saskatoon, Canada

Dear Roger:

It won't do, it really won't do. I mean your article in the *C.H.R.*

In Canada we have our cultural traditions. For scholarly work we favour the one-step-forward-two-steps-back style of reading, and a style of writing to suit. As I read our learned journal I have accustomed myself to taking notes, to help me remember what the writer said first, and to determine whether when he said it, he knew what he was going to say next. I hope you are still with me.

Now, this article of yours. I began reading it as I left the university today on the bus. Reading, I passed the new university monstrosity, the hospital, without a shudder and the architectural inanities of College Avenue without a glance. I found to my consternation that heedless of democracy you are in bondage to the laws of logic and style. I missed the familiar sensation of following a rope of sand. I forgot myself, relaxed, smiled, even laughed.

How dare you? Who are you to sport with the solemnity of the *Canadian Historical Review?* Who are you to attempt deliberately — I know you did it deliberately — to arouse interest in your subject, to write what is readable, to attempt to seduce your countrymen with the subtleties of style?

It won't do. Take warning by your hero and don't let us know you are clever; please don't let us be certain even that you are alive.

And please don't answer my abuse with irrelevancies. Of course the article is good. It's magnificent, but don't you call it *Canadian* history?

Yours with the maple leaf, forever.

Hilda[18]

INTRODUCTION TO *THE QUEBEC ACT: PROTEST AND POLICY*

A recent critic of Canadian education reports that school children complain bitterly of the series of "tidy little acts" pressed on their attention in the course of their study of the century following the cession of New France to Britain in 1763. If these "tidy little acts" are the enactments of 1774, 1791, 1840 and 1867, the complaint does indeed suggest that teachers and text books fail to do justice to the complexity of the problems which these statutes were designed to solve, or to the strenuous debates which generally preceded and followed them.

In this important group the Quebec Act holds a special place. It was the first Imperial statute to create a constitution for a British colony. This statute was passed at a great crisis in the affairs of the First Empire, and it has been seen by some as one cause of the American Revolution. It was destined to be cited as a precedent for similar enactments designed to suit the needs of the new kinds of colonies which composed the Second Empire. In some respects it even appears to embody the principles of the later Commonwealth. For all these reasons it has received special attention from historians of the British Empire. As it was also the first parliamentary statute to recognize the complexity of the relations between the two groups which together were to constitute the beginnings of the Canadian people, it has been considered a key piece of legislation by Canadian historians.

For all these reasons the Quebec Act has aroused much interest and much controversy. The purpose of this collection of papers is not so much to cast fresh light on the Act itself, as to offer it as an illustration of the way in which judgments are and must be made. Historians seek to reveal the truth. All good historians do reveal some truth. The particular truths they are able to show depend on time and circumstance, as well as on their own ability, diligence and good luck.

The Quebec Act has been praised by some as a just and humane piece of legislation because it recognized the claim of the Canadians to be judged in certain matters by their own traditional laws and customs and to continue the practice of their own religion without being officially rated as second-class citizens. Also, by refraining from imposing or granting an elective assembly, it left them, for a time, governed by a generally benevolent oligarchy and relatively free from taxation.

Historians have differed in their opinions of this piece of legislation for a number of reasons. No one is willing to admit that he is opposed to humanity and justice. But conceptions of what is just and humane change with the times. If it is agreed that the historian must attempt to distinguish between his own conceptions of justice and those which prevailed in the times of which he writes, it must be admitted that not all historians dealing with the Quebec Act have stopped to ask themselves what men of ability and goodwill would have considered just in 1774. For example, would it have seemed right to them to establish the British state church, to contrive an adaptation of the Gallican church, to arrange some sort of compromise, or even to identify and imitate the American experiments at voluntarism? Many writers have passed a rapid and generally favourable judgment on the religious settlement of the Quebec Act. Very few have stated in detail what this settlement was. The possible alternatives have not always received impartial examination.

The moral judgment here has been further confused by a natural inclination to consider the morality and wisdom of the measure as partly determined by motive and therefore to try to deal with the motives of the authors of the Act. Some writers have suggested that these motives were not only mistaken but discreditable. Not all have been precise in distinguishing their judgment on the possible motives from their decision on the merit or otherwise of what was done.

The commonest criticism of a historian, especially by the ill-informed, is that he is "biased." This word has been so overworked and abused that it is now freely applied (often with no supporting evidence) to any decided judgment, favourable or unfavourable, on men or events. The word thus used has no meaning in historical criticism. Historical bias, it may be said, is caused by some current of emotion which carries man's reason off the straight line which should lead him to an admission that there is not sufficient evidence for a final judgment.

Obviously all historians are in danger of letting any strong personal opinions they may hold on religion, ethics, politics, or the social order prejudice their treatment of historical issues. All good historians are aware of this occupational hazard and try to guard against it. Less obviously, all historians are likely to be strongly influenced in their judgments by what may be generally considered right or wrong, expedient or otherwise, in their own age and society. It is easier to discount one's own personal views, and to give their fair treatment to those of a dissenting contemporary, than to emancipate oneself from the whole climate of opinion in a given society, marking the subtle gradations from what may be accepted as eternal values at one extreme from purely temporary principles of expedience at the other. It may be very difficult for a historian so to emancipate himself from his surroundings as to give a fair judgment of what would have been right, wise or expedient in the very different times and circumstances of which he may be writing. It is his first obligation to be aware of the difficulty and to endeavour to overcome it. His success may well depend not only on his integrity and goodwill, but on the depth and the breadth of his scholarship.

A further complicating factor is that writers, especially Canadians, dealing with the Quebec Act may find their judgments on the motives and policy of the Act blending with their conclusions about its effect on the subsequent history of Canada. They find it difficult not to ask themselves whether it would have been "better" for Quebec, and for the future Canada and North America, the Empire and the Commonwealth, to have tried or tried harder to bring about assimilation of Canadians to a possible or probable Anglo-Saxon majority. Would such assimilation have been possible? The views of the historians on this question are likely to depend very much on the time at which they write — that is, on the current views on nationalism, liberalism and democracy — to say nothing of current population trends.

There are other and more obvious reasons for the differing views of historians on the Quebec Act. Some who have written have not had access to, or have perhaps not troubled to use relevant source material, or, using it, have not fully grasped its significance. The Quebec Act presents a special difficulty here because in two important areas of investigation the evidence is wholly inadequate. It is difficult to determine what were the general views and wishes of the Canadian people in 1774. As most critics would agree that justice and humanity demanded at least some attention to the wishes of the Canadians, this gap in historical evidence is a serious one. Formal petitions by Canadians have survived. Some other evidence exists. Unfortunately, the majority of Canadians at that time could not write and it may be assumed that many things written have not survived or have not been found. Among the clergy, especially, many whose views would have been interesting may have thought it wiser not to express them in writing. It is difficult even today with the aid of scientific polls to say what, at a given moment, a given group of people "want." On the wants of Canadians in 1774, it is inevitable that the fragmentary evidence surviving should be interpreted in different ways.

Evidence is also inadequate on the views and motives of those who gave the Act its final form. The papers of Carleton, which would presumably have been invaluable, were not preserved. The Quebec Act seemed to carry our views which he had expressed during his stay in Canada (1766–1770) but almost nothing survives of comments and suggestions which he must have made during his stay in England in the years preceding the passing of the Act (1770–1774). Nor is there much other confidential material apart from a few memoranda and drafts of the Act which have been preserved in the Dartmouth papers. Here again historians, trying to discern some pattern where too many pieces are missing, are likely to come to different conclusions.

The following selection of primary material presented as evidence on the situation in Canada preceding the Quebec Act, and on the motives and policy which may have determined it, is of course arbitrary. The intention, however, has been to make the sampling as representative as possible. It is hoped that this collection will add to the reader's understanding and appreciation of the judgments of various historians on the Act itself which are discussed in Part 5 of this book.[19]

HISTORY AND THE COMPUTER

How does the historian operate? I have already made some suggestions about this. Some say, as I have suggested, that he works by imagination and intuition operating on the evidence before him. For example, I say to myself, had I been the individual A faced with the situation X, would I not have done Y? If so, can I not say that X is the cause of Y? On the other hand some say that this form of sympathetic imagination, this getting yourself as one historian has said "inside the skins of other people" is not the way in which the historian should work. He should rather use a more logical or more scientific method. He should concentrate on human society as a collectivity, for that is really his field of interest. He should adapt himself more to the methods which sociologists, political scientists and psychologists have offered him. He should say something like this: if situation X is present, in any social context Y must follow after. Therefore, when we see X we look for Y; X being the effective cause of Y. We do not trouble ourselves about person A, B and C: they are, as it were, outside this beam of light which guides us. (As Karl Marx said "haves" — no matter when — always oppress "have-nots".) Most people, of course, do both; they put themselves in the place of

A, and they say confronted with X he may probably follow the course Y. He does so partly because of his character, tastes and interests. Yet, as his character, tastes and interests have been formed by the general environment, no matter who he is, that is, no matter if he is A, B or C he is likely to follow pretty much the same course. They do, however, try to see a combination of character, environment (and accident) as effective causes.

The trend in history, however, has been, especially in our increasingly populated and increasingly intercommunicating world to pay less attention to individuals, and to pay less attention to what could be called simple diplomatic and political history. We think less of A confronting B in a certain situation and wondering whether they are going to be able to compromise on X or what other form of action they will take and how character and luck may affect them. This kind of history, this concentration on important significant, powerful individuals and their reactions to their environment need not be simple or naive. It has been productive of much understanding and of extensive knowledge not simply of individuals but of masses. It has generally and rightly referred many motives to well understood maxims and principles of the civilization in which the individuals lived and of the beliefs of their age which they followed or neglected as the case might be. At the same time it assumes that characters are different, and that no situation will ever be precisely repeated.

But recent trends and our view of the new mass societies have tended to make us see the men less as free agents and more as products if not puppets of environmental conditions. We ask, therefore, is there not something we can detect in the situation X that will make *any* man or group of men in such a situation go on to Y? Therefore, we wonder if we have not been depending too much on our imagination; our imaginative reconstructions of say Henry VIII, Oliver Cromwell, Robespierre, Frontenac, William Lyon Mackenzie, or William Lyon Mackenzie King. Instead of saying when we find these people doing X we should think less about them as particular people and more about the Y (environmental situation) which in a sense operates them. That is, we should fix our attention on the general situation in which they find themselves which causes them to think and act as they do.

In other words, for a century and more historians and others have been spending a little less time on the leading ladies and gentlemen of the stage and a little more on the ever-moving stage and scenery, and on the vast nameless group of minor actors and stand-ins without which the stars simply would not shine or at least would shine differently.

The trend began perhaps not with historians at all but with others who were engaged in activities that attracted historians and helped them to see rather more and to think rather differently about the past. For example, in the early half of the nineteenth century England was wrestling with a problem of national relief for the destitute and unemployed which had taken on an entirely new shape, new to her and new in the history of the western world. It was occasioned by the very rapid progress and organization resulting from the introduction of heavy machines and of new forms of power into industry. One of the great civil servants who was concerned with this problem was a rather terrifyingly efficient, energetic and indeed opinionated man called Edwin Chadwick. Chadwick found that pauperism, which he wished to limit because it was very expensive and a burden on the economy, was very frequently connected with sickness on the part of the breadwinner of the family. This might well, of course, be due to insufficient food. Yet, although there was at this time no knowledge of germs, it was well known that diseases were contagious and Chadwick turned his attention to that. The authorities were led into a collection of statistics on the incidence of death in different parts of the country, urban and rural, and among people of different incomes. They found that in a predominantly rural area the well-to-do could expect to live to the age of 52; the poor to the age of 38. In Manchester, a rapidly developing, unplanned , insanitary cotton town, the corresponding ages were 38 for the well-to-do and 17 for the poor. One result, although a rather delayed one, of these illuminating statistics was the introduction of such health and housing measures as have made, until the new age of pollution has come upon us, urban areas often more healthy than rural, and perhaps (in the areas of over-affluence) the rich more vulnerable to sickness than the "poor".

For my purpose the importance of this is that these statistics, once they were discovered, gave the historians solid facts where before there had been only rough estimates and guesswork. Not only did these statistics confirm the impression that urbanization called for a somewhat higher standard of living and much better sanitary precautions than were necessary in the country to maintain an equivalent standard of health. They also going in quite the other direction corrected in part a misapprehension which was widespread. It had been believed (and I may say it is still repeated in countless textbooks) that children in general suffered in health from the unhealthy conditions in the factories where they went to work at an early age. This no doubt was true in some instances. However, the investigation found (a) a sharp drop in mortality after the employment age in many cases — a fact which may not be surprising, infants being more vulnerable than older children — but also (b) in some cases fewer deaths occurred among factory children than among children of the same age living in the same areas but belonging to the middle classes and remaining in their own homes. In other words, the factories apparently could be healthier and more sanitary, in fact better places for the growing child than his own home even if his home was not a paradise. I may say that I have not yet found the school text which has caught up with this very important piece of what I might call quantitative history although it has been available now for about 130 years. This is not because popular historians did not honestly deal with such facts as they had before them, but they were not looking for their facts in all possible places. For a very long time the historian was full of admiration for the reformer who wished to improve the lot of children getting them out of the factories and into schools. They were therefore concerned with the lives and with the somewhat selective statements of those concerned with limiting or ending the evil of excessive child labour. It was natural that these people did not dwell on or perhaps were not aware of the curious and interesting revelations of the statistics hidden in government bluebooks. Their impressions of the evils of child labour were generally right. What they did not realize was that child labour was not new — factories did not create it, and *occasionally* might mitigate the evil.

One of the increasingly important trends of this century is to look for these apparently lesser but collectively immensely important facts which together, creating as they do our general material environment, necessarily affect our tastes, our thoughts, our ambitions and even our moral and political convictions. In this examination of what I might call "facts in the mass" historians have found much to correct old assumptions even though these may seem to have rested on adequate evidence ....[20]

CHRIST THE CENTRE OF HISTORY

To the Christian this must be true. If the story of man on this earth has any meaning at all, it is the meaning given to it when God visited in a new way the world which He had created and the men made in His image; when He became not just a man, but a man for all men, and so created the community of forgiveness living always in Christ through the Holy Spirit. To become a Christian means to have seen this — and to be unable to forget it.

On the other hand, to the average sound historian the statement, if not untrue, is completely unproven, and as a dogma, must be repudiated out of hand. As stated, in his historical work the historian cannot entertain it for a moment.

Here then is a contradiction, apparently, that needs examination and, perhaps, resolution.

The problem did not much trouble the average man for many centuries, not, indeed, until modern times, about the eighteenth century when the modern study of history like so many other modern studies was coming into its own. Then the rationalists (although in no hostile fashion) challenged the Christian view. "You say," they stated in effect, "that your faith, your hope, your true life hang on the supposed fact of a Galilean who lived and died nearly two thousand years ago. This cannot be. This cannot make any change in you. An 'ugly broad ditch of history' lies in between. Your faith if sound must be nourished by an immediate experience, by something that happens to you in the here and now." They were, indeed, insisting on what I suppose we would call today an existential experience.

Obviously what they said was true, and Christians throughout the ages had recognized it, many without defining the problem. The "ugly broad ditch" is a reality. Many have suffered from it; it is with many not quite overcome.

> But, O dear Lord, we cry,
> That we thy face could see!
> Thy blessed face one moment's space,
> Then might we follow thee!

(F.T. Palgrave q. G.S. Hendry: *The Gospel of the Incarnation*, p. 149)

The importance of immediacy, of a direct and personal contact, was never absent. Paul told the Christians that Christ must be born *in them*; a well-known Christian hymn offers the same prayer; one source of the Protestant Reformation was the sense of insufficient immediate contact.

But the increasing study of history in modern times, and man's increasing sense of the vast flow of events of which he seemed to be the end product, constituted a real, if subtle barrier. Something like a theory of evolution current among historians before Darwin enthroned it over the biologists seemed to play down the importance, let alone the uniqueness of the death of an unimportant person in an unimportant place so long ago.

The Christian naturally and inevitably responds by casting aside the convention of history. This convention is our concept of time, pictured as a stream within which — constantly moving — human events work themselves out. Time, in the view of the Christian, is a mere convention. Eternity is the reality. Charles Williams [said] think, not of a stream, but of a circle, of a spiral if you like, but with Christ and His great acts, and His continuing action in the midst. He, in His work, is then always contemporary; He must become immediate to everyone, and He may; there is no "ugly broad ditch." Through the Holy Spirit He continues real and (in a sense) incarnate in the community of forgiveness, the community of the forgiven, and the forgiving, which is the Church.

This, I suggest, is something like the Christian view seen in the light of eternity. It is not and cannot be the view of the historical scholar *as a historical scholar*. History as a discipline is, by definition, a secular study. It is not anti-Christian or anti-religious, or anti-anything. It is *secular* (not eternal) in the primary sense of the word. It is a study *in time* of the *things of time* considered in *the light of reason*. (The historian does not say that reason is the only lamp; he says that, for him, it is the only legitimate means of illumination.)

The historian bases his work on certain conventions and methods which must be clearly understood if one is to appreciate his place in the task of knowing and understanding.

a. He accepts the convention of the flow of events in time. This does not mean that he is not concerned with forces that may delay, accelerate, disturb this flow. He is; he is always coming up with new theories. In recent times he is often, I must add, hovering on the edge of theology. But theology is not really his job. He cannot within his discipline throw off the impersonal domination of the flow of time.

b. He also goes on the assumption that some rational deductions about cause and effect may be made. That is, he is not concerned only with describing what he sees but with establishing some clear rational chain of cause and effect. He is hampered because many of the facts which might help him explain are gone beyond recall. He can't call back the witnesses; but he accepts the convention that if he could he would find a rational explanation for many more. His job ends where rational explanations end.

c. This brings me to the third convention: he must tell his story on the basis of precise evidence such as would be accepted in a court of law. He reconstructs the crime, and he may use all kinds of devices, but they must rest on and be consistent with his evidence. I don't say he never lets his imagination, passions and prejudices run away with him. So do many lawyers. It is for the judge to restrain them. The historian's judges are the public and — much more to be feared — his fellow historians.

On these bases the historian constructs a story of human relations, including the story of Christ and the Christian Church. Here they play an important place in the western and even in world history, but one cannot say that in the vast sweep of all human history viewed as the historian must view it they automatically take a central place.

One might ask, then, is history a pursuit for a Christian, compelled to ignore a truth that he knows; to treat matters, he must feel, in an artificial and affected fashion? The answer is, yes. Very often the only way to get the best understanding of a matter is to set aside temporarily our deepest convictions and let our reason operate on the surface of affairs. A well-known Christian historian argues that this is what the Christian should do if he is to understand adequately not only the world, but the Christian church. A possible analogy is that of the judge confronted with a man accused of some grave crime, a man whom he knows absolutely to be incapable of such a thing. He cannot and he should not ignore the evidence, but, on the contrary follow with the closest attention in order that he may understand completely the complex situation and (if he can) make it clear in his summing-up, to the jury. His belief in his friend's innocence is no greater at the end, but his knowledge and understanding, and his power to help not only him, but other wrongly accused people may be greatly enlarged.

So we may learn God's ways better by seeking, and honestly seeking, a rational and secular explanation as far as it will go; and also by not fearing apparent contradictions even though there may be no immediate prospect of resolving them. And, at the same time, we must bear in mind that not everything which we have happily associated with Christian belief is necessarily essential to that belief. There are such things as lazy Christians. God gave us our reason and set us in time (as well as in eternity) to worship Him; and that means not just acknowledging His ways but understanding them as far as we can.[21]

Plate 1.   Hilda, centre, at age 15, with her brother Allan and her sister Kate.

Plate 2.   The Neatby family on board the *Victoria* en route from England to Canada in 1906. In the centre are Mr. & Mrs. Neatby and in front of them is Hilda, 2 years old.

Plate 3. The Neatby homestead in 1916, located some miles west of the present Watrous, Saskatchewan. Mrs. Neatby stands in the centre, with Hilda's sister Margery to the left and her brother Kenneth to the right. The white house in the background was the family's second home. The shack to the right housed the Neatbys when they first arrived at the homestead.

Plate 4. Hilda Neatby, aged 21, in 1925.

Plate 5. This letter, dated January 22, 1933 and addressed to Kate, was written when Hilda was a doctoral student at the University of Minnesota. In it she discusses her application for the Royal Society fellowship.

Nos Universitatis Saskatchewanensis Cancellarius, Praeses, Artium Facultatis Decanus et Senatus Registrarius hoc Scripto testatum volumus

Hildam Marionam Neatby

Baccalaureum in Artibus Liberalibus rite renuntiatum esse, cunctaque consecutam esse Privilegia, Immunitates, Jura, quae hic aut usquam alibi Bonarum Artium Baccalaureis concedi solent. Cujus Rei quo major esset fides, Nos Sigillo communi appenso Chirographa apposuimus. Saskatoniae Anno Salutis Humanae millesimo nonagentesimo vicesimo quarto mensis Maii die secundo

Cancellarius
Praeses
Decanus
Registrarius

Plate 6. In 1924 Hilda graduated with a B.A. Honours Degree in History from the University of Saskatchewan.

Plate 7. After receiving her Ph.D. in 1934, Hilda taught history and French at Regina College for 12 years. This photograph of the college was taken in the mid-1930's.

Plate 8. The University of Saskatchewan campus in 1928. Hilda spent the years 1920–1924 at the university as a student and returned in 1946 as a professor in the History Department.

Plate 9. The Massey Commission ca. 1950. From left to right, Norman MacKenzie, Vincent Massey, Hilda Neatby, and Georges-Henri Lévesque, O.P. Missing from the picture is the fifth member, Arthur Surveyer.

Plate 10. Hilda with her nephew, historian Blair Neatby.

Plate 11. In 1967 Hilda was made a member of the Order of Canada. She is seen here posing with Roland Michener, Governor General of Canada, and Walter P. Thompson, President of the University of Saskatchewan from 1949–1959.

PART THREE

Hilda On ....

The purpose of this chapter is to show Hilda as a writer of Canadian, especially late eighteenth century Quebec, history. It can not be considered in isolation from Chapter 8 which showed her development as a historian both in style and theory. Much of the material in the first was Canadian. Development of theme will be noted in this chapter.

The first selection, "National History," was part of the report of the Massey Commission and was published in 1951. In this Hilda provides a survey of Canadian historiography and sums up the situation of the beginning of the 1950's by regretting the lack of biographies written by historians of Canada and the lack of work in non-Canadian history by Canadians — the very things that would come in the second half of the twentieth century. She also decried the lack of research funds that had so limited the work of her generation. She had a hand , on the national level, in providing research money. In Saskatchewan she concentrated on hiring historians of Europe. In her own work she provided a number of short biographical studies. One other failing of historians — uninteresting writing style — that she noted gently in her 1951 report she expressed more tellingly to Roger Graham in 1955 in a letter which is reprinted in Chapter 8.

To understand Hilda's development one should compare the second and third selections, exerpts from her first article, "The Political Career of Adam Mabane," published in 1935, and "Pierre Guy: A Montreal Merchant of the Eighteenth Century," written thirty-three years later. The first was much more anglophile, much less tolerant, much more traditional in approach. Or compare the conclusion of the Mabane article with its talk of nationalism and toryism within a constitutional framework with that of the fourth selection, "Racism in the Old Province of Quebec" from 1972 which speaks of "social-political conflict," "class domination" and "sense of community." The cynic might say that Hilda had picked up a few words but in reality had only moved from saying that it was an Englishman (or rather a Scot) who had given the French Canadians their start, to saying that some of the French Canadians shared the qualities of the English. There is some truth in the statement, in so far as Hilda's point of reference and preference remained nineteenth-century Anglo-Canadian. But, as can be seen by reading the other selections in this chapter and in Chapters 5 and 8, she continued to develop a fuller appreciation of French Canada.

In the years between Mabane and Pierre Guy, Hilda first worked at western Canadian history. Outside of book reviews, her only "western" article was "The Medical Profession in the North-West Territories" published in 1949.[1] Western Canadian historical writing might have been quite different if she had stayed with it, but when she had an opportunity to return to Quebec history she did so very happily, with the results that can be seen in the rest of this chapter.

"Servitude de l'Eglise Catholique: a Reconsideration,"[2] not reprinted because of space restrictions, shows Hilda at her debating best and with a more nuanced view of late eighteenth-century Quebec, a view that was uniquely hers, neither pro nor anti Québécois, a bit anglophile but also francophile — a view that won her at least grudging respect. This paper also illustrates Hilda's interest in the 1960's in the church in Quebec which she hoped would culminate in a biography of Bishop Briand, but which got no further than her presidential address to the Canadian Historical Association.[3]

The fourth selection, "Racism in the Old Province of Quebec" of 1972 illustrates Hilda's fully developed ideas about what was important in Quebec in the second half of the eighteenth century — the development of cultural and political nationalism out of religious conviction, political experience, economic development, and class consciousness. The sub-themes of survival and multifaceted outside influence, especially American, were partially formed by the times and political conditions within Canada when the essay was written. But like the dominant themes, they came also from Hilda's long years of study, thinking and maturing. Concern for American influence on Canada was a consistent sub-theme in all of Hilda's writing. The use of "survival" as a defining concept of Canada was not original with Hilda but she used it from 1954 onwards. In fact, it could be argued that much of her work in the last twenty years of her life, whether the subject was education, Canada, Christianity, or civilization, consciously or unconsciously, had the survival concept as a theme.[4]

The final selection, Hilda's conclusion to *The Quebec Act: Protest and Policy,* a collection of essays she edited in 1972, shows Hilda at the height of her powers both as a Canadian historian and as a reflecter on history.

NATIONAL HISTORY

An intelligent awareness of the past is generally considered to be a sign of maturity in an individual or a community; but the Canadian people, although showing unmistakable signs of political maturity, still regard their history with indifference tempered by distaste. Eminent authorities who are not historians have suggested that the situation might be remedied by "the sociological approach"; they deplore "the dry-as-dust constitutional history," and ask that history be written for "the common reader" — a rather uncommon individual. Such vague preachments from those whose presumed competence lies in fields remote from history are part of the penalty which Canadian historians must pay for their failure to produce works sufficiently varied to appeal to the many different types of readers who would certainly be interested in history, even in Canadian history, if they had the opportunity.

There is a general impression abroad that academic historians are a group apart, whose excessively dry books are read by reviewers and by their colleagues but by very few others. Although there is enough truth in this view to account for the low estate of Canadian history, it ignores the essential fact that these shadowy academic figures are, or should be, the historian's historians. They are the wholesalers from whom, for the most part, the popular and textbook historians procure the wares which they retail to the public. On the quality of their work and on their ability to inspire good popularizations must depend the general level of production and consumption in Canadian history.

It is not possible to explain or evaluate this fundamental academic work without touching briefly on the nature of Canada's past, and the problems that it has offered to all historians. Central Canada, the nucleus of the later Dominion, was, like the newly formed United States, an eighteenth-century by-product of an imperial struggle which covered the continent and the world. For the United States the problems of its own origin, nature and destiny could be expressed with revolutionary simplicity. The federated states were a group of communities born of a desire for freedom, now in maturity giving full expression to that desire, and demonstrating the will and the power to people a continent in the name of liberty and independence. In spite of minor disagreements and complications this single simple legend was there for historians to exploit to the full. It served a great purpose as a unifying national force. It probably still serves that purpose to a considerable extent in the popular mind, although serious historians have long been engaged on the work of demolition. What its cost has been in terms of isolation from the rest of the Anglo-Saxon world must be left to the sociologists to calculate.

Canada, fortunately or otherwise, has no such legend — no single love or hate. The nucleus was the French colony of the St. Lawrence, founded and for long maintained by the joint efforts of the missionary and the fur trader. In 1763, this colony was shorn at one stroke of leaders and of hinterland. The various groups which for the next century and more penetrated into or gathered around this nucleus had little sympathy with or understanding of it or of one another. They had no common loyalty at home and no common love or hate abroad, athough different sections for different reasons did possess a dislike or fear of the United States which one Canadian historian has compared with the parallel American dislike of Great Britain. Moreover, for well over a century after 1760, Canadians certainly were on no more common ground when looking forward to their destiny than when looking backward at their past. An able and distinguished statesman of the later nineteenth century not only believed in but publicly advocated the three very different destinies of annexation, independence and imperial federation one after the other in little over three decades. While the United States marched proudly on in the train of what was assumed to be manifest destiny, Canada, with no such guiding ray from the historian's Providence, had gropingly and cautiously to feel her way.

It should, therefore, be no cause for surprise that Canadian historians too had to grope and fumble, for as one of their great English colleagues has pointed out, the historian himself is the product of history. For nearly a century, Canadian history has been accumulating in a fragmentary, local and sporadic fashion. Excellent work has been done by scholars in many fields, but a clear philosophic concept of the whole is still lacking, and the gulf between the academic historian and the general public has not been bridged.

It was not unnatural that the first great Canadian history should be the French work of F.X. Garneau who wrote in the 1840's the story of survival against the perils from the wilderness, the Indian, the New Englander and the English conqueror in a volume which is still a classic. To Garneau and to the school which he founded, Canadian history was indeed *une épopée des plus brillants exploits.* This approach in its romantic aspects was taken up and developed by the genius of Francis Parkman who, although alien in sentiment to French-Canadian nationalism, was fully conscious of the epic qualities of the great struggle so much of which had taken place in his own land. Thus exploited in both languages, the heroic period of early Canadian history was opened in its romantic form to Canadians both French and English-speaking. The profound emotional and spiritual appeal, however, was for the French alone. English-speaking Canadians could and did admire Champlain, La Salle, Brébeuf and Talon for their characters and careers, but the true appeal of the epic in the nineteenth century was the racial and national appeal, the sense of being really a part of and belonging to the great deeds of the past. English-speaking Canadians, especially the Protestant Canadians, had no sense of proprietorship even in the pious and moderate Champlain, much less in the devoted and single-minded Brébeuf. They might have developed their own rival heroes in the men of the Hudson's Bay Company and other explorers of the West; but they did not, for these were even more alien to the historic past of Ontario and the Maritimes than were the Frenchmen of the St. Lawrence. They were, therefore, largely neglected until the westerner undertook his own history from a freshly sectional point of view.

The great interest of the Ontarian and the Maritime historian writing in and of the nineteenth century was the development of self-governing institutions. With the example of their nearest neighbour before them, and in keeping with the spirit of the great age of liberalism, it was quite natural that they should tend to adopt the familiar nineteenth-century theme of the struggle for freedom against tyranny. But Canadians unlike their superlative neighbour are condemned to the middle way. Apart from the fact that British tyranny in Canada had been of a very moderate kind, by the end of the century English-speaking Canada was coming strongly under the influence of the current sentiment of imperialism, and was most anxious to induce the rather hesitant French-speaking section to cooperate. Therefore the English-speaking Canadian historian in search of a patriotic pattern found himself condemned to a gentle rhythm of pros and cons instead of a fine roll on the drums of liberty. The ultimate decision to give Lount and Matthews, executed for complicity in the Upper Canada rising of 1837, an honourable burial, but to inscribe on the memorial stone their names only with no account of or comment on their deeds, typifies the plight of the responsible historian. He was compelled to write of relatively recent and stirring events in tones of studied moderation and compromise. He reflected, rightly and necessarily, the national policy of cautious empiricism; but such a safe and sensible policy does not produce the moving historical legend without which history will not capture the imagination of a people.

Yet much useful work was done. The beginning of the twentieth century saw the production in English of three great series which represented admirably the patient and laborious but still superficial and somewhat parochial investigations accomplished so far in the Canadian historical field by writers in both languages. These series mark the close of the semi-literary period in serious Canadian historiography. They were on the whole competent and careful, but they did not possess either the sound, meticulous, historical scholarship of a later day, or the strong imaginative literary appeal that at the cost of many false impressions may rouse a people to an awareness of itself. Yet they did show a dawning sense on the part of the historian of Canada's emergence from colonialism into a national entity. Moreover, the increasing attention to the whole Canadian community from its aboriginal beginnings to its modern development not only in political affairs but in economics, arts and letters represented an intellectual development and emancipation which paralleled constitutional growth.

During the last three or four decades the writing of history has been increasingly centred in universities and therefore "professionalized." Much more work has been produced and its extent is constantly growing. In every period and in every field of interest are being written short articles or longer monographs upon which more general histories can be based; without these no authoritative work is possible. The excellent constitutional investigations of the twenties in which Canadian historians profited much from the work of English and American colleagues in the same field have been followed during the last twenty years by important studies in economic history. These studies, carried on in Canada by Canadian historians, give a fresh and illuminating perspective on political and sectional wrangles and have been hailed as a notable achievement in North American historiography. Canadian history has also profited much from the elaborate and detailed investigations represented in the series of volumes on Canadian-American relations financed by an American foundation. Finally, there is a growing group of works on the west which, although occasionally somewhat charged with emotion, does help to give a new view not only of western but of all Canadian history. In general, it may be said that the body of Canadian history has been multiplied many times in the last few decades; and that level of scholarship has been much raised.

There are, however, certain grave deficiencies in Canadian historical writing. First, and perhaps most serious, is the almost complete lack of that class of historical literature which has a nearly universal appeal, the historical biography. From the viewpoint of a general popular understanding there could hardly be a more serious deficiency, for the average intelligent reader rightly feels that he can best learn his history through the men who helped to make it. Canadians, however, cannot do so. Most biographies of great Canadians combine a lengthy and often competent history of the age with an uncritical eulogy of the subject who is cast for the hero's part. Worst of all, the hero remains remote. We know what he said in public on the great issues of the day; we get the stock anecdotes always attached to popular figures; but we never really know him as a person. There is the occasional feverish reaction against the polite official biography as in the highly coloured works of W.T.R. Preston. The sad state of Canadian biography is emphasized by the fact that even these violent attacks failed to produce serious critical biographies of his principal victims, Lord Strathcona and Sir John A. Macdonald. The best Canadian biographies are probably those which follow most faithfully the Victorian tradition of lengthy and numerous citations from speeches and letters. This tradition which disappeared elsewhere in the debunking era of the twenties still survives in Canada with all its vices and virtues

For the poverty of Canadian historical biography the historian cannot be blamed entirely. There is reason for suspecting that some of our most successful Canadian statesmen have been very dull people; or that they or their families, by destroying or suppressing all evidence to the contrary, have wished them to appear so. Carleton, an early example, instructed his wife to destroy all his private papers at his death, and she, in a most regrettable demonstration of wifely obedience, has left us with no more than glimpses behind a formal facade of a curious and complex personality. Other equally interesting Canadian statesmen have succeeded in shrouding themselves in obscurity so complete as to defy the efforts of their would-be biographers.

Historians, however, cannot plead for their fault mere lack of material. The historical biography requires the combination of historical scholarship with literary skill and philosophic insight. It is probably the most difficult thing to do really well; the Canadian failure must be attributed to lack of skill and maturity on the part of historians as well as to dearth of material.

Another regrettable lack in Canadian historiography is the absence of works by Canadian historians in other than Canadian fields. One or two important exceptions only serve to emphasize the general provincialism which is a sign of our relative poverty and immaturity. The Institutes of Mediaeval Studies in Montreal and Toronto promise to broaden the general field of activities and to invite research in matters perhaps too much neglected in this age and on this continent.

The principal general popular works on Canadian history also come, as a rule, from professional Canadian historians. Some half dozen good ones have been published during the past ten years. During the previous twenty only two such histories appeared, one of them by an American and both written mainly with a view to school or college use. The more recent works, all by Canadians, although perhaps written partly for the college market, are also addressed to the general reader who wants to know and understand Canada and Canadians in relation to their history. With very wide differences in style, interpretation and arrangement, these volumes achieve on the whole a high level of excellence. The encouraging feature of this crop of the 1940's is not only its general excellence but the fact that after the appearance of five, a publisher in 1949 had the courage to put out a sixth, and in 1950 there have appeared two more. There are appearing also a number of historical novels and some stories for children. Most of the former, like the latter, exploit the exotic themes in our history. The historical novel of character is lacking, as might be expected in a country incapable of producing good historical biographies.

Good text book material for primary and secondary schools is wanting. Competent historians have written suitable texts; and there has been a good deal of writing down by writers of less repute. Some of this is very good, especially on provincial and local levels, but some is very bad. There is still a great field for good and able popularization on the elementary levels. There is a very general demand at the moment for one text book for all Canadian schools. That request is often, though not always, made by those who regard a history text book as a collection of vitamin pills requiring only to be administered at the right time and in the right quantity. At the present stage of our history and our historiography, a text that would suit the two cultural groups and the four great geographic and historic sections of Canada would be a pale and featureless mass of facts. If the time comes when we can produce a really good and living story which fulfils both the local and general needs of all schools in our vast and varied country, the need for one text rather than ten will be gone. No historian should ever assume a task which compels him to ignore any facts; and no teacher should ignore the fact that the best way to make history live for a child is to present it to him as an extention back into time of his own society.

An essential factor in historiography as in every form of literature is the scholarly review. In Canada, the *Bulletin des Recherches Historiques* and the *Canadian Historical Review* have for many years filled a role of increasing importance. The latter attempts to review all historical works relating to Canada in either language, and to give some account of all activities tending to encourage an interest in and understanding of Canadian history. The articles are nearly all in English and by English-speaking historians. Most of them relate to the period following 1760. Hitherto, the *Canadian Historical Review* has confined itself almost exclusively to Canadian material. It is proposed, in future, to accept articles in other fields of history.

The importance of the scholarly review in giving the young writer an opportunity to publish and in setting standards of achievement is very great. The *Canadian Historical Review* has performed an admirable service in stimulating scholarly work, in helping to open new fields and in co-ordinating research work done in university departments. That much of the material makes pretty dull reading may perhaps be blamed partly on an age that has convinced itself that the artist's sense of form is a menace to "scientific truth," and partly on other causes which must now be considered.

It is probably fair to say that for a young country only recently aware of its own increasing maturity among the nations of the world, the work done so far in Canadian history is of a high order, and is increasing in quantity and variety. For this Canadians must acknowledge their debt to the French group among their number who so early became aware of their history, and to distinguished British and American scholars, who by their work in Canadian history and related fields have helped set high standards which Canadians have maintained and developed. Yet, from the viewpoint of historical production alone, there are many discouraging factors to be faced, and these serve amply to correct undue complacency.

First, Canadian historians, few in number as they are, are divided into two groups by language and tradition. Between many individuals there is cordiality and co-operation, but the groups remain two. Practically all French-speaking historians are bilingual. Most English-speaking historians read French as a matter of course, but probably only a few could discuss their work freely in French with a French-speaking colleague. With very few exceptions, English-speaking historians have confined themselves to the period after 1760; French-speaking, to that before, or to their own communities. The exceptions to this rule lie mainly in semi-popular or in specialized works. There is a boundary which is not freely crossed by those engaged in original research. The maintenance of such a dividing line is a serious loss in a group already small and scattered in relation to the tremendous tasks before it. The division automatically operates to delay the development of any one general interpretation of Canadian history, inevitably bound to be a matter of dispute among the political, cultural, sociological and economic interpreters. This lack of a common philosophy is, of course, one conclusive answer to the demand for one text book, for contrary to the popular impression it is the common philosophy that must produce the common text book rather than the reverse process. Any standardized philosophy or interpretation must of course preclude real and live historical investigations, but some general ground of agreement and understanding would stimulate such investigation and help to create a real school of Canadian history. Today we have no school, only two groups each one divided somewhat within itself.

Moreover, at the moment, Canadian historians are not only divided but rather dispirited, being like the apostle beset on every side. Nearly all those who write history teach it. Those who teach it in universities find themselves departmentalized into the College of Arts, a despised group at the best, in which they may choose between attaching themselves to the humanities where at least they dwell with their peers in the lowest place or being accepted as the Cinderella of the social sciences. Whichever they choose they are likely to learn that they occupy a small and shrinking place in a changing world, where the modern scientist freely admits his debt to the anthropologist but rarely to the historian.

Most historians therefore find themselves cast in the role of artists whose art has gone out of fashion, and like the artist they must add poverty to the list of their woes. The historian's work is not obviously useful, and the history professor seldom gets the incidental employment which comes as a financial relief to his colleagues in other departments. This would be an advantage in leaving him freer for original work except for the fact that, unlike his scientific colleagues, he can seldom get grants for travelling, for research, or for research facilities. Poverty has few terrors for energetic enthusiasts, but poverty without any compensation in the way of opportunity for rewarding work, and with no hope of gaining any recognition for achievement, usually repels active and vigorous minds. It is probably doing so in the historical field. There are too many historical scholars unable to give a rational explanation or defence of the field of their endeavours. This is a dangerous symptom. Nothing comes of it, as King Lear said. This negative attitude is a symptom and it may well prove to be a cause of decay in Canadian historiography.

Canadians do not in general resort directly to the professional historian as the source of their historical convictions. They are influenced to a considerable extent by popular books, and in some measure by our scanty historical museums and our struggling historical societies. All these, however, depend on the universal foundation of what may be called involuntary absorptions through the efforts of these nationwide agencies, the school, the radio, and the film.

No final judgement can be made on the value of the historical contribution given by the schools, but some generalizations may be attempted. First, all provinces recognize the importance of history which holds a large place both in public and high school programmes. A study of these programmes does, however, reveal an embarrassment rather creditable to the school authorities who realize the importance not only of giving some general historical notions to all those children who leave school at thirteen or fourteen, but of including in their programmes, in addition to Canadian history, British, American and European history. One is forced to the conclusion that such a dispersal of energies must result in rather vague and cloudy notions in the minds of most pupils.

Second, in a well-intentioned attempt to bring history alive and to relate it to the rest of life, several of the provinces, particularly in the west, have gone in for a topical rather than a chronological approach and have merged history more or less completely in an omnibus subject called "social studies." The result is that the student almost literally loses all sense of time and very nearly all sense of place also. The unhappy combination of history and "civics" conveys him with more speed than accuracy from King John and Magna Carta in England to Baldwin,

Lafontaine, Howe and Responsible Government in British North America. This is supposed to teach him the truth about democracy; but the truth, if there is any, often rests on such a foundation of inaccuracies and distortions as to lead the historian to inquire whether even such an end justifies such means. Students emerging from the treatment can hardly be blamed for showing, as they have done in the past, a dislike for all history and particularly for Canadian history. Their ignorance is equal to their dislike. Groups of students in one junior college year after year, asked to name any well-known figure of the seventeenth century, after deep thought, would summon up Queen Elizabeth; a few might think of Cromwell; no one ever mentioned Louis XIV, Champlain, Frontenac, La Salle or any other well-known Canadian figure.

Nevertheless in the universities recently there has been a renewed interest in history, particularly in Canadian history. History departments in general feel that the prejudice against Canadian history, which used to be marked, is dying away. This change may perhaps be attributed partly to an increased consciousness of history, especially of national history, during and since the war; and partly to the group of good college and high school manuals mentioned above. More of these manuals on a more elementary level might do much to counteract the unfortunate tendencies in school curricula. However, in spite of encouraging signs of increasing interest, the universities are not turning out enough graduates in history to staff high schools, even with persons passably well qualified to teach the subject. Most universities attempt to give some graduate work in history, but in nearly all, staff, library and documentary materials are inadequate. Advanced graduate work may be done in a few institutions but most Canadian historians receive their training in the graduate schools of the United States, very often from expatriated Canadian professors.

There is no need to stress the possibilities of the radio for the popular historical "talk." They are only limited by what the public will take. Talks on historical and related subjects are a regular part of the C.B.C. programme, and during the last few years at least such talks have been given on Sundays. It may be assumed, therefore, that they have been found acceptable by a fairly wide audience. An examination of the talks themselves suggests, however, that there might be a more consistent effort to give what could be called "good" history, and to call more freely on the aid of the serious historians.

It must be admitted immediately that the professional historian is unlikely to have either the time or the capacity for the kind of popularization attempted. Such series as *Place Names, They Came to Canada, If You Had Lived Then,* and to a certain extent *Summer Fallow,* have drawn very largely on local colour, on historical anecdotes about well-known people, and on diaries of explorers and others. The style may be that of a chatty narrator, the incident may be thrown into semi-fictional story form, or it may be dramatized. Many people, it is true, will not listen to historical lecturers, but will have their interest sufficiently aroused by light programmes with some historical flavour to be willing to read serious history. Most professional historians would readily admit that this type of work may be very useful, and may be better done by the journalist or popular speaker than by themselves. It is a fact that C.B.C. script writers have shown very creditable energy and enterprise in their exploitation of colourful and relatively unfamiliar material. On the other hand, it must be emphasized that indiscriminate plucking from the quaint and the picturesque will not, of itself, teach the Canadian people anything of their history, or give them any sense of oneness with each other or with their past. Popular talks should be so grouped as to give some idea of continuity; they should at least suggest some general ideas on the growth of the Canadian community; and where local colour is used it should be authentic to the last detail. A strong and reliable historical foundation need not injure but may greatly enhance the popular appeal of the human interest material that overlays it.

To produce acceptable programmes of this kind may be difficult but is surely not impossible. Defects in historical broadcasts could easily be remedied without deserting either the popular appeal or even the popular speaker. Expert advice might be sought. Both in Montreal and Toronto, the centres where most of these talks originate, there are capable historians in complete sympathy with the need for popularization who could surely be induced not only to offer general advice when programmes are being planned but to cast an eye over the finished scripts in order to eliminate errors or faults of interpretation which might escape the notice of the amateur.

As a medium for the popularization of history the film is even more important and may be more dangerous than radio. Canadian history has not been entirely neglected by makers of commercial films. Hollywood had done its worst, and the Canadian Mountie has taken his place in popular myth with Mary of Scotland and Marie-Antoinette. The National Film Board has produced some historical films, or rather films on contemporary problems with an historical background, and more are contemplated. Here, as with C.B.C. talks, much care is needed. Without discounting the importance of accuracy, the film man may distrust the historical expert because of a conviction that he will not understand or appreciate the problem of interesting the public. The danger of bad and inaccurate history from the film is, however, far greater than from the radio. Information from the film given mainly through pictures may be far more subtly and powerfully misleading than anything in a radio talk.

There is no doubt of the honesty and sincerity of most of the individuals engaged on these historical films; but it would be unfortunate if, in their preoccupation with technical matters or with dramatic effect, they should come unconsciously to share the attitude of the Hollywood producer who wished his Sir Galahad to pose in a toga. To the protests of his expert he merely replied, "But it's all history, isn't it?" If our national educational bodies were to treat history as a pleasant and adjustable backdrop for what should be said about the present,

Canadian history could make little real contribution to the variety and richness of Canadian life.

It is difficult and dangerous to generalize in a field where very little exact information is available. It seems fair, however, to say that from the intellectual and philosophic viewpoint many Canadians are indifferent to any history, including and perhaps especially their own. A good deal of popular interest does go into local history; but here much energy and enthusiasm is lost because of the difficulty of bringing little groups scattered over the country to any consciousness of their common interest; and because of the added difficulty of giving coherence and continuity to those amateur efforts by the co-operation of the professional historian. The professional historian, operating almost exclusively within university walls where he is overworked and underpraised, has produced a sound and creditable, if not distinguished volume of work, but he has produced it too exclusively for an academic public. He has not reached or touched the Canadian people. Some of the reasons for this may be found in the handicaps already mentioned. The most important one has hardly been touched. With a few delightful and distinguished exceptions Canadian historians are extraordinarily dull writers. As has been suggested, they responded early in the century to the extreme doctrines of the pseudo-scientific school which in the interests of accuracy regards style with suspicion and imagination with horror. These prejudices are now happily passing, but the literary tradition is hard to revive, especially as so many of our historians are formed in universities, Canadian or American, where English is not important except in "English" classes.

The general reader then is not likely to find scholarly works on Canadian history inviting or even digestible. And our popular agencies, the school, the radio, and the film, in spite of evidence of enthusiasm and goodwill, do not fill the gap between the historian and his public. Too often they are convinced that good history must be dull and unprofitable, and they act accordingly, distorting the past for purposes of propaganda or entertainment.

The conclusion then must be that we have as yet no national history, and no genuine national consciousness of the past. "Historical background" is popular, but is usually only a highly imaginative *décor* for productions on current problems. This immature contentment with living in the present and the future is partly the outcome of an age of scientific materialism. The true appeal of history is philosophic, moral and aesthetic; it is killed by purely scientific dissection. However, our problem in Canada is more than the general problem of the scientific age. It is, as we have seen, the special problem imposed by the fact that two races, two religions, and two cultures, led by a strange combination of circumstances, are trying to create one state out of some scattered fragments of fertile soil strung along the border of another state, wealthy, populous and expanding. The undertaking is barely out of the experimental stage. It is perhaps unreasonable at this juncture to reproach Canadians because they have not yet contrived to explain themselves to themselves. It might be more appropriate to recognize the good work and the excellent promise of the many who realize that no community can achieve maturity without a sane and intelligent awareness of its past.[5]

THE POLITICAL CAREER OF ADAM MABANE

In the course of Canadian history since 1763, two factors are recognized as of outstanding importance: the triangular connection of Canada with Britain and with the United States; and the relations between the two principal races within her borders. These two factors stand out clearly in the political struggles of Lower Canada following the granting of representative government in 1791. Of the two political parties which then formed along racial lines, the French inclined to seek inspiration from the example of the rising American democracy, while the English appealed to the sentiment of loyalty and the value of the British connection.

These facts of common knowledge take on fresh interest when seen in contrast to the preceding period of rule by council. It has been perhaps not sufficiently realized that political as well as racial strife began during the first period of British rule. Until 1791, however, it was the English party that was tainted with the principles of democracy, while the French party carried the loyal banner. The French party, moreover, was led and organized not by members of its own race, but by an English-speaking group, and particularly by the Scottish doctor Adam Mabane.

Few individuals have enjoyed the personal power and prestige that belonged to Mabane for the period during which he dominated the political scene in the colony. He came to Canada in 1760 as a surgeon's mate in Amherst's army. A medical student at the University of Edinburgh, he had quitted his studies and enlisted in the army for reasons best known to himself. Life in the non-commissioned ranks of an army, many of whose soldiers were drawn from the scum of the population, and were controlled by a cruel and degrading discipline, cannot have been pleasant to a young man of energy and spirit. It was Mabane's good fortune that he came to Canada as a time when men such as he could carve out their own careers.

When Mabane arrived in Canada the triple set of relationships referred to above was already appearing. American merchants arrived on the heels of the British army, eager to secure the control of the rich fur-trade on which rested the whole commercial life of the colony. It is necessary here to do no more than mention the controversy which immediately arose over the form of the governmental and legal system to be set up in this new British possession. The French Canadians instinctively clung to the system to which they were accustomed, and acted on the theory — not entirely unfounded — that their interests would certainly be sacrificed in any American-made system of government. Without discussing the tangled legal and constitutional problems connected with the Proclamation of 1763, it may be said that the practical decision rested for the time being with Governor Murray. He refused to summon an elected assembly which, as the law then stood, would have represented the mercantile group only. In his council he tried to carry on the traditions of French paternalism, and although he was forced to adopt English civil law in the courts, he gave as much recognition to French-Canadian custom as he dared. From Murray's time may be dated the "French party" supported not only, or even chiefly, by the French Canadians, but rather by the military officers who in the first years had been responsible for the administration of the government, and by all whose energetic loyalty to Britain led them to regard with suspicion the turbulent and anti-French merchants from the Thirteen Colonies.

While these political groups were forming, Adam Mabane was making rapid advancement both in his private and public career. His regiment being sent to Quebec, he immediately began to profit by his peace-time leisure to work up a private medical practice in the city. Either his skill or his personal qualities commended him to the authorities, for when the surgeon of the garrison left, Mabane received the appointment in his place. This office carried with it commissioned rank, and therefore a greatly improved social standing. Further promotion of a different nature soon followed. During the years of the military régime, Mabane had not been an indifferent spectator of provincial politics. His natural loyalty to General Murray, his sympathy for the conquered, and apparently helpless French Canadians, and perhaps also, a dislike for the American merchants, ambitious like himself, led him to lend his hearty support to the French party.

This fortunate political leaning won for Mabane public promotion remarkable for a man who had so recently entered the province in a humble position, and without money, friends, or influence. In 1764 he was not only given a seat on the newly-formed council, but was appointed judge in the provincial court of common pleas, which, owing to lack of funds and to the absence of trained lawyers, was manned by unpaid amateurs. Since this was the court to which the French chiefly resorted, Murray was determined to appoint to it men who knew their language and understood their wants. As Roman Catholics were excluded by the oaths of office, the choice was limited. However, in Mabane and in his two colleagues, John Fraser, a retired army officer educated in a Jesuit college at Douai, and the Huguenot merchant Mounier, Murray seemed to have found men suited to his purpose.

Mabane as a judge fitted admirably into the paternal system advocated by the French party. He was kind-hearted, hardworking, and thoroughly honest. He even took the pains to add to these qualifications some knowledge of law, for after his elevation to the bench he seems to have studied diligently such law books, French and English, as lay within his reach. At the same time, he had serious defects which gave the English party a fair target for the criticisms which they lavishly offered. He was arbitrary, impulsive, and inclined to place too much weight on the personal factor in making his judicial decisions. He read his law books, but if law, and what he considered "substantial justice" appeared to point in opposite directions, so much the worse for the law. Legal subtleties did not impress him. He was not the man to mistake for the substance what he regarded as merely the shadow. The professional lawyer might well look askance at such a man; not so the professional soldier. In Mabane, Murray found exactly the man he needed to carry on the civil government of Quebec according to his views....

The nature of Mabane's power and influence at this time is shown by the proceedings in the famous case of *Haldimand v. Cochrane*. This case arose out of the custom of raising specie in the colony for military purposes by selling to the merchants the much-needed bills of exchange on London. Since all merchants secured their supplies from London the system worked well. There was a constant demand for bills of exchange, and the great risk and expense of sending specie across the Atlantic in wartime was avoided.

Unfortunately, the system was wrecked by the sharp practices of the Honourable John Cochrane, the financial agent charged with selling bills of exchange for Harley and Drummond, the remitters for the government in London. Before Cochrane's time merchants had occasionally been supplied with bills of exchange on partial credit. There were sound financial reasons for this practice, but it was a dangerous one, and required much caution and honesty on the part of the agent. Cochrane had neither. For his own ends he extended such lavish credit to the merchants that some of them were carrying on the bulk of their business with government capital. Worse still, he hoodwinked Haldimand into extending the mantle of his authority as governor over these evil deeds. The result was that when the war drew to a close, and the artificial war-time prosperity threatened to collapse, the merchants, through Cochrane, owed a huge debt to the government. Haldimand's reputation as an efficient governor depended on the recovery of this debt.

In this difficulty he naturally turned to Mabane, who readily came to his aid, and insisted that the merchants must be sued, and the money recovered. It was not possible, however, formally to sue the merchants, since, legally, they owed the money not to the government, but to Cochrane, and Cochrane refused to sue. Therefore, either Mabane or his friend Williams, a lawyer, and the clerk of the council, suggested the use of the *saisie arrêt,* a French usage similar to the garnishee. In this way Haldimand could sue Cochrane, and at the same time, from the very commencement of the suit, could effect a provisional seizure of the goods of the merchants who were technically Cochrane's debtors.

Haldimand decided to adopt this course. The suit was begun in Quebec, with Mabane and two others sitting on the bench. The prosecution certainly strained the principles of law, both French and English. Only the chaotic state of Canadian law at that time could have made possible a case conducted as this one was. The defence challenged the legality of the proceedings at every step, but it was not surprising that Mabane and his sympathetic colleagues should uphold the legality of steps which the former himself had approved, if he had not actually suggested them. Realizing this, the defence challenged Mabane's right to sit on the case at all, on the ground that he had been consulted beforehand by the governor, one of the parties in the suit, and that he had given his opinion and advice on the prosecution. The challenge was presumably good in French law, but it was rejected by the judges on the ground that, although they administered French principles of law, they did so in virtue of English commissions which did not allow them to be challenged.

Naturally, the decision was given in Haldimand's favour, to the wrath and discomfiture of the merchants. Mabane felt that he had deserved well of his country, and so he had, in a way. Through his means, the government was able at least to reduce the amount of its losses from Cochrane's speculations. He had played the part of an energetic and honest administrator. At the same time he had completely demonstrated his unfitness for the position of chief justice. The case was a political one. It was the government and the French party against the merchants, for, directly or indirectly, every merchant in the province was involved. For Mabane to carry out as judge the doubtful legal principles which he had presented as councillor, indicated a domination of the bench by politics, which, even in those days, caused no small scandal.

The years 1783 and 1784 saw Mabane and the French party at the height of their power. Their successful skirmishes with the merchant party in the council only invigorated them with a sense of power and righteousness. However, the peace of 1783 brought the beginning of the end. It would no longer be so easy to secure the support of the British government in governing Canada as a French colony, and in suppressing as American innovations all demands for English laws and institutions. The year 1784 saw the departure of Haldimand for England. His place was filled temporarily by Lieutenant-Governor Hamilton, the friend of the merchant party. With Hamilton's co-operation, several objectionable ordinances were forced through the council in spite of all opposition. In the summer of 1785 the reforms were checked, for Hamilton was dismissed, but the relief was only temporary. The large number of American Loyalists pouring into the colony, convinced the British government that important constitutional changes must be made. In 1786 they sent out Carleton, now Lord Dorchester, to investigate conditions, and make recommendations. With him, as his special adviser and assistant, came to Mabane's anger and disgust, the new chief justice, William Smith, the famous Loyalist chief justice of New York.

To Mabane, the arrival of Smith was a heavy blow, both personally and politically. It seems that ever since it had become clear that Livius would not return to Canada, he had nursed the hope that he himself might be appointed chief justice. Haldimand had encouraged the idea, and had written home to England strongly recommending him. It was an impossible ambition. The peculiar problem of the Canadian legal system, the racial difficulty, and the strength and bitterness of political factions in the colony, all required a man of balanced judgment, with high intellectual and legal attainments. Estimable as Mabane was in many ways, in no respect did he come anywhere near this ideal. However, with stubborn optimism he cherished the plan until his hopes were destroyed by a triple blow. The appointment had been given not to himself, but to William Smith; Smith was an American; and he had been appointed on the direct recommendation of his old friend, the governor, who relied implicitly on Smith's judgment. Carleton had sailed away from Canada, having dismissed an American chief justice in order to maintain Mabane and his friends in power. Now, as Lord Dorchester he was sailing back, bringing with him another chief justice, whose firm determination — it was shrewdly surmised — was to overthrow Mabane along with the principles for which he stood. There was a dramatic element in the situation, but poor Mabane was not in a position to appreciate it. Yielding to the persuasions of cautious friends, he accorded to Dorchester on his arrival the respectful attentions due to his position and made no reference to his own grievance. For Smith he had nothing but enmity, and it appears that his sentiments were heartily reciprocated.

Mabane and his party put up a good fight. If Smith controlled the governor's mind, they yet had at least as strong a party as he in the council. They also controlled the civil courts, for the provincial system confined the activities of the chief justice to criminal work, and to the court of appeals. When Smith in the court of appeals offered an interpretation of the Quebec Act which permitted the use of English law in purely English cases, Mabane from the bench flatly and publicly contradicted him at the next sitting of his own court. When Smith in council introduced a bill to confirm his new interpretation of the Quebec Act, Mabane and his party countered with a bill abolishing some of the few English usages which had been introduced into the courts. This proceeding, outrageous in Smith's eyes, inspired his great effort against Mabane. The American attorney-general, Monk, the close friend and ally of Smith, in supporting a petition to the council against the French party's bill, made outrageous accusations against Mabane and his fellow judges. They were accused of partiality, inconsistency, and complete and wilful ignorance of all the principles of law. Mabane, who had to sit in council and listen for six hours to a speech which ridiculed and insulted himself and the system he represented, must have felt that his humiliation was complete.

Unfortunately, it was only the beginning. Monk's accusations led to a long and bitter quarrel in the council. The English party demanded a judicial investigation into Monk's charges, which had, no doubt, been made with the single purpose of bringing about such a result. Mabane retorted that the pretended reformers were actuated by the sole desire to change well-established laws, and break the British connection — a remark which was to be echoed countless times during the political contests of the next century. In the end, Smith himself was ordered by Dorchester to preside over an investigation into the conduct of the judges. The inquiry was supposed to be conducted in a judicial and impartial manner, but it was really only a continuation of the factional fight in the council. Mabane's enemies exerted themselves to hold him and his colleagues up to ridicule and opprobrium, and they were abundantly successful. They concentrated on commercial cases where the law was in the greatest confusion. Mabane's lack of legal training, and his arbitrary disposition, added to his hearty dislike of the American members of the merchant group, made him a particularly unfit person to deal with these cases. He had frequently been betrayed into inconsistencies, and at times into at least a show of partiality. He might, however, have been expected to urge that the wretched condition of the laws was an excuse for most of his shortcomings. Unfortunately for his reputation, this excuse was not open to him. As the dominant political leader in the province, he had for years supported the legal system, or rather the want of one, which would have provided a plausible explanation for his apparent defects as a judge. To witness the practical condemnation of his system, and the parade of all the little faults and negligences in his administration of justice during the last ten years, must have been a very bitter experience for him.

The investigation ended, as it had begun, in the council, in a drawn battle between the parties of Mabane and Smith. Trivial details connected with the winding up of the affair were made the subject of a bitter political contest which was a disgrace to both parties. The conduct of neither had been above reproach, and each of the leaders hoped that the affair would end in the dismissal of the other by the authorities in Great Britain. In the end, the latter, realizing the political implications of the whole matter, took no steps beyond the dismissal of Monk, who was the apparent cause of the whole disturbance. This left Mabane and Smith free to continue their struggles in the council. Smith continued to bring in legislation calculated, as he thought, to increase the efficiency of the courts, and Mabane continued to oppose such legislation with all his might, as he was determined to oppose all of what he held to be American innovations.

In the council Mabane and his party at least held their ground. They were not always successful, but on many occasions they did succeed in thwarting Smith and the "American" policy of the merchant party. Until the constitutional change of 1791, Mabane kept his French system practically intact, and in that year he was able to hand it over to the safekeeping of the French national party in the new assembly. During this period, however, his private life was clouded with trouble and anxiety, which added to the vexations which he had to meet in his public capacity. He missed the easy and pleasant intercourse with his old friend,

Governor Haldimand. The old alliance with Dorchester was broken forever, and their relations seem to have been purely formal. Moreover, Mabane was suffering from financial embarrassments. The six or seven hundred pounds a year which he received in salary from his various offices was not sufficient for a man of his generous and extravagant disposition. His desire for the chief justiceship had been based on economic necessity as well as on personal ambition. When the appointment of Smith put that beyond his reach, he tried, through the influence of Haldimand and other friends, to be appointed to the office of lieutenant-governor, left vacant by the death of Henry Hope. Unfortunately this effort failed also, and his private affairs drifted from bad to worse. His faithful friend, Major Matthews, formerly secretary to Haldimand, strove to inculcate in him principles of financial as well as of political prudence, but with only a moderate measure of success. Mabane died at last in 1793, a poor man, not old in years, but worn with fatigues and disappointments, and oppressed with the most deadly of all disillusionments — the consciousness of the fact that his day was over, and his place gone.

Nevertheless, although Mabane died leaving his enemy Smith in possession of the field, he made a far deeper mark than Smith did on the course of Canadian history. He represents the first political articulation of the vague aspirations of French-Canadian nationalism in that early period. That he had no real understanding of, or sympathy with, what is called French-Canadian nationalism to-day, is beside the point. He held the political fort until the French Canadians found their feet. Mabane also contributed to later Canadian toryism. His warnings of the danger of democracy and of American innovations, and of the necessity of stubborn resistance to political change in the name of the British constitution, were faithfully echoed by the political heirs of those against whom he had breathed out threatenings in the council. The two parties to the constitutional struggle of the nineteenth century shared the political heritage of this half-forgotten leader.[6]

PIERRE GUY: A MONTREAL MERCHANT OF THE EIGHTEENTH CENTURY

The history of Canada in the eighteenth century has been too much the province of the diplomats and the generals, the lawyers, the constitutionalists, the patriots and the loyalists. It would be reckless to deny the fascination of the wars of Queen Anne, King George, the French and the Indians, or the great struggles which marked the American and French revolutions. It would be dangerous to question the importance of those constitutional milestones marked by every weary

Canadian school child: the Proclamation of 1763, the Quebec Act and the Constitutional Act, to say nothing of all the welter of despatches, reports, memoranda and debates that lie between.

And yet there is sometimes a sense that these great themes have been over-worked, or that their greatness and significance would be more apparent if we knew a little more of the ordinary men and women whose fates were apparently determined by the conspicuous events. What did they think and talk about? Were they as much concerned about their public events as we are? Did the Canadians in 1760, for example, suspect the immensity of the emotional impact which their sad fate would have on their successors? Did anyone imagine that the current satisfaction and frustration, rage or jubilation at the Quebec Act was to be the beginning of a paper war that would last for two hundred years?

We do not know, partly because, unhappily, the many ordinary but by no means uninteresting people of Quebec in the eighteenth century left very few personal records behind them, and of these many have been lost or perhaps just not found. At the same time not enough use has been made of letters and papers collected and preserved by careful and tireless hands such as those of the late Judge Baby. For example, not one in a thousand, or perhaps in five thousand, of the Montréalers who pass along Guy Street today know who Pierre Guy was or whether he pronounced his name in the French or the English fashion. There are, however, unprinted, but in easily accessible form, a long series of letters written to or by Guy and his acquaintances. Not all are brilliantly written; few would stand alone as of great historical significance. Yet, collectively, they give a remarkably vivid picture of Montreal in the late eighteenth century and of the men and women who lived and worked there.

They take the reader back to Old Montreal with its marketplace and its narrow streets, its busy wharves piled with great casks and small kegs, trunks, boxes, packs of furs, sacks of wheat, piles of staves; and its harbour filled with large and small boats, rafts, and sailing ships from the tiniest schooners to those large enough to have a draught of sixteen feet, the largest that could reach Montreal at that time. They take him into Pierre Guy's stone house on St. Paul Street with its storage vaults below and its garrets above, its kitchen and its parlour, its garden complete with stable and outhouse and they even show his enchanting little Indian slave maid who caused such emotional havoc in the heart of his sturdy Negro manservant that, unwilling to enlarge his human holdings, he was compelled to part with both.

The letters also show Guy's daily life as a merchant, his business problems, his family and, as the years go on, his development as a person with the comments, often satirical, and occasionally irreverent if not heretical, with which he amused himself and his friends. Guy is worth knowing as an engaging individual. If the serious historian demands also that he be relevant, it may be claimed that he does represent a significant group in the community in which that most reputable of scholars, the quantitative historian, is today taking some interest.

Little is known of Guy's background. His father, Pierre Guy, born in Paris, came to New France early in the eighteenth century, served in the army, probably established a retail business in Montreal, and died in 1748, when Pierre was ten. The boy went to school in the Seminary at Quebec, and also went to France before returning to serve in Canada in the Seven Years' War.

Meanwhile, Guy's widowed mother maintained the family business. In 1761, when the colony, having capitulated, was occupied by British troops, though not yet formally ceded to Britain, Mme Guy sent her son to France, to Bordeaux, where Denis Goguet, her wholesale supplier, had his business. She may have hoped to establish Guy with him, and to return herself to France if English rule proved objectionable. However, business was bad and Goguet had no place for him. He therefore settled down to eighteen month's study with tutors, waiting apparently until Canada's fate should be known or until his mother should make up her mind. Goguet, who was kind and hospitable, also sent home glowing reports on Guy's behaviour: "He is almost too good and regular in his life." Meanwhile Guy was sad and homesick, waiting in vain for letters, but receiving none from the fall of 1761 until the spring of 1763, when he got six all at once.

One of these letters apparently informed him that the Guys would stay on in Montreal, and summoned him home. Assisted by Goguet, he transferred his mother's funds and business to a French firm domiciled in London and made his way there, visiting Paris on the way. He made few purchases finding goods dear, and having satisfied himself that, many Quebec merchants being already over-stocked, he could buy more cheaply on his return. In the summer of 1763 he took ship for Quebec, arriving in the autumn, weary after three months' voyage, during which he suffered misery from seasickness. He may well have resolved then and there on the course he was to follow — to live henceforth and die in Montreal.

Having spent some weeks in Quebec purchasing and despatching his goods (and getting the English governor's licence to send up his load), Guy made his hostess in Quebec a present of apples and pears sent down from Montreal, and reached home at last, to the affectionate welcome of his mother and, one may hope, the grateful thanks of his sister Babette for the French cape and other luxuries he had brought her from Paris and from London. For two years thereafter he was in business with his mother. In 1764 he married, Mlle Hervieux, and in 1765 he began to establish his own independent business.

The adaptation of Guy and his family to English rule seems to have been carried out without serious loss or grave anxiety. This is worth noting, because it has been argued that the economic shock of the conquest destroyed the Canadian merchant bourgeoisie. It is true that they were in the end eliminated from major economic enterprises, but this was not done by the conquest. For twenty-five years, although on the whole they were smaller investors than the English, they remained more numerous, at least at first, in the fur-trade, and they lived and worked in a free and independent but not unfriendly rivalry with their English colleagues. Many of their sufferings and deprivations have been exaggerated by the nationalist school of historians. One may, however, descend to the frivolous and mention one source of suffering which has perhaps been too little noticed. A painful aspect of the separation from the beloved mother country was the loss of a certain luxury that was also considered a necessity. The red wines of France, some very cheap, others more costly, were part of a way of life, a special aspect of French culture which has been strangely neglected by Canadian nationalists in their preoccupation with the great themes of language, and of religion. Canadians at the time were certainly not silent on the matter, and the English governors sympathized with them and took their part, but in vain. The ingenuity of smugglers, who were indeed very ingenious, brought in French red wine from time to time, and the arrival of a cask must often have been the occasion of a party. Well-to-do Canadians, however, did learn to drink port and to enjoy it. Others gradually adjusted themselves to Boston rum. On one point, however, they appear to have stood firm. It is indeed astonishing that the great nationalists like Garneau and Groulx, in retailing the Canadian epic, have made so little of the heroic resistance of their compatriots to that almost unendurable aspect of British rule, the so-called British "brandy." "Vous savez, Monsieur, qu'il fait boire, et il est triste de le faire avec amertume," says one petition against this apparently odious beverage.

Guy's return to Montreal brings to an end the first series of business and family letters which reveal him as a most serious, diligent and businesslike young man, not yet displaying much sense of humour or originality of mind, but already showing that strong and quiet affection for his family and family life which marks all his correspondence, and which was abundantly fulfilled in marriage.

The twenty years from 1765 to 1785 see Guy enjoying his home with an increasing family, developing a many-sided and apparently profitable business, and taking a definite if cautious interest in the legal and political issues of the day. It is in the innumerable, although generally brief, references to his family that Guy is increasingly revealed as a truly sympathetic character rather than the almost over-virtuous, careful, cautious young man of the early letters. Always a man of character, early trained to his private duty (he was, apparently, the only surviving son of his mother), and ready to respond to any pressing public demand, he found his chief pleasure with his family and his friends. To his wife he was clearly devoted. Writing some years after her death to his sister in the convent of Three Rivers, sympathizing with her on the death of her Superior, he remarked, "I lost my Superior four years ago, and have not been able to forget it for a single day." One may hope that he made his wife similar pretty speeches in her lifetime, but the evidence in the letters is of a more material nature: twenty-five yards of white satin damask for a dress; a pair of earrings from Paris, smuggled into England not without some ingenuity by his friend Baby in 1774; a muff of marten skins to be selected by the same Baby. No letters to or from his wife have been found, and as most of the letters written during her lifetime were business letters, little is said of her until after her death.

Six children were born into the family. The eldest, a boy, died in 1771, when he was about six years old. Guy's letter to François Baby on the occasion is one of the most revealing in his correspondence, showing a depth of grief combined with a bitter resignation all the more moving because the reference to the child's death is inserted in the midst of routine business matters. He had no idea, said Guy, how much he would miss the child. "One should try not to spoil children, and not love them too much; then when they die the shock is less painful." It is the sad cry in this pre-medical age of the bereaved parent who knows too well that his grief is a common one and all too likely to strike again.

Guy's elder daughter, Lisette, is the subject of many comments, and his frequent reports on the state of her doll (the gift of an aunt, a member of the Ursuline community at Three Rivers), show his intimate fondness for his children. The doll, dressed as a nun, is to be called Mother St. Laurent. She is well named, says Guy; her martyrdom exceeds even that of the saint. She is rescued for a time and exhibited on the parlour wall, to the admiration of visitors. Later she seems again to have mingled with the world, for she has to be sent back to her maker to be given a new head. Lisette's story, retailed by her father, is that Mother St. Laurent offered to spend the night in church with *le petit Jésus* one cold Christmas and that her head and ears were frozen. Guy adds, "She has supported her trial with much patience. We have not heard her complain once since her misadventure."

These trivialities do not intrude much into the letters to Guy's chief correspondent during his married life, the merchant and later legislative councillor and intimate member of Governor Haldimand's circle of friends, François Baby of Quebec. The letters give a pretty clear idea of the variety and extent of Guy's business. Like his mother, he operated a general store, supplying local people at retail, and after 1773 also doing a wholesale business with the country merchants and fur traders going up-country. In 1767 Guy ordered 300 pounds of black beads and 100 of white which he had contracted to supply for the trade. He carried all sorts of imported and local supplies. He had regular dealings with London, at first with the French firm of Vialars, and later with the better-known Watson and Rashleigh. (Sir Brook Watson was a well-known merchant of London, deeply involved in American affairs, political as well as economic, and distinguished by a wooden leg, which earned him, very privately, the nickname of "Timbertoe.") From London came all sorts of dry goods, materials for ladies' dresses, and for the elaborate and expensive costumes worn by men on dress occasions; white silk and linen stockings, shoes of all kinds (ladies' dress shoes in those days being of considerable variety and also highly perishable). Although most building materials were supplied in the province, window-glass was an import. Tea, coffee, wines, sugar, cheeses, spices, and all sorts of other luxuries also came from abroad. These things would be included in Guy's overseas orders, but he might also supply himself from importers of Quebec . . . .

In spite of . . . warnings from English loyalists, Britain granted an Assembly in 1791. The project of the nonsectarian bicultural university, undoubtedly a project somewhat in advance of its time, was forgotten. It would be pleasant to be able to say that along with his fellow merchants, Canadian and English, Guy helped to carry out in the Assembly the reforms that they had all been demanding for some years — taxes to support a police force, repair to public buildings and roads, the provision of a gaol and courthouse, and so on. Unfortunately things did not turn out in that way. Fifty years later Durham had to lament that the failure of co-operation between French and English had resulted in the total neglect of these important matters. The name Guy does not persist along with those of his Montreal friends, the Frobishers, James McGill, and others, as representing a great business family. Although he did give his name to Guy Street in Montreal, his story ends on a somewhat diminished note.

Why this rather disappointing conclusion to the career of a successful businessman, moderate but liberal in his views, respected by Canadians and English alike? The general situation has been explained convincingly by Fernand Ouellet, who places, as suggested earlier, the decline of the Canadian merchant not in the years following the conquest but in the two decades after the treaty which recognized American independence and ceded much of the old province of Quebec to the United States. After 1793 the centre of the Montreal fur-trade was shifting from the Ohio country south of the lakes to the far northwest. The best furs were found there and Montrealers by almost superhuman efforts were able to bring them down the St. Lawrence, and to maintain a successful opposition to the men on Hudson Bay for nearly forty years. They developed this operation increasingly after the cession of the Ohio country to the United States in 1783 and for about twenty years even after the effective elimination of Canadians from the Ohio. But the very long-range trade demanded an organization quite different from Guy's family business. Guy's business was based on the co-ordination of a great variety of activities, wholesale and retail, but all centred in one relatively small area. The fur-trade inevitably fell into the hands of men who were able to form themselves as partners into a faithful but flexible group, each member of which was prepared to run great risks for high profits and to wait a considerable time for returns on his investments in the trade over this vast and difficult area. Such a business was unsuited to the Canadian temperament and to Canadian law. The long-range trade fell into English hands and English companies with a considerable degree of organization. The sons of Canadian merchants became priests, notaries, doctors, retail merchants, but they fell away from big business, unless it happened that they married into an English fur-trading family. Then they were likely to be assimilated.

Guy and his family illustrate with curious exactness this general pattern. After 1785 his letters tell less about his shop, although he continued at least a retail business, and very much more about the development of the lands that he held just beyond the little river of St. Peter, which flowed outside the walls of old Montreal, along the site of the present Craig Street. More and more of his time was spent on his farm while he left his daughters to mind the shop. In 1800 he was very busy on his land, where he was employing eighteen to twenty men clearing. He speaks of a piece of land which he said he was going to sell to the seminary for a graveyard. Every Montrealer knows this graveyard today, for it is the present Dominion Square. In Guy's day the land all about it was more pleasantly if less profitably used for orchards and wheat fields.

Meanwhile Guy's two elder sons, having no taste for the priesthood, but still thinking of business, awoke to the fact that for businessmen in the future Montreal would be bilingual. Each in turn in the 1790's made his way along Lake Champlain and the Hudson to New York, where, having paid his respects to Jacob Astor and other business friends of Guy senior, he made his way to Princeton University to learn English. Both boys reported that they should have started earlier. One suggested that the elements could be learned much more thoroughly in Montreal than in Princeton. Neither on his return got into business. The elder, and perhaps the second, became a notary. Etienne, the second son, in 1796 was elected to the Assembly. The youngest boy, Joseph, born in 1780, sowed far more wild oats than his father could tolerate and became the cause of much anxiety. Eventually he became his father's assistant in what was clearly a diminishing business. Guy could look forward to leaving his children a competence, but he lamented that the young men grew idle and mischievous because there were no openings for them in the business world. He made no reference to English rivalry. He simply saw that his own style of business was failing to grow.

Guy died in 1810. His business career held none of the excitement and challenge of those of the great fur traders, the lumbermen, the railway men, the wheat men, or the bankers, who have made business history on this continent. But in his time he and his Montreal friends, Canadian and English, did build up the modest prosperity of the immediate post-conquest period, adjusting with patience and skill to innumerable risks and uncertainties, including those of war and invasion. The Canadians among them seemed to have formed a special society, busy but tranquil, a society where money was indeed necessary and most important, but where the constant pursuit of more money was not the ruling passion. The libraries of these Canadians were preserved, their strong family links and loyalties were maintained, their cheerful wit continued to be enjoyed among many retail merchants and professional men of Montreal. But their kind no longer figured greatly in the main business and social life of the city. They retreated, leaving the field to St. James Street and the Beaver Club.

A generation later, Lord Durham remarked on the obvious cultural superiority, along with a somewhat injured sense of economic inferiority, which marked the social exclusiveness of the descendants of Guy and his fellow Canadian merchants. This was the sad sequel, not indeed, of the conquest, but of the American Revolution. Guy's life was that of a Canadian merchant, who could ignore barriers of race and religion, or at least without effort overcome them, and co-operate on something like equality in the economic and political life of the merchants' world, so long as a family business on a relatively small scale was profitable. It was inevitable that he and his group should be overlaid and smothered by the Scots and Americans, who, early working with each other, ready and able to make available adequate "risk capital," built up a great commercial empire on the St. Lawrence. This was progress. It is part of the historian's function, however, to note that progress, however inevitable, and even desirable, may also be costly; it is his privilege to recall with pleasure and regret some of the good things that have been lost.[7]

RACISM IN THE OLD PROVINCE OF QUEBEC

No one contemplating today what is often called the French fact in Canada can be blamed for assuming that the roots of the dangerous and occasionally even violent French-English racial-nationalist confrontation in the modern province of Quebec must have taken hold in the period immediately after the conquest. Superficial evidence supports this assumption, but recent research is showing the actual situation as more complex than has been supposed and the issues as far from fitting neatly into a racial-nationalist pattern.

It was in the years 1759–60 that a British naval force and British troops operating from bases in the British-American colonies completed the military occupation of the French province on the St. Lawrence and prepared for the events that resulted in surrender of the whole French empire on the mainland in North America to Britain in the peace treaty of 1763. This for Britain was a great but almost embarrassing victory. It necessarily involved London, at a time of great political instability, in a major reorganization of vast territories formerly ruled or claimed by France, territories in which almost every colony along the Atlantic seaboard had its claims and interests, at a period then there was considerable friction among the colonies themselves and a good deal between them and Great Britain.

The necessary reorganization eventually helped to precipitate American armed resistance to Britain in 1775, the American Declaration in 1776, and the ensuing war which ended in 1783 with recognition of the United States of America. Meanwhile, Great Britain had in 1763 created on the St. Lawrence a new province destined to be the nucleus of the later Dominion of Canada, the province of Quebec. This province was, roughly, a parallelogram extending along both sides of the St. Lawrence River from a little above the prosperous fur-trading town of Montreal to a little below the older, more dignified, government and military centre of Quebec, an area roughly 700 miles in length and something over 200 in breadth, a considerable extent but trifling compared with the other tremendous continental spaces now ruled by Britain. The province included most of the

Canadian settlements which were clustered along the banks of the St. Lawrence and Richelieu Rivers, as well as very considerable tracts of vacant land.

The Royal Proclamation of October 7, 1763, which had created this province, had also, and indeed as its primary purpose, established the tremendous area south of the Lakes, north of the Ohio, and east of the Mississippi, known generally as the Ohio country, as a large Indian reserve. Restless Americans and any others who wanted to settle there were strictly prohibited from entering; they were instead invited to occupy the vacant lands made available in the new province of Quebec and were promised, should they respond to the invitation, "the enjoyment of the benefit" of English law, and an elected assembly as soon as one could be summoned. This historic document, the basis of the first Canadian constitution under British rule, saw the beginning of a problem which has always looked large to Canadians, and has often not been much noticed by Americans — the problem of Canadian-American relations.

Not many frontiersmen or would-be farmer settlers responded to the invitation of the Proclamation, but some hundreds of others did. These were the traders and merchants from Boston, New York, and other American towns, and from London and elsewhere in Britain, all of them eager to supply the army and to take over the fur-trade in which, as was well known, merchants on the St. Lawrence had important natural advantages. Some of them no doubt also were interested in buying up seigneuries which might be made available by Canadians who, by treaty, were allowed to sell their property and return to France. On their arrival these new settlers found detachments of British troops at Quebec, Montreal, and elsewhere, troops which had been in occupation since 1760 and had administered the colony until the Proclamation made possible a return to civil law. These troops were also responsible for supplying the network of forts and posts maintained on the Great Lakes and in the Ohio country. The newcomers also found an English governor, or rather a Scottish one, General James Murray, and a few English-speaking officials. Apart from these their neighbours were the "new subjects," some 65,000-75,000 Canadians, the name then and for several generations later applying only to the ancient settlers, the French-speaking inhabitants of the former colony of New France.

This was the first contact, as fellow-citizens or fellow-subjects, of the French and English, who for a century and a half had been neighbours, and often bitter foes, in eastern North America. There were of course misunderstandings and tensions which were very obvious and which were given sufficient prominence at the time to make it natural for historians to adopt a simple French-English pattern as the theme of Canadian history from 1760 onward.

Canadians, so goes the story, first met the conquering army from Britain and found it surprisingly humane, benevolent, and tolerant of all their ways — their language, their laws and their religion. The later introduction of civil government in 1764, though vexatious in some ways, left them still with the humane soldier — Governor Murray. Meanwhile, however, they witnessed an influx of English and

American merchants, who (no doubt unthinkingly) treated Quebec as an English province and demanded that Murray establish English law courts, summon an elected assembly, presumably English-speaking and Protestant, and recognize more fully the place of the Church of England as the established Church. Murray, generous defender of Canadian claims, resisted and with his officials headed what came to be called the "French party" to oppose these English demands.

According to this version of history Murray's successor, Guy Carleton, continued to support and indeed to invigorate the French party, and secured that key piece of legislation the Quebec Act of 1774 as a "French-Canadian charter." The Quebec Act was indeed a remarkably tolerant piece of legislation in its concessions to a conquered people; it recognized Canadian civil law; it recognized the generous concessions already made in practice to the Roman Catholic worship and discipline; it instituted a special oath of office which would give Roman Catholics the civil equality not to be enjoyed by their co-religionists in England or Ireland until 1829; and it conceded that an assembly would be for the present "inexpedient." A concession to English merchants was the redrawing of the boundary of this formerly restricted province to include the enormous area of the Ohio country and the area surrounding the Great Lakes as far as the height of land which divided them from the Hudson Bay. The colonies to the south were outraged by the Act, and particularly by this provision, but that is another story. The English and Americans in Quebec protested at the provisions as an infringement of the rights promised them in the Proclamation of 1763 and, in practice, as injurious to commerce in its substitution of Canadian for English civil law.

For the next fifteen years the English demanded modifications, particularly the granting of an elected assembly and of at least some English commercial law. The "French Party" resisted successfully for about ten years, until the end of the American Revolutionary War, and the arrival in the province of thousands of displaced loyalists made it essential to consider some changes. As a result, after due consideration, the province, already greatly reduced by the concession of the Ohio country to the new United States of America, was divided, each part receiving an assembly. Surprisingly, the Canadians, who had supposedly been rejecting everything English in favour of their traditional institutions, took to the English ways like ducks to water and were soon dominating the assembly of the new province of Lower Canada, to the confusion of English merchants and English governors.

It has long been recognized that this French-English pattern, with English officials sponsoring the helpless French majority against the assimilating energies of the English, does not completely fit the facts. It was based on the official correspondence and legal documents most readily available to historians and these suited the nineteenth-century political national approach well enough. Even this interpretation, however, does not offer much suggestion of racial nationalism. There was, indeed, no tradition of race in New France as such. The Indians were referred to as *sauvages* but *"sauvages"* is a gentle enough word, and it was hoped that they would be converted to Christianity. The English were "heretics," but English children captured in Indian raids were rescued by the French, treated well, and converted in many instances. Racism appears, as one would expect, in relation to slaves. It is indeed something of a shock to find a Canadian merchant, charitable, kind, affectionate, and upright, bemoaning the love affairs carried on by his Negro servant in the attic, and regretting that the law forbade the surgical operation which was to him the only obvious remedy; or trying to sell his little *panise* — too attractive for the peace of mind of the Negro — to some trader of the West Indies. "Anybody would be glad to have her as she is so pretty." There were, however, only a few thousand slaves in the whole history of New France. A recent historian sets the French-English pattern aside altogether. This perhaps goes too far, but it is important to bear in mind that New France and its successor the old province of Quebec was an eighteenth-century colony, an integral part of a Western civilization not yet subjected to the violent national and racial patterns of the nineteenth and twentieth centuries.

What struck the soldier-governors, apart from the fact that the Canadians were a likeable people needing protection from the representatives of a conquering nation, was that this was a society ordered and decent, apt to fight but willing to obey, delightfully unlike the turbulent American colonies, who generally would neither fight nor obey. These saw in New France a kind of Roman colony, a placid but potent mass of habitants ranged in orderly obedience under priests and seigneurs. And one of them, Guy Carleton, who partly planned and chiefly implemented the Quebec Act, seems to have decided that this was a better kind of colony than Britain had ever devised. It was not merely that Carleton was willing and anxious to protect conquered Canadians against English bullying; he was moved at least equally by an admiration for the kind of government and society that he thought he saw in Quebec, and he wanted to preserve and maintain it as good for Canadians, good for English, and good for the British Empire in North America.

Unfortunately for Carleton's conclusions, he and the historians who have concentrated on his early dispatches overlooked a very important group of people. Canadians were not confined to priests, seigneurs, and habitants. There was a small but very significant class of Canadian townsmen: merchants, traders, and a few professionals. They were not powerful economically. Within a few years, for example, although their numbers were fewer, the English had decidedly the larger investment in the fur-trade, a development to be expected since the richer Canadian merchants, indeed all Canadians who could afford it, had returned to France.

The Canadians who remained, however, were culturally and politically significant. They were not merely literate; they had positive intellectual tastes and political interests. When the Loyalists arrived in the country after the American Revolution, they spoke much of the illiteracy of the Canadians in contrast to the

English, who maintained the Protestant tradition of literacy as a religious and moral duty. Yet the increasingly numerous Canadian merchants and professional men who could read generally made a serious business of it. In the 1770's one young merchant, ambitious and very busy, wrote to France to order the works of Voltaire, Rousseau, "and other good writers"; another accepted with gratitude a French edition of Blackstone from the English lieutenant-governor; a third, apparently after very little formal schooling, in letters written throughout his long life made frequent references to more or less serious reading and showed the fruits of it in his reflections and also in his increasingly mature and effective style of writing.

Some of these Canadian townsmen owned seigneuries, or intermarried with seigneurial families. They might share in some measure the seigneurial outlook, and they did not necessarily like or trust the English entirely. When certain of the English merchants in 1764 had launched a rather bitter attack on Murray and his policy through a Grand Jury presentment, a Canadian merchant, alarmed at his apparent hostility to Roman Catholic rights and the Canadian law, wrote, "If we are not careful they will destroy our nation." At the same time, while joining in petitions for concessions to Canadians, these men were very far from supporting the seigneurial demands for a "national charter," "sacred and inviolable," which should forever preserve the mummified structure of New France.

As early as 1765 a Canadian writer to the Quebec *Gazette* asked to be instructed in the true nature of the English liberties and rights of which he had heard so much and which as a British subject he now hoped to enjoy. Although there is a faint suggestion that this particular letter may have been written with tongue in cheek, it may have been genuine; and there is no doubt that the *Gazette*, a bilingual publication, offered a steady diet of articles on English rights and liberties to its Canadian readers. Moreover, in Montreal in 1766 there was a serious protest of Canadian and English merchants against an informal "assembly" that had gathered there to discuss Canadian problems; the merchants protested that it was composed of seigneurs only, and yet professed to speak for "the nation." On this occasion the merchants, Canadians and English, demonstrated together and tried to gain access to the meeting. When this was forbidden, forty-one of them, fifteen English and twenty-six Canadians, literally registered, in notarial instruments, two protests, one English and the other French, asserting the bad effect of a so-called representative meeting which did not include both Canadians and English, merchants and seigneurs.

It was not the Canadian merchants alone, however, but a legal pundit (who was also a small seigneur) who, when the Quebec Act was under consideration, organized some of his fellow seigneurs and some Canadian merchants to prepare a petition for an assembly which would secure to them, as they said, the rights of British subjects and enable them to protect their own laws and customs to an extent that under an appointed council they might not be able to do. The leading seigneurs, however, held aloof, and the English merchants, also asking for an assembly, refused to be as explicit as the Canadians felt it necessary to be in dictating the form of it. Therefore, in spite of interest at both Quebec and Montreal, and of efforts at co-operation, Canadians and English failed to agree, and the formal Canadian petitions which were presented made no mention of an assembly.

As a result the Quebec Act in 1774, representing ostensibly the desires of the Canadians, decreed as has been said that an assembly at the moment was inexpedient. This is not surprising and need not be attributed to current troubles with assemblies along the Atlantic coast, although the authorities were not unaware of these troubles. It would have been difficult, even had the neighbouring colonies been at perfect peace, to turn the colony over to a representative assembly composed chiefly of Canadians, yet an assembly which did not do so would, of course, have been a mockery of Parliament comparable to the one in Ireland; and the English probably thought that one Ireland was enough.

It seems quite certain, however, that in 1774 the Canadians were not united in the rejection of an assembly, and there is good evidence that some at least among the Canadian merchants were dismayed at a government which, professing to meet the wishes of Canadians, gave control to a partnership of the official "French" party and the leading seigneurs. Chief Justice Hey, who had been on leave in England, arrived in the province just after the Act came into force in May, 1775. He wrote a number of letters home during the summer and fall, giving his impression of the Canadian reception of the Act. He noted that, contrary to Governor Carleton's expectations, the Canadians had not in their gratitude, taken up arms to repulse the invading Americans. As he said, in complete astonishment, he must attribute the fact partly to pure ignorance preyed on by "malignant minds" — no doubt American ones. In addition, he saw clearly, and apparently for the first time, that the seigneurs as a class were neither liked nor trusted by the habitants. He reported that the Canadians had noted that Canadian members of the newly appointed council were all seigneurs, that these men were boasting foolishly and without cause of the great power now restored to them, and that they "have carried themselves in a manner very offensive both to their own people and to the English."

Fortunately there is also evidence on this matter from Canadians. The strongest comment comes from a Canadian merchant in Quebec, the same one who employed his winter leisure in reading Voltaire, Rousseau, and other good works. He wrote to his business correspondent in Montreal that, largely owing to the activities of the "monsters" — presumably the seigneurs — in Montreal, Canadians would be sorry that they had asked for a change in government; to which his Montreal friend agreed, congratulating him on being a bachelor and free to leave the country if he chose. Another merchant remarked that Canadians might soon find that they had changed "King Log" for "King Stork."

The conclusion must be, I think, that even before the American Revolution, Canadians, although aware of dangers to their language, customs, and religion, were almost, if not quite, as much interested in a social-economic resistance to their own seigneurs as in a cultural-national resistance to the English. Some indeed were beginning to see that the English had very good ideas about liberty and self-government which, with English help, might well be turned to French-Canadian advantage.

The American war, breaking out in 1775 immediately after the coming into force of the Quebec Act, put an end to effective political agitation for the time, but the diligent distribution of American propaganda undoubtedly enlarged Canadian ideas of English liberty, even though Canadians gave no very material assistance to the American invaders. Immediately after the war there is fragmentary but important evidence of political activity splitting the whole Canadian community and allying one section of it more or less with the English against the governor's "French Party." A small but significant incident occurred when the council was debating a piece of legislation long sought by the English but resisted by the official French party: a precise definition of the right of habeas corpus. The French party, in a delaying action, insisted that there must be a clause exempting religious communities from this dangerous privilege. Thereupon from the nuns of the Ursuline convent, cloistered but obviously well briefed on political events, came a message deploring the inclusion of any such unwanted exception. And the bishop, when applied to, supported the nuns. Meanwhile six English and five Canadian merchants had been jointly but vainly petitioning for admission to the council chambers that they might hear the debates on this important matter.

Even while this debate was going on in the council, a group of Canadian merchants, privately supported by leaders of the Church but not by the seigneurs, were sending a deputation to England to ask for permission to invite French priests to Quebec to fill the many vacancies in seminaries and parishes. Britain was naturally hostile to any such idea, being convinced that the French priest would always be also a political emissary. What is interesting is the supporting argument offered by the deputation, almost certainly inspired by American teaching and example, and surely not approved by the Canadian clerics, that religious freedom, "a natural right" promised them at the time of the conquest, must necessarily include the right to choose their own priests.

The failure in this primary demand led directly to another, a renewed petition for an assembly; "our only hope," said one of the disappointed delegates in London, "is this change." By the fall of 1784, English and Canadian committees were hard at work together on renewed petitions which were presented to the lieutenant-governor for transmission to Britain early in 1785. These were followed by counter-petitions against any such measures, which had been diligently circulated by the seigneurial party. Their opponents accused the seigneurs of having claimed as one of their manorial rights the privilege of transcribing to these counter-petitions the names of a number of their reluctant *censitaires*.

The Canadian petitions for an assembly did secure a formidable number of signatures, but their seigneurial opponents presented almost twice as many against the measure. Hugh Finlay, the provincial postmaster who knew the province well, believed that the majority of literate English and literate Canadians wanted an assembly; the habitants he thought were too ignorant to think much of anything except escaping taxes.

Government by assembly was granted in 1791. The province was divided into Lower Canada, which included Quebec, Montreal, and the old established seigneuries, and Upper Canada, composed of the new settlements of the Loyalists. The concession is generally attributed to Loyalist demands and to the penury of Great Britain, bent on local representative institutions because only through them could she now legitimately tax her colonies. During the five or six years preceding this grant, however, the political situation in the colony was involved, and was very far from conforming to an English-French pattern. Canadians were all somewhat resentful of the Loyalist assumption of moral and intellectual superiority, and of their often unconcealed contempt for the Canadian way of life, but the division between Canadian merchants and seigneurs had not been healed by this apparent English threat. On the contrary, fed by all sorts of propaganda from revolutionary France, Canadians were writing to the radical Montreal *Gazette*, pouring contempt on the idle and ignorant seigneurs and even on their priests. Now at last the national theme was beginning to emerge, but less as an attack on the English than as an assertion of the claim of the radical merchant and professional group that they, and not the seigneurs, truly represented *le corps de la nation*. Political and, still more, racial nationalism in Canada attained self-awareness not through the English conquest, but through the liberal and radical ideas disseminated first by the American and later by the French revolutionaries. These ideas, rejected by the seigneurs as damaging to their social pretensions and economic hopes, were eagerly received by the bourgeoisie and even by some of the clergy.

Meanwhile, national distinctions were being reinforced by economic and social factors. The Treaty of Paris (1783) surrendered to the United States the area of the Ohio country, hitherto the preserve of the Quebec fur merchants, both Canadian and English. Henceforth the fur-trade became, far more than it had been, a big business requiring extensive partnerships which could command large sums of risk capital. Such enterprises were alien to Canadians, who were generally devoted to the small, secure family business. As a result, the closing years of the eighteenth century and the beginning of the nineteenth century saw great prosperity for Quebec, but for English Quebec alone, since the English now controlled not only the fur-trade but also the rapidly growing commerce in timber and wheat. Canadians tended to move into the retail trade, into the professions, and especially into politics. Far from rejecting the assembly, said by the "French party" to be alien to their customs, they swarmed in, took possession, and dominated it with considerable skill and determination, eagerly claiming full parliamentary privileges from the English governor and from the now predominantly English council. At first linked with some English radicals, they spoke as before in the name of liberty; but, as the eighteenth century moved into the nineteenth and as greater prosperity and closer communications brought them nearer to the intellectual currents of Europe, they began, by a very easy and natural transition, to speak more and more in the name of the Canadian nation.

It is not accurate, then, to see Canadian nationalism as emerging immediately after the conquest in a homogeneous Canadian society. Canadians in the eighteenth century, like other peoples, were more excited by the new political ideas of liberty and equality than they were by the romantic ideas of nationalism. They were stirred by revolutionary thought before, during, and after the American Revolution. They were greatly stimulated by the French Revolution and by the experience of the English institutions which were given them at the very moment that similar institutions were being introduced into France. By the early nineteenth century a chiefly bourgeois group, which a decade or so before had associated political liberty with the right to import priests from France, was beginning to be touched with anticlericalism and was launching into a true racial-nationalist campaign against the Church, which had heretofore been benevolent, though naturally standing somewhat aside.

The generation after the conquest has, I believe, been misread. What happened was not a solid confrontation, French against English, with the French "chartered" by the Quebec Act, but a social-political conflict in which the dynamic Canadians joined the English in protesting against the Quebec Act, not because they were not potentially nationalist but because to them the Quebec Act was an instrument of class domination which denied them the one valuable fruit of the English conquest, political liberty. It was their co-operation in seeking the assembly and in learning to use it for their political purposes, and their increasing awareness of current European thought that led them on to a sense of community and to a possible national fulfilment.[8]

THE QUEBEC ACT: PROTEST AND POLICY

It is no more than fair that an editor who, however uneasily, has been sitting in judgment on the work of other historical scholars should be compelled to expose himself. If the foregoing examples of historical judgments have shown anything, it is that even those few who have dealt thoroughly with the available historical evidence have demonstrated that this evidence is inadequate.

Britain, after 1763, was faced with two problems inextricably entangled with one another, but in their nature distinct. One was the disposition of the Ohio country (where the local war had started in 1754) and the development of just and peaceful relations with the Indian peoples living there. The other was the determination of a mode of government consistent with the general law and practice of the British Empire, for a former French colony. The second problem was undoubtedly difficult, but the main lines of the settlement had already been sketched in the Articles of Capitulation and in the Peace Treaty. All that was needed was to apply the principles agreed on consistently with the general law of the British Empire.

The treaty was neither explicit nor very generous. It granted freedom of religion to the Canadians "as far as the laws of Great Britain permit." It confirmed the peaceful possession of property only to those Canadians who chose to sell it and leave the country within the space of eighteen months: "So that if they stay," said one commentator, "and claim under the Treaty only, they stay under condition of becoming, by their own free act, British subjects; and as such subject to British laws." The Articles of Capitulation were more generous. It was argued by some that these could be ignored as superseded by the Treaty. Lord Mansfield, however, was not alone in regarding the Articles of Capitulation as sacred. Advocate-General Marriott in making his recommendations for the Quebec Act dealt precisely with the issue: "But the Treaty made with the sovereign state of France . . . does not supersede the Capitulation made with the inhabitants; because I consider capitulations, in the eyes of the law of nations, to be not only national, but personal compacts and made with the inhabitants themselves, for the consideration of their ceasing their resistance. It is consistent with the honor and interests of this kingdom that they should be religiously observed."

The capitulations then were generally accepted as binding in honour. These promised the inhabitants, with certain exceptions for religious orders, complete enjoyment of their property and "the free exercise of the Catholic, apostolic and Roman religion." It was generally agreed, as the reports and deliberations of the law officers and officials clearly show, that the determination of the constitution for Quebec had to be consistent with these pledges. It is true that the request made to Amherst for a continuation of the custom of Paris under the capitulations for those who might choose to remain in the country under British rule was turned aside by his reply, "they become subjects of the King." Amherst naturally refused to commit himself as to the future laws which would govern the country should it be retained by Britain. But common sense as well as legal opinion agreed that the continued peaceful possession of property implied no abrupt or arbitrary change in the law by which the property was held. Murray and his legal advisors endeavoured to secure this in practice by the ordinance of September 17, 1764; the officials and lawyers and ministers in Britain criticized Murray openly for not giving greater security to Canadian law. The continuity of the bulk of Canadian civil law in Quebec was never in doubt; some Canadians complained that the council established by the Quebec Act could change it at discretion, but this council was under the direct supervision of the ministry in Great Britain which could and did cause unacceptable legislation to be disallowed.

It can be said that the continuation of much of Canadian civil law was never seriously threatened. Although the Proclamation of 1763 appeared to contemplate a change, any such intention was repudiated by British ministers, and condemned by Britain's law officers. The evidence indicates that no legislation by the British Parliament was needed, and that none would have been passed, but for the apparent blunder of the Proclamation in promising to confide legislative power to a hypothetical assembly which in the circumstances could hardly be summoned.

The obstacle to summoning an assembly was, or course, the religion of the Canadians. The religious question was more urgent and much more difficult than the legal one. It might have appeared to call for special legislation, but in fact, as more than one historian has noted, the Act gave the Roman Catholics very little that they did not already enjoy, and, rigidly applied, it would have restricted rather than extended their liberties.

The Capitulations had promised the free exercise of the Roman Catholic religion in Quebec; the request that the king of France continue to nominate the bishop was refused, naturally. Unfortunately, the question of the bishop on which Britain remained officially intransigent might have gone far to nullify the concession of "free exercise of worship." Roman Catholics could worship "freely" — in the sense of fully and entirely — only through the ministrations of priests duly ordained by a bishop duly consecrated under the authority of the pope. Britain, however, far from recognizing papal authority, was not prepared to countenance in Canada any "bishop" except the bishop of the established Church of England. This refusal was completely in accordance with the general practice of civilized nations of western Europe. The church was an aspect of the state; the bishop was not only a public official, he was part of the established structure of society of which the king was the head. Authorities in England were quite prepared to tell disgruntled merchants that they must accept Canadian law, as they would that of any other country where they chose to trade, but no one suggested that they must recognize or countenance any but a bishop of the English church in any British territory.

This delicate problem was solved in a manner typically British. What is important is that it was not settled by the Quebec Act. As far as any Roman Catholic in Quebec knew, it was solved by June 1766 when they welcomed the return from London of Jean-Olivier Briand whom they hailed as their bishop, and who had been consecrated as such on the authority of papal bulls by three French bishops. He dined at the governor's table, his authority was supported by the governor, he dressed like a bishop, he behaved like one — and he was treated like one, for like all his Canadian predecessors he had trouble with his flock. As for the government, he said, he had rather more freedom of action than he would have had under France.

Officially, Britain knew nothing of this. British officials continued to recommend that a "superintendent" be appointed for the "Romish Church" in Quebec, apparently oblivious of the fact that the church was fully superintended and that ecclesiastical business was going on as usual. This curious situation might be clarified by further research into the operations of the British cabinet, and the relations between ministers, members of the Board of Trade and law officers at this time. It is quite possible that the arrangement for Briand to go to France for consecration should have been made without leaving a trace on the official records. It is harder to understand how Charles Yorke and William de Grey, discussing benevolently in 1769 what could be done for the Roman Catholics in Quebec, should appear to know nothing of Briand's position and functions in the province. An examination of the relations in the inner circles of government and of the various ecclesiastical schemes proposed for Quebec prior to 1774 might show whether Yorke and de Grey were laboriously registering official unawareness of what was going on in Quebec, or whether they really knew nothing of it.

In fact the Quebec Act recognized a situation already universally accepted. The Act itself was even greeted by the bishop or "Superintendent" with some alarm. First the proposed oath of allegiance seemed to him inadmissible for Roman Catholics. It was reworded according to his request, but his fears were raised again when he saw in the final form of the Act that the free exercise of religion was "subject to the King's supremacy" according to the Elizabethan Act of Supremacy. It was Carleton who reassured him on this matter. The king, said Carleton, understood the beliefs of his Roman Catholic subjects and he would not interfere with them — "Just keep quiet and believe what you like."

Carleton would have needed to reassure Briand even more about the instructions on religious matters of which he had perhaps heard some rumour.

It may therefore be said that the essential concessions of law and religious freedom could be and were claimed under the capitulations. Apart from a constitutional technicality, the continuation of Canadian law could have been assured without any Parliamentary statute; and the Act, while enforcing, perhaps unnecessarily, the tithe, and providing in the instructions a salary for the "Superintendent," provided in the same instructions orders which can only be called harassing and degrading to the church. If the Quebec Act was a charter for Canadians, like some other charters it may be said only to have confirmed, and with some restrictions, what had already been conceded in practice.

One important exception must be noted to this statement. The granting of civil equality to Canadians by instituting a new oath of office which Roman Catholics were at liberty to take removed a degrading distinction. Even this, however, important as it was, was an application and an extension of the principle enunciated by the law officers in 1765 when they stated that Roman Catholics in colonies abroad ceded to the king were not subject to the disabilities imposed on Roman Catholics in the United Kingdom. Presumably, therefore, without a statute the governor might have been authorized to admit Canadians to office on condition of their taking a modified oath.

The main function of the Quebec Act so far as the Canadian community was concerned was to provide for a legislative body other than the promised assembly. Had an assembly been given it could not have been one from which Roman Catholics were excluded, as they must have been, had the usual colonial pattern been followed. The authorities, as was shown by the plan of 1769, were willing to experiment, but by 1773 they had decided that the risks from ignorance, inexperience, and "turbulence" were too great. Not all Canadians were satisfied with this decision. Chartier de Lotbinière complained that the Council was empowered to meddle with Canadian customs which should have been sacred. *Les Vrais Patriotes* . . . wanted an assembly and were willing to pay the price in taxes. Some years later they did get an assembly — and there is good reason for thinking that for all the talk of the seigneurial party about the Quebec Act, most politically-minded Canadians dated their "charter" from 1791 rather than from 1774.

So much for those parts of the Quebec Act that applied specifically to the internal affairs of the conquered French colony. Had the Act, or the British authorities without an Act, done no more than this, there would have been little controversy. Had the adjustments been gradual, as they might have been but for the constitutional doubts about the Council created under the Proclamation, there would almost certainly have been less controversy, less vehement attack from the merchants, less anxious probing of motive and circumstance from English and Canadian nationalists.

What made the Act a centre of the most violent and continued controversy was the geographical, economic, and historic connection of the St. Lawrence community with the Ohio country which inspired the boundary clause; and the coincidence in time of the evolution of a policy for the newly-conquered colony with the upsurge of revolutionary activity in the older colonies on the Atlantic coast.

It is impossible to separate the elements in a complex historical situation. It is hopeless to attempt to say what would have happened had one or other of the presumably operative factors been absent. It may, however, be useful, standing a little off from the problem and even from the records, to distinguish the various elements and to notice whether their association with one another is inherent or accidental. To force oneself to look at Quebec out of the context of the Ohio country, and the far North West, and the Atlantic seaboard, is, no doubt, an artificial exercise and therefore dangerous. It has, however, been the purpose of this work to show that historical research is dangerous; truth may lie at the bottom of a well both deep and dark.[9]

Strictly speaking Hilda taught at the pre-university level for only one year. In fact, though, much of her work in her early years at Regina College must have been very similar to high school teaching, at least because of the long teaching hours and the lack of time for herself, let alone research.

Hilda always felt close to school teachers and their problems even though the last thirty years of her life were spent in the university. Her experience as an associate editor of *The Bulletin* of the Saskatchewan Teachers' Federation provided some of the information that she used in her first article on education for a national audience "Education for Democracy" published in the *Dalhousie Review* in 1944 which is the first selection in this chapter. Nine years later, with her book *So Little for the Mind* just off the press, Hilda was the centre of a storm because her description of the problems of Canadian education and their origins was much more biting and public than it had been in the pages of the *Dalhousie Review*. Nowhere is her stance of the early 1950's more apparent than in the text of the statement she broadcast on CBC in November 1953 which is the second selection.

Hilda was genuinely surprised by the reaction to her assessment of the state of primary and secondary education in Canada. She had been concentrating on the essential message of *So Little for the Mind* — the intellects of both teachers and students were too often ignored in the schools. As a good historian should, she had frankly stated what she believed were the causes of the situation: bureaucrats and teachers too influenced by the educational philosophy of John Dewey and the presuppositions of the modern world. Later she would realize that she was not describing eighteenth-century Quebec and that she had made her opponents too angry for there to be the "temperate dispute" that she had hoped to initiate.

The third and fourth selections in this chapter, from *So Little for the Mind*, further illustrate the force of Hilda's attack. Any Canadian educational periodical of the years 1953–54 can be consulted to see (and feel) the bitter and violent reaction of educators.[1] Hilda replied with cunning, some elision, and a few twists in "My Small War with the Educators" which originally appeared in *Maclean's* on 15 July 1954 and is reprinted here as the fifth selection.

Many teachers and parents (and some professors of education) welcomed Hilda's book because it fitted their perception of the problem in the schools and gave hope for reform. During the next few years Hilda was often on the road speaking to sympathetic groups across Canada. She did not fear to address "the enemy." Her article "So Much To Do — So Little Time",[2] was originally delivered to the Canadian Association of School Superintendents and Inspectors in September 1959. The sixth selection "Educational Simony," sums up Hilda's views in the late 1950's as she was once again turning her attention to the university and to historical research.

When it was all over Hilda was disappointed because there were so few concrete results. There were at least two reasons for the absence of effect. Too many educational bureaucrats reacted negatively to Hilda's all-out attack. At least as important was the fact that too few people, professional educators or not, were willing to commit themselves to (or were even interested in) the elitist, intellectual, Christian future charted by Hilda in the conclusion to *So Little for the Mind*, part of which forms the last selection.

EDUCATION FOR DEMOCRACY

In a recent address to a meeting of English headmasters, Dr. John Murray, Principal of University College, Exeter, expresses his fear that English education in the post-war world is menaced by the growing tendency to equalitarianism and bureaucratic control. Because there are wide differences between English and Canadian systems of education, it is interesting to find that we ourselves are stricken by the very plagues that Dr. Murray dreads, although they appear under different forms. Some of the statements in this essay apply only to certain provinces, which may be retarded educationally; nevertheless, the diseases are spread throughout the Dominion, and perhaps can be studied best where the attack is most severe.

We derive our equalitarianism from certain misconceptions of democracy, curiously and inconsistently applied. It is urged that in a democratic society every child should have equal educational opportunities. Such counsel of perfection, however, operates only in the elementary schools. After that, economic circumstances govern education to a very large extent; to an extent, it may be added, unknown either in Britain, the leading capitalist country, or in Russia, the leading socialist country of Europe. Only in our North American isolation is this *laissez faire* attitude maintained.

We thus, undemocratically, allow a large number of our citizens to be automatically excluded from any formal education beyond that of the elementary school. On the other hand, for the pupils in the high school, in the name of democracy we maintain a disastrous equalitarianism. We glory in the absolute uniformity of curricula, text books, and examinations. More than this; we strive if not to overcome, at least to conceal the irritating irregularities which society admits or nature imposes, by our ingeniously contrived examination system. All high school pupils read the same text books; all examination questions must be rigidly confined to the very letter of the text. Any effort to introduce into an examination questions stimulating to thought and judgment, even if such questions are based on material in the test, is frowned upon. This is considered "unfair" to pupils and teachers in small schools and remote districts. Why pupils and teachers in country districts should be deemed incapable of reasoning, it is difficult to say. The truth remains that all examinations are confined to mere tests of mechanical memorization, ostensibly on their account. It is true that examinations are but a small part of education, and that the best teachers try to keep them in a subordinate position; but if parents, teachers and school boards regard them as the final test of the success of the educational process, the teachers are shackled. Some of the best ones, naturally, throw off their chains by leaving the profession.

This extraordinary narrowness and rigidity in the treatment of text books and examinations is seriously defended by educational authorities on the ground that it is the only democratic way. No child must be made to feel "inferior" either because fortune has denied him able instruction, or because nature has denied him reasoning power. All must be on a level, and inevitably, in practice, this is the lowest level. It is interesting, if not cheering, to find that this pathological form of democracy exists in Britain also, symbolized by a demand for "parity of esteem," or "parity of disesteem," as Dr. Murray says it should be called. The effort to keep the backward or slow child from feeling "inferior" and to mitigate the drawbacks of the rural school is admirable, but we are in serious danger of throwing out the baby with the bath. The fact that the slow child cannot reason is no reason for devising an examination system in which the bright child has not opportunity of reading. The fact that children and teachers in rural districts may have little opportunity for wide reasoning is no reason for not encouraging and even insisting upon it where libraries are available.

In certain schools, and particularly the elementary ones, there is a tendency to revolt against a mental discipline so lifeless that it can hardly be called educational. Many public schools, not subjected to a provincial examination system, are adopting what is referred to as "the new education." In this new type of education, class-room and school discipline are largely relaxed in order to permit "activities" and "projects." The general idea is that mental activity can best be stimulated through physical activity; that what is learned gladly and willingly is learned best; and that pupils can adequately prepare for citizenship only by working in the school on some joint project in which all may have a share.

This new education is widely praised in Canadian periodicals, both educational and popular. Teachers and parents are delighted with the interest and enthusiasm of the pupils. Superintendents find that the problem of the dull child is partially solved: "If the class decides to produce a play, not everyone can write an original script nor play a stellar role, but the girl who makes a gilt paper crown for the Queen is making a contribution to the success of the whole enterprise." Psychologists tell us that the shy child is disappearing in the free and easy activity of the new school life.

It would be absurd to deny that increased interest, self-confidence, and happiness in the children are good in themselves. Nevertheless, benefits may be purchased and abuses abolished at too great a cost. Without denying the admirable features of the new education, it is important to point out some serious dangers.

It is true that mental activity can often be stimulated by physical activity, particularly in mediocre or dull minds, hardly capable of abstract thought. On the other hand, many with the quickest imaginations and keenest intellects do not need such stimulation, and often get on better without it. Such children may spend days on constructing a medieval village about which nothing is more certain than that it is very unlike any original. During the same period their imaginations could have been nourished and their minds exercised by reading or hearing read tales from Froissart or Chaucer, which would bring vividly before them the whole medieval scene. Handicrafts are excellent as recreation for all, and as a full-time occupation for many. They become an abuse if able pupils are permitted to make them a substitute for thoughtful reading.

It is true also to a certain extent that children learn best what they learn gladly. There is, however, a danger that the new education may run counter to the best interests of the pupil and of society, by causing a mental confusion between work and play. Under the new system the children are happy, it seems. Happiness is a by-product of healthful mental entertainment and physical activity. It is also, in its purest and rarest form, a by-product of hard, exacting and even bitter labour, when that labour is intelligently undertaken and perseveringly carried through. Setting aside all question of social utility, do we judge it fair, while offering the child an easy and pleasant school life, to neglect the path to the best kind of happiness he can ever know? In other words, why encourage him in supposing that discipline is useless as well as pleasant, when human experience clearly indicates that, properly employed, it is the only means to the highest values that life has to offer?

Again, no one will question the value of joint undertakings as a training for co-operative citizenship. The danger is that these may trespass on other and even more important aspects of education. In the enthusiasm for joint activity, how easy it is to forget that thinking, if it is done at all, must be done alone! All real mental training is an individual process. There is a common ground on which rational minds can meet, but each must find its own path there. "Thinking," says a contemporary writer, "is a difficult and painful process" — and yet on it all the material and moral good of society depends. How disastrous if the attractions of the new education should lead to neglect of this difficult, painful, and solitary process!

One other aspect of the new education is worth attention. The teacher is not to order, but to encourage and guide. He is to "get the lead from the pupils." In order to encourage spontaneity and original activity, text books are frequently abolished. To anyone familiar with the abuses of the rigid text book and examination method, this seems a welcome change. In the hands of thoughtless enthusiasts, it too has its dangers. A teacher, discussing with her superintendent a certain course of study, remarked that she had found a good reference and meant to use it as a guide. He protested in horror. All set books and programmes were absolutely taboo. The teacher must "get the lead" from the class, without obtruding her own plans.

Although any intelligent teacher will automatically adapt his programme to the apparent interest and comprehension of the pupils, this interpretation of the new methods must lead to the worst consequences. The lead will not come from the whole class, but from the two or three most talkative members. A course on South America began with Trinidad because one child had an uncle who had once been there. Not only is such a hit-and-miss approach objectionable in itself, but it prevents serious study and careful planning by the teacher. Such a preparation is the foundation of all sound instruction even in the simplest of manual arts, and far more so when a large and complicated field must be presented. The suggestion that the teacher should get the lead from the pupils is therefore valid only in a very limited sense. Even if the teacher is a guide only, what guide ever gets the lead from his followers? If the idea is only to let the pupils *think* they give the lead, the whole thing becomes a farce which the pupils would be the first to despise.

It is worth remarking that the popularity of the new education in many quarters depends less on its virtues than on its vices. The educational leaders of this continent, in the grip of a pseudoscientific mania, take endless delight in measuring educational achievements and photographing educational processes. Class-room projects and activities are easy to measure and photograph and are therefore in high favour. Seeing is believing. Parents, teachers and children alike can see with their own eyes that education is taking place. Unfortunately, the true educational process is, as has been said, a matter of the individual mind. It cannot be seen with the naked eye, nor with the lens of the camera. Its returns to the individual and to society come in surely, but very slowly.

It is important to notice that the new education, like the system against which it revolts, finds much of its support in certain false notions of democracy. The increase in manual activity itself is, as has been shown, a partial concession to those who cannot think, and therefore may be a detriment to those who can — a dangerous sacrifice to democratic equalitarianism. Again, the insistence on pleasure in learning is a revolt against discipline as undemocratic. There is nothing undemocratic about discipline. No one ever achieved self-discipline without first accepting discipline from others. The stress on group activities represents the truth that democracy requires team work and co-operation; it ignores the equally important truth that democracies live by the achievements of solitary original thinkers. Without these, they are bound to collapse into the mass hysteria that throws up a Hitler. Finally, the notion that the teacher must get the lead from the pupils is an absurd reflection of the absurd belief of the 1930's that democratic leaders must be pushed from behind. No teacher worth the name would consent to be led by the class or any member of it, any more than Mr. Winston Churchill would consent to take dictation from his back-benchers.

Thus, education in many of our high schools is handicapped by a rigid and lifeless system which instructs but does not educate. In the elementary schools there is a new freedom and vigour, but again there is a danger of forgetting the true meaning of education. In both systems the confusion between equalitarianism and democracy results in a distortion of aim.

It is always easier to point out errors and deficiencies that to remedy them. What is needed above all is a new comprehension of the essentials of a liberal education, and a new interpretation of them in relation to democratic life. This cannot be done by any legislative or administrative reform. It must be done by the teachers themselves in their class-rooms. They may receive ideas from outside, but they themselves will determine how and when those ideas can be applied. It is safe to say that the soundest approach to educational reform is to raise the standard of the work done by the individual teacher. There are three ways in which this may be done: attract a larger number of highly qualified men and women into the profession; give them freedom to do their work in the best way; make education a national instead of a provincial concern.

Most people would admit that, with certain happy and important exceptions, the teaching profession does not generally attract the best minds. It is a safe profession, with few grave risks and few rewards; adventurous and ambitious minds look elsewhere. It is a profession which exacts a constant, heavy toll on nerves and temper; a brilliant but temperamental teacher cannot stand it, nor can his pupils. On the other hand, the phlegmatic lover of routine can get through, and often does. The professional hazards are grave; those who miss a nervous breakdown drift into stolid complacency, and all face a penurious old age.

We cannot remedy all these evils, but we can make the material conditions of teaching more tolerable. Salaries should be adequate, and promptly paid. Teachers should be allowed to devote themselves to teaching and to preparation therefor; their other social activities should be voluntary, and not thrust upon them by over-enthusiastic school boards and superintendents. Classes should be of a reasonable size; no one can teach a mob of fifty.

Even such simple and obvious reforms would do much to raise the standards of the teaching profession; first, by enabling the many able people now in it to do their best work; and second, by attracting many who have been going into other lines. A more important and fundamental reform, however, is urgently needed. The surest way of attracting the best people into the profession and of giving them a chance to do their best work is to give them freedom from excessive bureaucratic control, the second evil of which Dr. Murray complained. If British education is cramped by it, Canadian education is in danger of strangulation.

In most, if not all, provinces, normal schools are directly under the Department of Education and high schools under local boards. Both are departmentally controlled by a uniform system of text books and examinations. This means that the institutions from which many teachers are recruited are deprived of all initiative and freedom to improve and advance. Teaching, it should be repeated, is an individual process. Each individual must develop his own technique, each school staff must lay down, within certain limits, its own policy and programme, or the best possible results will not be achieved.

This does not mean that there should be no universal standards. At set periods students should submit to general examinations, but the examinations should test for understanding and power, not for a parrot-like knowledge of certain prescribed texts. Does it matter what the French class reads, so long as it learns good French? Does it matter whether students of English read Wordsworth or Shelley, Shakespeare or Milton, so long as they know and love good literature?

Surely, granted a broad general unity of aim, a healthy liberty to differ on special objectives and methods is the essence of democracy in education. The secondary schools of Britain, or some of them, have this liberty; until the secondary schools of Canada have it, Canadian education will not be worthy of the ability and money that we devote to it. Given this liberty, active and intelligent experimentation would soon sift the good from the bad in educational systems old and new. When all experiments are imposed on schools as a system from government departments staffed, at best, with teachers long retired, erroneous ideas become unbearable burdens and even sound ones become sterile in their application.

It is urged that department control is necessary to "keep up the standards." It serves equally well to keep down the standards. It will never make good teachers out of bad ones. It may easily cramp the good teachers, or drive them from the profession.

Better working conditions, and greater academic freedom, would automatically raise the standards of the teaching profession. One thing more is needed: a national system of education. If education is the key to the world of the future, why should Canadian education, at this crucial period in our national life, not be a matter of national concern? This does not mean that the Dominion should do in the future what the provinces do now. Instead of that, the emancipation of the schools from bureaucratic control should be accompanied by a broad national programme of education, which should maintain standards of achievement, but without any dictation of methods. For developing such a programme, and devising ways of promoting it, the best minds in the Dominion — and these are not confined to educational experts — should be secured. There need be nothing in such a national programme contrary to religious freedom, but quite the reverse.

At present, education in Canada is in danger of being starved by false ideas of democracy and strangled by bureaucratic interference. What is needed is a new comprehension of democracy, which translates equality not in terms of uniformity, but of liberty in unity; and a new comprehension of education, which translates education not in terms of examinations passed or of "projects" completed, but as the development of all human faculties not excepting the highest of all — the power of creative thought.[3]

CBC TALK, 1953

Good evening — One of the finest things in our democratic Canadian way of life is that there are so many matters on which we all agree. Our agreement is based not on intellectual indifference but on a devotion to the same virtues, an admiration for the same achievements, and a sincere liking for and understanding of each other. The advantage of such unity is that it leaves everyone of us free to criticize with enthusiasm what seems to him to be wrong in conception or ill-judged in execution. Even while we seem to attack each other we know that we are really defending common values and common aims. As attack is the best form of defence so may strife be the best as well as the most joyful form of co-operation.

I have recently been striving, a little, with the leaders of the vast educational pilgrimage which all Canadians are invited or compelled to join. I know that we are probably in agreement about what may be good or bad places for the pilgrims to reach. But I cannot help saying that I think they are driving the wrong kind of car along the wrong road; that if they continue in this way they will surely take themselves and all the rest of us where no one, no one at all, wants to go. There are two things chiefly that I criticize — what our leaders say and what they do.

First, they use bad language. They use words and phrases that many of us don't understand; they use far too many words; and they make not the slightest attempt to arrange their words and ideas in such fashion as to give them shape and form. They offer us no clear hierarchy of values, no priority system, no hint of what is the first and greatest commandment of all. I am going to give you as an example, a recent version of our progressive western views on education. It reached me only a few days ago, and it is a product of that device so dear to the educator, the "workshop." The great merit of the "workshop," it seems, is that it is entirely free from aristocratic or scholarly overtones; given these essential virtues, the fact that it is entirely unlike the traditional conception of workshop becomes apparently irrelevant.

This workshop undertook to determine the kind of educational programme we need, how we may get it, and what we should do about it immediately. I have read the workshop or rather the pamphlet which emanated from the workshop and I still don't know what its authors really think. I will offer you a sample to prove that my lack of understanding may not be entirely the fault of my traditional education. The qualities to be looked for in a good teacher are listed — sixteen numbered items. I have extracted from these items the following. I offer them to you in the order given: inspirational, stimulating, unprejudiced, well-informed, mature, emotionally adjusted, well-groomed, self-evaluating, economical in the use of school supplies, co-operative, sympathetic, patient, original, resourceful, sincere, tactful, fair, alert, healthy. Of course all these are good — I suppose. But we can't expect them all. What must we insist on, if anything? Should the teacher have a good mind? The workshop doesn't say so.

The teacher, whatever he is like, as one may learn from this and other pronouncements, is expected somehow to operate on the children and the community in all kinds of desirable ways and so to produce all kinds of desirable results. But it is so difficult to get a clear picture either of the teacher or of his job. Instead we sink into a shapeless mass of dull, shop-soiled words.

Not only do our educational leaders abuse our language. They are also careless of other things which deserve all their care: the minds of the children, and the priceless experiences of the past which it is their responsibility to transmit to the children. Nor are our leaders deeply concerned about the minds of the teachers, their scholarly foundations, or the necessity for their continued intellectual refreshment — such intellectual refreshment as may not be procurable at workshops or at teachers' conventions. How is it, that when so much is obscure in educational pronouncements, their indifference here is perfectly clear? The answer is simple. With certain notable and most welcome exceptions these matters are not mentioned at all.

I know that people who say what I am saying are accused even by their more indulgent critics of "not understanding what the schools are doing." Many of us might be quite willing to plead guilty, but with extenuating circumstances. However, I think I do understand partly what "the schools," to use the common expression, are doing. I understand it, and I don't like it any better than I like the language of educational leaders.

They are introducing their conception of democracy into the classroom in order to ensure, as they say, a truly democratic society in the future. It has been suggested by some that to introduce the teachings of John Dewey, who found God not only irrelevant but harmful, into an educational system supported by millions of Canadian parents whose views are by no means so advanced, is hardly a democratic procedure. I think that criticism can be pushed too far. The children have not been made to read John Dewey, and it would indeed be disastrous if teachers were to be offered no philosophy that would not meet the religious views of the average parent.

Certain other practices I do find alarming. One is the scorn of knowledge for its own sake and the determination to make every course from mathematics to social studies a tool for democratic indoctrination. It is true that this indoctrination as a rule is mild and harmless enough, but no one who has read the current tales of brainwashings can contemplate it without alarm.

Another dubious practice is the insistence on democratic equality. This does not mean, we are told, uniform treatment for all children. It means that each child is treated at once individually and as an integral part of a group; that all thus achieve self-fulfilment and a sense of success. It sounds so good that it takes a moment to realize how bad it is. The confused array of qualities and activities, and evidences of goodness in teacher, school and community conceal the fact that in the face of equalitarianism and group activities individual standards of achievement slide away; the individual sense of dedication to something outside and greater than oneself disappears; in simple and explicit terms, the overriding sense of duty as the governing force in life, is set aside.

We have, so far, discovered no modern substitute for an individual sense of duty. It is the cement which holds society together. We must have it. The true sense of duty is confirmed by a reasoned and voluntary dedication. When that fails we are likely to move, not forward to something modern and better, but backward to the ruthless imposition of obligations in a society on the way back to slavery. In our country we are still enjoying the freedom which is the fruit of an individual sense of duty rather slowly and painfully worked out in the course of building a free society. I do not see anything except this sense of duty to save our freedom from collapse. I would like to think I am wrong, but I cannot believe that socialized activities, a democratic climate in the classroom and a sense of security and purposeful achievement are any adequate substitutes.

I and others who criticize current pronouncements and practices are accused of not understanding the needs of a scientific, democratic and psychologically informed age. No one, I suppose, can claim a full understanding of such a difficult matter. When, however, I have become exhausted with the mass and weight of educational jargon, I like to recall a very old, very short statement of educational and social aims, appreciations and attitudes which seems to me quite extraordinarily appropriate to our modern perplexed and terrified society. This is it; you all know it. "What doth the Lord thy God require of thee, but to do justice, to love mercy, and to walk humbly with thy God?"

As an expression of educational philosophy I think it leaves nothing unsaid; those who do not care to refer their doings to a personal God are still left with the socially desirable qualities of justice, mercy and humility. They are, moreover, presented with a useful hierarchy of values which though simple, exact very considerable achievements of the intellect, the imagination and the emotions if they are to be realized. Justice in its widest sense, the sense of rendering to others all that we owe, demands from everyone precise knowledge and mature judgment as well as a sense of duty; mercy requires development of the imagination and the emotions as well as good social attitudes if it is to be wisely bestowed. Humility requires the avoidance of complexes both superior and inferior through the steady and serious contemplation of greatness.

There are other short ways of saying the same thing. I want to urge only that educational and social aims need not be such a clutter of nice things flung by well-meaning people into a sort of democratic catch-all. We should seek rather a simple and profound expression of the truths by which men have always lived; truths which may be abundantly developed and enriched by our imagination and our endeavours but which must not be smothered in professional jargon.

Not long ago I was asked to be practical; to say what I would do if I had a free hand in Canadian education. I can think of no more terrifying situation. I am relieved to think that I shall never have such freedom. There are, however, one or two things that I would like to try.

The Canadian Education Association is now engaged in a research project. They are spending, so they say, $335,000 on examining administrative problems. I would like to have enough money to find out *what* we are administering. I would look for half a dozen exceptionally able, highly educated, cultivated people — who know all about modern theories and techniques of education, to go into our schools and stay in and about them long enough to tell us what is being done there for the children's minds — and for the minds of the teachers. Someone has to deal, and to deal seriously, with minds. Someone has to see to it that the best minds at least are used to their fullest capacity. We must do justice to them, that they may be prepared to do justice to us — to render the best service of which they are capable.

While this school survey goes on I would like to get some more educated people to start half a dozen experimental schools which would concentrate on the old-fashioned acquisition of knowledge with hard work, real discipline, and of course games — but I mean games, not co-curricular activities — and attainments, real attainments, not just a sense of success. We would examine the children regularly, by the latest methods, to find out how many were becoming frustrated and anti-socialized by the new treatment. I would hope and expect to find that sound learning would develop their characters *and* increase their happiness. Of course this would all take time, as well as money. But, we could do two things *now* that would cost no money and would help enormously. First, external examinations for those leaving Grade 8 and Grade 12 — serious examinations, where the children take pen in hand and write; no recommendations; and no bonuses; no objective tests. Successful candidates would have to be able to express such ideas as they had in clear and simple English. Second, a stiff literacy test for all entering training schools — and another, even stiffer, before they leave. And, to go back to where I started, I would like one thing more. I would like our educational leaders to give themselves a little test: one page to be written in English, plain, ordinary English, on the meaning of knowledge and its place in education. They must write it without underlying objectives, reconstructing goals, building insights or evaluating values — and they must not adjust or integrate or socialize *anything*. If they could do that I think there might be hope even for Canadian education.[4]

SO LITTLE FOR THE MIND

Why could not the experts return to these simple and direct statements and build on them? The answer expresses how much of evil, as well as of good, Canadian education owes to the influence of Dewey. It is far easier to stop thinking than to start again, to renounce the habit of serious study, than to resume it. Dewey, as has been said, with all his services to education was in the long run anti-intellectual and anti-cultural in his influence. For several reasons this unfortunate tradition is tenacious. First, the rapidly growing industry of education has attracted and has even accorded responsible positions to many men of scanty scholarship and of intellects less than brilliant. They were only too glad to learn, or rather to think that they had learned from Dewey that it is much more useful and virtuous to bustle about working busily with their hands than to sit on a hard chair and try to think; it came to them as a revelation that this was what they had always suspected but had never quite dared to say.

Moreover, Dewey, it seemed, rolled off another burden. Most people reared in the tradition of western culture, acknowledging their debt to the past and their obligation to use its achievements at least for the improvement of their own minds, experience at times a sense of guilt at the thought of all that they have not read and of all that they do not know. It is, therefore, easy to understand that well-meaning men of restricted reading had a real if unconscious sense of relief at the suggestion that this was all old stuff prepared for idle aristocrats and only barely suitable for a working democracy. They could forget about the glory that was Greece and the grandeur that was Rome, in order to concentrate on concrete definable problems of school administration, school equipment, the latest findings of child psychology, and the "philosophy of education." Of course, there was a growing pile of "literature" in all these fields which left little time for mere culture.

Canadian educational experts have, therefore, allowed themselves to renounce the old sound traditions of a liberal academic education in favour of the faith of Dewey, "Seek ye first a natural environment, manipulative skill and co-operative enterprises and all these things shall be added unto you." Now they no longer believe this. They now admit the necessity of formal instruction, of cultural "values," of moral principles, and even of religion. But, impressed by what they have learned of psychology and related educational sciences, and obsessed with the magnitude of the "social engineering" task that they have voluntarily assumed, they insist on modern shortcuts which will make available to all, painlessly, all the real benefits through expert indoctrination in methods of thinking and in modes of conduct. They announce that we must "have faith" in the ability of all to "solve problems." Why do they not open to us all, as far as they are able, the best of our civilization in literature, science, mathematics, history, art, and then "have faith" that they, like their predecessors, will build on that foundation? The faith of our experts is not faith in the ability of all to solve problems but the reverse. The material which would enable the individual to work out his own salvation is practically withheld in order that he may be more receptive to the readymade solutions that are handed out. Few experts in education show any appreciation of the rewards of disinterested scholarship. And this is not surprising; few indeed have experienced them.[5]

THE PRODUCT OF THE TRAINING SCHOOL

. . . What kind of people, then, do train for the teaching profession? Some, certainly, who are devoted to scholarship, and many, for the elementary schools, who are devoted to children. These may be, and they often are, people of ability, admirably qualified for the profession. Others, however, are drawn into the profession by different and less desirable motives. Teachers may anticipate at present, in many provinces, security and reasonably good salaries. The work seems rather easy, with short hours and generous holidays. [This is a mistake, as many see later. Teaching is not easy. Lazy people would be well advised to try another calling.] Worse still, many are now attracted by the very fact that teaching is no longer a scholarly profession. Scholarship does not interest these people; administration does, "activities" do, social affairs do, athletics do; and the feeling of superiority which comes to the little mind from consorting with the immature makes perhaps the greatest appeal of all. The gravest evil stemming from the anti-intellectual and anti-cultural tendencies of the progressivists is the increasing attraction which the profession now holds for those incapable of using their intellects or of appreciating culture.

The training school does little to give such people any sense of their deficiencies. They suffer from a lack of content in their studies; that is, they are not really made free of the civilization which one might suppose it will be their duty to interpret to others. They remain ignorant, moreover, of the historic and the philosophic background of their work. The history of education is taught traditionally and with no real historic sense. Educational philosophy, if it takes in more than the twentieth century, does so only to condemn, with perhaps a qualified approval of Rousseau's *Emile.*

Teachers are thus deprived of those things which should nourish and stimulate their original enthusiasm for the profession they have undertaken. The great natural incentive of teaching is, after all, to be so pleased with one's subject as to feel an urgent need to go and tell someone about it. This desirable evangelical fervour should be at once disciplined and developed by a true understanding of the history and place of education in society and by a consideration of the principles and values enunciated by the great critics of all ages, including our own. No product of a Canadian training school can boast of such a preparation for his profession.

Many teachers-in-training realize and regret that their instructors do not even give them any sense of the greatness of their profession. They ask for bread and they are given a stone. A very able young man, qualified for university teaching, having experienced difficulty in securing a permanent post in the recent general reduction of university staffs, decided to take training as a high school teacher. He made the decision without regret for, as he said, he preferred teaching to research, and he was impressed with the need for well-qualified and enthusiastic high school teachers. After two months at his school, which is a most reputable institution, he was not at all embittered but he had been repelled by the coldness, the lack of enthusiasm for the profession, the slight regard for scholarship, and the fussily dictatorial methods of the place. He, and others whose need is far greater, are sent out to their work with a set of tools which, they are assured, are perfectly adapted for the work to be done. But they themselves are weak from lack of nourishment, and blind from want of vision.

What kind of people, then, come out of the schools? A generalization may be attempted. There are three types. First the open rebels, who defy everybody, get a bad rating, see no chance of professional advancement, and, therefore, either leave the profession or remain in it as chronic malcontents. Secondly, the independents; their views may be equally decided but their emotions are calmer and their wills are perhaps stronger. They want to teach and they know they have the capacity to do so. They derive such profit and such amusement as they can from their training, and having received their certificates and taken possession of their classrooms, they go their own way, so far as they can do so, harried as they are by activities, curricular and extra-curricular, supervisors, superintendents, conventions, conferences, committees and other teaching aids. The most able members of this group will, no doubt, do excellent work. The rest may eventually find their way, but they will inevitably spend much time groping and bewildered, having been cheated of the help and inspiration that they ought to have had.

There is a third class, the conformists. These absorb all that is offered and easily squeeze it back. Like those in the other groups, their abilities will vary from the very dull to the decidedly bright, although seldom are they really first-class people. It might, however, be supposed that the decidedly bright would one day bring their critical faculties to bear on their tasks and their teachers to such an extent that, if not rebels or independents, they would at least become friendly critics. This does not often happen. The intelligent conformists are soon identified and encouraged to proceed to the higher levels of the educational world. Their natural pleasure at praise and encouragement eventually dulls their critical faculties; and their natural ambition no doubt plays its part. If their critical faculties are too strong to be stifled, there may develop the hint of cynicism already mentioned. These are the "career educators." They do masters' theses on educational statistics, educational measurements, mental hygiene, curricular requirements, and other matters of supreme importance in the educational world. They continue at Teachers' College, Columbia, or in a comparable institution, and ultimately they return as professors, normal school teachers, superintendents and officials in provincial departments of education.[6]

MY SMALL WAR WITH THE EDUCATORS

"We welcome criticism, so long as it's constructive," said a leading Canadian educator and university professor recently.

This response to criticism seems very wise and tolerant until you write it down and look at it. No one really welcomes criticism; sensible people know they will be criticized, they learn to take it in good part and to profit by it if they can. Perhaps they do welcome it in a way; the way they welcome the verdict of the dentist who tells them he has decided on two large fillings and an extraction.

As for "constructive," what does it mean? To urge a man on his way to rob a bank to provide himself with a mask would be a constructive suggestion; to tell him to go home and forget about it would be destructive criticism — and also excellent advice. What is the mysterious virtue in this word constructive? Sometimes we really need a demolition squad. During the past six months I have learned much about the way in which leading Canadian educators welcome criticism. They have afforded me, as they would say themselves, an educational experience.

For some ten years I have been brooding over the changing educational scene wondering just how good were the changes and wondering, occasionally, just how bright were the scene-shifters. Two or three years ago I began trying to gather my ideas into a book.

Many months before it was published someone asked the inevitable but chilling question, "And who do you think will read it? It doesn't seem to appeal to any special audience." I said boldly that I thought teachers would read it; that teachers were the people who really know what happens in school; that many teachers I knew were anxious and discouraged; and that I depended on their evidence to arouse public interest and concern.

I was entirely, or almost entirely wrong. Many teachers, I know, have read the book, some have agreed with it, a few have written to me, and, even more usefully, to the newspapers in support of it. But it was not teachers, but the Press and the public generally that received the book with enthusiasm which even the vanity of an author cannot attribute to merit alone. The other and true explanation has reached me from every corner of the country. One lady (not a Canadian) wrote simply to say that she approved the book and would have written it herself if she had had time. Many Canadians have written more tactfully, that by putting into words their favourite thoughts I had achieved a subtle form of flattery which they found irresistible.

I cannot say with Byron that I awoke one morning and found myself famous. I can almost say that I awoke and found myself infamous. Not all responded to my flattery. The educational leaders have not remained silent but have indeed revealed surprising linguistic resources in their efforts to express themselves on this odious work.

Through patient and laborious "educational research" I have assembled a list of adjectives applied to the book. For convenience I have arranged them in alphabetic order: abusive, acid, angry, aristocratic, arrogant, unblushingly biased, biting, bitter, confusing, contentious, destructive, diffuse, dishonest, distorted, exaggerated, harsh, hysterical, impious (this is the one I like best), inaccurate, misleading, peevish, pitiful, prejudiced, repetitious, sarcastic, spiteful, splenetic, strident, tendentious, unbalanced, exasperatingly unclear, unfair, uninformed, unjust, unkind, unscholarly, unscientific, vindictive, virulent, vituperative and vulgar.

The work has also been described as "the most ibidness book I have ever seen" (whatever this means), "warmed-over Plato," "rightly titled So Little for the Mind," "a mass of exaggeration, sweeping generalization, personal prejudice and even spitefulness." And yet with all that "its effect . . . will be efficacious" (this is from the editor of a teachers' journal who it seems either does not possess a dictionary or has not yet acquired "dictionary skills").

So much for the book. The author is not neglected. "Public Eye Neatby," "Detective Neatby" with her "irritating air of superiority," with her "intellectual snobbishness" is "irritably allergic to experts" and "as a duellist lacks finesse" but "has a distinct relish for impaling her victims." And yet (according to this last authority) although "churlish" she is, rather surprisingly, "a well-intentioned sincere woman." Others, less charitable, find her "acidulous," an "embittered spinster," a "frigid introvert," an "educational McCarthy."

After all this it is refreshing to move to the great outdoors where we find that, "like a high-spirited and somewhat untrained bird dog she may frequently bark up the wrong tree, but she certainly does flush a lot of game," rather a pleasing picture even if it does leave one wondering what is the right kind of tree for a bird dog to bark up.

It is not for me to complain at this exuberance although even my free western upbringing has not entirely accustomed me to being referred to in print as "Hilda" by "prominent" educators to whom I have not as yet been introduced. However, as one (non-educator) who has been good enough to support my views has said, I gave no quarter and expected none. Those who speak frankly must expect frankness in return.

But I had the right to expect complete frankness and, if the expression is permissible, intellectual as well as emotional frankness. Educators have surpassed themselves in the epithets applied to my scholarship, my style and my personality. They owed it to me, and to the public whose attention they have endeavoured to engage, to examine and to answer my arguments also, and to do so with accuracy and with fairness. This they have not done.

Instead, there have been at best, in the general response, numerous variations on the theme "useful, but wrong-headed," supplied by a retired university professor. One reviewer after a lengthy denunciation, admits in a final sentence that many will agree with much of what I say, leaving us to guess that he may even number himself among the agreeable many. A friendly critic commenting on this article remarks, "Perhaps he was right to dissemble his love, but why did he kick her downstairs?" The official pronouncement of the Canadian Education Association reads in part, "The author has . . . perhaps rendered a service in her attack on pedagese, motivation through interest and the education of the whole child." This is unhappily typical. First, I did not "attack" all of these things, and second, did I or did I not render a service? If this authoritative reviewer cannot say, who can? If he had not at that time made up his mind on this essential matter, should he have rushed into print with an article which has been enthusiastically mined for material by faithful followers throughout the country?

The comments of this group fall roughly into three categories. A very few are purely abusive. One of these, first written in the form of a letter to a daily paper, was thought worthy of reproduction in the professional journals of two western provinces. Others combine with abuse some attempt at serious comment. The third group follows the pattern shown above with faint praise followed by loud and hearty damns.

"Some of what you say may be true but you are a liar; we question your motives and your scholarship; and how dare you criticize elementary and secondary school practices when you teach in a university?"

"But at least," say some of these critics, "the book has been useful in stirring up controversy." How? Is controversy useful in itself? A well-placed handful of mud will stir up controversy in almost any group, but is this really useful? Many critics now are beginning to think not. They suggest rather that educational leaders ("those at the top") should, as "gentlemen" (but not, surely, "aristocrats"), exercise restraint "over the whole unfortunate thing" until "the situation stirred up by Dr. Neatby" subsides.

There are educators, including even some at or near "the top" who, fervently agreeing that the book is a bad thing, have not been able to exercise restraint. With mathematical precision it has been adjudged 98 per cent wrong. The remaining two per cent have not been identified. A distinguished director of educational research has been good enough to place me in the headlines with Neatby Education Ideas Said Not Worth Nickel. "Dr. Neatby (he is reported to have said) . . . squanders a lot of $64 language on a lot of ideas which, if they were retailed at a nickel apiece, would represent profiteering." It is indeed churlish to criticize a pronouncement which sheds so much light on methods and attitudes deemed appropriate in educational research. Seriously, what business has this educational leader and many others to deal with the book without even attempting to answer the serious questions which I raised and to which I and all other Canadians have a right to demand an answer?

No one has attempted to answer the contention that the school's central purpose is or should be intellectual. An educational official described as a "director" of a branch of a well-known university in a "call for fair play" explains that "the business of education will continue its task of developing boys and girls who will have to work with their fellow men to make this Canada of ours a better place in which to live." They will do this by "the development of pupil intelligence, democratic leadership, peace and an inculcation of spiritual values," this development to be brought about apparently by teacher training "based on sound psychological, sociological and philosophical foundations." He then gives a list of five philosophies, remarks that whichever you pick you must consider "the welfare of young people" and ends with an "eclectic conclusion" in ten numbered statements which include, surprisingly, a brief statement on the causes of "Great War I, Great War II and the Korean War" and ends, not surprisingly at all, with "Education should develop an appreciation of the good, the beautiful and the true."

Yes, indeed, but does this educator believe, or doesn't he, that when children come to school the teacher has a direct and special responsibility to do something for their minds? We still don't know, and I am now convinced that he doesn't either.

Many other simple and important questions remain unanswered. Do we not need definite and ascertainable standards of achievement? Should there not be an official concern for scholarly achievement by the average as well as by the gifted child? After all, many average parents who acknowledge average children, think they have a right to expect that something be done for these children's minds. And finally, should there not be more concern for the intellectual endowment, the intellectual training and the continued intellectual enrichment of the teacher?

These questions which were asked, I believe, in clear and simple English have been clearly and simply ignored. Not one of the officials who attacked my book has said that schools are not primarily concerned with intellectual values, but not one says they are. And yet there is the critical question; for if the democracy apparently loved but most evidently not cherished by educators is to endure, we must have some institution which will give first place to matters of the mind. The question is not mine alone. Many during the last few months have shown concern for the supreme importance of the teachers' task which is, in effect, the creation of the intellectual climate of the next generation. My critics alone, apart from casual references to "the gifted child," maintain an attitude of complete indifference.

To say that educators have not answered the essential questions raised in my book does not mean that they have not dealt with the contents. They have maintained a kind of guerrilla warfare with frequent excursions into enemy territory from which they return happily laden with spoils, secured very often by those unorthodox methods which too often are associated with guerrilla warfare. The tactics are varied but they fall into three or four recognizable patterns.

There is, first, the "sweeping generalization" attack. This is easy and quite effective. It captures the booty by pure bluff. Sweeping generalization sounds very bad. Not everyone will reflect that scientific laws are nothing more than generalizations on known facts and that they are, indeed, sweeping generalizations. Sweeping generalizations as a term of reproach implies a statement which ignores one or more relevant facts. The soundness of the accusation must depend on the accuser citing such a statement, along with the facts which it ignores. And yet I have read dozens of such accusations without a single quotation from the book to support them. The reason is simple. I did not make sweeping generalizations. At the cost, occasionally, of sacrificing style to caution, I made a practice of modifying all general statements which dealt with matters of fact. Expressions of opinion — as for example that our current educational practices are anti-intellectual — should, of course, be received as expressions of opinion and no more.

Sweeping accusations of sweeping generalizations are often followed up by the expression "not a shred of evidence," again, as a rule, without a shred of evidence in support of the accusation. Many, however, do at this stage bring in the beloved "ivory tower — academic seclusion" cliché, not knowing apparently that ivory towers are as scarce as other types of housing in Canada today and that none are reserved for university professors. More practical than the ivory tower is the accusation that I have not visited classrooms and that therefore my views are based solely on personal opinion. But if I had visited classrooms, on what other than personal opinion could my views be based? Indeed, what right have I to offer the public any views which do not coincide with my personal opinion?

Admittedly my failure to visit Canadian schools might well have rendered my opinions more or less worthless if it had been my purpose to generalize on proceedings in the classrooms. I did not undertake to say what goes on in the Canadian classroom. Instead I tried to determine from their own carefully considered official statements, printed and circulated at the public expense, what our educational leaders think should go on in the classroom. These sources have been blithely brushed aside as valueless. Perhaps they are absolutely valueless in one sense. Perhaps they do tell nothing about classroom practices. They are, however, invaluable as evidence of what our educational authorities would like to think were classroom practices. Or if they do not, why do educational authorities produce them?

There is, indeed, something strangely inconsistent in the attitude of those who revile me for having dared to talk about the schools on the basis of written evidence without having visited classrooms in person; while scores of people who certainly have never visted *me* in person do not hesitate to describe me in detail on the basis of my book — which they may or may not have read. I am not prepared to admit that all the epithets which have been applied to me are accurate (they could hardly *all* be accurate) but if my critics insist on deducing the quality not only of my scholarship and my mind, but even of my character and disposition from my writings, they must allow me the privilege of drawing some conclusions on Canadian education from the official pronouncements of Canadian educational authorities.

One other device of the "sweeping generalization — not a shred of evidence" tactic is important. It is the cry of "false documentation" which gives critics the right to brand my book as "unscholarly" and/or "inaccurate" and/or "unacceptable even at the undergraduate level of research" and so forth. For these charges there are, indeed, two shreds of evidence, one very small and the other very misleading. The only real support for the charge of "false documentation" that has been presented to me or to my publishers is the omission in a footnote of the first publication date in a pamphlet which had been reprinted six years after its first appearance. Thus purely technical error might be important in a work of very intricate documentation; in my book, although I regret the error, I know and my critics know that it has not the slightest practical significance.

The second shred is even more dubious. A reviewer, a professor in a college of education, states that "the frequent use of references from 'unpublished manuscripts in possession of the author' denies to the reader the privilege of judging the competence of the authorities *from whom she draws much of her information* (italics mine)." Similar comments have been made by others, some of whom have been good enough to dignify the unpublished material with the title of "master's thesis." The truth is this: there are 377 footnotes in the book; four of them refer to unpublished material; about eight others refer to private information. This makes 12 out of 377 references which are "inaccessible to the reader." Moreover the "information" while interesting and pertinent is in no way essential to the main argument, which stands and was intended to stand on what educators themselves say about education.

Misrepresentations sometimes subtle, sometimes blatant, of what is actually contained in the book constitute the second type of guerrilla tactics. There is the charge often repeated in words such as these: "the author's main trend of thought is that schools should return to the aims and methods of the turn of the century"; "she would discard all that educators have learned in the last fifty years about the child and adolescent psychology and adjustment." I did suggest and I do believe that we are losing sight of many old and essential values because we have gone overboard in pursuit of the new professional learning. But many who have criticized my reactionary and "pendulumist" tendencies, including the critic who remarked that every time I mentioned discipline there was heard the swish of a whip, have overlooked an important section of the book which, as it happens, was given a particularly wide circulation through advance publication in a leading Canadian weekly.

I quote a short passage from this section: "This sympathetic and understanding attention to the child as an individual, to his physical well-being, to his interests, and to his moral growth must win the approval of all who are interested in children or in education. . . . Neglect of health and comfort, lack of sympathy and harshness, drill and discipline for their own sakes are as unfashionable today as their opposites were a generation or two ago. The educational system which undertakes to care adequately for all — the dull, the lazy and the misfits, as well as for the bright and industrious — is indeed a new and notable achievement."

There is, I believe, nothing in the book inconsistent with this position and much that specifically supports it. And yet the critic who accuses me of wishing to wash out fifty years of progress is a relatively mild representative of his group, and a man with a reputation for care and moderation.

Another misrepresentation which one can only hope is unintentional is the statement that I would reserve high schools for the intellectual elite. This has been many times repeated. Six critics, whose reviews are before me, even give approximate percentages of those whom I would remove from the school between the ages of 12 and 14; they range from 40 to 80 per cent. In fact, I made no estimate of numbers. I suggested only that instead of struggling to retain in school those "who have no interest in the school's purpose" (the words are those of a distinguished Canadian educator) they should be invited to withdraw before they destroyed the character of the school. As a result the word "aristocrat" has been shrieked up and down the country with a fervour worthy of the Jacobins; but it should be observed that no one has ventured to say that it is positively described to entice into the high school those who have no interest in the school's purpose.

There are numerous other petty misrepresentations. I did not "attack" the education of "the whole child"; I specifically approved it. I did not coin the expression "experts." That is what they like to call themselves. I don't care for their taste but it's a free country — still. I did not say that British schools are superior to Canadian in every respect; it happens that I do not even think so. I did not confine my discussion of American influences on our education to a sampling of the degrees of a small group of professors. I did not make light of educational research; I made fun of some of the unscientific nonsense that passes for educational research and I urged more attention to matters which educators themselves say are important. I did not recommend the abolition of all training schools; I suggested that (speaking of educational research) we follow an American example and institute *one* experimental apprenticeship course. I don't approve of the method, "Open your book at page   ." I even said so in so many words and was rebuked for being (by implication) unfair to traditionalists.

Finally, I did not say that Canadian educators employed the tactics of Hitler and Stalin. I said that they used, perhaps in ignorance, the same kind of argument that had been used in totalitarian states, when in the name of social welfare they demanded something like absolute power. I did not suggest and I do not think that they realize all the possible implications of their public statements.

A third tactic (also typical of guerrilla methods) is evasion. "I would imagine," says a reviewer, "that most administrators will shrug off her attack as an uninformed, prejudiced and cloudy bit of writing." This is not far from the truth.

They shrug it off, or shriek it down. Some of the critics even try both at the same time.

An example of a simple and crude method is the bare statement from a teachers' journal that everything is taken care of: "School people defended existing school conditions with facts from an informed point of view and in doing so 'exposed' the book as nothing but an opinion arrived at from a position of remoteness and isolation from the real, 'alive-and-kicking' educational community. Some things Miss Neatby mentioned are true but she did not prove them scientifically." Professional educators, it seems, must show their respect for educational research by ignoring all such contraband truth.

The educators or their allies have used one more device which would hardly be worth mentioning were it not for their own apparent faith in it. It is the cry of "Unfair, unfair!"

For example, one who presents himself as "a quiet voice" urging "a merger of opposing factors to submerge the errors and bring to the surface the best ideas of each" finds it necessary to speak in his judicial fashion severely of a certain radio debate on the book. He criticizes me for appealing to "natural public sympathy" (based on traditionalist sentiment), for being "cool and sharp with repartee," and for "university-debate logic," although he is good enough to add that I am "not completely to blame" for my "error" as the conditions of the debate encouraged it.

Since when, in a public discussion of a matter of public interest has it been an "error" to appeal to public sentiment, to remain cool and to make use of logic? One gets the impression that the use of logic and a successful appeal for public support are somehow not quite cricket. It is easy to understand that logic may be damned as remote and academic but it is hard for the abused author of an "ivory-tower indictment" to be blamed (in the name of democratic education) for enlisting "natural public sympathy" even if it is based on sentiment. I had not thought of my book as a sentimental production.

The most unfair thing of all, though, is my English. Educators speak of it as if, like logic, it were an unfair device, a smooth piece of business, almost a stab in the back. "Dr. Neatby uses English exceptionally well, a fact which to the poorly informed tends to lend an aura of plausibility to even her most implausible arguments," one of my most distinguished critics is reputed to have said. One can only admire the consistency with which the writer himself avoids the fault he condemns in others. In the new education, if logic is unfair, style is the specious device for those who would deceive.

I think I should not be guilty of prejudice, hysteria, impiety or even a sweeping generalization if I said that the public response to my criticism offered by official educators in the daily press and in professional journals has been undignified, unintelligent and supremely uninteresting. Loss of temper does not redeem most of the articles from dullness, jargon and pedantry. There is no evidence of the joy or even of the glee of combat. The pretext offered is that nothing can be secured by debate and we must all get round the table and talk. Debating is harmful, "choosing sides" pernicious. One wonders if educators even know how their own country is governed? Not exclusively by debate certainly, but it would be a sad day if debates were to disappear.

Educational leaders have been reminded of this. A moderate and carefully reasoned letter to an eastern paper urges that an attack which starts an argument is not necessarily a bad thing. "It would be a pathetic result of (Miss Neatby's) attack if those of us who are equally concerned with education should climb onto a stolid little rampart of self-justification." A parent writes that criticism is always difficult and criticism of those whose honesty and sincerity we respect may be painful. She adds, "But it is a mistake not to challenge ideas, when the only reason for not doing so is a reluctance to embarrass a genuine supporter of them." And a teacher adds, "What we ought to do of course if we believe Dr. Neatby is wrong is to find out why she and dozens like her feel it their duty to speak at all."

Moreover there is evidence in my own province and elsewhere that there are many holding responsible positions in educational administration and on educational faculties who refuse to close their minds to criticism even though they may find it unpleasant if not offensive. They are not prepared to toss out critics as mere logicians and stylists or to dispose of public concern as traditionalist sentiment. They do not write much to the papers. It may be that they prefer not to write until they have had more time to think.

The unfortunate result, however, is that in spite of a number of protests from teachers, the published views of professional educators follow the patterns which have been outlined. The impression is clearly given that it is themselves rather than their job that they take seriously, and that for all their talk of democracy they care nothing for individual freedom.

And these are not a lunatic fringe. Educators quoted or refered to in this article include important officials from all parts of the country, men who hold key positions. It was one such, not yet quoted, who indicated that one way to stop "vicious attacks" on education was "concerted official action . . . taken by educators" with a view to preventing publication. He cited, with apparent approval, an example of such a course which had, he believed, been followed in the U.S.

This attitude on the part of supposedly responsible and undoubtedly powerful officials, though it has its absurd aspects, is not funny. It is not, surely, an illegitimate appeal to public sentiment to say that our free society rests on freedom of speech; and that freedom of speech has no meaning if it does not involve freedom to differ, to debate and to criticize — negatively as well as positively.

As John Stuart Mill said a century ago, freedom of speech may be guaranteed by law but it will not work unless people agree that it is necessary and valuable. It must be tolerated; it must be welcomed. Mill was worrying about the danger of social tyranny. The danger of administrative tyranny was less obvious in an age when it could be argued seriously that education was the concern of parents only.

Are we not in danger of losing our freedom to criticize because we do not appreciate our right and our obligation to be criticized? It is hard to take criticism especially (as may sometimes occur) when criticism from hostile or irresponsible sources is directed at those who bear heavy burdens. It is hard; but liberty is hard; democracy is hard. In freedom we have chosen a hard and a noble way of life.

We cannot tolerate within ourselves that natural but dangerous shrinking from the necessary conditions of our life. There are those who say of my own criticisms that I did not mean them, that I wrote them with my tongue in my cheek, and so forth. I can only say that when I wrote these things I believed them to be true; now, fresh from reading a vast pile of angry nonsense, I am forced to the conclusion that they are proved beyond reasonable doubt.[7]

EDUCATIONAL SIMONY

We don't hear nearly as much as we used to about "education for democracy." For years eggheads and malcontents exposed ably (so they thought) but uselessly the crimes committed in its name. Only recently have the truly modern group activities and enterprises of Mr. Krushchev and his colleagues and the stern admonitions of practical men like Admiral Rickover broken in on professional complacency. We may even be in for something like a revival of learning in this country. The prospect tempts me to take another look at "education for democracy." Now that the expression is losing its sting it may be examined at leisure and without rancour. It is even possible to remember that it does represent one of the most noble conceptions of the western world, a moral and intellectual ideal almost lost in a mass of mechanical doing. However the words may have been abused the purpose they represent, and the roots from which it has sprung, should not be forgotten.

The democratic tradition emerged gradually in the modern age from more than one root. It is rooted, first of all, in the Judaic-Christian tradition. Every man has a soul; every soul is valuable in the eyes of God: if every soul is not equally valuable in God's eyes at least His standards differ from ours so greatly that we must accept each individual as having, from the standpoint of eternity, intrinsic and equal value. It is not for us to treat any person as a mere means to an end or to set one above another as having special value or importance. Men are distinguished superficially by their gifts and their virtues, by their achievements and their services, but in their fundamental humanity they stand on a level. No man is privileged in the eyes of the God who made him.

Moreover this Christian tradition assumes at once the frailty and even the wickedness of man, and his capacity for goodness and for righteous behaviour, with the aid of divine grace and, humanly speaking, a careful nurture in religion and morals. The Christian root of democracy implies a very great emphasis on education, and, to use the well known cliché, an education which lasts through life.

So much for the religious foundation of the democratic philosophy, of supreme importance and easily forgotten. There is another root, the rational one. By the eighteenth century at least it was being freely stated that all men are equal because all are endowed with the peculiarly human faculty of reason. All are more or less capable of grasping and apprehending truth, and of governing themselves accordingly. Men, it is true, behave irrationally but they do so through ignorance. If ignorance can be dispelled their reason will tutor and control their passions, and right conduct — to use a modern expression, socially desirable conduct — will result. Therefore every person individually, and society as a whole, has the right and duty to dispel ignorance and to build a peaceful harmonious society through the development of individual freedom. In short, the individual bound in chains of ignorance is a slave to his passions; this seems to justify arbitrary social control, the subjection of the lower orders, and so forth. By dispelling ignorance his reason may be set free and he can then safely be his own master and may claim an approximate equality with his fellows.

No doubt many rationalists of the eighteenth century would have looked very dubiously on this version of their creed. Voltaire who believed passionately in equality before the law and in a large measure of liberty certainly had no blind faith in the common man and his doubts were shared by others including many of the leaders of the French Revolution. But the notion of some sort of rational equality with liberty was an entrancing one. It underlies the radical thought of the late eighteenth and early nineteenth century on both sides of the Atlantic. It is the historic democracy of this period in its most extreme and simple form. Reason alone would not sustain it, but as a spiritual ideal it caught the minds of men and held them captive as it still does.

Its weaknesses, however, as a view of society were soon obvious. It could become an atomistic social creed. The principle of "laissez faire," of setting every individual free to go his own way, good and noble in a sense, can lead to social abuses. It could easily degenerate into the survival of the fittest. Men as a class may be reasonable beings, but the reason of some is much more powerful and competent than that of others. They needed to be reminded that they were not set free for themselves alone. Moreover men are social beings and one simply cannot maintain a society on competition alone.

The atomistic tendencies of democratic rationalism were, in fact, balanced in the nineteenth century by a number of forces. There was the philosophy of eighteenth-century Rousseau with his conception of the General Will, a social fusion of individual wills each one surrendering to the other. Democracies like totalitarian states have drawn much on Rousseau in their need for achieving social solidarity. Even in the age of reason he was ready to trust impulse rather than judgment and to set spontaneous feeling above critical thought.

There was also the later and typically nineteenth-century development of modern nationalism, that very complex movement emerging in part as a protest against Napoleon and his rational, if not very democratic rule. Nationalism emphasized the emotional and intuitive oneness of a people rather than the rational individuality of its members. With all its evils and dangers, among peoples who emphasized laissez faire in social and economic matters, it served as a powerful unifying force, and so made its contribution to the modern conception of a democratic society. So, in its own way did socialism with its direct protest against economic individualism and laissez faire, and its emphasis on the principles of harmony, co-ordination, organization or association instead of naked competition.

There was thus a number of different and even conflicting forces safeguarding rational democracy from reducing society to a kind of peaceful anarchy through its emphasis on individual freedom and laissez faire. There was also, of course, the abiding influence of that other great root of democracy, the Judaic-Christian teaching and tradition. The Christian claimed an essential equality and an entire freedom, but he was not free for himself alone. The whole basis of his thinking was community. No man lives unto himself; every man is his brother's keeper; one bears another's burden; if meat makes a brother to offend, you take no meat for his sake. The democratic rationalists of the late eighteenth and early nineteenth century did not acknowledge their Christian root. They were anti-clerical, sceptical, even atheist. Nevertheless the strong social solidarity of Christian philosophy imperceptibly tempered their views of the rights of man and brought together in the cause of a humane community men who had little else in common. The fervent evangelical Christian, Lord Shaftesbury, worked in the same field as the rational sceptic Owen against the right of any man to keep his factory open sixteen hours a day without a change of shift.

A modern thinker who carries democracy far from rational laissez faire brings us very near to education: John Dewey. Democracy, he said, consisted not in individual freedom, but in the shared and social experience. He was historically wrong; this was not the classic doctrine of democracy, the democracy that had moved and inspired Americans and French in the revolutions that shook ancient society and helped bring to birth the modern world. But if he was historically wrong, morally and psychologically he was right. Individual rights and freedom are only half man's life, only half his joy; the other half, paradoxically, is to use this freedom in sharing and giving, the sharing and giving that makes up the essence of community life. And in this conviction Dewey sums up the best moral tradition of the Jew and the Christian.

John Dewey confronts us with the great theme of education for democracy. What has democracy to do with education? If the conception of the two roots, Christian and rational, is accepted, of course democracy has everything to do with education. The Christian must give nurture and admonition in religion and morals or he denies his creed. And the rationalist must develop what he deems man's central and governing faculty, his reason. The rationalist would set every man free by dispelling the ignorance which limits and imprisons him. Everyone who has really learned has experienced the sense of liberation, of new breadth to life. He has travelled through new country and made it his own. And without ignorance, the individual is brought to the full development of his powers. He becomes free of what is his own.

And yet the danger of this form of education has always been recognized, consciously or unconsciously. The rationally educated man is much more powerful than the uneducated one, and he must be trusted not to abuse his new powers. Those who educate him must run the risk of seeing him more efficient in doing wrong as well as in doing right; they must be prepared for the almost equally painful experience of seeing him disagree with them and change the world that they have learned to like. If there has been a complete and honest effort to liberate and nourish the mind, people are free, free to do wrong as well as to do right, free to change civilization as well as to preserve it. The "safeguards" which have operated on laissez faire democracy have also operated on so-called democratic education. Rousseau, for all his Emile, when he planned a system of state education did not see it quite as a process of rational liberation. Nationalists have always had a good deal to say about education and so have socialists, and so, of course, have the exponents of the various branches of the Christian church. None of these groups has thought of it exclusively as a process of liberation. And the modern exponents of "socialization" and "life adjustment" must, in this respect, be put into the same category although they are less honest about it for they talk ceaselessly about democratic education when, in fact, in the sense of rational liberation, they are afraid of it.

Education, at first private, became increasingly a public concern in the evolving democratic societies of the western world. The comfortable moneyed aristocracies of the eighteenth century had inherited and developed from the Christian humanists of the Renaissance what they called "the education of a gentleman." It was the kind of education that was regarded as a legitimate object of ambition for every gifted and ambitious lad, and, as concern for public education grew, there was a desire to make it or something like it, available to as many people as possible. This was a perfectly proper and natural thing to do. The eighteenth-century gentleman, as one well known educationist has suggested, showed a great capacity and determination to secure the best for himself in everything: houses, gardens, food, furniture, pictures, books — and education. It was the noble ambition of the idealists in increasingly wealthy societies to open to all what had hitherto been the privileges and pleasures of the few. Democratic development was to be a process not of vulgarization but of an ever-widening distribution of the best to everyone.

The education of the gentleman has been described as knowledge for its own sake, "sufficient for itself apart from every external and ulterior object." This is the essence of intellectual freedom. Intellectual emancipation was to come through full understanding, complete enjoyment, and therefore in a sense control of the world looked at through the eyes of science, a rational view of human nature; the arts, a special non-rational approach, yielding insights apart from and beyond mere logic, an appeal to the deepest emotions. It is true that the formal education of the gentlemen was generally confined to the humanities, but the conception was not limited. It included universal knowledge, but always knowledge gained for its own sake.

This kind of education, often in a distorted and degenerate form and with various modifications, remained the standard for secondary schools everywhere until the early twentieth century. Then a vigorous attack on it and all its branches was launched by John Dewey, who attempted to translate into educational methods his conception of the new democratic society, built on science and on a new understanding of nature. To Dewey the natural world was not simply the scene or background of human life but a vast complex of which man was a part, with which he was logically continuous. Dewey had a horror, almost an unreasoning horror, of the aristocratic intellectual. He rather ungratefully ignored the fact that an aristocratic education had so nourished and liberated him that he was able to devote a long and fruitful academic life to attempting to destroy the very conception of it.

Dewey deplored all abstract knowledge, all information gained for its own sake. Education was to be a process of achieving immediate aims, from the viewpoint of the children. The purpose of the teacher must be to encourage the shared experience which was the essence of democracy. Although Dewey did admit some value in sharing experiences of past ages he seems to have been a pioneer in subordinating "subject matter" to methodology. "We may secure technical specialized ability in algebra, Latin or botany, but not the kind of intelligence which directs ability to useful ends. Only by engaging in a joint activity where one person's use of material and tools is consciously referred to the use other persons are making of their capacities and appliances, is a social direction of disposition attained."

Dewey was not unmindful of the value of disciplined thought or of useful knowledge. He does seem to have been suspicious of knowledge for enjoyment. He was greatly concerned, it seems, with interpreting democratic education in what might be called a measure of rational liberation and discipline guarded by sub-Christian values in the form of voluntary group activity and the shared experience.

Meanwhile the conception of education was also being transformed by the new science of psychology. The conclusions drawn from psychological findings have led many influential leaders to reject even the elements of a liberal education which might be derived from Dewey and to go overboard for pure "socialization" and "life adjustment." Their policy has been based on two new and important insights into the capacity and character of the child to be educated, a factor which should indeed be borne in mind.

The first of these insights is not new but has been given much publicity by the modern research which has accompanied the attempt to give every child an elementary school education, and even a secondary school education, not to mention the subtle suggestion which one senses in the air that there is something undemocratic in not providing everyone with some sort of "degree." While education has thus progressively broadened its base the startling inequality of natural endowments has been revealed with the remorseless precision, and, let us hope, accuracy, of the statistician. Men are certainly not born equal unless it is in respect of their rights and the number of children who cannot benefit, or who can benefit only very slightly, from their right to a rational and liberal education appears to be considerable. It was always so, but mass education and mass methods of testing in state systems of education have made it necessary to face the situation and deal with it by a suitable policy.

A second psychological discovery which has shaken the faith of some educators in a rational education is the revelation that most of us, no matter how able we think we are, are in many ways not rational at all but are the creatures of drives, frustrations and repressions. The fact that we are unaware of our captivity does not set us free.

The answer to both these revelations has been education directed not simply to rational enlightenment but to a process of conditioning, which does of course include rational processes, the object of which is to enable the individual to live happily and harmoniously in the society in which he finds himself. The object is not to set him free by extending his knowledge and cultivating his understanding but to engage him in activities and expose him to influences which will render undesirable unsocial actions improbable. This is "socialization" or "life adjustment." It is approved as democratic because it emphasizes group activities, democratic "sharing," and equality. It has moved a long way from the democracy which would make men equal by setting them all free. It rather looks forward to the fact hailed as the herald of a great new age by the Dean of Humanities in a certain famous academic institution, of "our approaching scientific ability to control men's thoughts with precision." The "life adjustment" approach permeates, if it does not dominate, much modern thought, educational and otherwise, to an alarming extent. "May we not," says Joseph Wood Krutch, "have philosophized ourselves into a question where we are no longer able to manage successfully our mental and spiritual lives?"

But democratic education has not been merely a projection of new psychological insights, it has also reflected the apparent needs of a materialist society seeing success in terms of technological advance.

Through the nineteenth and into the twentieth century pure knowledge increased with enormous speed. And in this great age all knowledge was increasingly being put to practical uses: industry, commerce, communications, the professions were all drawing on pure knowledge to show them how to do their work more efficiently, more rapidly, or perhaps to do things that they had never done before. The result was that knowledge increasing rapidly was almost immediately translated into "know-how." In a busy money-making age, when most of the people being educated were not "gentlemen" but would have to earn their living, there was a natural tendency to take the short cut and get the "know-how" rather than the knowledge. And again, there was a tendency to test the value of knowledge by asking whether it could be translated into "know-how." All this seems a natural and not such a bad tendency. But all true education, all liberating education, all "education for democracy" ends when you begin to ask of any piece of knowledge "What use is it?" What use is poetry, painting, music, history, philosophy? None probably except to enlarge and liberate the mind, set the spirit free, increase one's capacity for joy and for sorrow, enhance and enlarge one's whole being. Rule out everything that cannot be immediately translated into "know-how" and you have ruled out everything that really makes for human growth and human freedom.

There has recently been an awareness of the danger of this magnification of "know-how" even in terms of material success. From the scientists we hear increasingly of the important distinctions between applied, basic, and "pure" science, and of the danger of neglecting the last. . . . Pure science lies at the root of know-how and without pure science there wll be no know-how. But how does one secure advances in pure science? The "pure" scientist is by definition totally disinterested, completely unconcerned with the practical effects of his discoveries. How do those who are interested in something else produce pure scientists and secure from the fruitful labours? Is our technological society being driven back to something like the "education of a gentleman?" Are we prepared to risk production of the once-dreaded "élite" in the interests of national defence? Apparently we are. Our recent passionate concern for pure science because the Russians are outspacing us is an attempt to buy salvation, a kind of educational simony.

It can't be done. Our money will perish with us. The kingdom of heaven must be sought first and sincerely before the other things are added. We must have a revival of learning because true learning makes better people and better people make a better society. The threats of Mr. Kruschchev and the warnings of Admiral Rickover must obviously be heeded, but they have nothing to do with the definition of that true education we believe to be the foundation of a free life and of a character useful in the best sense. Such an education must be rescued from the false accusations of the equalitarians, from the pessimism of the non-rationalists, and from the false love of those who look only for the golden eggs which they identify with "research."

Our traditional education values must be revived. We all need "liberation," or freeing from ignorance as far as that may be achieved, and most of us are rational enough to be liberated in some degree. We all need moral discipline. We need to base our education on a belief in intellectual freedom, and in moral choice, and in spiritual values — values rather asserted than denied by those who, refusing to contemplate the possibility of heaven, teach themselves to look courageously on hell. All these things belong to our tradition and may be secured for our generation by diligence and devotion — but not by a calculating fear of the Communists or anyone else. The education of a gentleman is not for sale.[8]

THE RE-DIRECTION OF EDUCATION

Our educational systems would automatically right themselves if, by taking thought, it were possible to bring about a revival of civilization and to check the advance of barbarism within. Education, as Dewey has truly said, is a means of social continuity, and a society with a living belief will take adequate measures to secure its transmission.

Nevertheless, even if education is no more than a symptom, some symptoms require to be treated as if they were a disease. No one has ever questioned that systems of education do operate on the society of which they are the products. A serious attempt to revise our current systems in the light of human experience might do much to put new life into our vague and visionless society.

The key to the problem of education is obviously in the hands of the teachers. It is interesting to observe that in the recent report on Ontario education the matter of teacher training is dealt with at some length. Having stated that the teacher is the keystone of the educational arch and having rightly urged that teachers should be educated, the members of the commission, going on to the question of normal school instructors, make absolutely no suggestion that they should be scholars. Much emphasis is placed on their teaching and on their administrative experience. There is no suggestion that these people who are to train and inspire teachers should themselves be noted for their scholarship or for their culture. The report requires them to "possess high qualifications." These high qualifications refer to teaching and administrative experience, to personality and to health. There is no direct reference to scholarship or to cultural achievement. [A minority report dissents specifically from this attitude.]

Surely the proper procedure is to require all teachers and, even more, all those who teach teachers to do what every educated member of society should do; they should be allowed and encouraged to examine their roots, to look at the society in which they are to work and for the future of which they are in large part responsible, in relation not only to present phenomena but to the whole of its past. They should be invited to base their philosophy on a thorough understanding of the whole civilization and culture of which they and their society are products. They should be allowed to forget for a time about model kitchens and green blackboards, electric doors and intercommunication systems. They should be allowed to forget about custodians and counsellors, superintendents and supervisors and audio-visual experts. They might even forget for a moment the modern world and its problems in order to look at their whole civilization, at the spiritual and intellectual inheritance of which they are, in a special sense, the custodians. Let them look at their pupils not merely as so many units composed of reflexes and emotional drives, but as people, heirs of this civilization, capable of enjoying it and of enriching it. They should go out not as skilled conditioners trained to induce desirable attitudes but as evangelists with a genuine love of truth and with an urge to instruct and to inspire those whom they teach.

This idea is not original. Many people have been deeply concerned at the load of methodology and psychology under which teachers in training stagger. It is reported that one state in the American union has considered a plan whereby teachers should be trained simply through an extended course in the liberal arts supplemented by apprentice teaching (internship) under colleagues of competence and of experience [Reported in *Time*, November 12, 1951, and *School Review*, January 1952, p. 9.]. One of the authors of the scheme comments:

> A great many educators have felt for a long time that emphasis on teaching techniques has gotten out of hand in this country. Under-graduates who plan to enter the teaching profession have been spending an increasing amount of their time on the sort of subjects that are facetiously referred to as "blackboard engineering".... In some cases they spent more time studying teaching methods than they did studying the subject they would be called upon to teach.

There is no reason why such a scheme should not be tried in some Canadian province. It is, after all, followed in all universities where, it is generally agreed, there are at least some competent and inspiring teachers. With teachers sent into the schools not "trained" but educated, not completely briefed, but, one would hope, inspired with an enthusiasm for their fields of study and a zeal for the intellectual well-being of their pupils, facts might once more come into their own; and subjects (integrated by all means) might yet be allowed to stand on their own feet and perform their function of enlightenment without being forced inevitably to produce socialized attitudes.

As for what might be done in the schools by such enlightened teachers, they should surely begin by ceasing to urge the children to spare their minds and follow their fancies. He who saves his mind will certainly lose it. Educators, rightly concerned at the mass of facts which seem pertinent to modern life, have lost themselves in conveying useful information and inducing right approaches instead of insisting on the knowledge which is power and from which right judgment can grow. There is nothing so stimulating to the mind as a sense of mastery over a certain field, no matter how restricted. If it is retorted, as it certainly will be, that the object of the modern school is not just the conveying of facts but the building of character, the answer is obvious. No method of character building has yet been found which can replace the old way of "the vision of greatness." Our decayed democracy fears this vision of greatness. A certain Canadian educator, it is reported, deplores the study of Shakespeare because of his aristocratic approach. He has not apparently observed the snobbishness which lies all around him wherever he goes. What he fears in Shakespeare is the force and fury of the real people whose elemental passions refuse to fit themselves into his prefabricated categories. All psychological services, all devices of mental hygiene, excellent as they may be, are no substitute for the disciplining of the mind and the developing of the character through contact with the greatest deeds and the greatest characters of all ages. Children themselves feel this. They demand the superlative in character and if the real is not offered they will accept the synthetic, as the current vogue for crime comics abundantly proves.

Such a plan would no doubt be combined with the religious exercises and moral instruction at present carried on in so many Canadian schools. But it would surely be more reasonable to present accepted moral virtues as social axioms not open to discussion until the children had mastered enough facts to be able to discuss them intelligently. If good faith, duty, honesty, generosity and devotion to the dictates of conscience were presented in this way the present curious dichotomy of instruction which results from the combined worship of God and Dewey would be eliminated. Nor would there be any ground for charges of dogmatism, for the children would be admitted freely to all the wisdom of the ages and encouraged, as they matured, to think and judge for themselves. Provisional dogmas are conveyed to them now in a half-hearted sort of way. Such instruction might much better be given honestly and openly.

This is not to suggest that there is any form of the vision of greatness comparable to that gained from a study of religion and, in the view of this writer, of the Christian religion. Unfortunately the religious teaching now carried on in most Canadian schools is, as a rule, not an integral part of the programme. Like so many other things, it is pushed in as if in fear of missing something good. The whole problem of religious teaching in state schools is extremely difficult, however, and existing arrangements may be the best obtainable. It is encouraging to observe that in many places the matter seems to be receiving increasing attention. Quite apart from the development of character, it is a question whether one often achieves complete development of the intellect unless the powers are directed to something beyond the intellect. [An interesting and certainly a debatable point. If the rule is accepted, there are many distinguished exceptions.]

It will be argued that the strenuous intellectual, moral and even religious education here suggested is aristocratic in character and far above the heads of the majority of children. There are very many, however, who now share the view suggested in the preceding chapters that educators are disastrously under-estimating not only the capacity of the best but even the capacity of average pupils. Whether or not this is true, there is no doubt of the urgent necessity of giving to all who are capable as rich and strenuous intellectual training as they can take. If this necessitates grouping in classes or in schools, such grouping shall be undertaken and the social drawbacks, if any, should be faced courageously. We are told by educators that it is undemocratic to group children according to their intellectual capacity and that, therefore, they must be herded together in tremendous, elaborately equipped, composite high schools where, it seems, they are encouraged to do everything except sit down quietly and study. Such a proceeding cannot serve the cause either of scholarship or of democracy. It can only starve the minds on whose productive capacity the whole fate of our society depends. We must be able in the future to profit from the creative efforts of these minds. This is for us a moral and material necessity and no educational democratic dogmas can be allowed to stand in the way. The objection, after all, is rather childish. The children are perfectly aware of their different capacities for various tasks and, if they were not so indifferent, would doubtless be highly diverted at this elaborate adult conspiracy to conceal the facts of life.

A third reform should be introduced into all our high schools. We should stop worrying about "why our high school students quit." If they are offered abundant intellectual nourishment and if they prove themselves unable or unwilling to profit by it, they should not only be allowed to "quit," they should be obliged to withdraw. In our highly organized society, where only a specialist is allowed to substitute a new electric-light bulb for one which is burned out, it is obviously costly and even dangerous to retain in high school students incapable of studying, and when responsible educators explain that for the benefit of these students the whole scheme of the high schools must be reorganized, it is indeed clear that the keepers of the gate are opening the citadel to the barbarians. These high school students who ought to "quit" and who are encouraged not to, are rapidly ruining, body and soul, the diminishing group of real teachers who ought by every means be encouraged not to "quit" but to continue to do the essential work for which they have prepared themselves.

In conclusion, it is worth while to recall again that education is a major Canadian industry and the key Canadian industry, absorbing yearly hundreds of millions of dollars and the energy of more than two million people. The leaders of this industry, harassed and oppressed by the number of things they are required to do, are constantly demanding more money and more help. There is no doubt that much money is needed. There is equally no doubt that these leaders cannot and should not have unlimited money to spend. Too many worthy objects will always be crowding the budget. In this booming industry it is of the first importance to lay down certain basic principles which would serve to establish an inherent system of priorities.

This national problem should be dealt with on the national level. Obviously there are endless objections to such a proceeding. It is not the purpose of this study to list them or to suggest ways in which they might be met. It is sufficient to point out that we already have, through voluntary co-operation, national bodies investigating educational questions. If a national body can secure and spend nearly a quarter of a million dollars on studying the relationship between educational supervisors on the one hand and the general public on the other, is it unthinkable that a national body might not be formed and authorized to spend a reasonable amount of time and money on a consideration of the whole question of education and of its relation to the past and to the future of society? Surely a clear and precise statement of a Canadian philosophy of education based, not on an awkward synthesis of three or four mutually exclusive American schools of thought, but rather on a consideration of the essential values of western civilization would be a worthy project. It might even be considered so worthy that Canadians would not be compelled to go south of the border to ask for the necessary financial support.

The carrying through of such a project would be a difficult and a delicate task. There can be no serious discussion of education in any free society which does not provoke profound and even bitter disagreement. As Dr. Dewey has so rightly maintained, education is life and life implies strife as well as harmony. There will be much disagreement with what has been said in this final chapter on the ills of society and on the corresponding ills of our educational systems. Many will hold that our greatest need is less a renewal of faith than an elimination of bigotry. The whole question of the place of faith in society and in civilization, and of the place of religion in education, is a difficult and hazardous one. But, however much disagreement there may be on this and on many other questions, on one matter there will be very general agreement among the thoughtful members of a free society. The present preoccupation with body building and character moulding are useless and may even be dangerous so long as we neglect and starve the mind.[9]

11 | *On Universities*

The university by its nature cannot be diverted to practical needs or directed from the outside. The university is not one among many post-secondary institutions providing education from the high school to the grave. It is a unique organization with a unique function.[1]

These words written by Hilda in reaction to studies of post-secondary education in Canada in the late 1960's and early 1970's sum up her views on the place that the university should have in society. The universities had faults, especially modern ones:

They are costing more than society can or is willing to afford; we have too many of them; we are permitting or demanding too many things that we'd like but which we might perhaps do without; we are admitting too many and too many of the wrong kind of people and we are keeping them happy by letting them do the wrong thing.[2]

As for university administrators and teachers "University members are guilty of having prostituted themselves."[3]

Canadian universities are doing what Canadians so often do — follow the worse and not the better of two examples offered by our American neighbours. They are persuading themselves that they can have their cake and eat it too, that they can maintain university professors as communities of scholars dedicated to research and engaged in directing considerable numbers of research students; that they can at the same time give acceptable undergraduate training to the ever-increasing numbers that are asking for it; and that they can do all this at no exorbitant cost to the taxpayers at a time when university salaries are steadily rising.[4]

Whatever its failings in the present Hilda had an unbounded love for the university — past and present. Within the university Hilda had a special love for the Humanities and strove to explain them, their importance, and their goals to others and to humanists themselves who, Hilda thought, were more and more allowing themselves to be misled by social and natural scientists.[5] She also tried to explain the importance of the university to students both while they were on campus and for the future.[6]

As the university changed in the second half of the 1960's Hilda worried that both students and faculty were not what they should be:

I do not think that the university can fulfil its function unless it contains enough members capable of taking delight in pure knowledge to create and maintain something of their spirit throughout the whole group.

A second qualification for membership in the university should be a certain level of intellectual capacity. . . .

In spite of examinations and intelligence tests our means of identifying such people remain crude. One might perhaps hazard the guess that most of our students that achieve an average of under 65 to 67 per cent or even rather more could be released without grave loss.[7]

The result is that I am becoming increasingly depressed about education in all but highly selective university institutions. Not only are we being compelled to take people at a somewhat lower level of competence than we would have considered before, we are also being confronted with people of moderate competence who because of the rather high salaries now being paid have, I think, less of a sense of vocation than was common thirty years ago. This sounds like the cry of age against youth. I think rather that they are victims of circumstances. In my time few but people with keen intellectual interests got university positions and the salary was, as a rule, sufficiently small that they had to get their chief satisfaction from their work. There was not much time or money for other entertainment. Now there is, I believe, a rather patronizing attitude toward the teaching duties which it is thought do not bring promotion as quickly as research. Particularly there is a tendency to think that it is somehow unworthy or undignified to teach freshmen.[8]

In the late 1960's Hilda became concerned that students were demanding too large a role in the university and that the professors were wrong in allowing this to happen. "In some forty-five years of teaching I have always tried, directly and indirectly, to learn from students how to do a better job, and I have never presided over a course union and I never will."[9] She first fully expressed her concern in 1970 in a speech titled "The Role of the Professor in the Changing University."[10] In this version of her verdict, it is a society which used universities which received the blame, more than the students who had been formed by that society or the professors who gave into its demands. In a convocation address at the then Regina campus of the University of Saskatchewan in the fall of 1971, the students and especially the professors were blamed for the situation.[11] Her final statement was delivered to the Royal Society in 1972 and is the first selection in this chapter. The guilty parties — professors, university administrators, students and politicians — were all held responsible for the decline of the university. Those within the institution who wanted money and who misunderstood democracy received the most blame. To both students and professors Hilda's constant message was, realize what you are doing; realize that your actions have consequences for all and for all time.

However, even at her most pessimistic Hilda could find good in the university as illustrated by the second selection a short piece "A Perspective of Change," written in 1970. The love for students was also evident in an article she prepared for the Saskatoon *Star-Phoenix*, the third selection, in which she pleaded for the means to bring into the university all the "exceptionally bright." As in the schools, teacher and student together formed the important combination in the university. Hilda knew that good teachers were essential in both grade one and university, but without the students they were meaningless as teachers. The university professor could remain a researcher, a scholar; the grade one teacher would retain her educational theory, but without students they would cease to be teachers.

The student about whom Hilda cared so much needed help not only to develop his mind but also to preserve his faith. Though Hilda wrote favourably of Christian colleges,[12] she favoured the system developed in Saskatchewan — a religious college affiliated with a secular university. At this type of university a student had to be trained to use his intellect, while not losing his faith.

In the last speech that she wrote, the convocation address that she was to have delivered at the University of New Brunswick in May, 1975, which is the last selection in the chapter, Hilda admitted that Christianity was not as prevalent as it had been. Yet though she knew that secularization had taken place within the university she insisted on presenting her view, carefully and calmly, and was as convinced as ever that the truth would make one free within the limits set by conscience responding to God and to civilization. She hoped that the graduates would realize "that there is an absolute rule of right and wrong and that there are laws — which like the laws of health — cannot be broken without personal damage."

"FRUSTRATED, PREJUDICED, PARTIAL, BIASED AND UNDEMOCRATIC": SOME PERSONAL REFLECTIONS ON THE PREDICAMENT OF OUR UNIVERSITIES

I think that I should apologize for taking as the subject of my presidential address the predicament of Canadian Universities. Universities have been for the past many years too much talked about, examined, evaluated — and confronted. Moreover, we have on our programme this year an able young man — young to me — who has spent long months conducting a minute examination of one of our leading universities. What business have I to offer my purely amateur reflections, for this a speech without footnotes, on this much researched subject?

My excuse is largely sentimental, and I make no apologies. At my age I have a right to be sentimental if I choose. And as this is probably the last time I shall address such a knowledgeable and distinguished audience I'm going to exploit my advantage in order to explain my anxiety, my foreboding about institutions which have for over fifty years given me so much that I can never be grateful enough to those who over the centuries have founded and established them.

No historian can begin the most current of current topics without a little excursion into the past, and no reactionary like myself is going to fail to pay tribute to traditional functions. Those who fear today's excessive concentration on professional training are often reminded that the first European universities were professional schools. So they were. They served the church, law, and medicine. But they were always careful to keep to the "philosophical" aspects of their studies. They worked with general principles; so much so, that we hear of doctors refusing to touch their patients, and we know that barristers left such vulgar matters as the handling of property in the hands of the vulgar attorney or solicitor. It can be said therefore that the role of pure intellect so much emphasized by some as central to university life did ostensibly prevail in this early professional period, occasionally no doubt at the expense of professional training.

The close of what we call the Middle Ages and the period of the Renaissance brought an important development in the full opening to western Europe of the great works of the Greeks, and of ideas which corresponded almost miraculously to the ideas and feelings of this exciting age. There was immense emphasis on "pure" scholarship, but with an approach different from that which had consisted so largely of adding glosses or to engaging in debates over the sacred texts. Religious controversies which engaged much public attention at this time encouraged the new approach to the ancient texts. Sacred or secular they were still revered, but they now had to be hunted down to their originals and looked at with new eyes, a heightened imagination, a clearer understanding.

With all this came a new element in what was an increasingly secular age, a primary concern for the character and conduct of the ideal man for this world. This did not preclude the acceptance of the next world as a fact, but as one might say character and conduct were no longer left to the theologians. Education, according to the Renaissance ideals, must be whole education, concerned with the whole man. The twentieth century need not imagine that it originated that splendid slogan. "the whole child goes to school."

In harmony with the new age the new universities were less professional and were more concerned with training the whole man. From them emerged the ideal of a "gentleman" in a new form, the word being very slowly detached from its feudal origins and taking on a different and a broader meaning. For this splendid concept the English have somehow retained an everyday word, a word of which we are a little afraid today but which cannot be discarded because we all know that it stands for some excellency not unconnected with birth, character, early training, education, moral principles, but not exclusively dependent on any one of them. This concept of what Anglo-Saxons, if rather nervously, still call a gentleman, did become central in education and was maintained until modern times. As Newman argued in his classic, *The Idea of a University,* the real purpose of the whole university curriculum was to provide "the education of a gentleman," meaning the disinterested pursuit of knowledge and understanding as good for everyone with the   necessary leisure, and as one essential ingredient in the character of the gentleman. Newman very bluntly calls the knowledge acquired "useless knowledge" because it was not intended to serve any practical or material purpose.

This concept prevailed during the re-invigoration of the great universities that took place in Britian in the mid-nineteenth century and after. It is still inherent in the constitution and curriculum of the great English universities, and it still stands for courtesy, consideration, urbanity, and, fundamentally, respect for law and authority, respect for experience, regard (if not respect) for age, and repudiation of violence. All these admirable qualities, it was hoped, would be developed along with attention to the knowledge that Newman called useless because it did not contribute directly to the earning of a livelihood nor to obvious material well-being. This ideal did not destroy the notion of a university as a preparation for the professions or even as providing training in professions. The two concepts went hand in hand, each somewhat influencing the other.

It was to the great German universities, and to their pupils the American universities, that the twentieth century owed the second renaissance which made universities the accepted centres of pure research. The notion of pure research obviously did not originate in the late nineteenth century, but hitherto it had been largely voluntary, spasmodic, and (for one cannot make a speech on anything today without using this word) "unstructured." In the past century universities have, naturally, become so impressed with the possibilities of the university community as a research centre that there has been some tendency to forget the other function of maintaining an academic society dedicated to the pursuit and enjoyment of disinterested knowledge and of initiating the young into this enjoyment, accepting them into the community, and endeavouring over a period of years to communicate to them the essential foundations for the best character and the fullest life. Instead, universities have come to see their first glory as the promotion of pure research and especially of pure scientific research. This has become so true that, quite without shame, senior university members have admitted that their chief interest in undergraduate teaching is the opportunity for selecting the chosen few who may be fitted for initiation into the sacred rites. The others of course will be given a B.A. and told to go home.

From the Middle Ages until now universities have fulfilled three useful, indeed essential, functions: they have prepared candidates for the learned professions with emphasis on general principles and on non-technical knowledge; they have provided the education of gentlemen by admitting large numbers of young men, and later of young women, into the society dedicated to the disinterested search of, the enjoyment of, and the transmission of knowledge for its own sake; and they have made themselves the centres of small groups of men and women dedicated, especially in the natural sciences, to pure research carrried on singly or in groups and taking advantage of the essential and costly facilities that can only exist in a great and wealthy institution.

These functions cannot and perhaps should not be separated from one another, but they can be distinguished. Each I think comes closest to the others when it is being pursued on the highest level and at its best. Each may become degraded in a measure when it is carried on in isolation from the others. But, and I think this should be emphasized, what links all three is the love of knowledge and understanding for its own sake, and the willingness because of it to undergo severe discipline and to sacrifice many of the other pleasurable things in life.

My analysis of our predicament today can be stated very simply. I think that the large, very large, sums of money bestowed on universities in, and by, a democratic society, which has a tendency to translate democracy in merely equalitarian terms, has been sapping the life of these institutions, obscuring and smothering their essential principles until they are in grave danger of disintegrating and disappearing.

Through the nineteenth and twentieth centuries universities have received large sums of money from individuals, from trusts, and from governments. This has almost inevitably resulted in a most anxious concern on the part of university officials (who know that they are going to continue to need money) to do what these rich people or groups of people want done. Sometimes the influence of the money has simply been to create a special atmosphere, a kindly regard for — even an anxiety to know what is — the kind of university moneyed people like. But sometimes money comes through a special bargain, the university receiving such and such a grant if it will undertake to do such and such a thing, to carry on a special programme of research, establish an institute, open a new college, give new courses. And this easily develops the assumption that even annual grants from the public purse must be earned by anxious attention to what, at the moment, the public seems to want. The result of all this, hardly noticeable at first as more than one person has pointed out, has become increasingly harmful and has affected all three of the traditional university functions.

There has been an increased amount of applied research in universities, as in the acceptance of grants where there is an undertaking to solve or try to solve important practical problems. This has been brought forcibly to the attention of the public by the protests of students and others (with the spirit of which everyone must, in part, sympathize) against universities accepting research grants for military purposes, especially when those military purposes are purposes of which the students happen to disapprove. But there is no need to undertake the difficult task of evaluating the university research projects that are sponsored from outside. It can be said in general that there is a danger in any specifically applied research in a university. Universities traditionally deal with eternal principles and, in theory, the application of the principles should be left to other individuals and other institutions. This is of course quite impossible in practice, but what is important and what has almost disappeared is the constant awareness of where the emphasis should go, the constant reminder that the practical application of scientific principles is not the business of the university. The life is more than meat and the body more than clothing. As that admirable sociologist Robert Nisbet has pointed out in the United States, the eager competition among individuals for large research grants, and the fussy paraphernalia of assistants, secretaries, machines, and equipment of all sorts tends to occupy far more time and attention than is good for the health of any university.

In professional training a similar problem is apparent. Money is available to help establish schools, but the very success of the university in professional training has increased the pressure to introduce to the campus all sorts of professional training and other training that hardly deserves the name of either professional or technical. The influence of the longing for money, the root of all evil, in this matter is subtle and goes back a long way. It was in the early 1860's when discussing a measure of financial friction at Queen's University between the Faculty of Arts and Theology and the Faculty of Medicine that Principal Leitch urged peace and offered a formula of compromise adding urbanely (I need not add in a private letter) "let us prey on govenment and not on each other." Later we learn that the great Principal Grant, determined to make Queen's a great university but convinced that even his superhuman efforts to build up an endowment could not adequately provide for costly scientific training, had the idea of establishing a school of mining on the campus with government assistance, explaining privately that if this were done the cost of science instruction as a necessary preliminary to mining could be turned over to the government, leaving the college endowment to support Arts and Theology. I am not suggesting that this should not have been done. I am not even going to say that he who sups with the devil needs a long spoon. I think, however, that it is worthwhile to remember the grim warning that the love of money is the root of all evil, and to add to it the rider that the perfectly legitimate endeavour to earn subsidies for non-material purposes by providing material services has its dangers, and especially the danger that the material service, a good thing in itself, may be confused with the primary function of the university.

The same dangerous influence has operated on the third university function: providing the education of gentlemen. The anxiety to please can lead so easily to a willingness to teach anything that anyone wants; it can lead so easily to a resignation of a scholar's absolute right to pursue truth as he finds it, and to convey to his pupils what he thinks they ought to know in terms of the university's central purpose, the disinterested pursuit of knowledge. The danger is not a new one. Readers of that not very good novel, but admirable social document, Tom Hughes' *Tom Brown at Oxford,* will remember that St. Ambrose College, having become attractive to rich people, was betrayed into admitting "gentlemen commoners" who wore gold tassels on their caps, did very little work, and paid double fees. The results were becoming unhappily obvious before a generation had passed and, in that splendid mid-Victorian way, the Fellows recognized their sin and repudiated the gentlemen commoners in time to save the colleges. The fact that Hughes shows the work of regeneration as starting with the St. Ambrose boat crew, which makes the head of the river, need not obscure the moral.

Apart from too earnest pursuit of money, the other danger to which the university has been subjected and to which I think it has succumbed is the temptation to accept shallow and fashionable interpretations of democracy and the assumption that all its supposed principles must be applied to university life. There is no need to labour the various aspects of the equalitarian fallacy. They are obvious to anyone who has lived in a university and has thought about its current problems. In this day of extremely high income taxes much of the university's income must come from governments. Governments are supported by popular vote. Young men and women now vote at the age of eighteen. And the general social interpretation of democracy has not been that each individual has equal claims on society in relation to his own energy and aptitude, but rather that anything that is recognized as good for anybody must be equally good for all, and therefore all must share in it. The result has been to open the university doors, if not to everybody, to an enormous number who cannot profit by or contribute to essential university operations.

Worse still, during the last fifteen years the tendency has been increasingly to let these young people claim as a right participation in decisions as to what is to be done in the university and how. They are the voters, they say, and they are supporting the university by their taxes (even though in very many cases not they but the people who really do pay taxes are supporting them and the university). It is no criticism of them to say that they are not fit to exercise the powers they claim. If they were, there would be no need to maintain a large body of professors holding appointments for life. It is a truism to say that the greater and the more complex the institution, the longer the experience needed to guide it wisely and to preside over the changes that must come with changing times. To say that senior members of a university should be alert to the criticisms of students and should welcome very free and friendly communication with them is not to suggest that the final decision should not rest in the hands of the senior members of the hierarchy; and I must add that the junior members, the students, who at best are ignorant and at worst disastrously so, would be well advised to give most of their time and energy to the purpose for which they have presumably come, studying under experienced and expert guidance. Let me not overstate my case; universities need young blood and new ideas and the old can become hidebound. But we have reached the opposite extreme in our worship of youth.

The democratic fallacy affects every unversity function, even research. The very name "research" has become utterly degraded by our false and self-conscious democracy. Fifty years ago undergraduates looked for summer jobs. They preferred agreeable ones, but they had no false pride. Today the make-work programmes of governments consist chiefly of a long list of "research projects" to be carried on by any undergraduates who have not found more agreeable or gainful employment, and who almost certainly have not the remotest conception of the original meaning of this once dignified word, which now appears to be applicable to the gathering together of any two or three facts, significant or otherwise.

The result, then, of uncritical demands for and acceptance of money and of uncritical acceptance of popular democracy is inevitably that money and the average public taste have come to occupy, not too large a place, but an inappropriate place in the life of the university. The tail is wagging the dog. In the late Middle Ages groups of Cistercian monks began to move into remote places in northern England in order to have quiet and isolation for the meditation and prayer which were the purpose of their order. They raised a few sheep because this could be done in remote places, and because one must eat and wear something in order to meditate and pray in any climate, let alone a cold one. Able men, the monks raised good sheep. By a process of natural development the Cistercian monasteries became the mecca of continental wool-buyers, and the monks found themselves obliged, or at least inclined, to elect abbots shrewd enough to bargain with Italians. The lesser officials presumably dealt with prayer and meditation. Their duties, however, may not have been onerous, as most recruits attracted to the institutions in those changed times were more apt to deal with wool than with prayer. Their primary and traditional purpose gone, the monasteries disappeared, unwept, for they had taught others how to produce wool.

Traditionally universities have been communities of senior and junior scholars living together under their own law, hierarchies, and, at their best flexible, somehow combining decorum and discipline with free thought and free speech. Today the changing role of the university, the higher salaries, and the increase of prestige have attracted men and some women who are not particularly interested in scholarship, who do not understand or do not pause to reflect on what may be the merits of a hierarchical organization, but who love money, prestige, and power. Some of these recruits to the faculty have taken advantage of a lonely and frustrated generation of students to attempt to launch a social revolution, and thanks to "tenure," and to that great new slogan "academic freedom," they have done this generally with little or no risk to themselves.

For the unhappy state of affairs in which so many universities find themselves today the blame must be widely distributed and the sins (I have dared to suggest) are as much ones of omission as of commission. One great sin of omission must be noted, and I can think of no better place than this to do it: why have the leaders whose function it is to speak for all members of universities not intervened much more actively and specifically in the debate that is now going on to assert that universities, by their nature, are not government departments, and that they cannot be subjected to ordinary bureaucratic control and still remain universities? They can retain their true character only as communities of senior scholars working with a considerable degree of independence to preserve and extend the bounds of knowledge and to accept apprentices who are under authority and who accept authority because they need and want to be taught. This has not been said loudly and clearly enough by enough people.

More particularly, why has there not been a more explicit judgment on that regrettable document, the Wright *Draft Report*? As a senior member of a reputable university I do not feel complacent, and I have no thought of flattering my academic colleagues, but I must ask myself whether we have deserved this report, a staggering example of what democracy can fall to when it has lost the sound aristocratic principles that alone can keep it healthy.

The first cause for dismay was that the commissioners issued a draft report on which they invited public comment. Why? They were experts; they were given complete freedom to make their investigation, to consult whom they pleased, and to require any reports they chose. They were asked to give their opinion on the problem of education beyond the secondary level. The whole purpose, as I understand it, of a royal commission is to provide the government of the day with the opinion of experts on a practical solution to a given problem. It is not for the commission to consider whether their recommendations are going to be politically acceptable. That is for the government to decide. In other words, the commission offers the ideal solution. The members of the government, bearing in mind that theirs is the art of the possible, decide what they think best, what they can induce the public to accept. Therefore, when the public is presented directly with a draft report for comment it must surely mean either that the commissioners don't know what they want to say, or that they are afraid to say it, or that they are being used by the government of the day for political purposes as a test to see what the public will stand. I think that everyone must regret this melancholy conclusion, for the reputation of the government and for that of the commissioners.

The second depressing feature of this report is its style. Even a report addressed exclusively to members of the government might be expected to be, if not pleasant and easy reading, at least grammatical, logical, consistent and free from wearisome repetition. But the Draft Report, the commission admits, is addressed to the public, and the members of the public are asked to comment on it. Having spent forty years reading hastily composed undergraduate essays by young people whose grammar and syntax are weak and who often yield to the temptation to plagiarize, I have become an expert. I can say that I think I understand what most of the sentences in most pages of this report are intended to convey, except, and this is an important exception, when it is abundantly clear that the writers themselves do not know what they want to convey. I must sorrowfully admit that this is the worst educational jargon I have ever read.

As for the contents, the commission recommends post-secondary education for all. In any healthy, democratic society I think we would agree that opportunities for further improvement should be open to all. But at the moment they are. Libraries, museums, art galleries, musical conservatories, etc., offer services for very many tastes and capacities. If more "structured" instruction is needed, this too should be provided, as the commission recommends. The commission also urges persuasively that complete freedom of choice and the freedom to opt out of one line of study into another should be made possible. What is alarming is that all these proposed activities which are to be supervised by the state and which, rightly used, might take an intolerable burden from the universities, are apparently by the commissioners being confused with functions of the universities. The university, by its nature, cannot be safely adjusted to meet practical needs or be directed from the outside. The university is not one among many post-secondary institutions providing education from the high school to the grave. It is a unique organization with a unique function.

This does not mean that universities do not need close examination and fundamental reform. They are costing more than society can or is willing to afford; we have too many of them; members of universities are permitting or demanding too many things that may be good but are not indispensable; they have yielded to the temptation or to the pressure to admit too many and too many of the wrong kind of people, and they are keeping these people happy or trying to keep them happy sometimes by letting them do the wrong things.

The remedy may be a drastic overhauling of universities and a drastic reduction of costs and of activities. But if the institutions are to survive, the overhauling must be done from within and not from without. The public ought to remember, and responsible members of any administration ought to remind them, that although not many people are able or willing to give themselves unremittingly to pure intellectual pursuits civilization cannot survive unless some are allowed to do so in freedom. One might perhaps say that the true function of the university is to maintain a kind of worship. The scholar is akin to the artist, the musician, and the sculptor. He is dedicated to finding and revealing the truth; he knows what he looks for and he loves what he knows.

A month or two ago there was another report from Calgary even more clear and relevant and more devastating than the Wright Draft. Universities, according to this report, are looking after "post-secondary education" but at too great an expense and they must therefore be broken up. The work must be done by a variety of institutions under a rigid system of "cost accounting" and research institutions must be set up and subsidized, their activities being carried on according to a carefully devised system of priorities determined by the government.

We may agree that senior members and administrators of universities are guilty of having prostituted themselves, but it takes two to achieve an act of prostitution and it ill becomes ministers and deputy ministers of education, who have insisted on admission through pitifully inadequate entrance examinations, who have bribed and coerced universities to take in every kind of popular study, and who have allowed if not encouraged extravagant building and furnishing in order to let the public see what it was paying for, who in one province forced a take-over of all teachers' colleges with their staffs — it ill becomes them to drive these fallen women out into the street. What is needed is a frank confession of sin on both sides, and admission that many things done in universities could be done as well or better elsewhere. And along with this should go a repudiation of the nonsensical claptrap about élitism, and an admission that society will continue to need, even if on a reduced scale, some institutions like the ones that we know as universities, whether they are called universities, schools, colleges, monasteries, academies, or royal courts — the name and the place do not matter but the purpose matters and the people matter. They must be special and exceptional people, and they must be left free and at leisure to pursue their special purpose.

University administrators, professors, ministers, and deputy ministers of education have got us into our present predicament not through any ill will, not through any wrongdoing, but through doing a great many good things and at the same time committing an apparently small but in fact very great sin of omission, through what can only be called a kind of over-weaning pride in the great modern university. They have not remembered that institutions, like people, can sometimes gain the whole world and lose their own souls. The universities and those acting for them have in a sense voluntarily resigned their essential powers and responsibilities. If it is too late to resume them again, if the process of disintegration has gone too far, if the public has lost all sense of the unique function of the university, if many members of the universities themselves have perhaps lost it, we are then reaching the end of what has been a great age in the western world. Unless we are going to descend quickly into a new dark age, some other groups will presumably, after an interval, take up the responsibility of maintaining pure intellectual values. The future is uncertain. What we as individuals must do is to remember that, as the comfortable shelter of the institution falls away, the responsibility of those who truly care for learning and scholarship is immeasurably increased. That is why I am happy to have been able to offer these reflections to this particular audience.[13]

A PERSPECTIVE OF CHANGE

Fifty years ago the University of Saskatchewan was represented physically by four greystone buildings (including Emmanual College — primo in campo), some eight hundred students, and a handful of professors.

I shall take the professors first, that being the custom of those days. Most of them were young, but they were mature, they took their teaching duties very seriously, they expected at least outward deference and they got it. They were not all scholarly by today's standards (although one wrote a book which George Bernard Shaw found worthy of an enthusiastic foreword) but they were nearly all in their ways characters: Pompey, Galloping Mac, Teddy, Frankie, Thor, and the strikingly handsome young biology professor who became the third president of this university.

The undergraduates, for the most part, were older than those of today. They were shabbily but carefully dressed; long hair was worn by females only, and by nearly all females. Most of them came from farms or from small towns. Many had worked on the family farm or business as long as they could remember; many were now entirely self-supporting — and it would have been considered unusual if not discreditable not to be so before the age of twenty-one. University education was considered a privilege, and a costly one, even though fifty dollars would go most of the way to covering tuition, incidental fees and books. Many of the students had had few cultural privileges (though they had not suffered from the then non-existent radio and TV). They were often unpolished, narrow-minded and parochial in their outlook. They needed to be reminded to read the newspaper. They were anxious to learn what was "correct" and they did learn much. Even the president knew most of them by name. It was fashionable in those post-war years to be serious, responsible and ambitious. Convocation speakers reminded graduating classes that they might be leaders of the future, and that they all owed a debt to society. Many believed this. They had not heard that the world owed them a living. This was just as well since they would have to face Saskatchewan's grim thirties when the world acknowledged no such obligation.

Today, fifty years later, the original buildings stand in the midst of a university city. Staff, students and colleges have multiplied more than tenfold. Professors neither expect nor get deferential treatment, though they are better qualified, better paid (even allowing for inflation) and much more aware of their role in society. Deeply involved as many are with administration, research, and various forms of public activity, they have less time for teaching and communicating with the (proportionately) larger number of students.

Undergraduates are younger than their fellows of fifty years ago, better looking (as far as one can see), better-dressed, more poised, more demanding, less responsible and less secure. They are obsessed with "the generation gap" which fifty years ago was accepted as normal and not at all disturbing. They do not think the world owes them a living because they do not think anyone owes anything. It has become fashionable while repudiating the old conceptions of "right" and "wrong" to assume that the establishment is always "wrong," and that people under thirty have "a right" to anything they want if enough of them demand it loudly enough.

Fashions change like the surface of a stream. The whole moral climate appears to have changed radically in fifty years. And yet anyone who remembers 1920 must remember the smart set, the chronic idlers and the slick operators. And the generation gap is not so wide but that those who remember 1920 still see now what they saw then, serious, intelligent, hard-working, courteous students, frank and critical, but not malicious. The apparently reasonable pessimism of 1970 may be as groundless as the apparently well-founded optimism of 1920.[14]

ARTICLE FOR EDUCATION WEEK

The increasing costs of university education are impressive. Salaries and maintenance costs of all kinds are increasing; buildings and equipment call for very large capital expenditure. The costs are impressive but not alarming. In these years of relative prosperity they are borne without great difficulty. More important advanced academic, professional and technical training is now considered an economic necessity. "It pays dividends." Society is prepared, optimistically, to make a generous investment.

There is no harm, however, in asking how we can get the most for our money. One obvious way is to educate the right people and not to attempt to educate the wrong ones. It costs no more in money to give a B.A. or an M.D. to an able young man or woman than it does to one whose abilities are mediocre or less. In fact it probably costs less, as the able student will not be required to "repeat" any courses. Moreover, if any B.A. pays dividends to society a good degree will pay very much higher ones than a poor degree will.

We are told that about 10 per cent of all children are exceptionally able. Rather less than 10 per cent of the appropriate age group in the province attends the University of Saskatchewan. There are a number of exceptionally able students in attendance at the university, but there are many others who are no more than good or average. Obviously then, a considerable number of the exceptionally able students are not with us. Some no doubt go to universities outside the province. It is, however, reasonable to assume that many never reach university at all.

Their absence deprives us of a double advantage. First, they would leave the university with good degrees and would be capable of rendering very valuable service in their chosen callings. Second, a consideration often neglected, their presence in the university would raise the standard of work of their less capable colleagues. Every teacher knows how difficult it is to enable students to do the very best work of which they are capable, and every teacher knows too that his most valuable ally in this work is the eager and intelligent person who stimulates and sets the pace for the others. If we could attract to the University of Saskatchewan the 10 per cent of exceptionally bright people produced — statistically speaking — by every generation, all other students would do more and better work; all, that is, except the incurably dull and idle and they would probably withdraw from an atmosphere grown too intellectual to be comfortable for them.

The problem is, then, how to increase educational dividends by attracting to institutions of higher education the considerable number of exceptionally able people who now, apparently, cannot or will not take advantage of them. No doubt many of them will not. Not all able people are industrious. They may have discovered at high school that studying is hard work and have decided on some less strenuous pursuit. Others receive little encouragement at home, either in the shape of positive advice or in the general cultural influences that would naturally lead them on to more learning.

It is, however, reasonable to presume that a considerable number are repelled by the very high costs of higher education. Many can receive some help from their parents which may be supplemented by other earnings. Others depending on their own resources cannot meet the cost, and find it more prudent to accept the relatively attractive employment which may be immediately available.

It is this group which will be benefited by the scholarship scheme announced recently to the Legislative Assembly in the speech from the throne. All those who are interested in the intellectual future of our society, and in particular all those concerned with higher education will applaud the policy and will be eager for its implementation.

It seems clear that society which is spending so much money already on educational facilities would be well advised to spend a little more to ensure that enough of the right people take advantage of them. A scholarship system so calculated that no *exceptionally* able student need be excluded from university for lack of funds would not be prohibitive in cost; a more generous one giving help to the many very good students of second class ability would cost much more. The first is urgently needed. Mere prudence should forbid a waste of very exceptional talent. The second would be highly desirable.

In Ontario it has been proposed that all the exceptionally able should be given scholarships sufficient to pay the entire cost of their university career, and that efficient help should be given to others who are deserving. If this proposal is carried out not only the quantity but the quality of university education in the province should rise very sharply.

The details of a scholarship system require careful consideration. On the one hand it may be well to encourage thrift, self-respect and independence by limiting the amount of the scholarship to the sum a student requires over and above what he may be expected to earn in the summer. On the other hand the amount of money bestowed, and the conditions attached, may seriously affect the quality of the degree. Every university professor advises his students to read in the summer, knowing that a bare seven months crowded with lectures and conferences and examinations, to say nothing of student activities, simply does not leave enough time for the reading and reflecting necessary to a good degree. But the professor having offered this advice is almost sure to be asked directly or indirectly how much solid reading *he* could do after an eight-hour day of manual labour? The student is right, but so is the professor. It is a question whether the educational dividends derived from a summer, or a considerable part of the summer, spent in serious reading, would not justify the modest additional scholarship allowance that would be needed.

But whatever particular scheme is devised, there can be no two opinions about the general value of the policy. It is of immediate importance that society now spending millions on educational staff and "plants" should find a few thousands to bring in those who can derive the most benefit from what is offered at such cost.[15]

"KEEP YOUR HEARTS, MINDS"

I am very much honoured by the University of New Brunswick today. It is a great privilege to receive a degree from this ancient institution, and a great pleasure to be allowed to speak particularly to you the graduates on this day which means, and should mean, so much to you and to your parents and friends. I may say that I do not feel quite a stranger here, at this University provided the University of Saskatchewan — where I have spent nearly all my working life — with its first President, Walter C. Murray, who came west to found the new university in 1909, and who led it faithfully and valiantly for nearly thirty years.

I want to speak to you very briefly on the two matters which are, I think, of the utmost importance to you and to the country which has nourished and taught [you] — and which you, in your turn I know are preparing to serve. I found my title in one of the ancient benedictions of the church in which the apostle tells his flock that he is praying God "to keep your hearts and minds." I do not wish to affront those of you who may be atheist or agnostic. Such a prayer or heartfelt wish is entirely capable of a secular application. In our present moral and intellectual crisis it must find an application in all men and women of goodwill, unless we are to descend into anarchy.

You may think that in discussing the condition of your hearts I am treading on private ground and you may resent the intrusion. Normally I would agree with you. You will, however, understand that my words have no sentimental application. I am thinking of your hearts as the very centre and foundation of all your deepest convictions and principles: the firm but secret foundation of your character, and I am venturing to speak to you of these matters because the very security of our society depends more I think than ever before on your convictions, your character — on your hearts. Our moral crisis consists not only in the steady increase of lawlessness and the apparent bewilderment of our rulers — whom we have chosen — as to what to do about it. It goes far deeper down to a kind of general assumption that law is the enemy of freedom; freedom being the greatest good — supposedly — law must be at best a necessary evil; the "rule of law" — perhaps the proudest achievement of western civilization, has itself come under suspicion, along with all duly constituted authority. As the prime minister said, justly, I think, no one seems to respect government any more. It is, of course, obvious that we may have bad laws and bad governments — but to question the value, one could even say the necessity, of the rule of law, of government, is to try to destroy the foundation of our civilization.

Traditionally ancient peoples have been proud of their great law givers, have reverenced their memory. The proudest of all, the Jews, boasted that their law was given them by God — it was a compact, a covenant — between them and Him. A more secular approach was law as a sacred social covenant. The many revolutionaries have tried to replace what they thought a bad law for what they thought a better but until today convinced anarchists have been rare.

They are probably still more rare today, but we have undoubtedly lost our general reverence for the rule of law, and have been for some time replacing it by a kind of spurious reverence for freedom and personality. Children go to elementary school to "do their own thing"; in high, I have been told, they "choose their roles" — and the school is not to intervene, to interfere.

We can't go on much longer living on the moral capital of the past; and we can't go back. We can however recreate the element on which all law must rest: the firm moral conviction of the individual. What has been most alarming in the recent . . . scandals — Watergate and Harbourgate — is the apparent bewilderment among some principals as to what is right and wrong. They give the impression less of ignoring moral principles as of not having any.

I am now back with your hearts. I do not believe that you have passed through this university without receiving — and listening to — some encouragement to reflect on moral principles, to recognize with your reason as well as your conscience that there are absolute rules of right and wrong and that these are laws — which like the laws of health — cannot be broken without personal damage. A simple way of identifying your moral code is to ask yourselves two questions: first, What would I not do for any consideration whatever? second, What would I do, or try to do, at *all* costs? This should give you what the moderns would call your moral profile. You could go on from there — or stand fast as you are — "Keep your hearts." It is the best service you can do yourselves and your country.

And your minds: perhaps the second great crisis of our day is the intellectual one. We have experts; we have people highly trained in various skills. But, and I have said this before, our increasingly expensive schools seem to be increasingly unconcerned to offer children orderly and methodical discipline — that bad word — in those arts which are chiefly necessary to them in pursuing their own education — that is, in "keeping their minds" as they go through life. We have had a steadily increasing permissiveness, a constant increase of "options" in high schools and also in universities. It is now scarcely possible to be sure that a B.A. can read, and I know that many of them are not capable of expressing themselves on important subjects in clear and concise English.

I make an exception of course of the graduates of this university. I am sure that you can all read and write. But may I remind you that you are going out into a society that is increasingly illiterate, even barbarous. A well-known education professor (I will not say from where) recently defended the failure of the schools to teach reading by saying that we now possess a machine with buttons — of course. The child presses a button and gets the answer to the question he asks. What we do not know is how this child learns what questions are worth asking — which is what education is all about.

Once again I think we must admit that a general respect for learning, a real understanding of its pleasures and possibilities, a real capacity for critical reasoning, is growing very weak in our society. I would like to urge you again personally to "keep" those minds for which the university has done so much. If, as is possible, they have kept you so busy here that you have had no time to read, start reading now, reading for pleasure: history (of course!), biography (never I think have we had so many and such able biographies as are being produced today), travel, novels (old as well as new) and Canadian novels, too much neglected. I agree with the people in Manitoba, Saskatchewan, and B.C. who are waging something like a war to get more education in the schools: but I would suggest to you that here, as with the moral law, you may at first serve society best by treasuring and using what you have got: "Keep your minds" and enrich them.

May I once more offer you my congratulations, and good wishes on this very special day.[16]

If on the other hand we refuse to give our hearts and minds the thought and care that we lavish on our physical needs we may very easily use our wealth only to demonstrate a premature decadence and a relapse into barbarism.[1]

These words from a speech in 1954 sum up Hilda's approach to the world around her. History, religion, education; schools, universities, churches; learning, language, books of every sort: these formed Hilda's world. She was interested in painting; sculpture, music, ballet, and drama had a relatively small place in her life. She recognized their importance, but more in a context than in themsleves.[2] This attitude reflected not only her training but also her location. Until quite recently Saskatchewan had relatively little of the arts (with the partial exception of painting) accessible to those not directly involved as artists.

Yet Hilda, as a member of the Massey Commission, grew beyond her world to consider the place that all the arts should have in Canada. The first selection, "The Massey Report: A Retrospect," gives her assessment of the effect of the work of the commission five years after the fact, but before the Cànada Council, its most important contribution to Canada, had begun to function.

Hilda's work on the Massey Commission and *So Little for the Mind* gave her a national audience and a wider concern for the lives of ordinary people. The second selection in this chapter, "Canadian Leisure," is the best example of a fairly consistent concern that Hilda shared with a number of other intellectuals in the 1950's: What would Canadians do with their growing leisure time? In fact, though, Hilda had first written on the subject in 1937.[3]

Hilda began to become involved in lecturing on current events in Regina in 1934. Her first topic was Spain. War was next. During the late 1940's and through the 1950's she spoke about China, Poland, National Defence, and atomic warfare. Sometimes she prepared carefully, sometimes quickly:

I borrowed Father's biography of Elizabeth Fry from Margery and worked up her pension reforms, and then embroidered them all round with a beautiful theory of my own, that women have always been responsible for the well-being of the social culture, and that only the modern industrial city life has obliged them to remove their centre of action from the home to formal women's organizations.[4]

Hilda also wrote about world affairs. Between 1940 and 1943 she published in the *Bulletin* of the Saskatchewan Teachers' Federation nineteen well-written, objective reports on the unfolding of the Second World War. The one reproduced below as the third selection in this chapter was prepared for Saskatchewan teachers returning to the classroom in the fall of 1941. She tried to address the intellectual elite of Canada in the same year through the *Dalhousie Review*.[5] This article was not accepted, but a second "The Democratic Cycle," with a similar message, was published by that journal in 1943. "If twentieth century democracy cannot produce a synthesis in the form of freedom and individual worth translated in terms of common moral standards accepted and enforced, it will suffer annihilation, and justly."[6] Seventeen years later she delivered a speech "Hiroshima — Fifteen Years After," which presented her fully developed attitude toward the complexities and evils of the world as it actually exists. This is the fourth selection in this chapter.

Hilda was not always serious about the world around her. In the early 1950's one of her tasks as a speech writer for Vincent Massey was to prepare a speech for each city he visited on his first official tour across the country as Governor General. Each speech was supposed to draw upon the past and present of the city to produce praise for great accomplishments. The fifth selection in this chapter is the official speech prepared for the visit to Saskatoon (complete with notes to prepare the Governor General for conversation with the local dignitaries) — followed by the spoof of it which Hilda prepared for the enjoyment of Massey and his entourage.

During much of the 1950's education was the dominant theme of Hilda's speeches and writings. In her speeches a connected sub-theme was worry about the fate of freedom and the individual. She had voiced this concern at times in the 1940's in connection with the threat of fascism. In the 1950's, in common with many, she worried about the threat to freedom presented by Russian Communism. Just as important to Hilda was the fear that the West's reaction to Russia's growing military and scientific power would bring a subversion of liberty and excellence through the demands for the instant development of science and technology. These concerns are best seen in a speech she presented on a number of occasions in the late 1950's, "Educational Simony," which is printed in Chapter 10.

By the end of the 1960's western civilization, which, according to Hilda, had been endangered from without by Nazism and Communism and from within by scientism and false ideas of democracy propagated by the followers of John Dewey, was now, she believed, in grave danger because of a failure to teach the young to love religion, learning, and books. She had been warning of the possibility of the collapse of civilization for thirty years. The rise of student power now seemed to be a clear sign of the coming end — the rising up of the unlearned against those who were failing to teach. Hilda did not despair. She continued to teach and write. She protested to her peers as seen in the chapter on universities and reasoned with students as seen in her campus speeches and convocation addresses.

Hilda's explanation of a way out of the problems facing civilization was given to a Business and Professional Women's meeting in Saskatoon in 1970: reconciliation of group claims to individual justice and to the common good of society.

The closing words in this the seventh selection: "without a peaceful ordered society we have all lost what we value most" became the theme of Hilda's talks to students during the last five years of her life. This is illustrated by the last speech Hilda delivered, a convocation speech in the fall of 1974 at the University of Windsor, included as the last selection in this book.

THE MASSEY REPORT: A RETROSPECT

In June 1951 the *Report of the Royal Commission on National Development in the Arts, Letters and Sciences* was published. It is perhaps not indiscreet, now that five years have elapsed, to admit that the enthusiastic reception accorded to it by the newspapers from one end of the country to the other, the full spread, the special articles, the glowing editorials, were as astonishing as they were delightful to the gratified commissioners. "Culture," that forbidden word (and the word was sedulously avoided in the report), culture in Canada had personally achieved the front page.

And yet on the very day of publication a hard-headed radio commentator remarked that, for all the fanfare, when it came to action the government would follow those among the recommendations which reflected policies already formulated — and no others. And not long after, a sympathetic reviewer said much the same thing. "The chief danger is that the Massey Report will become merely another historical document. . . . It is already being brushed aside by 'practical' men as the work of long-haired high-brows. There is no other country in the world where intellectuals suffer from such low repute as in Canada."

To commissioners concerned, perhaps unduly concerned, with "canadianism,' such comments should have seemed far sweeter than all the front-page headlines, for they struck the authentic note of the Canadian intellectual: the resigned pessimism, the alarm at sentimental enthusiasm, the cold invitation to look at reality and to remember that it is almost certain to be worse than you think. From the vantage point of 1956 the precise and regrettable accuracy of the deflationary comments is evident. And yet the enthusiasm was genuine too, and significant and alive. It was perhaps an unexpected reminder of the fact that a nation does not live on pessimism and realism alone, useful as these qualities may be. At the lowest estimation the "culture probe" was more than a sentimental interlude in national life. It represented rather those profound sentiments and convictions which go far deeper than reason because without them life has no meaning.

Within its very general terms of reference the Massey Commission was required to investigate certain specific institutions: the CBC, the National Film Board, the National Gallery, and others. Examining and reporting on these bodies gave an initial point and precision to the assignment. It was, however, clear that (to borrow the phrase of a famous document) the generality was not to be restricted by the particulars. It was not. The inquiry was extended to the whole web of activities associated with the central institutions and to many other matters as well. Some of the briefs presented to the commission cast a very wide net indeed. Almost all were helpful if only indirectly.

It has occasionally been suggested that there was too much of cultural chauvinism in the briefs and in the evidence; and in the report that followed too much attention to the merit of being made in Canada, too much anxiety to be different for the sake of being different. It is not for the present writer to say that the commissioners did not fall into this sin, but, at least in their better moments, they were firmly against it. Moreover, neither they nor their critics could have supposed that there was any warrant for this in their terms of reference. It was not a question of Canadian culture but of culture in Canada. What place did the cultivation of the arts, letters, and sciences have in Canadian life? What place should it have? What could the national government properly do in the matter?

The assumption is that as economic activity is essential to life as existence, so cultural activity is essential to life as well-being. It is necessary for the well-being of the individual and of the community. The individual cannot live by bread alone; and the true life of the community must reside in those intangibles which derive their chief value from being enjoyed in common.

And yet there was an aspect of this question which might appear to involve actual chauvinism. There was no mention in the terms of reference to historical precedent, but inevitably the minds of those engaged in the inquiry turned to historical parallels. At no time in western history has any nation totally ignored the importance of national recognition of, and support for, non-material values. At no time has any capable ruler been unaware of the danger of neglecting these powerful forces or of allowing them to fall too completely into independent or alien hands. The new national monarchs of the sixteenth and seventeenth centuries, fearful of more than one rival influence, made themselves patrons of the arts and sciences not from personal taste alone, but as an important element in the prestige by which they claimed men's loyalty and support. Nor did they forget to patronize and even to attempt to control the church without whose moral support their power might either collapse or be compelled to rest unashamedly on naked force.

Such historical reflections do not certainly demand a "Canadian culture" such as Nazis might call for Aryan art or Soviet Russia for proletarian music. They do, however, suggest the impossibility of entirely separating political from cultural and moral community. To attempt to do so (and this is stated in the report) is to deny the moral character of the state. Moreover, Canada is attempting the almost impossible, to grow as a nation with "a small and scattered population in a vast area . . . this population . . . clustered along the rim of another country many times more populous," a country with which Canada has "peculiarly close and intimate relations." In such circumstances Canada cannot neglect those intangibles which other nations more secluded in their early development have found essential to their common life. Or to express the same truth from the individual viewpoint, the Canadian, like other men capable of reason, of a love of beauty, of aspiration toward the good, cannot give the full loyalty demanded by the modern nation-state to any organization which finds no place for at least some of these things which are so essential a part of himself.

Reflections such as these prompted the search for some brief and cogent statement which would bring to a point the vast intellectual and moral implications of the terms of reference. It was found in the quotation from St. Augustine printed at the beginning of the report and which, translated, reads: "A nation is an association of reasonable beings united in a peaceful sharing of the things they cherish, therefore to determine the quality of a nation, you must consider what those things are." The lines were found to be admirable for many reasons. It is clear that they leave plenty of room for Canadianism, and none for chauvinism. But if St. Augustine was right, the Massey Commission was concerned with the truest well-being of the Canadian nation and of all its neighbours.

The evidence and information accumulated and the conclusions drawn from them were presented at length in the report. It was important that the story should be told fully and roundly. A brief statistical survey would have suggested that Canadians taken as a whole were a nation of barbarians with little care for anything beyond political survival and material prosperity. Libraries might be accepted if the American foundations would pay for them, students sent abroad if other countries would offer scholarships, scientific laboratories equipped if "practical" applications were around the corner; but any evidence of spontaneous devotion to arts and letters as necessary to life would have been covered by the sheer mass of expenditures for armaments, automobiles, cinemas, chewing gum and comics.

A detailed examination of evidence showed that many Canadians were capable of material sacrifices for the non-material things that they truly cherished. It showed also that, apart from the provisions for formal education made by provincial authorities, governments at every level — dominion, provincial, and municipal — were concerning themselves with the general education of the community and with the encouragement of creative effort in many fields. The new institutions of mass communications, the CBC and the National Film Board, were working beside and in co-operation with the cultural products of a more exclusive age such as the National Gallery and the National Museum. There was every evidence of public appreciation of the services being given.

But these hopeful details could not obscure the general fact of undernourishment of the arts, of an excessive dependence on patronage from abroad, of inadequate facilities for communication between various parts of the country with an inevitable loss not only of what may be called moral understanding and goodwill, but also of the stimulation and enlightenment which the innumerable communities within the community could offer to each other. The individual capable of sustained and original thought may achieve nothing because he is incapable of the moral effort required to summon up his powers and set them to work. A consideration of the Canadian scene suggests that Canadians may fail even to acknowledge their vast debt to western civilization not from incapacity or ill-will but from sheer carelessness.

The Massey Report recommended that there should be a collective taking-thought about Canadian cultural affairs in order to strengthen the community by encouraging the freest and fullest development of the pursuits which are at the centre of life. In no civilized society have these pursuits "paid for themselves." They have lived through the gifts of those who cherish them. It was observed that individuals are doing much (and could do very much more); that provincial governments have in certain instances shown great imagination and enterprise.

It was believed, however, that Canada's needs could not be met without a greater expenditure of money and thought by the federal authorities. Apart from the important specific recommendations on radio and television, the chief recommendation of the report was the establishment of a Canada Council. This was to be a group of people appointed by the government, representative of the ablest and most devoted citizens, required to devote itself to the general encouragement and fostering of cultural activities, including the promotion of mature scholarship and the arrangement of international cultural exchanges. Such an organization would not be an organ of cultural regimentation. It would be a symbol of the concern of a free people for those things in human life that cannot be conquered or destroyed. It would, of course, be difficult to establish, and its path in a country like ours would be beset with perplexity and danger. But perplexity and danger are the necessary concomitants of life and freedom; refusing the first two, we are likely to be denied the second.

Looking back after five years it is possible to discern many encouraging signs which may be taken as the natural sequel of the enthusiasm which greeted the report. A number of specific recommendations ranging from financial aid to Canadian universities to the appointment of a trained historian to the Historic Sites and Monuments Board have been followed by the federal government. Provincial governments, especially in the West where there is a spate of anniversary celebrations, have been generous and discriminating in their encouragement to scholarship and to the arts. Even more interesting are the evidences of private enterprise and generosity. The astonishing achievement at Stratford is only the most sensational of new and bold undertakings in many different parts of Canada.

It would be presumptuous and absurd to attribute these welcome events to the Massey Report. They derive rather from the keen interest in the arts which the commissioners were privileged to observe and report on, and to the growing prosperity and confidence in the country which, also, the report remarked on but did not create. The appointment of the commission came at a critical phase in national growth, a time when a people may even make a conscious choice of destiny. The report was, in a sense, a symptom which in its turn became, no doubt, in part a contributory cause.

But the pessimists who discounted all sentimental enthusiasm are still right. The Massey Report recommended the preservation of the national broadcasting system in its integrity, and the appointment of a Canada Council. The broadcasting system is still under attack and in grave danger, and the Canada Council apparently has been played with until it is worn out. After all the polite speeches, on one or two essential matters and perhaps on both, the public voice has pronounced against the recommendations of the report.

The reasons are not difficult to find. Opposition to the principles of the report (as distinguished from numerous friendly criticisms) derives from three principal sources.

First there are the barbarians. Barbarians are of many kinds; some of them are admirable and others are charming persons. Seldom, however, are they both and often they are neither. They are those who from ignorance, stupidity, prejudice or greed or sheer carelessness shut their eyes to the wholeness of life and of society. They refuse to see that every part of existence is relevant to every other part; and they cannot understand that the price of truth and beauty — and even of simple honesty and decency — is eternal sacrifice, the casting of bread on the waters not in superstition but in reasoned faith. In other words, they reject the lesson which history seems to teach that man's happiness and even his security in society seem to depend on a continued reaching out after the unknown truth, the uncreated beauty. Barbarism in Canada provides an immensely profitable field for commercial exploitation. The exploiters, moreover, are aware that barbarians are made, not born, and that the potential field is as wide as the nation.

Second there are the exponents of what must, regretfully, be termed the outdated *laissez-faire* liberalism of the nineteenth century. The English Manchester School strove to confine the government more or less to the activities of the policeman and the soldier. They were optimistic enough to believe that even these functions would rapidly diminish in importance with the spread of the gospel of free trade. Twentieth-century Canada has paid these nineteenth-century Englishmen the tribute of preserving certain shreds of their ideas as dogmas while (necessarily) rejecting in its entirety their economic and political philosophy. Thus Canadians tenacious of the liberal philosophy contribute cheerfully to an immense defence budget, they maintain something approaching an economic dictatorship, and they implore a paternal government to take charge of the home and the school. But as Burke once said, every nation associates its freedom with some special object which is sacrosanct and with which government dare not meddle. In Canada the sacrosanct object appears to be culture. The traditional fear of government activity in this area dies hard in the minds of many who are very far from being barbarians. This fact has not escaped the attention of those who find it profitable to swell the ranks of barbarism.

The third area of opposition is to be found precisely in that part of Canada where *laissez-faire* liberalism has no very strong hold and where barbarism, though ever present, is most fiercely resented: French-speaking Quebec. Many French-speaking Canadians who would not acknowledge a rabid or intransigent "nationalism" cannot accept, or cannot accept completely, the concept of Canadian nationalism inherent in the terms of reference of the Massey Commission. Canadian federalism, they believe, is a useful constitutional and political device within which two nations maintain a friendly but separate existence. The idea of two cultures thriving within one nation seems to them impossible. The close ties between English-speaking Canada and the United States must, they believe, lead to complete absorption of the minority group unless Quebec can support a distinct culture with a considerable degree of economic and political independence.

Such views cannot be lightly dismissed, however dismaying they may be to the English-speaking Canadian who sees the culture of French-speaking Canada as a source of enrichment and inspiration but not as a barrier to the freest exchange and intercourse. It is not to be expected that those who have considered the amazing phenomenon of *la survivance,* and who have been formed and nourished in that remarkable environment, can lightly accept any new scheme which seems to menace the cultural community which is so precious to them. The English-speaking Canadian may condemn their view as short-sighted or distorted. He may urge that this cultural nationalism is providing a perfect ground for the virulent disease of racialism, the curse of the twentieth century, the foe of cultural values of all kinds, and above all the foe of the church which has done so much to nurture French-Canadian culture.

These arguments are all sound. Even if they satisfied the reason of the cultural nationalist they would not quite overcome his instinctive distrust of too-close association with those whom he cannot quite call Canadians. They will not reconcile him wholly to a Canada Council. By an odd combination of circumstances — odd, that is, except by Canadian standards — the Massey Report, criticized for chauvinism by its friends, attacked with vehemence by barbarians and *laissez-faire* liberals, meets its most competent and sustained opposition from a group by definition opposed to barbarism, suspicious of *laissez-faire,* but itself hovering on the brink of chauvinism. A commission ordered to explore "the variety and richness of Canadian life" has at least pointed up the variety.

And that, perhaps, is all that can be said. The report, I believe, was on the whole an honest report, and, on the whole it has been honestly received. The report itself and the treatment accorded to it are symptomatic of our national life with its divisions and cross-currents, and its fears. They are symptomatic also of that toughness, that will to survive, along with that fundamental acceptance of the conditions of life as it is which has produced what we call the Canadian nation.

The report was addressed to and written for the government which had commissioned the investigation. But that government was commissioned by a nation living according to democratic principles and the report was necessarily offered to the nation as well as to the government. It has been widely and carefully read. It is much quoted even yet. Democratic life depends on honest and competent decisions of men of goodwill dealing diligently with their common concerns. Given honesty, goodwill and competence, sooner or later what was sound in the report will be recognized, what is good in the recommendations will stand. Such platitudes are, perhaps, a poor consolation to those who can see only so much to do in so little time. But there is nothing else to say. In a dictatorship things may get done more quickly and more neatly; but this report, in spite of some suggestions to the contrary, was written in the interests of freedom for a free people.[7]

CANADIAN LEISURE

Canadians are impressed by their achievement in reducing the work week from fifty hours or more to forty or less in the course of a generation. Convention speakers (who absorb a good deal of Canadian leisure time) speak optimistically about the future of our civilization. The quality of civilization depending, it is said, on leisure, we are asked to compare ourselves with the ancient Greeks who gave leisure only to the privileged few, whereas we give it to everyone. The conclusion is irresistible.

But, it is, to put it mildly, optimistic. In the first place, the amount of effective leisure time is much less than the stated hours of work suggest. "Moonlighters" take a second job after hours; married women take advantage of modern kitchens to do the same. And the general effect of short hours and high pay is to reduce free time by taking work from the expert and giving it to the amateur as in the extreme cases of those who use their ample free time to build their own houses because the ample free time of the carpenter makes him too expensive to hire.

Moreover, in its influence on civilization free time is not at all the same thing as true leisure. It is safe to say that most Canadians will spend their extra free time not in "cultivating that preserve of . . . undiminished humanity which views the world as a whole," but in seeking escape from their working world in various ways, and especially in resorting to the roads where every national holiday is celebrated by our urge to make human sacrifices to the necessity of escaping even the bare possibility of quiet contemplation.

There are notable exceptions, like the carpenter whose hobby was medieval history. To the amazement of the local bookseller he carried home a rare and weighty volume for which he was quite content to spend seventy-five dollars.

Such carpenters and such booksellers are rare. Canadians are reading more than formerly, but those who are rated as "urban" still spend six times as much on alcohol and cigarettes as on books.

Obviously all Canadians are not like those of the ancient Greeks that we know must about. Probably the other ancient Greeks were not either. Civilization depends, no doubt, on the "creative minority" which is expected to make proper use of its leisure time. That many Canadians are truly concerned with the cultivation of their "undiminished humanity" is testified to by a real and rapidly growing interest in the arts, in literature and history, and by the insistence of many different groups on the creation of the newly-formed Canada Council for the encouragement of the arts and literature.

Unfortunately, the shorter hours do not always benefit those who might be expected to make the most use of them. The brain worker still takes work home at night, thinks himself fortunate it he does not take his problems to bed with him, probably does a good deal of voluntary work in the community, and, in the absence of domestic help may have to do much of his quiet contemplation as he dries the dishes or taxis the children to their evening engagements. Nor is it the custom in Canada to encourage a long summer break for people with particularly heavy intellectual responsibilities. There are quite understandable reasons for this, but it means that some of the ablest people may find their humanity very greatly diminished.

And yet, in fairness it must be admitted that it is not want of opportunity alone that is the enemy of true leisure even in the supposed intellectual classes. The fine traditions of leisure, both religious and humane, in our civilization have been somewhat obscured by the more recent traditions of mechanical efficiency, of self-help, and of ever more specific "education" with a view to professional advancement. That these good things may be the enemy of the best is suggested by the feeling that it is always well for the children even of the well-to-do to take a summer job for the long vacation rather than to take advantage of their last opportunities for summers of leisured and uninterrupted reading. Many Canadians who see and rejoice in the possible advantages of the shorter working week are not unmindful of those sobering considerations.[8]

CURRENT AFFAIRS

The accelerated pace of the Axis activity noticed in March and April has been continued through the summer months. In May the centre of interest was in the near East, with activity in Iraq, Egypt, Crete, and later in Syria. In June came another of the great, yet not entirely unexpected shocks of the war, the German invasion in Russia. Through July the Russian resistance was maintained; then came the fresh diversion, again not unexpected, of the Japanese move into Indo-China and towards Thailand. Behind all these events, three important factors operate: the increasing and serious pressure of the Battle of the Atlantic; the increasing pressure of Germany on Vichy France for greater collaboration; and the seemingly growing resentment against Germany of many of the conquered nations of Europe, along with the determination of the people of the United States, expressed by President Roosevelt in proclaiming a national emergency on May 27, that "we will not accept a Hitler dominated world."

In April Germany's spectacular advance through the Balkans and to the very tip of Greece was paralleled by her success in driving back the British from Libya into Egypt, thus again menacing the safety of the Suez. In May occurred in rapid succession a series of moves calculated to drive the British completely out of the near East. The drive on Libya — halted by the stubborn defence of the almost isolated outpost of Tobruk — was only one of the thrusts which made many observers feel that Britain must resign herself to the loss of the whole Eastern Mediterranean area. This sentiment met with prompt opposition from Winston Churchill. "We intend to fight with all our strength for the Nile Valley and its surrounding country, and to command the Mediterranean." The area is indeed vital to Britain in every way. From Iraq through the oil pipe line to Haifa she obtains the oil for warships, planes, and motorized units. Through it she maintains her influence over the 40,000,000 people of the "Arab World." By it she secures free passage through the Suez Canal, the gateway to her whole eastern Empire.

For these advantages she had to fight hard through the month of May against direct and indirect attacks from the Axis powers. Early in April a coup d'etat put the government of Iraq, once a British mandate, in the hands of a pro-Axis faction. Fighting broke out between British and Iraqi forces early in May, when the oil pipe was damaged. Britain struggled to put down the disturbance before the Moslem world should be roused, and before the Germans could render material assistance. In spite of the bombing of British bases by German planes operating from Syrian air fields, Baghdad was captured, and peace was restored before the end of May.

Meanwhile this indirect German attack on Britain's position in the Mediterranean was paralleled by a very direct one, an all-out sea and air attack on the island of Crete, eighty miles from the southern tip of the Greek peninsula. A furious air attack put the island bases out of commission and gravely embarrassed the navy. Troops were flown in in large gliders, and were landed from transports, in spite of serious losses. With the air defence disabled, the fate of the island was almost a foregone conclusion. A hasty and partial evacuation took place twelve days after the beginning of the battle. Germany now had a good air base only 340 miles from Alexandria, the chief British naval base in the eastern

Mediterranean, and the same distance from the island of Cyprus, guarding the Syrian coast.

In the first week in June the direction of the next German move seemed to be clear. The rising in Iraq had failed for want of reinforcements, but a German move through the French mandate of Syria might have better success. Syria could also be used as a bombing base for Suez and Alexandria, and as a base for a land drive through Palestine and Transjordania to Egypt. Already German planes had used Syrian airfields against Iraq. Now more men and planes were filtering in. The British, with American approval, determined to forestall this new attack. While Britain's ships endeavoured to guard against possible German landings by sea, Free French and British forces marched against the comparatively weak Vichy France force which held the country. Some of the Vichy French yielded readily, others fought stubbornly, but by the end of June the Free French and the British were in control, and a serious menace to the British position in the Mediterranean was removed for a time, at least.

The explanation for the comparative German inactivity in the Near East was presumably her pre-occupation with Russia. In the summer of 1939 those who still hoped that war might be averted pinned their faith on an alliance between Britain and France on the one hand, and Russia on the other. This would deter Germany by the old fear of a "two-front war." For various reasons the alliance was not concluded, but in August, with the British and French negotiators still at Moscow, Russia signed a treaty of neutrality with Germany. This meant that Germany could push her attack first on Poland, and then on France without fear of any movement against her from the Russian mass to the east. Russia was loudly blamed for perfidiously plunging Europe into war. Her action, however, was dictated by political realism. Knowing that all the Western powers hated and feared her, she felt it wise to turn their mechanized forces on one another while she prepared her great resources for defence, and possibly for attack. Since the beginning of the war she has concentrated on defence preparations, and on securing strategic protection on the west by gathering in the Baltic states with certain key points in Finland, a large part of Poland and Bessarabia.

As the war has proceeded, there have been many rumours of an approaching rift between Russia and Germany. Germany, it was thought, must be angered at Russia's advances in the Baltic, and Russia must be dismayed at Germany's rapid successes in the Balkans. However, relations between the two countries remained outwardly friendly, and close economic co-operation was reported until the early part of June. Then Germany was supposed to be making demands for sweeping economic concessions which Russia was resisting. On June 21, Hitler proclaimed war against Russia, and early on June 22 his troops marched.

The reasons given for Germany's action are many and varied. The two simplest and most obvious are, first, her urgent need of raw materials, especially wheat from the Ukraine, and oil from the Caucasus; and, second, her conviction that she could not safely invade Britain with unconquered Russia — a nominal friend, but a potential foe — behind her. It is also suggested that Germany, convinced by the American aid to Britain programme that the war must be a long one, has decided to "dig herself in" in Russia, and exploit the vast resources of that country at her leisure. Another suggestion is that Germany, having failed to win a signal victory over Britain, either through invasion or in the Eastern Mediterranean, is beginning to "fumble" in her search for a spectacular success. Optimists recalled the precedent of the Napoleonic invasion; pessimists, the weakness of Russia's mechanized forces, and the ease with which Germany, having mastered the Ukraine and reached the Caucasus, could turn the British flank in the Middle East, and even proceed through Iran to an invasion of India.

So far neither prophecy has been fulfilled. Germany proceeded in three great movements across the plains of eastern Europe towards Leningrad, Moscow, and Kiev, the chief city of the Ukraine. How the campaign has gone is a little difficult to say, since the Russian and German reports differ so widely as to be absolutely irreconcilable. However, it is clear that seven weeks of war have not placed Germany in possession of any one of her three main objectives. At first German reports were jubilant, but gradually they became cautious. Bad weather and bad roads were mentioned, and the Russians were alternately praised as good fighters, and blamed for not fighting fairly. They make use of mean tricks like pretending to be dead, and then springing to life at the approach of the German infantry, and they fight stubbornly and to the death instead of surrendering at the proper moment. All this costs German lives and German material, and more provoking still interrupts the harmonious routine of the *blitzkrieg*.

Meanwhile Britain has accepted Russia as an ally (subject to Churchill's personal reserve, that he still dislikes Communism) and the United States has offered help similar to that available to Britain under the lend-lease programme. Russia is still fighting in isolation, but heavy R.A.F. attacks by day and night over France and western Germany are thought to have diverted a part, at least, of the German air force from the Russian front. In spite of good Russian resistance, and this indirect British aid, the Russian forces are steadily retreating. The Germans claim to be approaching Moscow, to be encircling Kiev and to have reached Odessa on the Black Sea. The present Russian policy is one of orderly retreat, to keep the Red Army in being, and of "scorched earth" tactics, so that Germany shall get no profit from her victory. It is said that the population of the Ukraine is moving eastwards in a mass, taking along the produce of the harvest. Gangs of workmen and farmers are left behind with orders to produce and send goods eastward as long as they can; when they must retreat, expert saboteurs are to make a clean sweep of all supplies and equipment that can be useful to the Germans. The Russians hope to make an efficient retreat to the newly developed industrial and agricultural area behind the Ural mountains and from there to harry the enemy.

It has often been remarked that a definite Axis push in the West is generally accompanied or followed by a corresponding Japanese push in the East. The German move against Russia has put Japan into a position of some perplexity, since, although a member of the Axis, she has also recently signed a non-aggression pact with Russia. Moreover, somewhat exhausted by the war with China, it is said that she does not wish to undertake hostilities with Russia, nor does she wish to see a victorious Germany in the Far East. However, she is no longer master of her fate, and like Italy must, it seems, move at the command of Berlin, subject always to her fear of war with the United States. Late in July, having re-organized her cabinet, she occupied various air fields and stations in French Indo-China. Vichy France, presumably under German pressure, gave consent to Japan's co-operation in her "defence." With Japanese bombers and warships and some 40,000 troops stationed in Indo-China, Thailand, with good reason, began to look to her defences. Meanwhile in the Dutch East Indies, Singapore and the Philippines there was serious alarm. Japan's project for a "greater East Asia Co-prosperity sphere" found no favour with her neighbour across the Pacific. The United States froze Japanese assets within her territory, Japan responded in kind, and the United States thereupon prevented the shipment of aviation gasoline and oils to Japan. As Japan can produce only a fraction of her own oil needs, she must use her reserves or invade the oil fields of the East Indies or British Borneo, The situation remains acute (Aug. 12).

A final diplomatic success for Germany is just announced. Vichy France, after a week-end of closed cabinet conferences, has announced her full "collaboration" with Germany. Admiral Darlan, pro-Nazi and anti-British, has complete military command in unoccupied France, and Weygand has returned to Africa with instructions to follow Darlan's orders in everything. The fruit of this victory to Germany is expected to be concessions in the West African ports.

Throughout the summer developments everywhere have tended to extend the war area to the Western Hemisphere. The occupation of Iceland by American troops is only one indication of the increasing activity of the United States in measures short of war. Whether recent developments in the Far East and in Vichy France will draw her in still further is the question of the moment.[9]

HIROSHIMA — FIFTEEN YEARS AFTER

HIROSHIMA

On August 10, 1945, Japan offered her surrender to the Allied Powers, and August 14 was proclaimed V.J. Day. In England preparations were made for thanksgiving services in innumerable little parish churches. In one church in East

Anglia, however, there was no such service. In spite of protests the vicar forbade it. He would not, he said, permit a formal service of thanksgiving for a victory achieved through such odious and iniquitous means.

The vicar's concern is ours today. The victory, as all remember, had been finally achieved by dropping an atomic bomb on Hiroshima, a fan-shaped city lying on six islands in a river estuary, with docks and the sea to the south and mountains round the other three sides. It contained on the morning of the bombing, about a quarter of a million people. The blow came early in the morning. Some who survived speak of an intensely white light, then a frightful concussion and roar, intense heat, fires everywhere, everything at the centre of the blast wiped out by intense heat. More than half the population were instantly killed (64,000) or injured (72,000). The injured suffered bad burns, injuries from glass or timbers, radiation injuries. Three hospitals were left standing out of forty-five, twenty-eight doctors were uninjured out of 290, and 126 out of 1,780 nurses. Means of communication, water mains, pipes were destroyed. Survivors were presented with cases of intense suffering, the more horrible because in hideous and bizarre forms. Hiroshima still stands out as a horrifying event in an age of horrors.

The question asked then, and since is "Why did the Americans who, throughout their history have stood sincerely if not always quite consistently for human rights, for mercy and humanity, for peace, develop and use this most horrible weapon?" In suggesting answers to this question and to others throughout the paper I would remind you that in determining courses of action we are governed by two sets of considerations: moral and expedient. Ideally we do not consider a choice of expediencies until we have ascertained the necessary moral limitations. In practice it is sometimes difficult entirely to separate the two although the moral person tries to do so. In arriving at reasoned judgments on men's conduct we must keep in mind the distinction between what is right and permissible on the one hand, and what seems necessary, desirable or pleasing on the other. If you say "It's not right and anyway it doesn't pay," or "It doesn't pay, and anyway you shouldn't do it," you are confusing two categories of thought. The result is muddled thinking and no sure conclusion.

The American development and use of the bomb certainly seemed to be expedient: First, they had what they believed was good information that the Germans were working on just such a weapon and would use it. Until Germany's defeat this was an argument for the practical necessity to do the same. Second, although Germany was out of the war before the bomb was used it was believed that it would bring a speedy end to the war which the Japanese were apparently prepared to end suicidally. It would thus save life on both sides. Thirdly, it would forestall the Russian entry into Japanese territory with the possible consequent extension of Russian control over this strategically important area. It might even impress Russia sufficiently to make her more reasonable in her claims over European territory.

It did seem expedient then to make use of what Secretary of State Stinson referred to as "the most terrible weapon ever developed in human history."

It might be expedient, but was it morally right? That is, was this a legitimate means of achieving even an admittedly most desirable end?

The question is a very difficult one and should not be oversimplified by saying merely "This is too horrible; it must be wrong" — although that, in the end may be the right answer.

One must ask, however, if war is right at all? Fundamentally it is an appeal to force when reason fails. We all know that might does not make right. Our only defence of war is that, if we are sure we have both might *and* right on our side we may restrain a madman or a criminal and that it is even better for them that we should do so.

May you then use *any* means to restrain them? What means would you refuse to use? These are difficult questions to answer, even in the rather simple cases of the individual confronted with a murderer or homicidal maniac. In war, men of our civilization have, through the ages, developed certain roles to "humanize" or "civilize" the process, fantastic though that may seem. Over the centuries we have introduced adequate and equal care of sick and wounded of both sides, humanity to prisoners, immunity of non-combatants, especially women and children, and elimination of cruel weapons. The close of the nineteenth century saw the highest point of the movement to "play the game according to rules." It does make the game less revolting perhaps. A duel is less offensive than a stab in the back even though the unskilled swordsman may just as certainly be killed. But, apart from the devastating parody of *The Bridge Over the River Kwai,* the twentieth century has ended much of that. There are no non-combatants, and offensive weapons became steadily more and more terrible and destructive, from the first feeble scattering of bombs in World War I to the awful devastation of Holland and Germany in World War II.

And yet the issue did come up, being pressed, I believe, chiefly by certain scientists, in relation to the atom bomb. They did not say (most of them) that its use was absolutely wrong. They pleaded first that it should not be used without a warning and some sort of demonstration to Japan; and second that it should be used only under the authority of the United Nations. This does not, however, it seems to me, deal with the moral issue. If the atom bomb is so terrible a weapon that its use is wrong, it is just as wrong for the United Nations as for the United States.

These arguments were set aside, partly, it seems, because the civilian leaders felt some uncertainty whether the thing would really work. If it didn't, the less said about it the better. If it did, the psychological effect, the shock — would be very much more effective. If one seeks a moral justification it must be on the ground that one evil was accepted in order to avert an even greater one. It was determined to kill and maim in a horrible and terrifying fashion a limited number of people in order to save, ultimately, a greater loss of life. It must be said that the

Americans had evidence that the Japanese although accepting the certainty of ultimate defeat were prepared to offer a suicidal resistance; and it is fair to remember that, on the whole they had not been merciful foes.

I do not find these arguments entirely convincing. I would like to find evidence — there seems to be none — that those who took the decision reflected sufficiently on the horror of their action. At the same time, they might well ask whether their action differed in kind or only in degree from the terrible concentrated bombings of German cities which had helped to secure the European victory.

WHERE DO WE STAND NOW?

We are now fifteen years away from that first nuclear attack. The United States, Russia and others have acquired or are acquiring large stockpiles of these hideous weapons. They remain a permanent threat not merely to peace and civilization, but even to human survival. The threat is so frightful that the thought of atomic war waged on largely urbanized societies must remain with most of us an intellectual concept only. If we have the courage we scarcely have the capacity fully to imagine the awful picture.

Meanwhile radioactive fall-out is a real, and perhaps a great — we cannot say precisely how great — danger to health and efficiency in this and succeeding generations. Estimates of exposure and of our capacity to tolerate it differ, but no one denies the possibility that damage is being done now in some areas. It is certain that it will continue and increase if tests continue unaltered.

The stock-piling of weapons and the tests continue not in our own country but in that of our close ally. We, like they, constitute a democratic society, and our government can, in some measure perhaps, influence theirs. As individuals it is our responsibility to inquire, consider, and endeavour to reach a decision on what ought to be done. Only there is a moral limitation on democratic freedom of speech which is easily forgotten. No one has any moral right to give judgment without a very serious examination of the facts, and a courteous consideration of both sides of the question, if there are two sides. And, on a momentous issue of practical politics before attempting to influence public opinion, it is important to be sure that the course you recommend is the one you would follow if you were in a position of full power and full responsibility — a very awful position in times like these.

WHAT ARE THE POSSIBLE COURSES OF ACTION?

First, the bomb could be condemned utterly in the western world, and all tests stopped. This would amount to unilateral disarmament and conventional forces in the West do not match those of Russia. The possession of even a limited number of these dreadful weapons has been as a useful deterrent against the aggression of a country who with its satellites is very much stronger than we are.

The arguments of those who would, nonetheless abolish the bomb are practical and moral.

Practical — The bomb defended as a deterrent may even cause an atomic war through working on the fears of our potential foe. Without the bomb there would be no danger of nuclear warfare. No country would wage it against an enemy equipped only with conventional arms; the physical destruction and psychological antagonism caused would be too great.

Moral — The argument here must be simply that to use this weapon or to threaten to use it, or to do anything to make its use possible is morally wrong. And, it may be argued, that settles the matter. The moral man does what is right, and ignores the consequences. This is a powerful and persuasive argument. On this principle, many of the noblest men and women in our civilization have ruled their lives. But it is, I think, important to remember that a completely dogmatic moral code is only possible for those who firmly believe in the revelation of a God to whom men are accountable, whose decrees they obey, though not always understanding them, and to whom, in faith, they leave the consequences of their obedience. But such a dogmatic system will hardly do for any humanistic system of morality. With such a system the probable and possible consequences of any action must always be borne in mind, and action rationally determined in relation to them. This does not mean a selfish calculation of course, but a calculation of good not to ourselves but to society.

It does mean, however, that it is difficult to say "This single action of loosing an atomic weapon is absolutely wrong and I can have no part in it." One would have to say, rather "I am convinced that the ill effects will outweigh any conceivable good ones" — and of such a proposition it is very hard to be sure. What one is tempted to say is, "I regard atom bombs as utterly loathsome and I will shout them down" — but that is allowing one's practical and moral judgment to be strongly tinged with emotion.

Second, an alternative course to the elimination of the nuclear weapons, and of all testing is to maintain nuclear weapons and even fresh tests, but to look for "clean" weapons of limited power; and to seek for a system of international control which shall be a complement to a complete disarmament.

This is not satisfactory. It leaves us in awful peril. It leaves us with a sense of guilt, inadequacy and helplessness. It leaves us in a condition of patient groping, accepting a condition of "neither war nor peace" as a recent writer puts it, when we long for some decisive, heroic gesture.

And yet it can be defended.

Moral — The moral defence, admittedly, is not easy. The nuclear weapon as we know it is odious, cruel and destructive beyond imagination. But, if we eliminate in on *moral* grounds do we tolerate all other means of man's destruction and torture? The answer may be yes — reluctantly — because nuclear weapons do threaten the integrity and survival of the race — the most elementary humanistic morality cries out against them. If only as a mere statement of the will to survive they should be unilaterally outlawed. This may be sound, so long as we accept the possible, many would say the certain alternative of a world organized by Soviet Russia. There are moments when we would most of us be prepared to do so.

Practical — This brings me to the practical arguments in favour of retaining and "cleaning" nuclear weapons.

1. The nuclear deterrent it is argued *is* a real one. To say that we wish the bomb had never been made or used in 1945 does not mean that we should renounce its use today. The powers now sit facing each other, each holding a weapon too terrible to be used, as they well know. It may be presumed that it will not be used — a risky presumption, but we live in a risky age. It is certain that without nuclear weapons in the West there would be nothing to contain a Communist Eurasian power.

2. Not only may the existence of nuclear weapons prevent a war between great powers; it may prevent disputes and wars between small powers from spreading and perhaps has done so — over Berlin, the Suez Canal, Jordan, Lebanon, Quemoy, Tibet and Laos.

3. By continuing patient and hopeful, we may work through without war, or without major wars, to some genuine international understanding.

These are not exciting or heroic considerations. They may be sound ones. The whole matter deserves patient and thoughtful study. No one should take the easy way of rushing at decisions which he is not responsible to carry out. Historical analogies are dangerous, but it is impossible not to think of the many ardent self-styled "pacifists" of the thirties. They did not, they would not ask themselves whether they only hated war as all decent people do, or really refused even to consider it as a means to an end. They were in part responsible for the appeasement of Hitler who played on them as (it has been suggested) Russia plays on the West's strong and righteous loathing and shame over having produced and used nuclear weapons.

I have said the historical analogy is dangerous. I think so, and I do not press it. I would only point out that in this appallingly difficult age hatred of evil is not enough. We will never be presented in any important matter with a clear choice of good and evil. Our task is rather humbly and painstakingly to make our way in a labyrinth that seems all evil toward the faint glimmer that is the light of day.[10]

SASKATOON — REPLY TO ADDRESS OF WELCOME

May I say first, Mr. Mayor, how deeply I appreciate your kind and cordial welcome. Thank you very much for all that you have said. It is a great pleasure to be here, and I am particularly glad that my visit should so nearly coincide with the seventieth anniversary of the founding of Saskatoon, and the celebrations connected with it.

These celebrations, I understand, began appropriately with a tribute to Saskatoon's pioneers. Saskatoon today, Mr. Mayor, has the reputation of being pre-eminently a beautiful city of quiet homes and gardens. It is fitting then that your first tribute should be paid to those quiet and determined people who banded together to found new homes and a new community in what was then, to all appearance a barren and an empty land.

Energy and enterprise, and even speculative adventure were, I understand, to be found among these quiet people. Conquering the hardships and solving the problems of the early years, Saskatoon survived and flourished. It became very soon, I understand, first the distributing centre of a great area which subsisted first on cattle-raising and then on the still experimental operations of dry farming. Various factors, including, I am told, the determination of Saskatoon citizens, made the place one of the great railway centres of the province.

Long before reaching complete maturity, Mr. Mayor, your city was called on to play its part in the First World War. Later, as one of the leading cities of the chief wheat producing province of Canada, it suffered severely from the prolonged period of drought and depression which preceded the second test of war, even more severe than the first one. In that war Saskatoon played an important part in the Commonwealth Air Training Plan, and the city later co-operated most ably with the university authorities in providing educational facilities for many hundreds of veterans from all the services.

Saskatoon's seventy years, Mr. Mayor, have not been without labour and sorrow. It is clear, however, that they have been brightened by optimism, and that they have marked the steady endurance which this country demands, and which your pioneers and their successors have given in full measure.

For the present you enjoy much prosperity and the future promises great, perhaps very great, expansion. May I offer to you and to the citizens of Saskatoon my very best wishes. I am very happy to be here with you today.

(Saskatoon does pride itself on being a beautiful city. The *Star-Phoenix,* I recall, editorialized its beauty not so long ago. Also it is remarkable for the number of small homes with really beautiful gardens, even though they can only bloom 3–4 months out of the twelve. It is extremely difficult to find a comfortable flat in Saskatoon, and always has been difficult, because people like even small houses much better. It is important, however, not to forget how energetic and businesslike we are, or our Boards of Trade will be offended. Our position as a railway centre is a subject of modest pride; we were almost by-passed on two occasions, but the citizens by fair means or foul got the railways here, and then called Saskatoon "the Hub City" in honour of the achievement. They also fought a stout battle for the capital and lost, and another for the university which they won.)[11]

SASKATOON

I wish I could say that I was glad to be in your beautiful city, but the truth is, my one desire at the moment is to be comfortably at home assured only of this: never to see another mayor, never to hear another address, and *never* to make another speech.

As for your city it may be tolerable in summer, concealed as far as may be under the scanty and grudging foliage which is all this wretched climate affords. Now under this lead-coloured sky with a raw wind driving the dust from the naked plains through your squalid dwellings and along your sordid streets I must tell you plainly I never saw anything more revolting. It is worse, if possible than it was three years ago when I imperilled my health and the future of this Dominion by sitting in a frigid town hall listening [to] ignorant ———[12] supporting the cause of private radio.

I understand you have recently been celebrating your 70th anniversary. Why the 70th? Why celebrate the completion of your allotted span? But perhaps after all you are right and you may find others to join you with heartiness if not with goodwill.

You ———[13] of prosperity. I should be glad to hear that at least you are making money, but I am not. I could respect those who chose this place from the call of duty or who — if it could be so — were sent here by law for the comfort and security of other citizens in more civilized areas. To choose such a place from mercenary motives forfeits at once my respect.

I have said enough, Mr. Mayor. Some may think I have said too much, but this is my day for being frank. Good morning.[14]

SPEECH FOR INTERNATIONAL NIGHT — BUSINESS AND PROFESSIONAL WOMEN

To anyone interested in history, the very word "international" invites a two-volume commentary. What does it mean? What does nation mean?

Without going to the length of two volumes, it is worth while to spend a few moments on the word "national," because its correct meaning is under discussion and represents one of the most important problems in the world today — one that is of particular interest to Canada.

The modern conception of "nation" emerged from a profound reaction against the eighteenth-century assumption that man's most conspicuous, valuable and universal quality was his reason. As men who reason correctly must come to the same conclusions, reason would unite all peoples and classes — through education. And educated reason could procure a good life for men who were naturally good, and who erred only through ignorance.

It was during the romantic reaction against the over-stressing of reason that nationalism emerged. It was argued, and particularly by politically suppressed groups — Germans, Poles, Italians and others — that men's emotions are as truly a part of them as their reason, and that emotions are as important as reason in achieving truth and goodness. And men's strongest and best emotions (it was argued) bound them to their language, their traditions, their literature, their history — in fact to their own land and people as a special entity having a character different and distinct from other like entities — and rightly demanding their allegiance. From the French Revolution — roughly — to the end of the First World War the great *political* concern, the great political ideal for many, was to ensure that each "nation" — each group claiming a separate identity in virtue of language, race, tradition, culture, should become a self-governing political unit, a state with a moral claim to a kind of equality to all other states, large and small. This moral claim came to be accepted by many liberals in the nineteenth-century. One of its most eminent exponents was President Woodrow Wilson, whose intervention in the First World War, and in the ensuing peace discussions, was such a potent force for good, and for evil too.

But nationalist idealists like Wilson, and like the Italian Mazzini, understand very well that national hates and rivalries may be as strong and dangerous as dynastic ones. During the emergence of many new nation states (which was paralleled by the development of modern communications) countless numbers of men and women of goodwill recognized that our common humanity bridges all racial and cultural differences. Accepting the sovereignty of the nation states they strove to build along horizontal lines international operations and organizations that would pass over or through the vertical material walls.

Many such operations, of course, preceded in time the era of the nation state. Two great and rather different kinds of people in the western world have always taken the world for their parish. The business man (or woman) will go where his business takes him, by his occupation, if not his convictions free of prejudice. From the time of the Romans particularly trade has been a great factor in international exchange. The Christian church has also been, again by definition, international, rising above, if not indifferent to, local differences. And, rather more recently, the professions, and the scholars, have created international organizations, recognizing that skill and learning are not "national," but international.

Through the nineteenth century a host of international organizations developed from all these sources. Two eminent ones, not belonging specifically to any of the categories mentioned, are the International Postal Union and the International Red Cross.

After the First World War, and again after the Second, those who now realized that national rivalries could be even more dangerous to peace and justice than dynastic ones, made serious attempts to put into practice a very old dream, a world government. The idealists hoped for something as efficient as the old *Pax Romana* but based on free consent and on democratic decisions. Until something like that could be developed, they settled for the League of Nations, whose members "outlawed" war and agreed on certain procedures for the peaceful settlement of disputes.

Wise people, however, realized that an organization existing chiefly for the settlement of quarrels is at best negative. The League therefore asserted that one of its great functions was to encourage and assist international organizations of any kind for all peaceful and useful social purposes. It wished to associate with itself those already existing, and to foster others.

After the failure of the League and the Second World War, the United Nations did the same thing, even more systematically. *Unesco,* the United Nations Educational, Scientific and Cultural Organization, was founded and endowed with the idea of establishing a world community of the mind — a community for promoting all those peaceful and useful and pleasurable activities which emphasize ideas we have in common, which give big dividends to peaceful co-operation, and inspire a corresponding natural penalty or national hostility. In addition the Economic Social Council, of which the [International Federation of Business and Professional Women] is a consultative member, is concerned with more immediate and pragmatic aspects of international co-operation.

The International Federation of Business and Professional Women was, as you know, founded in the period between the wars. The date of its birth was peculiarly inauspicious for international operations and for women. Although Communist Russia asked women to fill a role in society comparable to, and equal to, that of men, Russia was not on good terms with the West. Moreover, the opposing ideology, Nazism, emphasized strongly a militant nationalism, hostility to international organizations, and the subjection of women. I do not know how successful the first [Federation] meetings were. I do know that in 1936 I attended a meeting of the International Federation of University Women held in Cracow, Poland, and in spite of many hopes no members from Russia, Italy or Germany were permitted to attend.

In the last twenty years, however, international organizations have taken on new life and energy, partly because of increased freedom of operation, partly because of the new and lively nations of the Third World — Africa, South America, Asia, who are eager to assert and develop their independent status and the special contributions they have to make. In these states, for the most part, it is taken for granted that all educated people must accept their responsibilities — and the traditions which limited the activities of women, like so many other traditions, are being rapidly thrown aside.

This new aspect to international operations is emphasized by the recognition that wealthy nations, of which ours is one, must help the new nations, most of which are situated in poor or rather underdeveloped countries. This is recognized as a work of humanity and also of self-preservation. It is not possible for countries so rich that the big problem for many of us is to avoid the penalties of over-eating and over-drinking, to live permanently and peacefully next door to those in which the majority live at or near the starvation level. And it is wrong not to feed the hungry when we can.

The problem is that "hand-outs" are resented, and that they are not the practical answer. Richer countries are, as you know, trying to bring up the level in poorer ones by loans to be used for machinery, construction materials and labour that may equip the poorer ones to use their own resources to the best advantage. The most valuable of all gifts — and this we can give — is "know-how."

It is impressive to read of the various activities of the I.F.B.P.W. in giving this sort of aid abroad, and in associating women of every country in carrying out their responsibility to ask for and use the right to fill various positions and perform various services formerly reserved to men. I was much impressed in the fall issue of *Widening Horizons* to note the plea for continued help to young women training in the Middle East (Ramallah) in spite of difficulties caused by national animosities.

It is, however, impossible to leave this international theme without raising (as I suggested earlier) the current and very difficult question of the meaning of "nation." Most international organizations have to translate it as meaning "a people calling itself a nation which through one means or another has got itself recognized as a state by other states" — as, for example, Biafra called itself a nation, but having been defeated (and I express no opinion on the merits of the issue) is not a nation, and almost certainly will not be so. It is perhaps too easy to refer to law and to "international law superseding national law" — to forget how much in many countries each law rests on force. (This is not a reason for over-throwing disagreeable laws by force. Anarchy is much worse.)

Another question I think must occur to many on International Night. If "international law" supersedes national law, what does the I.F.B.P.W. think of national laws of Rhodesia and South Africa and their effect on the women of these countries. I am sure these matters have come before the leaders of your organization and that they are a matter of deep concern to them. Our society today is deeply concerned, one might almost say obsessed, with group rights — women's rights, students' rights, black rights, Indian and Eskimo rights — and innumerable others. I think it is fair to say that *so far* the women's movement has *on the whole* only been concerned to assert the right of a woman as an individual. This perhaps gives them a peculiar ability to bring their knowledge and experience to the more modern claimant groups and to say: "Claim equality as individuals, but do not claim privileges — the moment you claim a special privilege you forfeit your claim to equal rights." And also to say, "Claiming equality for yourselves: are you equally concerned with the needs of other suppressed groups?"

More and more I think intelligent people must address themselves to the problem of reconciling group claims to two other values: first, justice to every individual and second, the common good of society — for without a peaceful ordered society we [have] all lost what we value most.[15]

CONVOCATION ADDRESS, UNIVERSITY OF WINDSOR OCTOBER 5, 1974

When I say that it is a pleasure and privilege to be allowed to address you today, I am not using the empty language of politeness. For nearly fifty years I have been speaking to young men and women on subjects that interest me keenly; captive audiences they have been, no doubt, but I have a strong and grateful memory of their honesty, their fairness and their kindness. We may as well face facts. Many professors are bad lecturers. What has struck me in my whole career has been the generosity of students. They do not condemn harshly anyone who is really doing his best, especially if he has an honest enthusiasm for his subject. If he has not, of course, he had no business wasting their time. So I ask your indulgence. What I have to say to you today I am saying because I think it is important. You may not agree but I know you will hear me with patience.

All of us today — like every generation of mankind since Adam — are concerned at the perilous state of human society. Young people, naturally, blame the previous generation, and, no doubt, receive the obvious retort, "We didn't inherit a perfect world either." As I reflect on our most pressing problems, two occur to me as being acute. Each is closely linked with every aspect of life in society and each arises fundamentally from moral weakness. One is the decay through carelessness, laziness, and sheer dishonesty of one of the great languages of the western world. We have not quite lost the means of communication, but we are destroying the qualities of language that raise communication above mere material needs. I am not so fit to judge the situation of the other great language we claim as our inheritance but I understand there are problems there too.

The other, of which I wish to speak more particularly, is the decay of "law." "Law" has now become a bad word along with rules, discipline, conformity and so forth. We now concentrate on individual rights and on "doing our own thing" as the glory of our way of life. The ideal of individual freedom is indeed one of the achievements of our civilization. What can so easily be forgotten is that our individual freedom has grown very slowly and very painfully in any given society, and that it has always had to grow within the framework of a rule of law. From the arbitrary law of the Romans which yet appealed in general to the individual sense of justice and right reason, to the freer systems of the modern western world where law was a common possession to be adapted by the common will to changing social needs, and to a developing social conscience, freedom has developed not in opposition to law — although there have been conflicts — but within the shelter of the community conception of law as an ideal.

In a modern free society the law must rest, in some sense, on the private moral convictions of each individual: "This I would not do for any consideration; this I must do at all costs." If one could know the private moral imperatives and moral prohibitions of each individual, one could gauge his moral character. Some, of course, have very short lists; many, alas, have undertaken no private moral inventory.

But to return to the law, on the one hand a good law for a free society must rest on some consensus of free and moral individuals in society; and on the other hand, young people growing up into conscious moral priniciples are profoundly affected by the law under which they live.

I come now to our present crisis which could, I think, be destructive of all freedom if not of all happiness. We are losing the sense that respect and obedience to the law of the community — imperfect though it may be — is essential not only to freedom but to any kind of security. And it is not the traditional "lawbreakers" who have lost this sense. It is worthy, respectable people whose moral conduct probably is above reproach, but whose awareness of the significance of law in history is sadly defective. This is the essence of our crisis. It is not that "bad" people are breaking the law, but that the good are tolerant or even ready to give their approval if the motive of the law-breakers appears to be good.

This matter first came forcibly to my attention a few years ago. I was visiting friends in the Eastern United States when two young people, relatives, turned up, having travelled from the west coast in the comfortable and casual fashion of today, wearing jeans and almost without luggage. They were on their way to the Middle East to do international good works. Both had graduate degrees, one a Ph.D. We discussed recent developments on university campuses, including the horrifying death by a bomb of a young mathematician at Madison, Wisconsin. These young people acknowledged that his death was a pity, but they had no condemnation for those who had planted the bomb. It was too bad, they said, but the attention of authorities must be drawn to injustices, incompetence, and inequality. We — the older members — agreed that bad laws should be protested somehow, but not, we argued, *anyhow,* and never or almost never by the cold-blooded murder of an innocent and unsuspecting person. Our arguments were received politely, but were not convincing. And yet these young people were truly kind, intelligent and highly educated. They must have tens of thousands of counterparts in the U.S. and in Canada. Were they just trying to get a rise out of their elders? Even this laudable aim hardly explains or justifies a light-hearted approach to murder. And some who are tolerant of lawlessness are not young. This tolerant approach is immoral; it is also irrational and inconsistent. If one of these two young people had been murdered or maimed, either by a bomb, or, say, by gang murder, the other would have assumed that the whole force of the state would be brought to bear in the interest of what, I think, they would call not vengeance, but justice.

I may be labouring a point completely clear to all of you. But perhaps I am not. Perhaps all the combined inequalities, injustices and general idiocies of some of our laws have led you to ignore the fundamental condition of freedom. Reverence for the rule of law — not necessarily for any particular law — is the primary condition of a free, happy and useful life for you and for millions less privileged and more helpless than you are. At the moment, this great western ideal — a just law as underlying true freedom — is discredited. It may be restored by a fresh understanding, especially if there is added a conviction of the truth I mentioned earlier: in a free society the ultimate sanction and support of the rule of law is the moral imperative which governs each individual. If you ask for a rationalization of such a moral imperative I may refer you not to the sanctions of religion, powerful though these may be for some of us, but to a remark of your own president which impressed me greatly when I read it:

> I press you to consider certain fundamental bases for the framework of your lives. The first of these is that we are all here as part of a greater purpose, of some larger design. If we are not part of such a major intention then it does not matter what we do. But such a conclusion violates our deepest instincts and affronts our common sense.

I think it does. I ask you in the light of your sense of this larger design to review your own convictions and you own obligation to the inheritance of law with freedom which, at great cost, has been preserved for you, and which is now in grave peril.[16]

PART FOUR

More Words about Hilda

Hilda spent much of her life thinking and trying to apply her conclusions to her life and to the lives of others. The attempt to transmit her convictions to others was carried out through her ability to convince others rather than through force. This book has concentrated on her attempts at persuasion through writing and formal speeches. Her day-to-day efforts to change attitudes now exist only in anecdotes. The recordings of Hilda that exist were made on the formal occasions of radio and television broadcasts.[1]

Reading what Hilda wrote and said reveals that there were constants, variables, paradoxes, and contradictions in her thought. Her constants can be summed up by the words woman, Presbyterian, historian, teacher. The variables were in her attitudes toward Christianity and civilization. The paradoxes existed because of her simultaneous beliefs in an intellectual aristocracy and democracy, in freedom and truth, and in freedom and law. The contradictions reveal themselves in her view of Canada, Britain, and the United States, in her regard for accuracy, and in the stance she took in facing the world.

Hilda was a woman and this, partly because of biology, partly because of society, gave her insights not shared by her mostly male colleagues. At times this brought within her a war between duty and compassion, the particular and the general, the practical and the theoretical. The war did not create a dual personality, however. Hilda developed as a woman scholar facing a somewhat hostile male world with resources provided by her own talents and convictions, by the example and training of her father and mother, by the support of her family, especially her sister Kate, and by the influence and support of friends — especially of Frank Underhill, who broadened her moral sense, Vincent Massey, who reinforced both her sense of propriety and her courage, Eugene Forsey, who taught pugnacity, and Georges-Henri Lévesque, O.P., who both appreciated her and provided broad-mindedness.[2]

Hilda's mature convictions were particularly influenced by her Presbyterian religion and her study of history. The Presbyterian influence reinforced the sense of being "chosen" and special that had come from her family. This feeling was always mixed with the uncertainties that also came from a full understanding of Presbyterianism and from growing up English on the prairies. Hilda at one and the same time knew she was able and doubted her ability; knew that she was right and yet hesitated to impose herself too much. Her study of history and her efforts to teach it convinced her of the complexity of the world, of humans, of life. She came to realize that there is no simple approach to life, no single response to difficulty. She summed it up for herself in a letter to Frank Underhill:

> When I was young, of course I thought I was a liberal. Now, I think I am a conservative by taste, a liberal by disposition — sometimes anyway — and a socialist by conviction — again sometimes.[3]

Hilda came to recognize, at least in others, the problems that the tendencies within her created:

> It is difficult for anyone who has read Haldimand's letters not to believe that he was a man with a steady determination to do his duty, and to be kind as well as just. Yet such people can be irritating; they make errors of judgment and may cause more hardship to others than they intend or wish. The merchants who resisted Haldimand so deeply may not have been altogether unreasonable.[4]

The first variable was in her attitude toward Christianity. Hilda's experiences led her to modify, to relax a bit. She became less insistent on a narrowly defined Christianity. There came to be room for Anglicans and even Roman Catholics on one side, and members of the United Church on the other. Beyond Christianity Hilda was willing to respect those who sought God through faith and reason or who accepted the norms of what she considered civilization: freedom constrained by reason and law.

Hilda remained a convinced Presbyterian, but her dissenting tradition, influenced by her historical studies, her experience, and her feminine insight, led her to accept that "in my father's house there are many mansions." She both supported ecumenism and fervently hoped for religious revival among all Christians.

The second variable in Hilda's thought was of a different nature. Concern for civilization was a constant, but her ideas on the source of the major threat to civilization varied. The variation was influenced by her growing knowledge and understanding as well as by the world around her. Her concern about Fascism in the 1940's, Communism in the 1950's, and anarchy in the late 1960's were commonplace. The strength of her convictions and her willingness to act were not.

Reason was not equally present in all human beings; therefore, Hilda believed

that there had to exist an intellectual aristocracy, which should be encouraged —
given privileges. Yet everyone should be free. Civilization was freedom constrained by reason and law in a mix that was difficult to determine. Put together,
these beliefs created paradoxes that Hilda could not solve, but with which she
could live. Faith, reason, freedom, and order all needed to exist and deserved
different emphases according to the temper of the times: "If artificially preserved
from failure you will never know success; and if you are not prepared early to live
in and respect a society based on law you will never know what freedom means."
"There can be no justice without law." "Can one argue that science is only safe for
society as long as Galileo knows that he just might be burned?"[5]

Despite the paradoxes, Hilda could and did prescribe cures for the predomi-
nant evils of each time. Her books, articles, and speeches reveal both her attacks
and her remedies. In the 1940's protection was needed against both totalitarianism and an extreme reaction against it — democracy poorly understood. After
the war her first fear was that with totalitarianism defeated, a false idea of
democracy, developed by educators under the influence of John Dewey, would
destroy both reason and the intellectual aristocracy. Later in the 1950's, she
feared that the race to catch the Soviet Union in the development of science and
technology would destroy the humanities.

During most of the 1960's Hilda was tied up in the day-to-day concerns of
developing a history department in an expanding university. She was worried
about the outcome. In a sense the worries were those of the fortunate — how to
be sure that as much quality as possible would be built into the new university.
Hilda was careful in hiring. Others throughout North America were not or could
not be as careful.

The world was changing. The new generation felt restricted by traditions, the
existing power structure, and, in some cases, the standards in place. First the
younger members of the faculty and then the students began to demand a larger
voice in the governing of the university. Hilda saw this demand as an attack on
reason, liberty, and the intellectual aristocracy. Once again it was a case of
democracy poorly understood. This time she feared that the result would be more
than poor education. She foresaw the possiblity of the disappearance of the
university and not only the end of the intellectual aristocracy, which was rotting
from within, but of civilization itself. Hilda came close to despair; then she
rallied. Her last speeches were an effort to establish contact again with the young
on terms acceptable to both generations in the interest of civilization.

Because she was human, there were contradictions in Hilda. The three major
contradictions were her love for all humans combined with her very high
standards, her insistence on accuracy in tandem with a tendency toward
inaccuracy, and her devotion to Canada and Quebec history in face of her English
preferences.

Hilda truly loved human beings, wanted to be charitable and to give people
the benefit of the doubt; yet there was so much in the world that was wrong

and that should be righted. The Dean of Regina College put it succinctly, if discreetly, when approached by the President of the University of Saskatchewan about the possibility of Hilda's brother Leslie teaching at Regina, "from my knowledge of him I would have some fear that two of the same family, inclined to be dogmatic and censorious, might be a little overpowering for our small staff."[6]

It was not just a family fondness for argument and searching for truth that formed Hilda's approach to the world. In the world she was always perceived as different: as a child because she was very English and very religious, as a student because she was very intelligent, as a professor because she was a woman, as a woman because she was a professor, and as an intellectual because she was a religious woman westerner. Hilda was aware of these perceptions. This led her to maintain a reserve that some interpreted as haughtiness.

Hilda considered some to be beyond redemption in their stupidity. Sometimes she went too far. Yet she could be faced down, could be reasoned with by those who were persistent and either intelligent or civilized — and she could always be approached as a fellow human being.

Hilda was very conscious of accuracy, rules, and style. She resisted with vigour the attempts of editors to change her words.[7] She took it upon herself to correct others. Her war against "hopefully" was legendary.[8] In her book reviews she constantly criticized poor proofreading and inaccurate citations. Yet Hilda herself was inaccurate. Some of this might be excused on the grounds that she was poorly served by her typists until the last ten years of her life.

She did not, however, become noticeably more accurate in her last decade. The fact is that Hilda hurried too often. She did not have the time nor perhaps the patience to proofread carefully. She did not always take careful notes; she did not always recheck citations herself. Hilda was aware of her failing. She wrote Roger Graham in 1966 after reading her book on Quebec: "I must confess that as I reread it although parts satisfy me the many little slips and ambiguities stand out."[9]

Despite her awareness of the problem, her collection of writings about the Quebec Act was saved from appearing with numerous textual inaccuracies only because of the efforts of others.[10] The typescript of the book on Queen's that she left behind at her death had many errors that had to be corrected. The last might be excused on the grounds of ill health were it not for the habits of a lifetime of a woman for whom there was much to do.

The third contradiction in Hilda was her attitude toward Canada. She was a convinced Canadian, aware of her country's virtues and failings. She was very aware of her own and her country's British roots; she had a thorough historical understanding of the unique role of the French in Canada. She had also a clear picture from personal experience and study of the influence of the United States on Canada. She could not, however, quite bring all of this together.

Quebec was the big problem. She studied its history carefully for more than forty years and understood its meaning for Canada. She appreciated French Canada and had warm relationships with individual Québécois. But they were different, a different "race" with different attitudes. Above all Hilda could not accept what happened in Quebec in the 1960's. She spoke of "the atmosphere of obscurantism which isolated French Canadians and has made them such a very difficult element in the nation today."[11] Immediately after Charles de Gaulle's *Québec libre* speech in 1967 she wrote:

> I agree that the danger of dictatorship in Quebec is even more alarming. The greater the emotionalism in which they indulge, the greater the danger of a dictatorship because they simply demand from their politicians that they be emotionally excited rather than informed. I don't know that we have much right to cast stones, but at the moment the danger is greater in Quebec than anywhere else.[12]

Hilda thought that the origins of the trouble in Quebec ultimately came from outside. In her view most of the French who stayed in Canada after the mid-1760s adapted to the new situation. Trouble came from south of the border in the form of the Protestant Loyalists escaping from the American Revolution: "An arrogant and unimaginative people," who caused great resentment in Quebec.[13] The problem was compounded because at first the British had refused to allow priests to come to Quebec from France and then had admitted clerical refugees from the French Revolution. This led to the obscurantism referred to above. The French Revolution was also responsible for nationalism in Quebec.

> It is no wonder that the intoxicating sense of nationalism released by the French Revolution took on in Canada an especially tenacious form, expressing itself in a fashion peculiarly hostile to the British who had conquered and divided them and to the continuing Britishness even of the Americans who appeared to be engulfing them.[14]

Hilda understood the development of Quebec, but she could not accept it because she did not want Quebec to be separate from the rest of Canada in any significant way and because she remained "British."

Remaining British explains part of Hilda's attitude toward the United States. Growing up British on the prairies she must have associated American immigrants, whose numbers were substantial in Saskatchewan, with the discrimination she felt. She wrote to her sister Kate when she went to Minnesota in 1931 that to her amazement the Americans there were not at all like the ones they had known at home. Her experience in Minnesota gave her a more positive attitude toward the States. This was strengthened when Kate settled in the U.S. As with the *Québecois,* Hilda could relate warmly with many individual Americans. But the country remained a threat to British ways and to Canadian civilization, especially because the civilization was so fragile. It was fragile because there were so few people, so divided, spread so far, with so little encouragement and so little time.

Minnesota had not been Hilda's first choice for a graduate school. At first she was not particularly proud of having an American Ph.D. Yet she would have gladly accepted a teaching position in the U.S. if she could have found one. As a member of the Massey Commission she worked hard to find the means for Canadian scholars and artists to develop for the sake of Canadian civilization. The result was that they became part of the international community of scholars and artists at a time when international often meant American. Faced with the need in the 1960's of developing a Canadian university and a shortage of Canadians who were trained in fields other than Canadian history, she hired Americans (except for the teaching of American history — she hired British scholars for that).

Hilda had contradictions within her, partly because the world is a complicated place, partly because of the nature of her country, partly because of her heritage, partly because of her personality; largely because she was in such a hurry to do so much. However, excluding the ignorant and bigots, Hilda had fewer contradictions than most people.

Hilda's ideas might be summed up in a series of quotations:

> Western civilization has grown normally through the fruitful action of individuals in groups.
> The freer you are the more you will feel the weight of it, but the more joyfully you will carry it.
> Why, then, study history? Because it is useful, it is inescapable.
> The education of a gentleman is not for sale.
> I am bothered by a sense of intellectual vagueness . . . a want of intellectual integrity.
> Seek the guidance of the Holy Spirit and use your own common sense.
> The test of a Christian is not what you do but what you are.
> Our task is rather humbly and painstakingly to make our way in a labyrinth that seems all evil toward the faint glimmer that is the light of day.
> Keep your hearts . . . "Keep your minds" and enrich them.[15]

How original was the combination of ideas that were Hilda's? This question cannot be answered because the intellectual history of her generation has not been written. It is not yet time for that history to be written. The present generation of historians are the intellectual children of the Canadians born during the first decade of the twentieth century. Historians born during the late 1950's and 1960's should be far enough removed from Hilda's generation to study it without undue emotionalism.

When the proper time comes this book should be of some help whether Hilda is found to be either an exception or a spokesperson (how she would have hated that word) for her generation. She spoke forcefully on history, democracy, education, and religion. She was heard and people reacted. Her work on the Massey Commission and her book *So Little for the Mind* at least have earned her a permanent place in the history of Canadian civilization.

Having admitted that it is, at this time, impossible to assess Hilda's role in Canadian intellectual history, it can do little harm to suggest a few possibilities.

Hilda contributed to the understanding of eighteenth-century Quebec. However, she could not be called a historian of the first rank. She did not establish a stable of followers or propose a theory to be argued over; but we do know more because of her work. She was not a profound philosopher of history; but she said well what her contemporaries with similar backgrounds and training were thinking, with an added twist of intelligence and determination.

So Little for the Mind was written as Hilda approached fifty. While meant for young parents and young schoolteachers rather than for her own generation, the book did express the ideas of many — perhaps most — of her contemporaries, except those who were part of the educational bureaucracy. The effect was not lasting. She attracted significant attention to the ideas of her generation by publishing a vigorous attack on the existing educational system and was helped in gaining attention because there was a similar attack underway in the United States. What happened remains to be discovered by historians of North America: Overkill? Too old-fashioned? Too intellectually demanding? Smothered by the educational bureaucracy who controlled teacher-training and promotions? Or merely lying dormant until parental disgust with schools reaches another peak after being buried by the combination of prosperity and "student-power" in the 1960's and concerns for "student rights" in the 1970's?

As a historical theorist Hilda was both of her time and open to new influences. As an educational theorist she was either behind or ahead of her time. In neither realm is Hilda likely to have a lasting influence, though no history of Canadian education could possibly ignore her role. Because of two other endeavours Hilda continues to be influential. She formed a coherent, effective History Department at the University of Saskatchewan just before the hiring stopped, thus ensuring its preservation until the end of the twentieth century. She was an effective driving force within the Massey Commission which, because it spoke out and was listened to at a crucial moment, has had a determining effect on the molding of Canadian culture that will probably outlast the century.

Hilda fashioned a History Department not in her own image, but to her liking, which was able to reorganize itself after her retirement yet preserve her sense of devotion to scholarship, teaching, and university and public service. The department continues to play a role and have an influence beyond what its numbers would warrant within both the University of Saskatchewan and the Canadian historical community.

Hilda did not originate the idea of the Canada Council, the National Film Board or a reformed CBC, but she played an important part in molding the suggestions of others into a forcefully stated, coherent programme that captured both public attention and political support. Through the Massey Commission Hilda contributed significantly to the establishment of a formal Canadian system of encouragement for the arts, letters, humanities, and social sciences.

Many of Hilda's ideas were communicated primarily to her students. She was above all a teacher of history. There can be no doubt that she left her mark on her students and that more often than not the mark was a positive one.[16] A limitation on the influence of a teacher is that it lasts only as long as the students do. Some of her last students are now over thirty and most much older. Some of them will pass her ideas along, though in an altered form. That is the basic law of intellectual history — it is not what one says but what others hear that makes a difference. That is the great advantage that writers of ideas have over sayers. Even though written ideas also are misunderstood, it is possible for later generations to return to the text, and, perhaps, reach a better understanding of the ideas. That is why this book needed to be.

What others think one has said depends on their prior formation and subsequent life. Only Hilda was Hilda. She had been formed differently from her students, and she could not bring back a different time and a different place.[17] There were too many other influences. It is tempting to say that her time and place had never existed outside the Neatby house on the prairies, but that was not so. She was more demanding, less compromising, and more consistent than many others of her generation. She also accomplished more than most. At the same time many of her ideas were congenial, at least in theory, to many Canadian intellectuals trained in the 1920's and eary 1930's.[18] When that group is studied it will be easier to assess the positive role in the preservation of civilization of Hilda Neatby, the western-Canadian, Presbyterian, woman, teacher, and historian who had "so much to do and for the doing so little time."

NOTES

ABBREVIATIONS

AUS   Archives of the University of Saskatchewan
PAC   Public Archives of Canada, Ottawa
SAB   Saskatchewan Archives Board, Saskatoon and Regina

N.B.   The footnotes of the original texts have been omitted, except where noted, since almost all are simple references to historical sources. Obvious typographical errors have been silently corrected; other anomalies are noted.

NOTES TO THE INTRODUCTION

1. Frederick W. Gibson in *Queen's University, Vol. I, 1841–1917* (Montreal, 1978), p. xiv; Roger Graham, "Hilda Neatby, 1904–1975," *Proceedings of the Royal Society of Canada,* ser. 4, 14 (1976): 92–95. See also *Canadian Historical Review* 56 (1975): 510–12.
2. Hilda Neatby, *So Little for the Mind* (Toronto: Clarke Irwin, 1953), p. 335.
3. Hilda Neatby, "The Dangers of History," *La Nouvelle Revue Canadienne* 1 (1951): 32.
4. Hilda Neatby, "Are Women Fulfilling Their Obligations to Society?" Speech delivered to the Canadian Federation of University Women, August 1952. SAB, A139, no. 199(1).

NOTES TO CHAPTER 1

1. *Thomas Neatby, A Memorial,* edited by his wife (Glasgow, n.d.); *Marion Jane Neatby, Mother and Granny,* ed. Mary Elizabeth Neatby (Poole, 1930); Kate Neatby Nicoll, *Paths They Have Not Known* (n.p., 1978); L.H. Neatby, *Chronicle of a Pioneer Prairie Family* (Saskatoon, 1979).
2. SAB, A139, no. 3(8).
3. A hint of Thomas Neatby's control of his environment is to be found in his youngest daughter's words about her mother, "To my mother, who revered with passionate *abandon* the spiritual qualities of which she always deemed herself destitute, it seemed the privilege and honor of her life to be the wife of such a man" (M.E. Neatby, *Mother and Granny,* p. 23).
4. Nicoll, *Paths,* p. 31.
5. Quoted in *ibid.,* p. 10. Kate felt that it was their accent, puritanical standards, and her father's dogmatism when he was in charge of the local school district that caused the problems (p. 93). It was not just being English in Canada. Edith wrote to Kate in 1934, "When I was a child [in England] the sense of our being wholly different from, and infinitely superior to the rest of mankind, was very strong" (Edith Neatby Hedlin to Kate Neatby, 22 June 1934, SAB, A139, no. 219).
6. Quoted in Nicoll, *Paths,* pp. 91–92.
7. Convocation Speech, Regina, 1971, SAB, A139, no. 198(15).
8. L.H. Neatby, *Chronicle,* p. 66.
9. Ibid., p. 90; Nicoll, *Paths,* p. 29.
10. PAC, MG30 A25, vol. 5 (Kenneth Neatby to Eugene Forsey, 1 July 1954).
11. Nicoll, *Paths,* p. 66.
12. Graduation Address, Alma College, 7 June 1969, SAB, A139, no. 198(14).
13. Nicoll, *Paths,* p. 120. It was Mr. Neatby who wrote to the University of Saskatchewan in September 1919 to see if Hilda could begin even though she was not 16 (AUS, Presidential Papers, Ser. I B111).
14. Neatby, *Chronicle,* pp. 59–60.
15. PAC, MG30 D204, vol. 6, Frank Underhill to graduate dean, University of Minnesota, 10 March 1931: "She was in-

variably the best student in the course."
Hilda's marks for the first three years of
university are in AUS, Presidential
Papers, Ser. I B80 (nine firsts, seven
seconds); her marks in the fourth year
were all firsts).

16. AUS, Presidential Papers, Ser. I, A51.
7 October 1930.

17. *University of Saskatchewan Yearbook*,
1924, p. 12.

18. Letters from Mary Carr Travis, Florence
Kirk, and Gordon Grant, SAB, A139, no.
219.

19. Hilda described him to her mother in 1924,
pleased that he was helping her get a
scholarship, "Professor Morton certainly
is a duck. I miss him ever so much" (SAB,
A139, no. 3[2], undated letter [Nov.]
1924). In 1930–31 Morton would have a
crucial influence on Hilda as described
below. In the 1930's Hilda was unsure of
his attitude toward her. He continued to
write glowing letters of reference for her.
His letters to her were cordial, and on
occasion he helped her with her work (see
AUS, Morton Papers, I: 33).

20. The quotations are from "Memorandum
on Frank Underhill," prepared in 1966 for
W.D. Meikle, SAB, A139, no. 3(7).

21. Morton, in AUS, Morton Papers I: 33;
Burt, in PAC, MG30 D103, vol. 4;
Underhill, in PAC, MG30 D204, vols. 6,
13.

22. SAB, A139, no. 3(2), Hilda to her father,
16 and 23 June 1923, describes her
summer reading, done while she was
taking care of her brother, his expecting
wife and their two small children. The
final paper is now in Morton's papers in
the archives of the University of Saskatchewan, I, V, 12.

23. AUS, Presidential Papers, Ser. I, B80.

24. Ibid.

25. Ibid. The second payment was made at the
end of April 1925 (SAB, Education, no.
26).

26. AUS, Morton Papers, I, 33, Hilda Neatby
to Morton, 11 January 1925; Hilda eventually chose the topic "La traite indienne
dans le Canada français au XVIIe siècle."
The director of her thesis was Georges
Pages; SAB, Ed., 26, Hilda to D.P.
McColl, 31 March 1925.

27. SAB, A139, nos. 3 (2–4), 31(2).

28. SAB, A139, no. 3(2), Hilda to her mother,
23 November 1924, has a classic description of registration at the Sorbonne.

29. Ibid., Hilda to her mother, 5 October
1924. Miss Carr became Mrs. Underhill.

30. M.E. Neatby, *Granny and Mother*, p. 173.
Few men got along with Hilda that well in
those years. Clement, however, was her
uncle by marriage.

31. SAB, A139, no. 3(2), Hilda to her mother,
7 December 1924.

32. Ibid., 11 January 1925.

33. Ibid., Hilda to Margery Neatby Hedlin,
14 January 1925.

34. Ibid., Hilda to Kate Neatby, 14 December
1924.

35. SAB, A139, no. 33(1); AUS, History
Department, Morton to secretary of the
Royal Society of Canada, 28 January
1933.

36. SAB, A139, no. 3(4), Hilda to her mother,
26 April 1925.

37. AUS, Presidential Papers, Ser. I, B 38/36.

38. AUS, Minutes of the Board of Governors,
30 October 1926, 10 May 1927, 25 March
1929, 25 May 1930; Presidential Papers,
Ser. I, B54; Walter Murray to various
members of the faculty, April 1930.

39. AUS, Presidential Papers, Ser. I, A51;
Hilda to Walter Murray, 21 November
1930.

40. Ibid.

41. AUS, Presidential Papers, Ser. I, A51,
Murray to Hilda, 26 November 1930;
SAB, A139, no. 19, Hilda to Kate Neatby,
30 April 1933; Ibid., Edith Hedlin to Kate
Neatby, 10 July 1934. Murray may have
been using a convenient situation to save
money. His daughter was paid through a
deduction from his own salary. The
$2,100.00 saved provided the exact
amount needed to balance the university
budget (AUS, Presidential Papers, Ser. I,
B54). The most curious document connected with this series of events is a letter
from Murray to the premier of Saskatchewan, J.T.M. Anderson, explaining the
salary arrangement. The two key para-
graphs are typed on a different typewriter
than the preceding and following para-
graphs (ibid., B6, 28 December 1931); for
Hilda's later support of Jean Murray see
Ibid., Ser. III, B95, Hilda to W.P.
Thompson 28 October, 3 November 1958.

42. PAC, MG30 D204, vol. 6, Hilda to
Underhill, 20 January 1930.

43. Ibid., 27 October 1930.

44. Ibid., 19 November 1930.

45. Ibid., 1 April, 7 August 1931.

46. Ibid., 7 August 1931.

47. There is a letter to her sister Kate almost every week between November 1932 and March 1935 with a scattering for earlier 1932. The letters are both a pleasure to read and an excellent historical source for graduate life in the 1930's and the condition of women in Minnesota, London, and Regina. A few of these letters are printed in Chapter 6 to give an idea of Hilda both as graduate student and as letter writer.

48. SAB, A139, no. 19, Hilda to Kate, 23 July 1933.

49. Ibid., Hilda to Kate, 15 January 1933.

50. Ibid., 6 November 1932.

51. Religious and very Anglo-Canadian (see Burt's speeches at the University of Alberta in PAC, MG30 D103, vol. 1, pp. 502–17).

52. SAB, A139, no. 19, Hilda to Kate, 30 September 1934.

53. PAC, MG30 D204, vol. 6, Hilda to Underhill, 26 November 1931.

54. SAB, A139, no. 19, Hilda to Kate, 20 November 1932.

55. Ibid., 13 November 1932.

56. Ibid., 1 April 1934.

57. Ibid., 18 March 1933. Hilda added "I except students and people you work with of course — you can always get along with them if they are decent at all."

58. Kate Neatby Nicoll to Kay Graham, 17 July 1976. In Mrs. Graham's possession.

59. SAB, A139, no. 19, Hilda to Kate, 9 April, 3 December 1933.

60. Ibid., 15 January 1932.

61. Ibid., 25 November 1933.

62. Ibid., 18 April 1933.

63. Royal Society Correspondence formerly in the possession of Jean Murray, now AUS, Jean Murray Papers, Presidential Papers, Ser. I, II, 42.

64. Ibid., Murray had also strongly supported Hilda's application for an assistantship at Minnesota in 1931 (AUS, Presidential Papers, Ser. I, A48, 2 March 1931).

65. SAB, A139, no. 19, Hilda to Kate, 9 April, 14 August, 13 November 1933; 3 March, 23 April 1934.

66. PAC, MG30 D103, vol. 4, Jean Jenness to Hilda Neatby, 23 September 1971; Hilda to Jean Jenness, 26 September 1971; SAB, A139, no. 19, Hilda to Kate, 30 April 1934.

67. SAB, A139, no. 19, Hilda to Kate, 6 May, 29 June, 12 July 1934.

68. Ibid., 6 May 1933.

69. Ibid.

70. Ibid., 6, 12, 22 July 1934.

71. AUS, Presidential Papers, Ser. I, A51, Hilda to Walter Murray, 10 July 1934; Murray to Hilda, 12 July 1934.

72. SAB, A139, no. 19, Hilda to Kate, 10 September 1934. In her second year Hilda got $1,608, without room and board. In September 1936, she became an assistant professor with a salary of $2,100 on the condition that she teach university-level French as well as history (though without classes at Moose Jaw). By 1944 this had risen to only $2,700; $3,300 by 1946. SAB, A139, no. 148, and AUS, Minutes of Meetings of the Board of Governors, 29 May 1935, 9 May 1936; AUS, Presidential Papers, Ser. I, B88, Murray to W. Ramsay, 15 February 1936, Murray to Hilda, 27 June 1936. Hilda's suspicion that she was being underpaid relative to others at Regina was accurate.

73. Greta Rempel to her son Richard, 15 October 1981, SAB, A139, no. 219. For details of Hilda's hiring see AUS Presidential Papers, Ser. I, B88, 11–14 September 1934.

74. SAB, A139, no. 19, Hilda to Kate, 7 October 1934; see also October 13 as the situation became more serious.

75. Ibid., 5 March 1933.

76. Ibid., 4 November 1934. Kate wrote in 1981, "Hilda was devoted to the Smith's little girl — she loved small children. While they were out one day the child fell and cut her tongue, and Margaret MacRae, the nurse, rushed her to the hospital. They gave her a general anesthetic to stitch it, but the child was allergic and died instantly. This was a frightful grief to Hilda, and she had to watch the parents cope with it. You say that they thought alike, but I don't think they shared Hilda's firm faith and that was part of what troubled her — she said that during the burial a dreadful Saskatchewan dust storm came up which practically blotted them out. I still remember her letter" (Kate to author, 18 February 1981, SAB, A139, no. 219). The letter referred to no longer exists.

77. "It was well known that Hilda loved a debate, and I have often seen her carried away by the logic of her own argument" (Margaret Belcher to author, 7 April 1980, SAB, A139, no. 219, she added "But she also had an honest and open mind, and

she surprised many people, as they got to know her better, by her intellectual modesty." The quote concerning teas comes from a letter to Kate of 12 January 1935 (SAB, A139, no. 19).

78. Ibid., Hilda to Kate, 11 and 18 November 1934; AUS, Morton Papers, I: 33; Hilda to Morton, 9 May 1935; Morton to Hilda, 20 April, 30 May 1935; see also AUS, Presidential Papers, Ser. I B88; and SAB, Regina R2.481a, Academic Faculty Meeting, Regina College, 5 October 1937, 17 January 1938, 10 March 1938.

79. SAB, A139, no. 217, Jake Rempel to Kate and Ted Nicoll, 15 May 1975. The force of these words is particularly apparent to those who remember Jake Rempel's speech of protest against government interference in the university's affairs presented with force in the presence of the premier of Saskatchewan in the midst of the supposedly decorous installation of the first and only principal of the Saskatoon campus of the short lived double campus university of Saskatchewan on 8 December 1967.

80. W.A. Riddell to author, 11 March 1980, SAB, A139, no. 129, reporting the words of Cliff Blight, former associate registrar of Regina College.

81. AUS, Presidential Papers II, A45, G.W. Simpson to J.S. Thomson, 13 June, 17 July 1942; B23(4), 151(7), correspondence concerning Toronto's original offer; B22 (11), Board of Governors Minutes, 23 March 1945, the second offer; B151(7), Hilda's return to Regina; PAC, MG30 D204, vol. 6, Hilda to Frank Underhill, 12, 18 and 19 March 1946, Hilda to Ruth Underhill, 13 October 1945.

82. For the 1939–40 search, see AUS, Presidential Papers, Ser. II, B12 (12); for the 1946 search and the correspondence between Thomson and Thompson, ibid., B85 and Arts and Science, Dean's Office A; for Dean and Acting President Thompson's insistence that Simpson did not oppose Hilda's appointment, ibid., B133, 24 May 1946; see also ibid., B13 and B151(8), Basterfield to Thomson, 16 April 1946.

83. PAC, MG30 D204, vol. 6, Hilda to Ruth Underhill, 29 April 1947; see also SAB, A139, no. 36, Hilda to George Simpson, 29 July 1949.

84. PAC, MG30D204, vol. 6, Hilda to Ruth Underhill, undated (1948); see also AUS,

Presidential Papers, Ser. II, B85, and B65 (the latter for an idea of the impossible introductory course combining broad philosophy and minute history that Hilda taught with President Thomson.

85. PAC, MG30 D204, vol. 6, Hilda to Frank Underhill, 30 May 1949; Kate Nicoll to author, 20 Dec. 1981, SAB, A139, no. 219.

86. *Report of the Royal Commission on National Development in the Arts, Letters and Sciences, 1949–*1951 (Ottawa, 1951): 9.

87. Hilda Neatby, "The Massey Report: A Retrospect, *"Tamarack Review* 1: (Autumn, 1956): 45. The whole article is reprinted in Chapter 12.

88. J. Pickersgill, *My Years with St. Laurent* (Toronto, 1975), p. 139. David A.A. Stager, "Federal Government Grants to Canadian Universities, 1951–1966," *Canadian Historical Review* 54(1973), 287–97.

89. Fr. Lévesque has said that St. Laurent created the commission to help Canadians realize the richness of their cultural patrimony and to find the best ways to protect and develop it, "comme un des principaux facteurs d'unité nationale." According to Père Lévesque, Massey was chosen because of his "valeur personelle" and also to prepare him to be the first Canadian Governor General. Then St. Laurent and Massey chose the other members together, with Fr. Lévesque being the first choice of both as a French Canadian who could work closely with Massey. His hypothesis for the reason Hilda was picked is that St. Laurent probably wanted an historian and that both Norman MacKenzie (already chosen) and Massey "Qui connaissaient très bien la competence professionnele de Hilda," suggested her. Fr. Lévesque thinks that her bilingualism and perhaps "l'excellente reputation scientifique" of her brother Kenneth "dans les hautes sphères d'Ottawa" helped (Fr. Lévesque to author, 25 January 1981, SAB, A139, no. 219).

90. See SAB, A139, nos. 38, 40; for those special studies that most influenced Hilda see nos. 93, 94, 102, 106 with her markings; Fr. Lévesque to author, 25 January 1981; see also SAB, A139, no. 36, Norman MacKenzie to Hilda, 16 September 1950; and ibid., Francis Leddy to Hilda 3 June 1951: "From conversation volunteered by various people here [Ottawa] I gather that the considerable share which you under-

took in drafting the report is freely acknowledged in Ottawa and very much appreciated."

91. SAB, A139, nos. 41–2. See, for example, Hilda arguing with an ardent advocate of immense doses of classical music on CBC in no. 41, Winnipeg Sessions, pp. 41, 212A. If Hilda discussed the matter with her sister Edith, a prairie housewife, she would already have known of the liberating effect of radio on women, though Edith preferred the Metropolitan Opera and plays to soap operas (Edith Hedlin to Kate Neatby, 29 January 1933, 4 November 1934, ibid., no. 219).

92. Ibid., no. 42, p. 342.

93. Donald Creighton, *The Forked Road* (Toronto, 1970), p. 185.

94. Frank Underhill, "So Little for the Mind; Comments and Queries," *Transactions of the Royal Society of Canada* 48, Ser. 3 (June 1954): 15, 31.

95. Arthur Lower, *History and Myth: Arthur Lower and the Making of Canadian Nationalism,* ed. W.H. Heick (Vancouver, 1975), p. 123. Originally published in *The Canadian Banker* (Winter 1952).

96. *Report of the Royal Commission,* p. 18.

97. Ibid.

98. Ibid., p. 5. Present day proponents of regional culture rather than national must remember how little there was of this in 1950 and how much the efforts of the Massey Commission did to generate the money now available to them. Ethnic cultural development has also benefited at least indirectly from the work of the Massey Commission.

99. Ibid., pp. 274–75.

100. SAB, A139, no. 36, Vincent Massey to Hilda 1 February 1951; Georges-Henri Lévesque to Hilda, 6 February 1951; in a letter to Hilda on 1 March 1951 Massey added a comment in his own hand, "You have been a pillar of strength throughout and I can't begin to say how grateful I am, "(ibid.); see also, ibid., no. 12(1), Massey to Hilda, 5 February 1951 which includes MacKenzie as part of the group. Surveyer and MacKenzie attended fewer of the sessions than the other three members.

101. Ibid., nos. 12, 1(1), the Massey-Neatby letters and Hilda's diary for 1956–60. Hilda's presentation copy of Massey's collection of speeches while Governor General, *Speaking of Canada,* now in the Shortt Collection of the University of Saskatchewan, has her discreet pencil marks next to the speeches she wrote. She was responsible for 33 and partially responsible for three more of the 44 speeches printed in the volume. Massey did not acknowledge her role either in the preface or in the inscription he wrote on the fly leaf. The method used to produce the speeches is best seen in ibid., 12(2), Hilda to Vincent Massey, 15 September 1952, and 12(4), Hilda to Lionel Massey, 10 September 1953.

102. Ibid., 12(2a), Hilda to Vincent Massey, 15 September 1952.

103. Ibid., no. 12(3), 7 April 1953. Lionel Massey, Vincent's son and secretary, wrote on 17 September 1952, "The drafts are perfect and give me everything I need, so there is very little left for me to do," ibid., 12(2).

104. PAC, MG30 A25, vol. 5, Hilda to Eugene Forsey, 12 July [1954].

105. SAB, A139, no. 3(5), 2 February 1955.

106. Ibid., no. 12(2), Hilda to Massey, 15 September 1952.

107. *Queen's Quarterly* 71 (1964): 271. In a letter after Massey's death Hilda said she regretted Hart House and Massey College but that the Massey Commission was his monument (SAB, A139, no. 3(9), Hilda to Lillian Chase, 9 January 1968); see Irving Abella and Howard Troper, "'The Line Must be Drawn Somewhere,' Canada and Jewish Refugees, 1933–39," *Canadian Historical Review* 60 (1979): 203–5.

108. SAB, A139, no. 12(3), Hilda to Lionel Massey, 16 May 1953; see also ibid., 12(4), notes to herself in September and October 1953 in which she complains of "chilly formal face saving" and adds "Surprised myself at what it has done to me — but so it has . . . . Must clear up because poisoning relations. Am falling into habit of looking for slights and resenting trifles which I should never notice."

109. PAC, Sound Archives, no. 1980 – 47. *Take 30,* CBC, 6 December 1962.

110. Hilda Neatby, "Education for Democracy," *Dalhousie Review* 24 (April 1944): 43. See Chapter 10.

111. See, for example, SAB, A139, no. 41, Regina, p. 139, Saskatoon, pp. 128, 143–44.

112. Ibid., no. 12(1), Hilda to Massey, 5 May 1952; Massey to Hilda, 13 May 1952.

113. Ibid., Massey to Hilda 19 September 1951; no. 175(1), Hilda to Donald Greene, 26

November 1953; no. 12(3), Hilda to Massey, 30 April 1953. For Hilda's sources see no. 179.

114. Ibid., no. 12(3), Hilda to Massey, 30 April 1953. Hilda wanted half of the royalties to go to the Massey Foundation. Massey refused, saying all belonged to Hilda (ibid., Massey to Hilda, 1 May 1953).

115. Ibid., no. 176, Marian Scribner to Hilda, 24 March 1952; no. 12 (1, 3), Massey to Hilda, 7 April 1952, undated, 30 March 1953. Hilda later lent the forty-three page "discussion" of Dewey to a professor of education at the University of Saskatchewan. He returned it, but no trace of it has been found (ibid., no. 175 (1), Hilda to C.A. Bowers, 13 May 1963; C.A. Bowers to author, 27 April 1981, ibid., no. 219).

116. Ibid., nos. 6, 175 (1).

117. Ibid., no. 175 (2). Note dated 21 December 1953, mailed from Saskatoon.

118. Underhill, "Comments and Queries," p. 15.

119. SAB, A139, no. 7. Radio broadcast transscript, CKOY, 5 March 1954; see also Hilda to Forsey, 2 October 1954, PAC, MG30 A25, vol. 5.

120. PAC, MG30 D204, vol. 6, Hilda to Underhill, 31 January 1954; see also ibid., 22 February 1954; and Underhill to Hilda, 16 January 1954, SAB, A139, no. 175 (3).

121. For example, between 23 February and 12 March 1954, Hilda spoke seven times: in Toronto, Kingston, Montreal, and Halifax as well as speaking on radio (PAC, Sound Archives, 1980: 63, no. 1). In April and May she spoke in the West (SAB, A139, no. 6; PAC, MG30 A25, vol. 5, Eugene Forsey to Hilda, and Hilda to Forsey, February to June 1954; see SAB, A139, no. 203 [1-2]).

122. See Chapter 10. Hilda believed that professional educators educators tried to ignore the book until they realized how popular it was becoming and then launched an all out attack (SAB, A139, no. 180).

123. SAB, A139, no. 175(8), Hilda to T.J. Allard, 12 October 1954.

124. Ibid., no. 3 (7) "Memorandum on Activities," 6 March 1963.

125. PAC, MG30 A25, vol. 5, Hilda to Eugene Forsey, 12 July 1954.

126. Ibid., D204, vol. 6, Hilda to Underhill, 21 June 1954.

127. SAB, A139, no. 175 (10), Laura Ferrier to Hilda, 23 June 1955; Hilda to Laura Ferrier, 28 June 1955.

128. Ibid., nos. 175 (3-11), 178, 204.

129. Ibid., no. 178 (2). Hilda's answer began "Our great shortcoming is lack of incentive. We suffer from enervating effects of anti-intellectual trends in school and society and from a terror of words like duty and discipline." It ended with a defence of the humanities, "Neglect of humanities will mean neglect of human values. If so why not let Russia take over at once. Neglect of humanities does not produce scientists only technicians and often bad ones."

130. PAC, MG30 A25, vol. 5, Hilda to Forsey, 1 March 1958.

131. SAB, A139, no. 178, Hilda to Arthur Lower, 3 March 1963.

132. Ibid., no. 6. The reason for insistence on control of the text was that Roger Graham had just had a difficult time with Clarke Irwin over the wording of his book.

133. PAC, MG30 D204, vol. 12, Hilda to Underhill, 25 April 1957; see also Hilda's diary, SAB, A139, no. 1(1). The comment about fatigue was written into the Christmas 1956 entry on 26 December 1958.

134. PAC, MG30 D204, vol. 12, Hilda to Underhill, 25 August 1957.

135. SAB, A139, no. 1(1).

136. Ibid.

137. SAB, A139, no. 1(1). AUS, Arts and Sciences, B37, 1954–60; Department of History, I, fvi, ix, 1959–62; Presidential Papers, Ser. III, B95.

138. PAC, MG30 D204, vol. 12, Hilda to Underhill, 1958. See also AUS, Principal's Papers, I, 5Bxvi.

139. SAB, A129, no. 151, Hilda to J.P. Smith, 13 July 1965.

140. AUS, History, I, Civ, Hilda to A.M. Watson, 12 January 1967.

141. SAB, A139, no. 3(10), Hilda to S.R. Tompkins, 22 May 1969.

142. Ibid., no. 219, Hilda to Ivo Lambi, 10 September 1972.

143. PAC, MG30 A25, vol. 5, Hilda to Forsey, 28 June 1954; PAC, Sound Archives, 1980: 63, nos. 1–2 (Citizen's Forum 25 February 1954, 10 March 1955).

144. See, for example, SAB, A139, no. 113, and AUS, Principal's Papers, I, 5Bxvi. The student from the late 1950's was Lloyd Rodwell now of the Saskatchewan

Archives Board. The student from the late 1920's was James F. Rae replying to a questionnaire on university life. The description of the method of teaching first year classes is from AUS, History Department, I, B, 22 January 1957.

145. SAB, A139, no. 33(2).

146. Ibid., no. 114.

147. Francis Leddy to author, 13 May 1981, ibid., no. 219.

148. PAC, MG30 D204, vol. 6, Hilda to Underhill, 15 March 1952; SAB, A139, no. 189, Hilda to W.L. Morton, 19 November 1956, Morton to Hilda, 17 November 1964; ibid., no. 175 (16), Hilda to W.P. Thompson, 29 June 1955; ibid., no. 194(1), Hilda to G.W. Brown, 19 December 1956.

149. Ibid., no. 190, no. 161(2), Hilda to Fernand Ouellet, 20 September 1962; AUS, History Department, I, fvi; Hilda to Ivo Lambi, 10 December 1965; see also ibid., I, fix (for her activities as president of the Canadian Historical Association, see SAB, A139, no. 161, 91–92).

150. See Chapter 9.

151. Hilda to Roger Graham, 18 January 1967, in Professor Graham's possession. Hilda had approached Lambi as early as 1966 about the possibility of taking the headship one day. At first he refused.

152. SAB, A139, no. 3(10). Hilda to Sr. Francis d'Assisi, 12 March 1969; ibid., no. 136, passim; ibid., no. 3(5), Eric Harrison to Hilda, 17 May 1955, Hilda to Harrison, 24 July 1955.

153. Ibid., no. 113, Hilda to J. Joyce, 10 September 1969, 5 February 1970; ibid., no. 219, Hilda to Ivo Lambi, 18 March 1972; ibid., no. 210 (account book, 1973).

154. Ibid., no. 219. Hilda to Lambi, 11 August, 10 September and 2 October 1972. Lambi to Hilda, 30 August, 20 September and 4 October 1972. To the end, Underhill remained Hilda's favourite professor. See her speech on his eightieth birthday (ibid., no. 3[10]).

155. Ibid., no. 1(2), diary entries, 19 September to 19 December 1970; see also Kay Graham, "Hilda, the Person Behind the Professor," *Queen's Alumni Review* (July-August, 1976): pp. 2–5, and letter of Professor Madden to author, 30 January 1981, SAB, A139, no. 219.

156. Ibid., no. 34. Her honourary doctorates were from Toronto (1953), Brock (1967), Regina (1971), Windsor (1974), Carelton (1974), and New Brunswick (1975).

157. The first direct quotation is from Graham, "Hilda," p. 4. The second from Fr. Lévesque to author, 25 January 1981, SAB, A139, no. 219. The indirect quotations are from members of her family in conversation with the author.

NOTES TO CHAPTER 2

1. "Are Women Fulfilling Their Obligations to Society?" speech delivered at the Canadian Federation of University Women's Triennial Meeting, August 1952, privately printed, unpaged; partially reprinted in *Food for Thought* 12 (November 1953): 19–23.

2. "The Woman Thou Gavest Me," speech to the Edmonton University Women's Club, 11 January 1954, pp. 12–13, 19, SAB, A139, no. 198(6).

3. "Not the Possible," *Journal of the YWCA*, November 1955, pp. 5–6.

4. Hilda to J.A.S. Reid, 14 April 1961, SAB, A139, no. 151. She added, "At the same time, I would defend the administrator who hesitated to take the risk."

5. Hilda to R.A.H. Robson concerning the Royal Commission of the Status of Women, 20 November 1968, ibid., no. 132(2).

6. "Women and the Christian Community," speech delivered to the Women's Auxilliary Dominion Board, 9 October 1953, pp. 7–8, ibid., no. 198(6).

7. "Are Women Fulfilling Their Obligations to Society?"

NOTES TO CHAPTER 3

1. Hilda to A.W. Plumstead, 11 February 1963, SAB, A139, no. 20.

2. Hilda to C.B. Riddehough, 25 August 1955, ibid., 75 (10).

3. One other piece is "Birth of the Scottish Reformed Church," ibid., 198 (3).

4. Hilda Neatby to Kate Neatby, 25 November 1934, ibid., no. 19.

5. "Inheritance and Stewardship," St. Andrew's Presbyterian Church, 29 October 1967, ibid., 198(12).

6. Hilda Neatby to Kate Neatby, 5 August 1933, ibid., no. 19.

7. "The Protestant Church: A Historical Essay," ibid., 198(3).
8. "Address: St. Andrew's College Dinner, 17 February 1956," ibid, 198(7).
9. "The Vitamin Virtue," a talk to the Varsity Christian Fellowship, 9 February 1967, ibid., 198(12).
10. "The Pure in Heart," a talk to the V.C.F., 7 March 1968, ibid., 198(13).
11. "Sermon: Third Avenue United Church, 24 May 1970," ibid. The ellipses mark blanks in the typed text.

NOTES TO CHAPTER 4

1. *Saskatchewan History* 1 (1948): 29–30.
2. "Some Western Canadian Paradoxes," unpublished speech, late 1950's, SAB, A139, no. 198(8). The ellipsis marks a missing word in the text.
3. Ibid., 198(14), "Address of Welcome, Farm and Home Week," 15 January 1969, Unpublished.
4. "The Canadian Historical Association, The *Canadian Historical Review*, and Local History: A Symposium," Canadian Historical Association, *Report of the Annual Meeting*, eds. R.A. Preston, G.F.G. Stanley, and L. Lamontagne (Ottawa, 1952): 46–50.

NOTES TO CHAPTER 5

1. "Religious Liberation: A Canadian Bi-Centenary," *Chelsea Journal* 1 (January–February 1975): 47.
2. "Canadianism — A Symposium," Canadian Historical Association, *Report* (1956): 74–76.
3. "The English in Canada," composed probably in 1953 by Hilda and her brother, Leslie for inclusion in an encyclopedia (SAB, A139, no. 198(6)).
4. Ibid., 198(2); "La Co-existence au Canada. This was given at Laval University in 1957 and over the RTF network in France along with a companion piece by Fr. Lévesque. Hilda wrote the speech in English, had it translated by Margaret Cameron, and then adjusted it herself.
5. "Canadian Bi-Culturalism," *Rotunda* (1967): 15–19. Also delivered as a speech to the Canadian Catholic Alumnae Association in 1963.

6. "Ethnic Groups: Assimilation or Integration," 1967, SAB, A139, no. 198(12).
7. Letter to the Editor, Saskatoon *Star-Phoenix*, 2 January 1969.
8. "Cultural Evolution," in *Canada's Tomorrow*, ed. G.P. Gilmour (Toronto: Macmillan, 1954), pp. 187–91, 221–23. The rest of the article discusses the arts, universities, publishing and broadcasting and their funding in Canada. This theme was developed in a number of speeches in the early 1950's, for example, in a speech to the Canadian Club in 1951 "Are Canadians Growing Up?" (SAB, A139, no. 198[6]).

NOTES TO CHAPTER 7

1. "The Problem of Survival," a speech to the Women Teachers' Association of Toronto, 15 December 1962. This quotation, slightly different from the printed version in *WTA Newsletter* (15 December 1962), is from the typescript, SAB, A139, no. 198(9), pp. 10–11.
2. Ibid. "The Art of Teaching: Reflections of an Amateur," unpublished address to Saskatchewan Teachers' Association, 5 October 1962.
3. Ibid., 198(15), "The Obligation of the Teacher" unpublished speech, 1970. In making this speech at McArthur College of Education Hilda was in part replying to the remarks of an earlier speaker to the same group. She disagreed with his proposition that teachers were and should be looked to for inspiration and guidance on current topics.
"History Teaching; Hope or Menace," *Prince Albert Daily Herald* 4 May 1968.

NOTES TO CHAPTER 8

1. Carl Berger, *The Writing of Canadian History* (Toronto, 1976), pp. 179, 180, 183, 225.
2. Mason Wade, "While the Old Order Crumbled," *Toronto Globe and Mail,* 10 December 1966. The major reviews of her three historical books are: *Administration of Justice under the Quebec Act, Canadian Historical Review* 19 (1938): 420–22; *American Historical Review* 44 (1938–39): 139–41, *Annals of the American Academy of Politics and Political Science* 198, (1938) pp. 201–2; *American Political Science*

Review 32 (1938): 387; *Quebec, the Revolutionary Age, 1760-1791, Canadian Historical Review* 48 (1967): 159-60, *Saskatchewan History* 20 (1966): 39-40, *English Historical Review* 84 (1969): 617-18, *Canadian Forum* 47 (1967-68): 184-85, *Revue du Centre d'étude du Québec* 1 (1967): pp. 51-54 (curiously, neither the *Revue d'histoire de l'Amérique française*, nor the *American Historical Revew* reviewed *Quebec*); *Queen's University, 1941-1917. And Not to Yield, Canadian Historical Review* 60 (1979): 495-98.

3. *Revue du Centre d'étude du Québec* 1 (1967): 54.

4. PAC, MG D204, vol. 12, Hilda to Underhill, 25 August 1957.

5. Ibid., 17 September 1958. Her strongest comments were reserved for a historian in her field, one of which referred to his "rather serious ignorance of any but the special subject which he has chosen" (SAB, A139, no. 194 [1], 14 July 1966).

6. The fullest expression of this idea is to be found in Hilda's debate with the representative of the Social Science Research Council during the Massey Commission hearing (SAB, A139, no. 41, pp. 475-80).

7. "The Theology of Hope: The Historian's Insight," unpublished speech, ibid., no. 198(15), p. 8.

8. " 'Christian' Views of History: Toynbee and Butterfield," *Transactions of the Royal Society of Canada* 52, Ser. 3 (June 1958), section 2, pp. 33-42. A fuller version is in SAB, A139, no. 202. One of the two sections dropped to meet the space restrictions of *Transactions* was a rejection of Toynbee's interpretation of Christianity: "he corrects history by religion and religion by history, happily accommodating himself to two variables with no constant." The second section dropped was a paraphrase of her development of Butterfield's ideas (ibid., pp. 10, 13). Originally she had intended to include a discussion of Christopher Dawson (Hilda to M. Ross, 31 January 1958, ibid., no. 171[1]).

9. " 'Neutralism': Is It Possible for a Christian," ibid., no. 198(4).

10. Hilda to William Dray, 4 July 1962, ibid., no. 139(3).

11. "The Theology of Hope," p. 8.

12. Ibid., pp. 9-10.

13. "Imperial Sentiment in Canada (1867-1896)," Master's thesis, University of Saskatchewan, 1927, pp. 1, 16-18, 26.

14. *Pacific Northwest Quarterly* 35 (1944): 273-74.

15. Read on the CBC programme "Critically Speaking," 9 October 1955.

16. *Revue du Centre d'étude du Québec*, 1 (1967): 47-50.

17. PAC, MG30 D204, vol. 6, Hilda to Underhill, 9 September 1947.

18. Hilda to Roger Graham, 16 May 1955. In Professor Graham's possession.

19. *Quebec Act: Protest and Policy* (Toronto: Prentice Hall, 1972) pp. 1-4.

20. "History and the Computer," unpublished speech given in Kingston and Chalk River, Ontario, spring, 1970. (SAB, A139, no. 198(15), pp. 3-6, 7c-12, 14-15). Originally Hilda meant to condemn the computer. After careful consideration she found it to be useful if employed with intelligence and historical understanding.

21. "Christ the Centre of History," unpublished, ibid., no. 198(4).

NOTES TO CHAPTER 9

1. *Saskatchewan History* 2 (1949), 1-15.

2. "Servitude de l'Eglise Catholique: A Reconsideration," *Study Sessions 1969*, Canadian Catholic Historical Association, pp. 9-25. See also "Canadians and Their Church in Old Quebec," SAB, A139, no. 198(1).

3. "Jean-Olivier Briand: A 'Minor' Canadian," Canadian Historical Association, *Report* (1963): 1-18.

4. "The Survival Theme in Canadian History," unpublished speech delivered at Laval University, November 1954 (SAB, A139, no. 198(6); see also "La Co-existence au Canada" (ibid., no. 198[2]; for the origin of Hilda's interest in the survival theme, see Hilda to J.M.S. Careless, 31 August 1953 (ibid., no. 5); for Hilda's assessment of work needing to be done in eighteenth-century Quebec history, see Hilda to Mother McManus, 14 July 1966 (ibid., 194[1]).

5. "National History," *Royal Commission Studies* (Ottawa, 1951), pp. 205-16. This is a shortened and revised version of the original which is to be found in SAB, A139, no. 103.

6. "The Political Career of Adam Mabane," *Canadian Historical Review* 16 (1935): 137-39, 144-50.

7. "Pierre Guy: A Montreal Merchant of the Eighteenth Century," *Eighteenth Century Studies* 5 (1972): 224-30, 239-42.

8. "Racism in the Old Province of Quebec," in *Racism in the Eighteenth Century,* ed. Harold E. Pagliaro, (Cleveland: Case Western Reserve University Press, 1973), pp. 279-92. See also Hilda's last article, "The Impact of the American Revolution on Canada: Some Neglected Aspects," in *1776,* eds. John Browning and Richard Morton (Toronto, 1976), pp. 93-107. Hilda first developed the theme in "French Canadian Nationalism and the American Revolution," *Centennial Review* 10 (1966): 505-22, and her Quebec book.

9. *The Quebec Act: Protest and Policy,* pp. 137-42.

NOTES TO CHAPTER 10

1. For example *The Saskatchewan Bulletin* 19 (December 1953): 42-45; 20 (February 1954), (March 1954): 14-15, 26-31.

2. "So Much To Do — So Little Time," *The Western Producer,* 22 October, 1959, pp. 21, 28.

3. "Education for Democracy," *Dalhousie Review* 24 (1944): 43-50. Strictly speaking, Hilda's first article on education was "The Use of Cultural Education," *The Bulletin* 4 (March 1937): 38-39. Her first development of the theme used in the *Dalhousie Review* article was "The New Education," Regina *Leader-Post,* 11 November 1942, p. 9.

4. A six-page typescript headed "on CBC November 1953" (SAB, A139, no. 198[6]).

5. *So Little for the Mind* (Toronto: Clarke Irwin, 1953), pp. 57-59.

6. Ibid., pp. 123-27. Bracketed material comes from the footnotes.

7. "My Small War with the Educators," *Maclean's,* 15 July 1954, pp. 7, 50-54.

8. "Educational Simony," unpublished speech, late 1950's, SAB, A139, no. 198(2). The ellipsis marks the omission of a long quote from Anton Pegis. This speech seems to have developed out of the ideas in another speech "Education for Democracy," also known as "Some Reflections on 'Education for Democracy.' " The same ideas are found in various partial combinations in "So Much to Do — So Little Time," "The Survival Problem," and "Educational Totalitarianism" among others. Hilda chose "Educational Simony" as her contribution to an Underhill *festschrift* that never materialized.

9. *So Little for the Mind,* pp. 326-35. Bracketed material comes from the footnotes. The problem of a Christian education in a secular society concerned Hilda. See, for example, "Education: Through Fear or Faith," *The Journal* (of the Canadian Dietic Association) 20 (1958): pp. 19-26 and "The Challenge of Education to the Christian Church," *Canadian Journal of Theology* 1 (1955): 35-43. Her solution to the Problem "Neutralism: Is It Possible for a Christian?" is quoted in the introduction to Chapter 6.

NOTES TO CHAPTER 11

1. "Notes on the Wright Report and on the Calgary Report," SAB, A139, no. 198(5).

2. Ibid.

3. Ibid. Hilda used the words of the "Notes" in a restrained fashion before the Royal Society of Canada in 1972 as can be seen in the first selection in this chapter.

4. "Hilda Neatby Makes the Case against Production Line Education," *Maclean's,* January 1963, p. 4.

5. See the last selection in Chapter 7.

6. See, for example, "How Can an Arts Degree Help Earn a Living?" SAB, A139, no. 198(9), and "The Humanities," ibid.

7. SAB, A139, no. 116, Hilda to Ivo Lambi, 16 May 1966.

8. Ibid., no. 178(6), Hilda to J.H. Willits, 17 November 1966.

9. "Sorrows of a University." *Queen's University Alumni Review,* 45 (May-June 1971): 69.

10. Speech to University Women's Club, SAB, A139, no. 198(15).

11. Ibid., no. 198(8). See also "The University/ Academic Authority and Student Power," Toronto *Daily Star,* 9 March 1970. Her first public statement on the subject may have been a 1968 speech, "Student Power," SAB, A139, no. 198(13).

12. "The Christian College in the Life of the Church," *The Christian Scholar* 40 (1958): 210-22.

13. " 'Frustrated, Prejudiced, Partial, Biased and Undemocratic': Some Personal Reflections on the Predicament of Our Universities," *Transactions of the Royal Society of Canada* ser. 4, 10 (1972): 137-47.

14. "A Perspective of Change," *Auricle* 2 (April 1970): 25.

15. "Article on Education Week submitted to the Editor of the *Star-Phoenix* the request of Mr. K.M. Benson," SAB, A139, no. 198(3).

16. "Convocation Address U.N.B.," hand-

written draft, SAB, A139, no. 34. The ellipsis marks on indecipherable word.

NOTES TO CHAPTER 12

1. "The Artist in Canada," presented to the Manitoba Registered Music Teachers' Association, 22 April 1954 and privately printed by them.
2. Hilda attempted to place the arts in a Christian context in "Christianity and the Arts," SAB, A129, no. 198(6); in a Canadian context in a speech "Opening — Art Gallery, 11 December 1953," SAB, A139, no. 198(6).
3. "The Use of Cultural Education," *The Bulletin* (of the Saskatchewan Teachers' Federation) 4 (March 1937): 38–39.
4. Hilda to Kate Nicoll, 12 June 1935, SAB, A139, no. 198; see also "China in the Post-War World," *The Bulletin* 9 (December (1943): 20–22; "The Polish Problem," *The Bulletin* 10 (February 1944): 42–43; The Massey Report and National Defence," SAB, A139, no. 198(6). In the national defence speech delivered to the Current Affairs Course for Officers of the Canadian Forces at the University of Saskatchewan in 1957, she worried about the possibility of the development of a military oligarchy and the danger of rejection of the necessity of defence. Her remedy was to keep people's minds on what it was that they were defending and the spending of significant amounts of money for the development of Canadian culture.
5. "The European Problem," returned by the editor of *Dalhousie Review* on 30 September 1941 with the comment "Sorry to send this back. There is good stuff in it, but I am overwhelmed with material: much accepted work I have had to hold over. Try me again" (SAB, A139, no. 198[6]).
6. "The Democratic Cycle," *Dalhousie Review* 22 (1943): 475.
7. "The Massey Report: A Retrospect," *Tamarack Review* 1 (Autumn 1956): 37–47.
8. "Canadian Leisure," SAB, A139, no. 198(2). This piece appeared in *The Times* of London in November 1957, and in *The Western Producer,* 3 April 1958 as "Free Time for History or Handicraft."
9. "Current Affairs," *Bulletin* 7 (September 1941): 21–23.
10. "Hiroshima — Fifteen Years After," SAB, A139, no. 198(8).
11. "Saskatoon — Reply to Address of Welcome," SAB, A139, no. 12(1).
12. Originally "women" but crossed out and replaced with an indecipherable word.
13. Indecipherable word.
14. "Saskatoon," SAB, A139, no. 12(1).
15. "International Night — Business and Professional Women," 23 February 1970, ibid., no. 198(15).
16. "Convocation Address, University of Windsor," 5 October 1974, ibid.,198(17). The speech was given at the request of Hilda's old friend Francis Leddy, then president of the University of Windsor.

NOTES TO CHAPTER 13

1. In addition to those broadcasts now in the PAC Sound Archives listed in the bibliography, a few more may still exist in the uncatalogued section of the CBC Archives.
2. A.S. Morton and A.L. Burt influenced her historical method and style. The most poignant example of support from friends comes from a diary entry of 24 June 1959, "Chatted with Bernadine on our common sense of depression and frustration and she drove me home" (SAB, A139, no. 1[1]).
3. PAC, MG30 D204, vol. 12, Hilda to Frank Underhill, 27 November 1960.
4. Introduction to A.L. Burt, *The Old Province of Quebec* (Toronto, 1968), xiii–xiv.
5. SAB, A139, no 34, "Freedom the Underlying Prinicple," handwritten speech, early 1970's; *Administration of Justice,* p. 25; Hilda to A.R.M. Lower, 7 September 1962, ibid.
6. AUS, Presidential Papers, I, B151(7), S. Basterfield to J.S. Thomson, 17 April 1945.
7. SAB A139, nos. 171(1), p. 200, Hilda to C.E. Dolman and Dolman to Hilda, October-December, 1966.
8. Ibid., no. 171(2), Hilda to the secretary of the Royal Society, 3 December 1968.
9. Hilda to Roger Graham, 10 November 1966, in R. Graham's possession; see also SAB, A139, no. 188, Conway Turton to Hilda, 28 June 1971, concerning the errors to be removed from *Quebec, the Revolutionary Age* before reprinting.
10. Ibid., nos. 171(4), 192.
11. Ibid., no. 10, Hilda to J.K. McConica, 2 March 1962.
12. Ibid., no. 3(9), Hilda to S.R. Tompkins.
13. PAC Sound Archives, 1974 — 113, *Ideas,* CBC 10 October 1974.

14. "French Canadian Nationalism and the American Revolution," *Centennial Review* 10 (1966): 522.

15. In the order cited the quotations are from: "The Menace of the Herd," *Temperate Dispute* (Toronto, 1954), p. 45; "The Burden of Freedom," Convocation address, Mount Saint Vincent College, 15 May 1962, SAB, A139, no. 198(9); "Why History?" ibid., 198(4); "Educational Simony," ibid., no. 198(2); letter to Frank Underhill 9 September 1947, PAC, MG30 D204, vol. 6; "Neutralism: Is it possible for a Christian," SAB, A139, no. 198(9); "Hiroshima — Fifteen Years After," ibid., 198(8); "Keep Your Hearts, Minds," Convocation address intended for University of New Brunswick, 15 May 1975, ibid., no. 34.

16. An example of a negative reaction came in answer to an alumni questionnaire. A survivor of Hilda's first effort as a university teacher in 1926 jotted down, "Woman French teacher, forget her name, think it was Nesby, dull uninspiring, not helpful, sarcastic," in possession of author.

17. "I have often said to students that I was divided from them in that I could remember the time before we went over Niagara in 1914. There has been no such dividing line since — although I can still remember reading a paper in 1933 and thinking in disbelief — 'But the Germans are a civilized people' " (Hilda to Underhill, 3 January 1970, PAC, MG30 D204, vol. 12).

18. A curious example of this is the sermon preached in a Unitarian Church in May 1954 by Earle Birney, one of Hilda's fellow Royal Society Fellowship "failures," in defense of *So Little for the Mind* (SAB, A139, no. 204, Birney to Hilda, 31 May 1954). Another example is the Christmas card Hilda received from the author of *Sarah Binks* — "I have just been reading with envy and delight 'So Little for the Mind' by one Hilda Neatby of Saskatchewan. Permit me, therefore, a stranger, to wish you a Merry Christmas. Sincerely, Paul E. Hiebert."

BIBLIOGRAPHY

I. Sources used for Biography and Introductions

Public Archives of Canada.
    Manuscripts.
    MG30 A25, Vol. 5. Forsey – Neatby Correspondence
    MG30 D103, Vols. 1, 4. Burt Papers
    MG30 D204, Vols. 6, 12. Underhill – Neatby Correspondence
    Sound Archives.
    1974 – 113. *Ideas.* CBC FM. 19 October 1974
    1980 – 47. *Take 30.* CBC, 6 December 1962
    1980 – 63 nos. 1, 2. *Citizen's Forum* 25 February 1954, 10 March 1955

Archives of the University of Saskatchewan.
    Presidential Papers. Series I.
    A48   Correspondence – Moore
    A51   Correspondence – Neatby
    B6   Correspondence – Anderson
    B8   Applications and Appointments
    B38/36 History Department, 1912–37
    B54   Board of Governors, 1908–1937
    B80   Paris Scholarships
    B88   Regina College
    Series II
    A38   Correspondence – Neatby
    A45   Correspondence – Simpson
    B12 (12–13)   Appointments
    B13   Applications and Promotions
    B22 (11)   Board of Governors, 1945
    B23   (4) Board of Governors – Executive, 1943–44
    B65   Examinations, 1944–48
    B85   History Department, 1946–49
    B133   Political Science, 1938–48
    B151 (7, 8)   Regina College, 1944–47
    Series III
    B12/40   Annual Reports, History Department
    B19   Armed Services: Current Affairs Lecture
    B95   History Department, 1949–59
    Series IV
    B14/77   Annual Reports, History Department
    B137   History Department, 1959–71
    Principal's Papers   I 5Bxvi History Department, 1967–73
    History Department   Ib Meetings, 1957–1970
                       If Internal Correspondence, 1956–69
    Board of Governors Minutes   1926–30, 1935, 1944–45, 1955

Arts and Science, Dean's Office   A General Correspondence
                                   B19/15 Forward Planning Committee
                                   B37 History Department
                                   B65 Regina College
Jean Murray Papers   Presidential Papers, Series I
                      II.42 Royal Society
Morton Papers   I, 30–32 Students
                33 History Department

Saskatchewan Archives Board.
Education 26 Paris scholarships
R. 2.48 la University of Regina, Minutes of Academic Faculty
A 139 The Hilda Neatby Papers, (sixty-five boxes)
        Provisional arrangement
            1 Diaries, 1956–60, 1968–73
            2 – 28. Correspondence
           29 – 35. Souvenirs, Honours, Awards
           36 – 111. Massey Commission (42–111, briefs and special studies)
          112 – 33. University of Saskatchewan
          134 – 43. Queen's University
          145 – 74. Societies and Conferences
          175 – 205. Writings, Speeches, and related correspondence
          206 – 19. Miscellaneous
Since numbers but not file titles may be changed in the future the file titles corresponding to the
numbers used in the footnotes are given below:
    1. Diaries
    3. General Personal Correspondence
    5. CBC Correspondence
    6. Clarke Irwin Correspondence
    7. Forsey Correspondence
   10. McConica Correspondence
   12. Massey Correspondence
   19. Kate Nicoll Correspondence
   34. Honours and Awards (includes last speeches)
   36. Massey Commission Correspondence
   37. Massey Commission, Memo to Chairman
   40. Massey Commission, Draft Report
   41. Massey Commission, Transcripts
  112. University of Saskatchewan, general
  113. U. of S. correspondence with administration
  132. U. of S. University Council
  151. C.A.U.T. Correspondence
  171. Royal Society Correspondence
  175. So Little For The Mind: Correspondence
  180. Education, correspondence & articles
  190. *Quebec,* Correspondence
  198. Speeches, Articles and Reviews, 1941–1975
  200. Speeches, Articles, Reviews
  204. Education, Correspondence
  209. Royalties
  217. Letters of Sympathy

OTHER BOOKS AND ARTICLES CITED

Creighton, Donald, *The Forked Road:* McClelland and Stewart Toronto, 1970.
Fulford, Robert, Christine Newman, Sandra Gwyn, "The Year They Created Modern Canada."
        Saturday Night 92 (June 1977): 18–25.

Lower, A.R.M., *History and Myth: Arthur Lower and the Making of Canadian-Nationalism.* Edited by W.A. Heich. Vancouver: University of British Columbia Press, 1975.

Massey, Vincent, *Speaking of Canada.* Toronto: Macmillan, 1959.

Neatby, Leslie *Chronicle of a Pioneer Prairie Family.* Saskatoon: Western Producer Prairie Books, 1979.

Neatby, Marion Jean, ed., *Thomas Neatby, a Memorial.* Glasgow, n.d.

Neatby, Mary Elizabeth, ed., *Marion Jean Neatby, Mother and Granny.* Poole, 1930.

Nicoll, Kate Neatby, *Paths They Have Not Known.* N.p., n.d. (1978).

Pickersgill, J.W., *My Years with St. Laurent.* Toronto: University of Toronto Press, 1975.

Report of the Royal Commission on National Development in the Arts, Letters and Sciences, 1949–51. Ottawa; E. Cloutier, 1951.

Underhill, "So Little for the Mind: Comments and Queries." *Transactions of the Royal Society of Canada,* 48, ser. 3, section 2 (June 1959): 15–23.

II. Bibliography of Published and Unpublished Works of Hilda Neatby

BOOKS

The Administration of Justice Under the Quebec Act. Minneapolis: University of Minnesota Press, 1937.
The Debt of Reason. Toronto: Clarke Irwin, 1954.
So Little For The Mind. Toronto: Clarke Irwin, 1953.
A Temperate Dispute. (A collection of 4 speeches: "A Temperate Dispute," "The Group and the Herd," "Is Teaching a Learned Profession," "The Debt of Our Reason"). Toronto: Clarke Irwin, 1954.
Quebec, The Revolutionary Age 1760–1791. Toronto: McClelland and Stewart Ltd., 1966.
The Quebec Act: Protest and Policy. Scarborough: Prentice Hall, 1972.
Queen's University, 1841–1917: And Not to Yield. Montreal: McGill, Queen's Press, 1978.

THESES

"Imperial Sentiment in Canada (1867–1896)." M.A. thesis, University of Saskatchewan, 1928.
"The Administration of Justice under the Quebec Act." Ph.D. diss., University of Minnesota, 1934.

INTRODUCTIONS

Burt, A.C., *The Old Province of Quebec.* 2nd ed. with an introduction by Hilda Neatby (I: ix–xv). Toronto: McClelland and Stewart, 1968.
Introduction in *Man and His World.* Edited by Helen Hogg, p. 47. Toronto: University of Toronto Press, 1968.

PARTS OF BOOKS

"Cultural Evolution." *Canada's Tomorrow.* Edited by G.P. Gilmour pp. 187–223 Toronto: Macmillan, 1954.
"That Great Street; the St. Lawrence." *Water Resources of Canada,* edited by C.E. Dolman, pp. 49–62, Toronto, University of Toronto Press, 1967.
"The Impact of the American Revolution on Canada: Some Neglected Aspects." *1776.* Edited by J. Browning and R. Morton, pp. 93–107, Toronto; S.S. Hakkert, 1976.
"National History." *Royal Commission Studies,* pp. 205–16; Ottawa: E. Cloutier, 1951.
"Racism in the Old Province of Quebec." *In Racism in the Eighteenth Century.* Edited by H. Pagliano, *pp. 279*–92. Cleveland: Case Western Reserve University Press, 1973.
"Is Education Possible." *In Education and Social Policy, Local Control of Education.* Edited by C.A. Bowers, Doris Dyke, Ian Housego, pp. 129–137. New York: Random House, 1970.

ARTICLES AND PUBLISHED SPEECHES

"Abstract of the Difficulties of the Hudson's Bay Company's Penetration of the West." *Saskatchewan History* 2 (January 1949): 30–32.
"Alfred Leroy Burt." *Canadian Historical Review* 52 (1971): 478–80.
"Canadian Bi-Culturalism." *The Rotunda* (1967): 15–19. Originally given as a speech to Canadian Catholic Alumnae Association, 21 August 1963.

"The Canadian Historical Association, *The Canadian Historical Review,* and Local History; A Symposium." C.H.A. *Report* (1952): 46–50. Delivered at CHA Meeting June 1952.

"The Canadian History Teacher and the Paperback Revolution." *Saskatchewan History Teachers' Association Newsletter* 5 (January 1968): 35–36.

"Canadianism — A Symposium." CHA *Report* (1956): 74–76.

"The Challenge of Education to the Christian Church," *Canadian Journal of Theology* 1, 1 (1955): 35–43.

"Chief Justice William Smith: An Eighteenth Century Whig Imperialist," *Canadian Historical Review* 28 (1947): 44–67.

"China in the Post-War World," *The Bulletin* (of the Saskatchewan Teachers' Federation) 9 (December 1943): 20–22.

"The Christian College in the Life of the Church." *The Christian Scholar* 41 (1958): 210–222.

" 'Christian' Views of History: Toynbee and Butterfield." *Transactions of the Royal Society of Canada* Ser. 3, vol. 52 (1958), section II: 33–42.

"Current Affairs." *The Bulletin* 7, 4–6 (September–December 1941): 21–23, 16–19, 16–18; 8, 1–3, 5–6 (February–December 1942): 33–35, 27–29, 31–33, 20–22, 33–35; 9, 1–3 (February–May 1943): 39–41, 46–48, 41–43.

"Current Events." *The Bulletin* 4, 1–3, 5–6 (February–December 1940): 31–34, 33–35, 34–36, 27–29, 22–25; 7, 1–3 (February–May 1941): 26–28, 7–8, 33–35.

"The Dangers of History." *La nouvelle revue Canadienne* 1, 3 (1951): 21–33.

"The Democratic Cycle." *Dalhousie Review* 12 (January 1943): 470–75.

"Dr. Hilda Neatby Comments on the Cameron Report." *Calgary Herald,* 23 November 1959, pp. 1, 15. Reprinted in the *Edmonton Journal,* 24 November 1959, pp. 1–2.

"Education for Democracy." *Dalhousie Review* 24 (April 1944): 43–50.

"Education is *Not* Everybody's Business." *Chatelaine,* April 1958, pp. 14–15, 74–75.

"Education: Through Fear or in Faith." *The Journal* (of the Canadian Dietetic Association) 20 (1958): 19–26. Originally given as speech, 9 June 1958.

"The Empire, Sanctuary of Liberty," Regina *Leader-Post,* 23 May 1941, p. 11.

"For the Sake of Argument," *Maclean's* 69, 28 April 1956: 4, 71–73. An abstract of "Do we Need Aristocratic Education?" SAB, A139, no. 198(7).

"Frank Hawkins Underhill." *Proceedings of the Royal Society of Canada* Ser. 4, vol. 10 (1972): 99–100.

"Free Time for History or Handicrafts." London *Times,* November 1957: *Western Producer,* 3 April 1958. Original title, "Canadian Leisure." Cf. SAB, A139, no. 198(2).

"French Canadian Nationalism and the American Revolution." *The Centennial Review* 10 (Fall 1966): 505–22.

" 'Frustrated, Prejudiced, Partial, Biased and Undemocratic': Some Personal Reflections on the Predicament of our Universities." *Transactions of the Royal Society of Canada* Ser. 4, vol. 10 (1972): 137–47.

"George Wilfred Simpson, 1894–1969." *Proceedings of the Royal Society of Canada,* Ser. 4, vol. 7 (1969): 101–2.

"Hilda Neatby Makes the Case Against Production Line Education." *Maclean's* 76, January 1963, 3–4.

"History Teaching, Hope or Menace?" Prince Albert *Daily Herald,* 4 May 1968, p. 7.

"Is Man the Measure of All Things?" *The Chronicle* (of the Canadian Federation of University Women) (1951–52): 69–72.

"Jean-Oliver Briand: A 'Minor' Canadien." Canadian Historical Association, *Report* (1963): 1–18. C.H.A. Presidential Address, 6 June 1963. Partially reprinted in *The French Canadians* Edited by C. Nish, pp. 107–12. Toronto, 1966.

"The Massey Report: A Retrospect." *Tamarack Review* 1 (Autumn 1956): 37–40, 43–47.

"The Medical Profession in the North-West Territories." *Saskatchewan History* 2 (1949): 1–15.

"My Small War with the Educators." *Maclean's,* 15 July 1954, pp. 7, 50–54.

"The Myth of Versailles." Regina *Leader-Post,* 8 July 1941, p. 9.

"The New Education." Regina *Leader-Post,* 11 November 1942, p. 9.

"Not the Possible." *Journal of the YWCA,* November 1955, pp. 4–6.

"Our Educational Dilemma," *Drum Beats* (Saskatchewan Indian Teachers' Association), 1958, pp. 2–6.

"Our Tragic Waste of Minds and Money." *Star Weekly Magazine,* 21 April 1962, pp. 2–5.

"Pierre Guy: A Montreal Merchant of the Eighteenth Century." *Eighteenth Century Studies* 5 (1972): 224–42. Originally given at the Royal Ontario Museum, February, 1968.

"Perspective of Change." *Auricle* (University of Saskatchewan) 2, 4 (April 1970): 25.

"The Polish Problem." *The Bulletin* 10 (February 1944): 42–43.

"The Political Career of Adam Mabane." *Canadian Historical Review* 16 (1935): 137–50.

"Queen's College and the Scottish Fact." *Queen's Quarterly* 80 (1973): 1–11.

"Reading Aloud." *Canadian Library Association Bulletin* 16 (1959): 17; reprinted in *The Saskatchewan Bulletin* (of the Saskatchewan Teachers' Federation) (October 1959), 17, 39; *Union Farmer* 10, 9 (November 1959): 2.

"Religious Liberation: A Canadian Bi-Centenary." *Chelsea Journal* 1 (January–February 1975): 41–47.

"The Report of The Royal Commission on Education in Manitoba." *Winnipeg Tribune,* December 1959.

"Servitude de l'Eglise Catholique: A Reconsideration." *Study Sessions* (1969): Canadian Catholic Historical Association 9–25.

"Social Goals for Canada: Education." *Letter to the Laos* 3, 1 (January–February 1962): 2–3.

"Social Studies: Hope for the Future." *Annual Conference of Social Studies Teachers of Nova Scotia,* 1965.

"So Little for the Mind." *Saturday Night* 69, 17 October 1953, pp. 7–8.

"So Much To Do — So Little Time." *Western Producer,* 22 October 1959, pp. 21, 28. Originally given to Canadian Association of School Superintendents 14 September 1959. Translated into Ukrainian and published in *New Pathway.*

"Sorrows of a University." *Queen's Review* 45, 3 (May–June 1971): 68–69. Originally delivered to The Newman Club in Kingston.

"The Survival Problem." *W.T.A. Newsletter* (Women Teachers' Association of Toronto), Originally a speech given 15 December 1962, titled "The Problem of Survival," 198(9).

"The University/Academic Authority and Student Power." Toronto *Daily Star,* 9 March 1970. Reprinted without full permission in *Making It: A Canadian Dream,* pp. 120–23. Toronto, 1972.

"The Use of Cultural Education." *The Bulletin* 4 (March 1937): 38–39.

"What are Women Doing for Education?" YWCA *Journal* 13 October 1955.

PUBLISHED BOOK REVIEWS

1943

Pares, *Russia;* Davies *Mission to Moscow. The Bulletin* (of the Saskatchewan's Teachers' Federation) 10, 5 (October: 33–36.

1944

Creighton, *Dominion of the North. Pacific Northwest Quarterly* 35: 273–74.

1948

Ewing, C., *The Individual, The State, and World Government;* Herman, *Freedom and Order. International Journal* 3: 67–68.

Macleod, ed., *The Letters of Letitia Hargrave. Pacific Northwest Quarterly* 39: 238–39.

McCourt, *Music at the Close. Saskatchewan History* 1, 2: 29–30.

History of the Regina Local Council of Women. Saskatchewan History 1, 3: 28–29.

1949

MacEwan, "The Sodbusters". Saskatchewan History 2: 37.

1951

Rich, ed., *James Ishan's Observation on Hudson Bay, 1743. Pacific Northwest Quarterly* 42: 250–51.

1952

Turner, *The North-West Mounted Police, 1873–*1893. Saskatchewan History 5: 78–79.

1953

Careless, *Canada A Story of Challenge, Canadian Historical Review* 34: 354–55.

MacEwan, *Between the Red and the Rockies. American Historical Review,* 58: 670–71.

Rich and Johnson, eds., *Cumberland House Journals. Pacific Northwest Quarterly* 44: 35–36.

1954
Frémont, *Les secrétaires de Riel. Saskatchewan History* 7: 115–16.
Taylor, *On Education and Freedom, Queen's Quarterly* 61: 381–83.
1956
Stanley, *In Search of the Magnetic North, Pacific Northwest Quarterly* 47: 62–63.
1957
Katy, ed., *Canadian Education Today: A Symposium. Canadian Historical Review* 38: 74–75.
Sabine, ed., *Historical Memoirs . . . by William Smith. Canadian Historical Review* 38: 146–48.
1958
Phillips, *The Development of Education in Canada. Canadian Historical Review* 39: 155–56.
1960
McDougall, *Our Living Tradition. Queen's Quarterly* 67: 683–84.
1961
MacKinnon, *The Politics of Education. Queen's Quarterly* 67: 683–84.
Brebner, *Canada: A Modern History. Queen's Quarterly* 68: 176.
Hersey, *The Child Buyer. Queen's Quarterly* 68: 519–20.
Moir, *Church and State in Canada West. Canadian Journal of Theology* 7: 69–71.
"The Course of Progressive Education." Review of *The Transformation of the School* by Cremin.
       Dalhousie Review 41: 394–99.
1962
Livingstone, *The Rainbow Bridge. Dalhousie Review* 41: 543–44.
Soisin, *Whitehall and the Wilderness. Canadian Historical Review* 43: 225–26.
Walcutt, ed., *Tomorrow's Illiterates. Queen's Quarterly* 69: 519–20.
1964
Massey, *What's Past is Prologue. Queen's Quarterly* 71: 271.
Vachon, *Histoire du notariat Canadien, 1621–1960.* American Historical Review 69: 559–60.
Upton, ed., *The Diary and Selected Papers of Chief Justice William Smith, 1784–1793,* I. *Canadian
       Historical Review* 45: 315–16.
1965
Klinck, *Literary History of Canada. Canadian Historical Review.* 46: 352–54.
1966
Upton, ed., *The Diary and Selected Papers of Chief Justice William Smith,* II. *Canadian Historical
       Review.* 47: 361–62.
1967
Ouellet, *Histoire économique et sociale du Québec. Revue du centre d'étude du Québec.* 1 (April):
       47–50.
Hatch, *The Mountbattens. Canadian Journal of History.* 2: 114–15.
1968
Lower, *My First Seventy-Five Years. American Historical Review* 74: 780–81.
1969
"A Canadian Enigma." Review of *The Mackenzie King Record,* II, ed. Pickersgill. Winnipeg *Free
       Press,* 25 January, p. 15.
Wilson, *The Clergy Reserves of Upper Canada. American Historical Review* 75: 620–21.
1970
Careless, Brown, eds., *The Canadians. Winnipeg Free Press,* 10 April.
1971
Moir, ed., *Character and Circumstance. Canadian Journal of History* 6: 223–24.
1974
Oury, *Marie de l'Incarnation. American Historical Review* 79: 1669.
1975
Paquet and Wallot, *Patronage et pouvoir dans le Bas-Canada. Journal of American History* 61:
       1158–59.

BOOK REVIEWS — PLACE OF PUBLICATION UNKNOWN

Bissel, ed., *Canada's Crisis in Higher Education* SAB, A139, no. 198 (7)
Kidd, *How Adults Learn,* ibid., 198 (8)
Kline, ed., *Soviet Education,* ibid.

LETTERS TO THE EDITOR

Exchange (University of Saskatchewan), 7 Nov. 1968, p. 2.
New York Times, 24 Jan. 1973, p. 40.
Saskatoon, *Star-Phoenix,* 2 Jan. 1969, p. 21.

ENCYCLOPEDIA ARTICLES

Dictionary of Canadian Biography:
Burton, Ralph, 3: 88–90.
Price, Benjamin, 3: 541–42.
Leitch, William, 9: 460–62.
Machar, John, 9: 495–96.
"The English in Canada" for *Encyclopedia of Canada,* evidently unpublished.

MISCELLANEOUS

"Article for Education Week, submitted to the Editor of the *Star-Phoenix* at the request of Mr. K.M.
  Benson," SAB, A139, no. 198 (3)
"The Crown," for brochure welcoming Queen Elizabeth to Saskatoon, ibid., no. 198 (8)
"Why History," ibid. 198 (4)

RADIO AND TV PROGRAMS

November 1952
Critically Speaking. Review of *The Young Politician*, by Creighton. SAB, A139, no. 198 (6).
30 August 1953
"Pioneer Eating Habits," CBC. International Service.
27 November 1953
Speaker's Choice. Fifteen minute talk on her views of education. CBC. SAB, A139, no. 148 (6).
25 February 1954
"Education, the Canadian Controversy." *Citizen's Forum*. CBC. PAC Sound Archives, 1980–63, no.
1.
17 March 1954
Fighting Words. CBC. With Robertson Davies and Blatz.
1954
Fighting Words. CBC. With Woodhouse and Blatz.
10 March 1955
Citizens Forum CBC. PAC Sound Archives, 1980–63, no. 2
9 October 1955
Critically Speaking. CBC. Review of *The Old Chieftain by Creighton*. SAB, A139, no. 148 (7).
31 January 1956
Taped Radio Speech, CBC.
4 March 1956
Critically Speaking. CBC. Review of *Restoration of Learning* by Bestor. SAB, A139, no. 198 (7).
23 September 1956
Critically Speaking. CBC.
30 December 1956
Critically Speaking. CBC. Review of *Commercial Empire* by Creighton and *Firebrand* by Kilbourn.
  SAB, A139, no. 198 (7).
February 1957
Critically Speaking. CBC.
October 1957
La Co-existence au Canada. R.T.F. SAB, A139, no. 198 (2).

? March 1958
Fighting Words. CBC.
25 October 1958
CBC-TV
29 February 1959
Fighting Words. CBC.
5 March 1959
Exploration. CBC.
September 1959
Hundredth Anniversary of Fall of Quebec. CBC–TV
21 February 1960
"Fighting Words." CBC. With Fernand Hayek, Marcus Levy, and Lawrence Lynch.
6 December 1962
Take 30. CBC–TV, PAC Sound Archives, 1980–47.
10 October 1974
Ideas. CBC–FM. PAC, Sound Archives, 1974–113.
Date Unknown
Critically Speaking. CBC. Review of *The Historical Approach to Religion* by Toynbee, and *Personalities and Powers* by Namier. SAB A139, no. 198 (7).

PRIVATELY REPRODUCED SPEECHES

"Are Women Fulfilling their Obligations to Society." Canadian Federation of University Women. Ottawa, August 1952. SAB, A139 no. 199(1). Partially reprinted in *Food For Thought* 13 (1952): 19–23.
"The Artist in Canada," "The Group and the Herd." "Is Teaching a Learned Profession." Manitoba Educational Association 1954 (Speeches at Convention 1954), pp. 13–25. SAB, A139, no. 199 (2).
"The Burden of Freedom." Convocation Address, Mount St. Vincent College. 15 May 1962. SAB, A139, no. 198 (9).
"History and Christianity." 7 February 1955. University of Saskatchewan. SAB, A139, no. 198 (7).
"The Massey Report and National Defence." Current Affairs Course for Officers of the Canadian Forces, University of Saskatchewan, 1952, 1953. SAB, A139, no. 198 (6). AUS, Presidential Papers, III, B–19.
"The Theology of Hope: The Historian's Insight," St. Andrew's College, 1970. SAB, A139, no. 198(15).

UNPUBLISHED ARTICLES

"The European Problem." Turned down by *Dalhousie Review* 30 September 1941. SAB, A139, no. 198(6).
Untitled on education in Canada. Original 1961, rev. 1967. SAB, A139, 198 (9).

UNPUBLISHED REPORTS

"The Canadian Conference on Education — Higher Education." SAB, A139, no. 198(8).
"Comment on 'Proposed Statement of Policy on Disarmament.' " SAB, A139, no. 198(4).
"Comments on 'Is Education Possible' by Jules Henry." 11 October 1967. SAB, A139, no. 198(12).
"Impressions of the Ottawa Conference." SAB, A139, no. 198(3).
"Memorandum of a Conversation with Dr. Kaye Lamb." SAB, A139, no. 37.
"Memorandum of F.H. Underhill at the University of Saskatchewan, 1920–1926." SAB, A139, no. 3(7).
"Memorandum to the Chairman of an Informal Investigation of Television Programmes made in and near New York May 1949, by Dr. Hilda Neatby." SAB, A139, no. 37.

"Memorandum to the Chairman on Mr. Surveyer's dissenting views on television." 8 February 1951. SAB, A139, no. 37.
"Memorandum to the Chairman: on the Dissenting Views of Mr. Surveyer on Broadcasting." 1 February 1951. SAB, A139, no. 37.
"Notes on John L. McDougall, 'Radio in a Free Society' Private and Confidential." SAB, A139, no. 198(4).
"Notes on the Wright Report and on the Calgary Report." SAB, A139, no. 198(5).
"Report on 'The Training of Teachers in Elementary and Secondary Education' by David M. Robb." SAB, A139, no. 179(5).

UNPUBLISHED SPEECHES

"The Abuses of History." University of Saskatchewan Faculty Club 13 February, 1948. SAB, A139, no. 198(3).
"Are Canadians Growing Up." Canadian Club, 29 March 1951. SAB, A139, no. 198(6).
"The Art of Teaching: Relfections of an Amateur." Saskatoon Teachers' Association 5 October 1962. SAB, A139, no. 198(9).
"The Birth of the Scottish Reformed Church." SAB, A139, no. 198(3).
"The Canadian Conference on Education: Achievements?" 3 September 1962. SAB, A139, no. 198(9).
"Canadians and their Church in Old Quebec." SAB, A139, no. 198(1).
"The Christian and the Rule of Law." 9 October 1969. SAB, A139, no. 198(14).
"Christianity and the Arts." SAB, A139, no. 198(6).
"Christianity and Western Civilization." Address to St. Andrew's Young People's Society 21 March 1960. SAB, A139, no. 198(8).
"A Christian View of Education." SAB, A139, no. 198(2).
"A Christian View of History." SAB, A139, no. 198(8).
"A Christian View of Man — Current Philosophy of Education." S.C.M., 13 July 1960. SAB, A139, no. 198(8).
"Christ the Centre of History." SAB, A139, no. 198(4).
"La Coexistence au Canada." SAB, A139, no. 198(2).
"The Decay of the University." 198(3).
"The Democratic Struggle for Survival." 198(4).
"Educational Simony." 198(2).
"Educational Totalitarianism." Montreal Canadian Club, March 1955. SAB, A139, no. 198(7).
"Education — Duty and Dedication." Address to Saskatchewan Alumni Association (Winnipeg) 3 February 1962. SAB, A139, no. 198(9).
"Education for Democracy." SAB, A139, no. 198(9).
"Education for the Future." Queen's University, February 1954. SAB, A139, no. 198(6).
"Ethnic Groups: Assimilation or Integration." 23 September 1967. SAB, A139, no. 198(12).
"A Few Points on the Military Occupation of Quebec, 1760–1764." The Humanities Association, Kingston, 23 March 1971. SAB, A139, no. 198(15).
"Freedom: The Underlying Principle." Early 1970's. SAB, A139, no. 34.
"The Genesis of the Quebec Act." University of Windsor, January 1971. SAB, A139, no. 198(15).
"Hiroshima — Fifteen Years After." 6 August 1960. SAB, A139, no. 198(8).
"Historical Research." Address to the Graduate Students. SAB, A139, no. 198(4).
"History and the Computer." University Women's Club, Kingston 14 October 1970; slightly revised for Chalk River, 13 November 1970. SAB, A139, no. 198(15).
"How Can An Arts Degree Help Earn a Living?" 1961 or 1962. SAB, A139, no. 198(9).
"The Humanities." Address to the Academic Competition Candidates Dinner, 14 May 1961. SAB, A139, no. 198(9).
"Impression of the Ottawa Conference." SAB, A139, no. 198(3).
"Inheritance and Stewardship." Sermon, St. Andrew's Church, 29 October 1967. SAB, A139, no. 198(12).
"In Honour of Professor B. Bujilla." 28 April 1967. SAB, A139, no. 198(11).
"Keep Your Hearts, Minds." 1975. SAB, A139, no. 34.

"Let's Abolish History Courses." 1967 or 1968. SAB, A139, no. 198(4).

"Medicine and the Historian." Address to First Year Medical Students, University of Saskatchewan, 15 October 1962. SAB, A139, no. 198(9).

"Morality and Education." 27 July 1965. SAB, A139, no. 198(10).

"The Near and Middle East." SAB, A139, no. 198(4).

"Neutralism: Is it Possible for a Christian?" Lutheran Students, 23 January 1963. SAB, A139, no. 198(9).

"The Obligation of the Teacher in Terms of the Role of the School." 1970. SAB, A139, no. 198(15).

"Our Anxious Age." Lutheran Students Dinner, Spring, 1958. SAB, A139, no. 198(8).

"Our Educational Dilemma." SAB, A139, no. 198(2).

"The Place of History and the Humanities in the Aims and Purposes of the University." Hazen Conference, May 1952. SAB, A139, no. 198(6).

"The Protestant Church: A Historical Essay." SAB, A139, no. 198(3).

"The Pure in Heart." V.C.F., 7 March 1968. SAB, A139, no. 198(13).

"Re-Discovering Basic Values in Inter-Personal Relationships." Introductory address for group discussion, Canadian Conference of Christians and Jews, Saskatoon, 18 February 1961. SAB, A139, no. 198(9).

"Reply to Toast to Canada at the Welsh Dinner." March 1968. SAB, A139, no. 198(13).

"The Role of the Professor in the Changing University." University Women's Club, Saskatoon, February 1970. SAB, A139, no. 198(5).

"So Little for the Mind." Teachers' Convention, October 1953. SAB, A139, no. 198(6).

"Some Reflections on 'Education for Democracy.' " (Same as "Education for Democracy)." SAB, A139, no. 198(3).

"Some Western Canadian Paradoxes." 1958. SAB, A139, no. 198(3).

"Soviet Russia and the Western World." April 1956. SAB, A139, no. 198(7).

"Student Power." 23 March 1968. SAB, A139, no. 198(13).

"The Survival Theme in Canadian History." Laval University, November 1954. French version translated by Margaret Cameron. SAB, A139, no. 198(6).

"Thanksgiving." 20 October 1971. SAB, A139, no. 198(5).

"Toynbee." September 1956. SAB, A139, no. 198(7).

"The United Nations and the Individual." SAB, A139, no. 198(3).

"Useless Studies." Saskatchewan Association of Music Teachers, 16 April 1968. SAB, A139, no. 198(13).

"The Vitamin Virtue." V.C.F., 9 February 1967. SAB, A139, no. 198(12).

"Wasted Personality." SAB, A139, no. 198(4).

"What Can One Expect from University?" SAB, A139, no. 198(2).

"What does the University Want High School Students to Know About History?" SAB, A139, no. 198(4).

"What Should We Expect of Our Schools?" SAB, A139, no. 198(3).

"What the University Expects of High School Students / How They Are Measuring Up?" 1960 or 1961." SAB, A139, no. 198(8).

"What We Expect of The Schools." SAB, A139, no. 198(8).

"The Wholeness of Man: Man and His Mind." S.C.M. Summer School, 10 July 1956. SAB, A139, no. 198(7).

"The Woman Thou Gavest Me." Edmonton University Women's Club, 11 January 1954. SAB, A139, no. 198(6).

"Women and the Christian Community." Women's Auxiliary Dominion Board, Edmonton, 9 October 1953. SAB, A139, no. 198(6).

Without Formal Titles

Address, Academic Competitions Banquet, 1965–60. SAB, A139, no. 198(10).

Address, Conference on Canadian Studies, 15 November 1969. SAB, A139, no. 198(14).

Address, Convocation of Emmanuel-St. Chad. 3 May 1967. SAB, A139, no. 198(11).

Address, Emmanuel College, Colour Night. 4 March 1966. SAB, A139, no. 198(11).

Address, Graduation, Convent of Sion. 15 May 1968. SAB, A139, no. 198(11).

Address of Welcome Farm and Home Week. 15 January 1969. SAB, A139, no. 198(14).

Address on Miss Jean Murray. 28 April 1968. SAB, A139, no. 198(13).

Address, Regina College Closing Exercises. SAB, A139, no. 198(8).

Address, Residence Dinner. 23 March 1968. SAB, A139, no. 198(13).

Address, St. Andrew's College Dinner. 17 February 1956. SAB, A139, no. 198(7).

Address, S.T.M. Graduate Divine [sic]. 1 March 1974. SAB, A139, no. 198(17).

Address to Emmanuel and St. Chad Banquet. 8 March 1969. SAB, A139, no. 198(14).

Address to Regina Campus Fall Convocation. 23 October 1971. SAB, A139, no. 198(15).

Address to the Anglican Synod at Winnipeg. 20 January 1960. SAB, A139, no. 198(8).

Address to the Saskatchewan Home Coming. October 1971. SAB, A139, no. 198(15).

Comment on Robert M. Stamp "Does Educational History Have A Place in the Classrooms." 17 April 1968. SAB, A139, no. 198(13).

Convocation Address, University of Windsor. 5 October 1974. SAB, A139, no. 198(17).

Convocation, University of Toronto. June 1953. SAB, A139, no. 198(6).

International Night, Business and Professional Women. 23 February 1970. SAB, A139, no. 198(15).

Introduction, Dr. Underhill. 17 January 1961. SAB, A139, no. 198(9).

Luther College Commencement Address. 19 April 1966. SAB, A139, no. 198(11).

Opening, Art Gallery. 11 December 1953. SAB, A139, no. 198(6).

Presentation of Fr. Lévesque for Honourary Degree, University of Saskatchewan. 11 May 1961. SAB, A139, no. 198(9).

"The Religion of Hope." St. Andrew's. 17 May 1970. SAB, A139, no. 198(15).

Reply to Toast to Professors, V.C.F. Banquet. 20 March 1959. SAB, A139, no. 198(8).

Review of The Comfortable Pew by Pierre Berton. SAB, A139, no. 198(4).

Sermon, Third Avenue Church. 24 May 1970. SAB, A139, no. 198(15).

Speech at Underhill Dinner. 26 November 1969. SAB, A139, no. 198(14).

Speech, Faculty Dinner. 24 April 1970. SAB, A139, no. 198(15).

Speech, Nutana Collegiate. 8 May 1970. SAB, A139, no. 198(15).

Speech to IVCF. November ? 1958? SAB, A169, no. 198(8).

Talk, St. Andrew's College Chapel. 23 November 1966. SAB, A169, no. 198(11).

To the Graduating Class of Alma College. 7 June 1969. SAB, A139, no. 198(14).

Untitled, on Cynicism to Lutheran Students. 23 February 1966. SAB, A139, no. 198(11).

Untitled on Queen's University. 30 March 1971. SAB, A139, no. 198(15).

Untitled, Upper Canada College. 1954 March. SAB, A139, no. 198(6).

Index

Permissions

I wish to gratefully acknowledge the permission granted by the following to include the selections listed below. Grantors are also identified in the footnotes. The order followed is that in which the selections appear.

For "Are Women Fulfilling their Obligations to Society?" The Canadian Federation of University Women.
For the review of *Music at the Close, Saskatchewan History.*
For "The Canadian Historical Association, the *Canadian Historical Review* and local History: A Symposium," the Canadian Historical Association. .
For "Letter to the Editor," the Saskatoon *Star Phoenix.*
For "Cultural Evolution," Westinghouse Canada, Inc.
For "History Teaching: Hope or Menace?" Prince Albert *Daily Herald.*
For "Imperial Sentiment in Canada, 1867-1896," The University of Saskatchewan.
For the Review of *Dominion of the North, Pacific Northwest Quarterly.*
For *Quebec Act: Protest and Policy,* Prentice-Hall Canada Inc.
For "The Political Career of Adam Mabane," The University of Toronto Press.
For "Pierre Guy: A Montreal Merchant of the Eighteenth Century," *Eighteenth Century Studies.*
For "Racism in the Old Province of Quebec," American Society for Eighteenth-Century Studies.
For "Education for Democracy," *Dalhousie Review.*
For *So Little for the Mind* by Hilda Neatby © 1953 by Clarke, Irwin & Company Limited. Used by permission.
For "My Small War with the Educators," Maclean Hunter Ltd.
For "'Frustrated, Prejudiced, Partial, Biased and Undemocratic': Some Personal Reflections of the Predicament of Our Universities," The Royal Society of Canada.
For "The Massey Report: A Retrospect," Robert Columbo.
For "Current Affairs," The Saskatchewan Teachers' Federation.
For "Canadian Leisure," *The Western Producer.*
For all of the unpublished material, The Saskatchewan Archives Board.